WAR DIARY

1939 – 1945

WAR DIARY

1939 – 1945

CHARTWELL
BOOKS, INC.

Published in 1995 by
Chartwell Books, Inc.
A division of Book Sales Inc,
110 Enterprise Avenue,
Secaucus NJ 07094

ISBN 07858 0280 0

Copyright © Marshall Cavendish 1995

Printed and bound in Italy

Some of this material has previously appeared in the Marshall
Cavendish partwork
IMAGES OF WAR

contents

1939 – 1945

CHAPTER 1

BATTLE DIARY

DUNKIRK – IN VICTORY AND DEFEAT

When World War II began in September 1939, France and Britain were confident that the Poles would hold Nazi Germany in the east, and that the superior strength of the old World War I Allies would produce a victory. What followed was a frightening surprise: Poland fell in only about a month.

In April and May 1940, after eight months of so-called Phoney War, Germany invaded Denmark and Norway and, on May 10, Belgium and Holland. Three French armies and the British Expeditionary Force responded by crossing the border into Belgium to hold the Dyle Line. Holland, attacked by land and air, fell on May 15. The same day, tanks and infantry of German Army Group A, headed by Panzer Group V, punched through thin French defenses at Sedan and began a drive for the Channel coast, reaching Boulogne on the 25th. After a heroic defense by British forces Calais fell a day later.

A day later at 19.00, Vice Admiral Bertram Ramsay launched Operation Dynamo, the seaborne evacuation of more than 330,000 British and French troops in northern France and Belgium, which surrendered on May 28. The Allied troops were trapped but, believing that the Luftwaffe, the German air force, would stop the Allied evacuation and destroy the pocket concentrated around the port of Dunkirk, Hitler ordered his tanks to stop rolling.

Although larger ships could use the harbor at Dunkirk, the Royal Navy asked small-boat owners to assist in the evacuation as they could approach the sandy coast and ferry men to larger ships off shore. By the small hours of June 4, the flotilla of vessels that answered the navy's call had helped rescue around 338,000 men, over six times Ramsay's original estimate. The cost had been high: six British and three French destroyers had been sunk, along with 56 other ships and 161 small craft; the Royal Air Force had lost 100 aircraft. But the spirit and success of the evacuation turned an English defeat into a byword for national pride.

IN VICTORY AND DEFEAT

The heroes of Dunkirk—the personal accounts of the men who were there. Their memories of one army in defeat and another in victory.

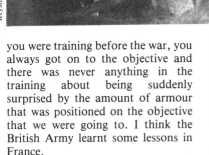

Keystone Collection; Inset: Imperial War Museum

Only when veterans of Operation Dynamo look back does the enormity of the undertaking and the sheer doggedness and courage required to see it through emerge.

Corporal George Andow of the 4th Royal Tank Regiment was evacuated in a ship which narrowly escaped being blown apart. In retrospect, his memory is one of being woefully unprepared for the savageness of Blitzkrieg—and of how very desperate and piecemeal the British escape really was.

❝ We were all very low when we reached the town, very low in spirits . . . but we were still getting rations from somewhere. If I remember rightly I still had some iron rations when I got to the other side.

Any organisation, at least so far as regimental organisation was concerned, was pretty non-existent. You might come across a group of chaps who had been together for a while, but that was as far it went. Not all of them had weapons. If you saw one lying around you picked it up.

By this time, the tanks had gone into this rearguard action. We did not see them again. And all the personnel with them were either killed or taken prisoner of war.

The voyage took six hours maybe, I wouldn't like to say. We just had this one bad attack with these six planes—whether they were Messerschmitts or not I wouldn't like to say off-hand now. I daresay they were floating around us for four or five minutes, in which time they could do quite a bit of damage . . . but for some unknown reason they just went down the port side. They never did the starboard side at all.

The thing is—and I've thought about this a lot—that whenever

W Fowler Collection; Inset: Bildarchiv Preussischer Kulturbesitz

◄ **Stop press from the front** – neutral nationality journalists report from an *al fresco* office in Compiègne. Inset: a regimental bugle – a picture worth a thousand of any journalist's words.

you were training before the war, you always got on to the objective and there was never anything in the training about being suddenly surprised by the amount of armour that was positioned on the objective that we were going to. I think the British Army learnt some lessons in France.

Back home, I think the general public was rather surprised at how fast the advance had gone; we were ourselves. But I don't think the public itself could grasp the situation until the troops had come back from Dunkirk and Calais and so on, and told them what was really taking

▶ **British Bren gun carriers move in** – as lines of dejected refugees stream out, down the Brussels-Louvain road.

place out there during the retreat.

When we got back to England, naturally enough the newspapers and the radio were getting information left, right and centre—and I don't think it was censored too much. After all, you can't gag thousands upon thousands upon thousands of troops, can you? ❞

▼ **The lucky ones who returned safely** – with good cause to be cheerful, despite their ignominious rout. A week's leave – then back to training for the return match.

Topham Picture Library

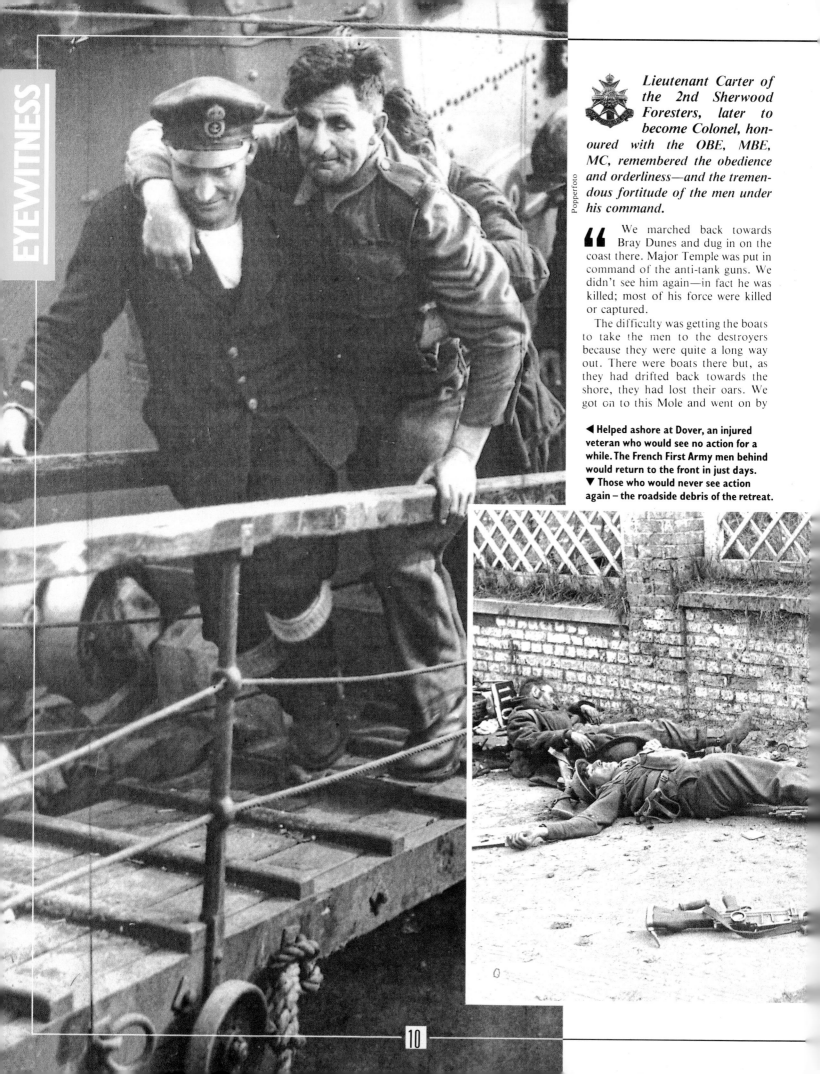

Popperfoto

Lieutenant Carter of the 2nd Sherwood Foresters, later to become Colonel, honoured with the OBE, MBE, MC, remembered the obedience and orderliness—and the tremendous fortitude of the men under his command.

"We marched back towards Bray Dunes and dug in on the coast there. Major Temple was put in command of the anti-tank guns. We didn't see him again—in fact he was killed; most of his force were killed or captured.

The difficulty was getting the boats to take the men to the destroyers because they were quite a long way out. There were boats there but, as they had drifted back towards the shore, they had lost their oars. We got on to this Mole and went on by

◄ **Helped ashore at Dover, an injured veteran who would see no action for a while. The French First Army men behind would return to the front in just days.**
▼ **Those who would never see action again – the roadside debris of the retreat.**

companies, quite quietly and steadily. I remember putting a brave young officer in charge of getting the wounded on—there were quite a lot of wounded there. We got every man in, every man carrying his weapon, you see, and this awful Boys anti-tank rifle was taken solemnly aboard.

I don't know what the papers said but I don't think anybody knew very much what was happening. A lot of the soldiers go back for old times' sake, but it was a defeat, and that's all there is to it. **"**

▼ **West Mole evacuees, risking their lives on an escape route dangerously close to oil storage tanks on the dock.**

Times Newspapers

S.I.R.P.A./E.C.P.A. France

Brigadier F P Barclay, DSO, MC, then a Captain in the 2nd Royal Norfolks, recognised the debt owed by those who got away to the last defenders of Dunkirk. The British Tommies' indomitable spirit was a credit to them.

" Well, the first thing I'd pay tribute to is the men and the morale that we had in the battalion, which was absolutely wonderful. It was the most thrilling feeling to experience the spirit of the chaps who were with you.

On the other side, I think we were shockingly badly equipped. Some of the equipment we got we'd not trained with. It only joined us when we were mobilising.

So far as training in the orthodox forms of warfare went, we were fine, but we hadn't done enough movement at night by transport.

We had tremendous courage in our men and the way they held out when the Dunkirk withdrawal was going on—they never got to Dunkirk themselves—they were stopping the Germans interfering with the withdrawal of thousands and thousands of other people. Which they did successfully and I mean, the battalion was practically wiped out doing it. But, such was the determination to put the biggest possible spanner in the Germans' advance that it succeeded in letting the better part of the British Expeditionary Force get back to England. **"**

Private Samuel Valentine Love of the Royal Army Medical Corps, interviewed many years later, recalled conditions on his rescue ship and then, later, the same man's shocked return to France without even setting foot on British soil.

" I bet there were thousands buried on them beaches that nobody knows nothing at all about, because the bombs were coming down that thick and fast. One would make a crater and a bloke would fall in it and the next bomb would cover him over.

What condition was the town in?
Burning and blowing up. We'd get in a doorway, and I used to say 'Let's go' and we'd go—and as soon as ever we'd gone that building went as well.

How was the crossing?
This boat that we got on had had a hit. We had to back out and they were after us—Jerry was after us all the while we were trying to get out. Four or five miles after we left Dunkirk harbour, we lost three destroyers in twenty minutes.

What happened at Dover?
We were turned round and sent to Cherbourg. Do you know, the troops lined up along the rail and they were going to shoot that captain if he didn't take us to Southampton.

Eventually there were 146 wounded and 26 of them that had died on the voyage to Cherbourg.

How was the Cherbourg hospital?
They fussed over me properly when they found out what I was and what I'd done. A sister offered me sleeping draught—I said I didn't need it—I'd had no sleep for a fortnight. I could sleep on a clothes line''. The next day Private Love sailed home. **"**

Bildarchiv Preussischer Kulturbesitz

▲ **Littered with rubble and deserted – the beach at Dunkirk within hours of the invaders' arrival.**

Pilot Officer John 'Chalky' White, of No. 32 Squadron of the RAF, saw Dunkirk from above while giving air cover to the rescue boats.

" We arrived at Wittering for a break, and learned that we had to leave for Dunkirk.

We patrolled it the best we could—the town was covered by a huge pall of smoke and it was very difficult indeed to see any low-flying enemy aircraft such as Stukas. We were ordered to patrol at 15,000 ft in Hurricanes with Spitfires at 30,000 ft.

I met two young officers who had been posted to our squadron at St Pancras. It was about 4.30 in the morning when we finally reached Biggin Hill. We had to go straight out to the aircraft, and I remember telling them, 'For heaven's sake keep your eyes open all the time'. I was worried stiff as they were brand new to the squadron and there they were—expected to fly into the heat of the action within the hour.

Over Dunkirk we got mixed up with a whole lot of 109s. It was a question of flying around in tight turns and firing at any 109 you could, while making sure that no-one was on your tail. Those two poor youngsters were both shot down and killed on that first mission—that was the end of their war experience.

I know a lot of the troops on the ground said that there was no Air Force protection—I can assure you

▶ **Primed for terror – a Stuka Ju-87.** Although they caused chaos on the undefended beaches of Dunkirk, they lacked the speed of the RAF fighter planes, so seldom survived in a dog-fight.

▼ **A cautious German advance through a deserted French street.** Already wounded and not wanting to be bayoneted, a French soldier lies, submissive, on the cobblestones.

that whatever aircraft and men we had were out there trying to provide air cover from above the smoke.

Troops were coming back without equipment—bedraggled, grey, dusty and dirty—and I remember thinking 'My God, this is the pride of the British Army'. 〞

Reporting back from a visit to the front, one of General Maurice Gamelin's liaison officers bore witness to the terrible rout of French Army.

〝 Complete disintegration. Out of 70,000 men and numerous officers, no single unit is commanded, however small . . . at most 10 per cent of the men have kept their rifles . . . Out of the thousands we sifted, it wasn't possible for me to form one company for the defence of the bridge at Compiègne. However, the losses had not seemed to be high. There were no wounded among the thousands of fugitives . . . they don't understand what has happened to them. The sight of an aeroplane induces terror in them. Service troops broke up before the infantry and spread disorder. 〞

Jean Murray, a French gunner on leave from his infantry regiment, was awaiting transport to the front.

〝 We marched incessantly, with a surprising continuity for two long hours, and then the column suddenly stopped. A powerful light was fixed upon us at a turn in the road . . . profiting from this unhoped-for halt, men sat down on the side of the road. A quarter of an hour passed, then an officer came to the back of the column, to announce that we were prisoners and that we must throw away our arms. The commander had already been taken away by the Germans . . . I threw my rifle away in a ditch. How simple this had all been! 〞

Fritz Kanzler, a soldier with the Panzerschütze (tank crew member) recalled the apparent ease of the advance— it all seemed too easy . . .

〝 It's through the speed of the Panzers that we've managed to come round to the back of the English. We are travelling north-east. Our second company has been on the move all night in order to be at the arranged place to meet the artillery battalion. We can still feel a pleasant warmth from the burning town we've just come through.

The Tommies would not let themselves be taken and are still shooting at us from a distance. An abandoned English anti-tank gun stands at the fork in the road—an evil looking thing with considerable gauge and power.

Another battalion is arriving from a different attack which they had started the previous day. There are still many fallen German soldiers laid out on the road from this assault.

The artillery follows closely after the Panzers. So far, everything is going as if on the practice ground, but still everyone had the feeling that the enemy, who are holed up in positions in the hillocks over there, are only letting us advance so as to be able to wipe us out at the closest possible proximity.

Suddenly there are new orders. The Panzer division splits immediately from the artillery unit and quickly makes the crossing of the Canal at Merville to pursue the English who are in retreat . . .

Unfortunately we have very little cover and I'm lying near the others, out of breath and panting. Just as I raise myself up to join them, another shell whistles above us into the masonry. As I'm lying there, I cut the boot from the foot of the Lieutenant next to me and bind a splint to his broken leg. **"**

▼ Protection and camouflage – behind these BEF men is a fire pit, in which an anti-aircraft gun lurks, scarcely visible in the soft Dunkirk sands.
▼▼ Dockside destruction at Dieppe.

▲ German casualties are removed from the battle zone and treated by highly trained medical units, whose speed and efficiency also saved the lives of many injured British prisoners of war in the Dunkirk campaign.

◄ Digging into the dunes on the outskirts of Dunkirk, a German anti-tank gun takes up position to pick off Allied air cover, on a beach covered in debris.

CHAPTER 2

BATTLE DIARY

JULY

10	First day's bombing
11	Attacks on Portsmouth
24	RAF lose 5 aircraft
	Luftwaffe lose 15 aircraft
25	Luftwaffe lose 19 aircraft

AUGUST

8	Weymouth convoy attacked
11	Eagle Day set
13	Eagle Day
30	RAF lose 35 aircraft
	Luftwaffe lose 76 aircraft
31	RAF lose 41 aircraft
	Luftwaffe lose 39 aircraft

SEPTEMBER

15	Battle of Britain Day
27	Day planned to smash the RAF

OCTOBER

	Luftwaffe lose 19 aircraft
15	RAF lose 15 aircraft
29	Luftwaffe lose 16 aircraft
31	Battle ends – TOTAL LOSSES

RAF   1,023 aircraft
Luftwaffe 1,887 aircraft

BATTLE OF BRITAIN – HEROES OF THE AIR

The defeat of France in 1940 fulfilled Hitler's dreams. It was assumed that Britain would also sue for peace, but Prime Minister Winston Churchill remained defiant. Hitler decided that the islands would have to be invaded and the navy and army began work on Operation Sealion. The Channel would be blocked by mines to prevent the Royal Navy from attacking the invasion force, and the initial wave would come in nine divisions landing between Worthing and Dover.

The British fighter and bomber squadrons were still intact and so the first priority was for the 2,800 aircraft of the Luftwaffe to destroy the 700 fighters of the Royal Air Force. The first attacks began on July 10 and were directed at the Channel ports and shipping, effectively closing the Channel to merchant convoys. The next target on August 10 was the RAF airfields along the south coast. The British were assisted by radar and by high-level intelligence from German coded signals sent by Enigma machines, which they were able to intercept and decode. In ten days' heavy fighting the Luftwaffe lost 602 aircraft and the RAF 260. Even so, had the Luftwaffe continued, the attrition could have destroyed the RAF.

An RAF night-raid on Berlin, in retaliation for an accidental Luftwaffe attack on London, caused Hitler to demand that London and the major British cities be attacked. These began on September 7 and on the 15th the Germans lost 56 aircraft. Two days later Operation Sealion was cancelled, although the night raids known as the Blitz continued into the spring of 1941. Between July and October 1940 the Luftwaffe had lost 1,800 planes and more than 2,500 aircrew, while RAF Fighter Command suffered losses of 1,100 aircraft and 550 pilots. The British fighter pilots who took part in defending the island would earn themselves the praise of Churchill: 'Never in the field of human conflict was so much owed by so many to so few.'

HEROES OF THE AIR

These are the fliers of the Battle of Britain. The Few and their Luftwaffe opponents recall the heat of the battle in the summer of 1940.

Fighting on different sides and under orders to wipe each other out, but with the same sense of duty, the aerial heroes of the Battle of Britain recall summer 1940.

⊙ *Flight Lieutenant Peter Brothers of 32 Squadron, now Air Commodore, CBE DSO DFC, made flying his entire life, and was at the forefront of the action in the south east.*

The philosophy of taking on German bombers and fighters was based on the fact that the Hurricanes should attack the bomber formations and the Spitfires the fighter cover. Of course it never worked out like that. Either you weren't together with the Spitfires when the raid happened or, by the time the first flight went in to attack the bombers, the fighters were already coming down—so one of you had to play rear guard action and take on the fighters. This usually fell to my lot, although I did get mixed up with bombers on occasions.

If you had the time and the height, you got into a favourable position up-sun—but again that didn't usually work out, because one was always scrambled on the late side. This was because, until the controllers were certain that it was a raid and not a spoof to draw you into the air, there was no point in launching you. If it was a spoof, by the time you were refuelling, the main raid would come—and this was what the controllers were trying to avoid.

As a result, it was rather late when we got the word 'Go'. That usually meant that you were at a disadvantage heightwise, so you'd have to take the bombers head-on. That, we discovered, was one of the best ways. They didn't like that, as they didn't have forward-firing guns—or very few of them did.

You could break up a formation and, once you'd scattered it, you had a good opportunity of shooting down individual aircraft without being involved in crossfire from the rest of the formation. Also, by the time the fighters got as far as London, they were at the limit of their range.

◀ **Spitfires in formation – the Glamor Boys of the RAF, photographed from a Defiant. Göring asked Adolf Galland what they needed to smash the RAF – his reluctant answer: 'A squadron of Spitfires'.**

The Germans had one formation where they were not in close cover with the bombers—this was with the fighters stacked up above, giving them a very favourable position. Once you were attacking the bombers, they could build up speed diving down to attack you. The 109s could dive much faster than we could. If they carried on their dive you hadn't a hope of catching them.

The 109s had fuel injection, with the result that they could take inverted load without the engine cutting. Whereas, if we pushed the stick forwards and went into a steep dive, we got a momentary cut in the engine—which didn't help build up speed. The only thing to do was a half roll, so the engine didn't cut, then an aileron turn down straight after them. On occasions we'd catch them like that, but that was usually because the chap was inexperienced.

Life was much simpler afterwards, when we were doing sweeps over France—you planned those. During the Battle of Britain, there was a lot of time for sitting around and waiting—and then there was the panic of the scramble.

The game was, you were shooting aeroplanes down—the only time I felt positively sick was when I hit a chap straight in the cockpit. I thought 'I didn't mean that—I only meant to hit a wing off'. That was the game side of it—we all rather hoped the chap

▼ **Relaxing at Hawkinge, pilots of No. 32 Squadron. Seated third from right, Flight Lieutenant Peter Brothers, second from right, Pilot Officer Keith Gillman, whose face became familiar on RAF posters.**

Peter Brothers

▲ **'When I was 15, my father paid for me to learn to fly, so I could get it out of my system' – Peter Brothers.**

would jump out and be taken prisoner of war rather than be killed.

One got very tired. When we were operating, we were at readiness half an hour before first light at about half past three in the morning, and we'd finish about half an hour after last light—say 10.30 at night.

By the time you'd gone over to the mess and had a meal (and I often used to go back and take a crate of beer for the ground crew, and had a chat with them to thank them) and were in bed, it was around midnight. Then you were back down at the aircraft by 3.30, with time for breakfast beforehand "

RAF Museum, Hendon

▲ **The emblem of No.32 Squadron, based at Biggin Hill in C Sector of Park's 11 Group, and at the forefront of the counter-attack in south-east England.**

▼ **It was not only in the air that a pilot had to keep an eye out all round – Fighter Command could ill afford to lose aircraft through careless maneuvering on the ground.**

RAF Museum, Hendon

Crown Copyright (Biggin Hill). Insert: RAF Museum, Hendon

▶ An RAF pilot acknowledges 'The 109's performance was that little bit better than the Hurricane's – they could dive faster than we could'. Luftwaffe fighters were ordered to fly in close formation above the bombers to try to prevent losses.

Daimler Benz. Inset: Suddeutscher Verlag

▲ Bombs away. A Do-17 drops its deadly cargo on target. 'I don't know why they chose to stop bombing aircraft factories and air bases, but as it was, they really took the bite off us at the right moment' – Flying Officer Peter Matthews.

▼ The emblem of No.249 Squadron, based at North Weald in Sector E of 11 Group.

◀ Hurricanes take off. 'It was a delightful aeroplane – not as agile as the Spitfire, but had a very good gun platform. It was very steady and took a tremendous amount of battle damage without appearing to worry too much.' Inset: Pilot Officer R G A Barclay.

R A F Museum, Hendon

Imperial War Museum. Inset: R F Barclay

Pilot Officer *R G A Barclay* with 249 Squadron based at North Weald, kept a diary during the battle of Britain. Excerpts for 15 September read like this.

❝ I followed three of our Hurricanes climbing up on the left of the bombers for a head-on attack— but lost patience and turned to do a beam attack on the leader. At the same time, the leading Hurricane turned to do a head-on attack and we almost collided above the bomber.

I remember diving earthwards in the middle of the bomber formation. I opened fire with more than full deflection and let the Do fly into the bullets like a partridge.

The Me 109s escorting the bombers were far above and behind and did not trouble us—I believe due to Spitfires engaging them. Owing to lack of fighter opposition, there was no need to break right away downwards, so I came back and did a short quarter attack. The Do 215 then broke away from the formation, and I saw that the engines were just idling as it glided down.

We were scrambled again later—and very shortly after reaching our height of 16,000 ft, we sighted fighters above us and about 20 Do 215s, for once at the same height as ourselves. The squadron went into the attack on the beam, except one, who went into some Heinkel IIIs he saw coming up behind the Do 215s.

As we attacked, I noted the cannon fire from the top rear gun positions of the Dos—little spurts of white smoke flicking back past the twin rudders in the slipstream, like intermittent squirts from a hose pipe.

After my attack, the Do 215 dropped behind the formation a bit and one parachute came out underneath. I then noticed all the Dos jettisoning their bombs. The Dos had broken up on our first attack and some dived for the clouds, but stayed just skimming the clouds and did not go right into them and instrument fly home. Inexperience? **"**

▼ The scramble. 'It affected people in different ways – one man used to be violently sick on the way to his aircraft, and we all swore we'd never have a phone in the house after the war'.

Crown Copyright (Biggin Hill)

RAF Museum, Hendon

▲ The emblem of No.1 Squadron, based at Northolt in Z Sector of 11 Group. The Squadron was formed in 1912 as part of the Royal Flying Corps.

◉ *Group Captain Peter Matthews, then a Flying Officer with Number 1 Squadron based at Northolt, had been in France since the start of the war—so the start of the action came as no surprise.*

" We came back on June 18, three days after the French packed up. We left everything behind—I left my golf clubs, saxophone, some marvellous records, a gramophone—all for the Germans to find. We were called out so often that we slept under the wings of our aircraft.

I was flying Hurricanes—there were more Hurricanes than Spits in Fighter Command at the time. We'd get to bed just after dark and try to get a few hours sleep—then up again. We spent a lot of time waiting for the phone to ring.

We were all pretty scared, really. The waiting was the worst part—we'd sit about playing poker, with that tension in the pit of our stomachs—it was almost a relief

▲ 'The worst part of it, I suppose, was the hanging around and waiting for the phone to ring to scramble us'. Here, pilots play a waiting game.

when we heard the phone ring to scramble us.

In a day we might be scrambled three, four or even five times—then you were probably only in the air for half an hour or 45 minutes. It's amazing that time went so fast. I suppose we all stood up to it because we were young.

I remember one attack we made on a big formation—we went in head-on. We wanted to get higher and avoid any fighters and shoot down the bombers from that position, but we couldn't gain the height in the time. So, we made a head-on attack on a bunch of 110s—we were very successful and must have shot down three or four.

Our Hurricanes weren't as fast as the Germans, but we were more manoeuvrable, if slower in climbing. Those Hurricanes took a hell of a lot of punishment—you could get badly shot up and still be safe. **"**

Peter Matthews

▲ Flying Officer Peter Matthews of No.1 Squadron, who claimed modestly: 'Northolt wasn't a very forward base, but we were jolly busy'.

Hulton Picture Library

THE LEGEND WHO LIVED TO FLY

Squadron Leader (later Wing Commander) R R Stanford Tuck—otherwise Bob, found being a fighter pilot 'the most fascinating occupation in the world'.

By the time of the Battle of Britain, he had already secured a name for himself in RAF history as one of its most successful pilots. Tuck joined No 92 Squadron of Spitfires on 1 July 1940 and was posted to No 257 Squadron of Hurricanes as Squadron Leader on 11 September.

Having downed eight German planes over Dunkirk, his reputation grew. 'He always seems to be around when the Nazis turn up', said a friend—after Tuck had shot down two enemy aircraft while out on what he termed 'a pleasure spin'.

During the Battle of Britain he was credited with 5½ (a shared hit) Ju 88, 1 Bf 110 and 3 Bf 109 aircraft.

By the time he crash-landed his Spitfire and was taken prisoner in France in 1942, he had made 29 'kills'.

Imperial War Museum

▶ Tuck in his Hurricane, showing a good number of kills to his credit.

RAF Museum, Hendon

▲ The emblem of No.92 Squadron, based at Biggin Hill.

Formal reports cite an incident on 18 August 1940 as follows: 'Spitfire N3040. Abandoned over Horsmonden, damaged by return fire from Ju88 2.15 pm. Crashed by Tucks Cottages, near Park Farm. Flt Lt. Robert Stanford Tuck baled out and was slightly injured in heavy landing. Aircraft a write-off'. To Tuck of 92 Squadron, it was like this:

❝ Spotted two Ju 88s that had passed over me at 15,000 ft, heading SSW or S. I turned on them and gave chase. As there was no cloud, the two E/A (enemy aircraft) put down their noses and went straight on to the surface of the water.

I flew straight ahead of them as fast as possible and then turned head-on and fired at the number 2 E/A. After passing close over the top of the E/A and pulling straight up, I observed that he had gone straight into the water with a terrific splash and disappeared. (Up 'til this time, I had only been hit in the wings and through the left side of the perspex on the windscreen.)

I then flew straight ahead again to attack the E/A that was left. Just when I had opened fire on this head-on attack, I saw a large greeny bluish flash from the nose of the Ju 88. Immediately following this, there was a loud crash on the underneath front of my aircraft. This seemed to tip my tail up and I thought I should hit the water. However, I pulled straight up and left the Ju 88 heading off on the same course, leaving a trail of oil on the water. I was now approximately 35 – 40 miles south of Beachy Head at 4,000 ft. My aircraft must have been badly damaged, as there was excessive engine vibration and glycol

▶ 'We passed as close as this!' A German pilot swaps experiences with a colleague after the day's mission.

▼ The cramped cockpit of a Spitfire. The machine gun firing button is sited at the end of the central joystick.

Imperial War Museum

John Frost Collection

◀ An RAF morale-booster. A painting provocatively titled 'Off with the old – on with the new'.

and oil temperatures were very high.

I managed to reach the coast, but dense fumes were coming from the engine and under the dashboard. I could feel myself being overcome by these fumes, so decided to abandon my aircraft. Jumped clear at 800 ft. Could not say whether my aircraft was straight and level or not, as fumes had blinded me. My aircraft landed ½ mile away from me **"** in a wood and did no damage.

✠ *On only his second bombing mission, Ober-leutnant Hans Gollnisch of the Stab II/KG30 bomber unit was ground-ed by an RAF fighter as he approached his target.*

" In early September 1940, my unit was transferred from Denmark to Chievre, near Ath in Belgium, in order to concentrate bomber groups for bigger raids on England. It was my second mission of this kind when on September 9 we took off from Chievre to meet about 200 bombers at 5,000 metres over Cap Gris-Nez.

After a wide swing eastwards, we headed for London, escorted by hundreds of German fighters. The targets were the docks and shipping in the Thames, and could already be seen, when we were suddenly hit by a very short burst of fire from the machine guns of the RAF fighter that had evidently approached from

Bildarchiv Preussischer Kulturbesitz

▶ Luftwaffe bomber crew into action. A pilot and navigator read their map in the cockpit of a Ju 88. Inset: Oberleutnant Hans Gollnisch, whose Ju-88 was shot down at Barcombe, near Lewes in Sussex.

Andy Saunders

below and behind, unseen by the escorting fighters and our rear gunner, Unteroffizier Diebler.

Our plane was badly damaged and the situation was grim—the control column didn't work any more, as a bullet must have severed the elevator cables, and both engines were hit, the right losing gasoline, the left oil.

Then, the observer, Unteroffizier Rolf, reported that Diebler was lying dead in a pool of blood, a bullet having pierced the artery of his neck. I gave the order to shed the cockpit roof in order to bail out, but then I found that I could just about control the aeroplane by the trimming wheel, which to some extent replaced the elevator. Thinking of our dead gunner, I decided to stay in the plane and make for the Channel. If our

▶ A Luftwaffe poster. Strength, discipline, power and their conquest of the skies reassured pilots of their natural superiority.

Süddeutscher Verlag

Topham Picture Library

▲ Oberleutnant Gerhard Kadow, the first of many German fighter pilots officially taken prisoner during The Battle of Britain, lands safely in Britain and is taken prisoner.

▼ The personal emblem of Oberst Adolf Galland – a Mickey Mouse with a cruel streak.

engines kept going long enough, we could get down on the water and maybe get back to France in the rubber dinghy which was carried on board. So I turned south for the shortest route and jettisoned our bombs. However, we now had no guns to defend ourselves against further attack, as these had gone with the roof, so I dived for cover in the clouds 3,000 metres below.

Unfortunately, in the clouds the engines stopped and didn't want to start again. By now we were too low to bale out, so had no choice but to make a very difficult landing with no use of the control column. I couldn't even let out the flaps, because the electrical system had failed!

I was very lucky to make a good landing as another problem was that of all the fields being covered in all sorts of poles and obstacles like old cars—as a defence against a possible landing by assault gliders in an invasion.

However, I got us down in one piece and after we had lifted out the dead gunner, we set fire to our aeroplane and gave ourselves up to police and soldiers.

✠ ***It was on a fighter mission to escort Stuka bombers that Oberleutnant Gerhard Kadow with the 9th Staffel, Zerstörergeschwader 76 (9 Squadron, Destroyer Group 76) became the first German brought down and taken prisoner on British soil.***

❝ On 11 July, I flew Me 110, number 2N + EP, with my wireless operator and air gunner, Gefreiter Helmut Scholz. My squadron was stationed at Laval, and we flew from here to Dinard for refuelling and from Dinard to England at about 12.00 noon.

My squadron, together with two others, had orders to protect Ju 87 Stuka dive-bombers, which would attack targets on the south coast of England in the vicinity of Portland.

Before we started, our commander, Major Grabmann, told us that it was vital that no Stuka be lost. This meant a considerable risk to our lives.

At the English coast I counted

▲ Stukas on the attack. 'We had some good days against Stukas—one could get amongst them and dodge the fighters fairly easily'. Inset: the black, ominous protector—a Bf-110 fighter.

some twenty dark spots in the distance, somewhat higher than we were. I was certain they were RAF fighters, but couldn't recognise whether they were Hurricanes or Spitfires—but knew that our twin-engined machines were no match for these single-engined fighters.

However, it was our duty to protect the Stukas, so that they could bomb unhindered. The main strength of the Me 110 was the two 20mm cannons and four machine guns in its nose. I pressed the firing buttons and bullets flew like water out of a watering can towards the enemy. The closing speed was high, and at the last minute both I and my attacker had to break away to avoid a head-on collision. Whether I scored any hits or not, I don't know.

The next moment, two fighters were on my tail and had opened fire. Almost immediately both of my engines stopped and a return to the

THE ACES IN THE GERMAN PACK

Major (later General) Adolf Galland, a veteran of the Spanish Civil War, was a flamboyant character (he had a special tray installed in the cockpit of his fighter to accommodate his favourite big, black cigars). 'Dolfo' Galland led a Bf-109E group of the Luftwaffe's 26 Fighter Wing, then took command of the Wing on 21 August 1940.

Top-scoring German pilot in the Battle of Britain, he eventually shot down 103 aircraft. At 30 he was the youngest General in the German forces.

An unsmiling introvert, Major (later Lieutenant-Colonel) Werner Mölders was one of Germany's top fighter aces, and the first to shoot down 20 enemy planes in 1940. For this, 'Vati' (Daddy) Mölders received the coveted Knight's Cross.

The youngest Kommodore in the Luftwaffe, he commanded 51 Fighter Wing of Bf-109s from 27 July 1940. Surviving a vicious dogfight with 'Sailor' Malan on 28 July, but badly wounded in the legs, he recovered and shot down a total of 55 aircraft in the Battle of Britain.

Süddeutscher Verlag

▲ Time off for fighter aces, Werner Mölders (left) and Adolf Galland on a hunting trip. Inset: the Luftwaffe pilot's badge.

Continent was clearly impossible. The enemy saw his success and stopped shooting, but watched me from behind.

I flung off my cabin roof for a quick escape and hoped it would hit him. I ordered Helmut Scholz to do the same. He radioed that the mechanism to ditch his cabin roof would not operate as a result of bullet damage.

▼ The end of one man's war. Gerhard Kadow's Messerschmitt Bf-110, shot down at Povington Heath, near Weymouth. Kadow spent the remainder of the war in captivity.

I couldn't bail out and leave Scholz to his fate, and for the same reason a ditching in the sea seemed unwise. The only alternative was a crash landing on British soil.

After we had landed I found I could not leave my cockpit—a high explosive bullet had hit my seat, causing a big hole. The torn aluminium 'fangs' around the hole had nailed themselves through my parachute pack and tunic and on to my flesh.

I pulled myself forward, and suddenly was free. I left the aircraft and smashed the cabin roof of my

gunner so that he could get out. He was hurt only by shell splinters. The first thing to do was destroy the aircraft. We didn't have a self-destruct charge, so opened the fuel caps and tried to ignite the petrol with the muzzle flash from my pistol.

I fired eight shots, but had no success. In hindsight, this was just as well, otherwise the aircraft would have exploded and killed us. ❞

▼ The emblem of Galland's Jagdgeschwader 26, one of the Luftwaffe's foremost fighter units.

CHAPTER 3

BATTLE DIARY

JUNE 1941

22	Beginning of Operation Barbarossa
29	Minsk pocket closed

JULY

1	Fall of Riga
5	German forces reach River Dnieper
9	Rivers Dvina and Dnieper crossed, Smolensk threatened
12	First Luftwaffe bombing raid on Moscow
14	German forces reach River Luga
17	Dnieper crossed at Mogilev
27	Smolensk pocket closed
31	Army Group North reaches Lake Ilmen

AUGUST

1	Russian counter-attack begins from the Pripet Marshes
7–8	First Russian air raid on Berlin
12	Army Group Center splits to send Panzers north and south
29	Finnish army captures Viipuri

SEPTEMBER

12	Kiev pocket closed
15	Leningrad cut off from the rest of the USSR
25	Start of the siege of Sevastopol
26	Kiev pocket eliminated – Germans now only 200 miles from Moscow

BARBAROSSA – SCORCHED EARTH

On June 22, 1941, Hitler launched his attack on the Soviet Union, codenamed Barbarossa. Three army and Panzer groups bore the brunt of the fighting, along with troops from his Italian, Romanian and Hungarian allies. The odds seemed overwhelmingly against the Germans: with only 3,332 tanks, they were massively outnumbered by the Soviets' 24,000. They did, however, have the advantage of *blitzkreig,* or lightning war, based on quick movement and surprise, and were well supported by the Luftwaffe, which on only the first day of the campaign destroyed 1,489 Soviet aircraft on the ground. Within a month, they had destroyed nearly 5,000 planes. On the ground, meanwhile, Army Group North pushed along the Baltic coast to encircle Leningrad, while Army Group Center headed towards Smolensk and Moscow. Army Group South drove towards Kiev, reaching Rostov by December 5.

The initial Soviet resistance was ineffectual, and as the German army rolled into the Soviet landmass, fighting huge battles of encirclement, it exacted a heavy toll. Of the 12 million men the Red Army mustered for what proved the greatest land battle in history, around a quarter were taken prisoner, while the Germans also captured around 15,000 tanks. Despite their own 800,000 casualties and the loss of the majority of their tanks, the Germans were convinced by the end of 1941 that the huge losses had broken the back of the Red Army.

As the Reich's stormtroopers advanced, however, they found progress increasingly difficult. Poor roads turned from dust to thick mud; the retreating Red Army fought a strong rearguard action, and destroyed vital bridges and industrial sites in a scorched earth campaign that finally brought the Germans to a halt in the snow outside Moscow.

SCORCHED EARTH

Against the backdrop of the longest and most savage land battle ever fought in history, combatants from both east and west tell of how they experienced the epic confrontation.

A s the Russians pressed their antiquated forces into action, Wehrmacht troops swept into the Soviet landmass—not all of them convinced of the rightness of their headlong thrust into Communist territory.

 Konstantin Simonov, a Russian novelist and poet, was sent as a war correspondent to join a unit at the front. His train's progress was blocked, so he set out on foot with an artillery captain to hitch a lift and join up with his unit.

" German aircraft were circling the town. It was desperately hot and dusty. At the exit of the town, near the hospital, I saw the first corpses. Some were lying on stretchers, others without. I don't know where they came from—they were probably bomb victims.

Troops and vehicles were going along the road, some in one direction, some in the other. It was impossible to make sense of it all. Having discovered that the petrol filling point was 15 kilometres out of town, we went there, picking up a supplies officer and two or three soldiers on the way.

Everything was quiet at the filling point, although we had been told en route that the Germans were there. While we were filling the tank with buckets of petrol, the captain went to the commander of the point to explain something. Following behind him, I saw a strange sight; the captain

◀▼ The German invasion force presses on east of Kiev, devastation in its wake. Inset: The Waffen SS storms into action.

with whom I was travelling and a colonel were pointing their pistols at two officers in sappers' uniforms, who had been disarmed. One of them wore medal ribbons. It turned out that they had been sent to discuss the possibility of demolishing the point, and either they had given the impression of already being on the point of destroying it, or there had been some kind of misunderstanding, but in any case, the captain and colonel took them for diversionists and for five minutes held them at pistol point. When it was all cleared up, one of the sappers, an elderly major with two decorations, began to shout that nothing like this had ever happened to him before, that he had been wounded three times in the Finnish campaign, and that after this insult, the only thing left was to shoot himself. It was quite difficult to calm him down. **"**

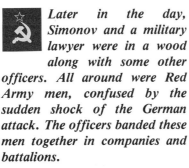 *Later in the day, Simonov and a military lawyer were in a wood along with some other officers. All around were Red Army men, confused by the sudden shock of the German attack. The officers banded these men together in companies and battalions.*

" Half an hour after I arrived, the Germans discovered our assembly from the air and began to machine-gun the wood. Waves of aircraft flew, one after the other, at intervals of about 20 minutes. We lay down, pressing our heads against the gaunt trees. The trees were not very dense, so it was easy to shoot at us from the air. Nobody knew each other and with the best will in the world, it was difficult for people either to give or to take orders.

Finally, after three o'clock, a flight of IL-15s flew over. We jumped up, elated because our own planes had turned up at last. But they gave us a good shower of lead and several men nearby were wounded—all of them in the foot. They had been lying in a line.

We thought that this was an accident, a mistake, but the planes came back and went over the wood a second and a third time. The stars on their wings were clearly visible. When they went over for the third time, someone with a machine-gun managed to bring one of them down.

Quite a few people ran to the outskirts of the wood, where the plane was burning. Those who had gone there described how they dragged the half-burned body of a German pilot

▲ With smoke still pouring from a bombed-out town, a unit of German 38(t) tanks, commandeered from the Czechoslovakians, drives on to hammer the last nails into its coffin.

▶ In the heart of Russia, rural calm is shattered by the arrival of the Waffen SS Division 'Das Reich' – at this stage optimistic and unimpeded by the rigors of the icy Russian winter.

from the cockpit.

I do not know how this came about. Probably the Germans in the first day captured several planes somewhere and showed their pilots how to fly them. In any case, it left a very depressing impression on us.

I walked to the edge of the wood, where the forest road joined the Minsk highway. Suddenly, five paces away, a soldier with a rifle jumped out on the highway. His eyes seemed to be crawling out of their sockets, and had an insane look about them as he shouted out in a strangled, tearing voice: 'Run! The Germans have surrounded us! We're finished!' One of the officers standing by me shouted, 'Shoot him, shoot that panic-monger'. He began to fire.

I also pulled out my pistol, which I had obtained just an hour before, and began to shoot at the fugitive. Now, later, I think that he was probably a man maddened, a psycho case, not having been able to stand the terrible events of that day.

Evidently we did not hit him, as he ran off further. A captain jumped out in his path and, trying to hold him, grasped his rifle. It went off and, frightened still more by this shot, the fugitive, like a hunted animal, turned round and with his bayonet, rushed at the captain. The latter took out his pistol and shot him. Three or four men silently dragged the body off the road.

"

◀ **The Battle of Minsk is over and the city is in German hands. Surrendering voluntarily, Russian soldiers tear off their insignia and accept imprisonment.**

Bundesarchiv-Koblenz

Dmitrii Gavryushin, an infantry battalion commander, was amongst the many Russian troops cut off behind the advancing German front line, trapped by the sheer speed of their attack. His escape from captivity was to last an agonizing three months on the run.

"Having fought for 14 days without a break, I was bruised, but stayed in action. I was later wounded in the arm and hand.

On 24 July I was put in the Mogilev hospital. On 26 July, the town was captured by the fascists and the hospital was not evacuated because it was encircled.

Another two days later I, and some soldiers from my battalion, fled from the hospital. We changed our clothes in someone's home and set off in the direction of our troops.

We went in the guise of civilian prisoners who had been working at the airport and had been wounded in the bombing. After five days, the fascists detained us at the front. We were held for three days, and then sent to one of the Smolensk hospitals.

Having spent three days there, and having carried out an appropriate intelligence appreciation, we ran away

▼ Heavily muffled against the cold, Red Army soldiers check over a Russian KV-I, a strong, maneuverable heavy tank, first tested and designed in 1940.

Süddeutscher Verlag

from this hospital and after 15 days, caught up with the front line near Shmakov, where they again detained us.

After five hungry days, they put us in a truck and sent us forwards. Catching up with a group of our prisoners of war, they put us out of the lorry, joined us to the column, and hurried us on. Hunger, and the pain of my wounds, stopped me keeping up with the fit ones, and I lagged behind, with the fascist escort all the time pushing me on with rifle-butt blows to my back. Having spent the night gathering our strength, we ran away in the morning. After several days, we reached the settlement of Stodolishche and bumped into our surgeon. We asked him to change our bandages. He uncovered our wounds and they were already gangrenous, with little worms crawling about."

Eberhard Wagemann led a platoon of 13 Company in Regiment 67 of the German 23 Infantry Division in the advance into Russia. Contrary to popular German belief, the Red Army turned out to be a formidable adversary.

"Returning to Regiment 67 in 1941, detailed to lead a platoon with the 13 Company, I would frequently go and see my contemporary from my training period, Ekkehard Maurer, who was then Adjutant to Captain Heinemann, Commander of III Batallion. He had gained a special respect from the members of the regiment because of his fearlessness, even towards leading party figures, his military prowess and soldierly bearing.

Once the news began to spread of the proposed Russian campaign, he left us in no doubt as to what he thought of it. 'This is the end for Germany'—still, he remained a soldier and a Commander, served his Fatherland and his comrades and had no illusions about the prospects of this war. As a cadet schooled in Berlin in the Prussian tradition, he called it 'something I just damn well have to do'. All his life he remained a model for us.

We felt no sense of injustice towards the Soviet Union. We knew about the Party's monopoly of power and of Stalin's Terror. We were convinced we were superior to the Red Army, which had been weakened by Stalin's purges, and had hardly given a convincing account of it-

Roger-Viollet, Paris

self in the war against Finland in 1940-41. But it was the great expanse of Russia we feared, in which even Napoleon had had to fight to the bitter end. We knew of the Russian soldier's courage and stamina.

The III Batallion had its first taste of this directly behind the frontier of Eastern Poland, which had been annexed by the Soviet Union in 1939. The garrison in the newly-built bunkers of Sklody defended them down to the last man. During the advance march we were confronted with the horrific effects of modern weapons of war, as we passed alongside mile-long columns of Russian tanks, which had been destroyed by our Stukas.

However, our batallion was soon to see the other side of the Russian

▲ Marshal Budenny's defending army is in retreat—behind it a trail of abandoned Russian equipment—weapons and vehicles. In the calm before the invasion force arrives, painfully gaunt horses browse amongst the wreckage.

soldiers during the attack on Brunitschi and Mogilew—their courage and military skill.

The attitude of the indigenous population towards us was one of cautious trepidation at first, but they became increasingly friendly. The people had clearly been fed horror stories about the German soldiers.

Particularly in White Russia, the old men, women and children welcomed us with bread and salt, and they would show us their crucifixes and icons, which they stashed away in 'God's holy corner'. As for provisions, there wasn't much for us to take—initially a bit of poultry, sometimes, though rarely, a calf or cow for the field kitchen, all of which we had to pay for, of course. So long as you continued to behave decently towards them, you could get along quite well with the Russian people.

However, the partisan warfare, which was just then starting up, had been prepared and orchestrated, as it were, at arms' length, by the Red Army and the Party. I had taken over 9 Company from the wounded 1st Lieutenant Petersen by the Desna. Following the battle of Wjasma, I had been ordered to 'clean out' an area of woodland with this company, after shots had been fired from there at our vehicles. As we got into the wood itself, we could see that the whole area was one large partisan camp, extended and occupied in peace-time. The paths had been covered over with camouflage

▲ A German mechanized unit in a Mk IV Panzer arrives to an indifferent reception in a small Russian town.

Bruce Quarrie

netting—underground passageways linked bunkers and fighting positions, which were dug into and magnificently camouflaged in the overgrown forest floor. It was possible to mount an all-round defence of the area from the combat positions—the underground passages followed a path with various corners.

At first sight the wood looked deserted—however, as the first volunteer stepped on to a ramp, he was shot in the stomach.

The operation had to be called off—Stukas were called for. **"**

Martin Hirsch, age 28, was an NCO with the 3 Panzer Division 'Brandenburg', which advanced into Russia in summer 1941. He had fundamental disagreement with Nazi tenets, and eventually became a 'Verfassungsrichter' in Germany—one of the most senior-ranking constitutional judges.

" I was brought up in an actively democratic and republican family, and the schools I attended were run along the same principles, so that I was completely immune to the ideas of National Socialism. As a student I marched through the streets chanting, 'If you elect Hitler, you elect war. Smash the fascists wherever you find them'. Unfortunately, we were proved right, but it wasn't us that smashed the fascists—they were smashed by others, in the war, that is.

When I was first called up, I was passed unfit for military service on grounds of health, but when the war came along, the circumstances were not so favourable, and this time I was passed fit.

I was with the 3 Panzer Division 'Brandenburg', which was mobilised for operation 'Barbarossa'. My first recollection is of crossing the Bug in the direction of Brest-Litovsk—we were standing around waiting for orders, and there were, at that time, various rumours going round, quite absurd now, looking back on them. Rumours like, there would be no war in the east as such, instead the Brit-

▼ Red Army machine-gunners, heavily camouflaged in woodland greenery, lie in ambush. Their grim determination, courage and patriotism made sure that the German forces had no hiding place and no time when they could relax from the fear of attack.

Popperfoto

▶ Ill-prepared for winter combat, men of 'Der Führer' regiment, Waffen SS, wear improvised camouflage clothing.

S.I.R.P.A./E.C.P.A. France

ish would go in with us to encircle the Russians and liberate the world from Communism. This was obviously rubbish, but that was the kind of rumour that was usual then.

The first heavy barrage from the Russians that I experienced was during the advance on Brest-Litovsk. We had crossed the Bug and camped down. On the advance into Brest-Litovsk I got my first taste of the horror to come. There was a huge field full of corpses and wounded Russian soldiers. These had, I think, been hit by the advance bombing by the Luftwaffe. One Russian soldier was bleeding heavily and I tried to bind his wounds, when suddenly a soldier from another unit, whom I didn't know, came over to me: 'What are you doing here?' he asked. I told him I was bandaging a soldier. He said it was not my job to look after these 'Untermenschen'—he did actually use this word—but I remembered from my training that our instructions were that a wounded enemy soldier was no longer an enemy, and it was our duty to help.

He told me he would report me, but I never heard anything more from him. He struck me as quite a callous Nazi, and I was pleased that I never caught sight of him again.

The war went on, and my memory of the individual experiences is not very clear. My major preoccupation throughout the whole of the Russian campaign was to ensure that I would

▲ The horse-drawn regiment 'Gross-Deutschland' plods through the sludgy roads of early winter as cold sets in in Russia.

Bruce Quarrie

Bundesarchiv-Koblenz

▶ The end of one man's war—the driver of a Russian T-26B tank surrenders to his German captor, August 1941.

Roger-Viollet, Paris

▲ Carnage in the streets of Rostov in southern Russia, as motorized and horse-drawn units of the German invasion force take control.

▲ Crouched in scant cover at the edge of a Russian town under attack, German soldiers prepare to open fire with a machine-gun.

not be promoted to an officer.

There were others who felt like me, but we were a minority, and any actual meaningful resistance in such a theatre of war was impossible. Had I been at the Western Front, I'd have tried to go over to the other side.

What I remember of the daily routine of the early part of the war is mainly the sheer tedium of it all.

I remember sleeping in bedclothes thick with dust, dirt, cockroaches and lice which plagued the motorised units—I was then with the artillery—for whom, it was said, conditions were relatively good.

My worst experience during the initial advance was in August of '41 The unit was based in a village—I can't remember which, and we were hit by heavy bombing from the Russians. We were in our quarters, and some of the men were sitting around a table. We could hear the whistling of the bombs which seemed to be quite a distance away. Then the noise was more high-pitched . . . the bombs were dropping closer. I dived under the table. All the people who had been sitting at the table were killed in this attack, one had his head ripped to pieces. I don't know how I came through. **"**

Alex Vanags Baginskis was a young teenager when Germany invaded Latvia. He recalls the people's delight at being freed from the existing oppressive Communist regime, and their subsequent disillusionment.

" I was living in Riga, the capital of Latvia, with my mother when the Soviets invaded. We woke up one morning—June 17 1940, and the tanks were in the streets. I was thirteen years old and very intrigued. I looked at the tanks and the soldiers—they were scruffy, their uniforms didn't look nice and they were all armed.

At the beginning, they said that nothing would change—but it did.

I remember very clearly reading in a Soviet paper in April 1941, a little, insignificant notice about German troops going through Finland. They were just passing through Finland to Norway. I was good at geography, and I wondered to myself . . . .

People were hoping that the Germans would come. They are our

S.I.R.P.A./E.C.P.A. France

Süddeutscher Verlag

historical enemies. They arrived with the Bible and the sword in the 12/13th Century and subdued our people, forcing Christianity on with them. They ruled us until World War I, but even the Germans would be better than the Russians.

Early in 1941, the Soviets suddenly started increasing the number of troops in Latvia. Artillery moved through at night, the horses' hooves wrapped in rags. We couldn't hear them, but we could see them.

In spring 1941 the Russians suddenly wanted to build 80 or 90 airfields in Latvia. Most of them were bomber airfields—and you don't build bomber airfields for defence—they were planning something.

In June 1941, whispers started going around that the Soviets would deport people. These people were described by the Soviets as 'socially dangerous elements'. One night, over 35,000 people, out of a population of about 1,600,000, were deported. Quite a number were shot as well. You can imagine the shock of going to visit my uncle next morning to find the whole house empty.

A number of people, including my mother, took to the woods to stay with a family who lived near a farm. There were about 30 or 40 people living there with us in the woods.

About a week later, the war began. Suddenly, early one morning, the German aircraft arrived over Riga. We were up on the roof, binoculars in hand, watching the dive-bombers and the anti-aircraft guns firing. The Germans didn't bomb the town—they bombed gas tanks, oil tanks.

Within two days, the Red Army was retreating. Single German aircraft would fly over in the evening dusk and fire on the road. You could see the tracers. Once I saw a Soviet fighter take off, trying to catch a German plane. His aircraft was shot and exploded in the woods.

▼ **Time off from their almost religious drive against the Communist 'Untermensch', a group of German soldiers enjoy the privilege of some unguarded relaxation and a taste of the local spirits.**

We returned to Riga a couple of days after the Germans arrived. A home guard and scout groups were organised. I was a scout. There was still some hard fighting to do—there was a lot of street fighting in Riga old town with the remaining Soviet troops or local communist militia.

There were burnt-out tanks with skeletons inside which had sunk into the pavements and we couldn't move them. They remained for a long, long, time. There were lots of things for kids to do—aircraft and tanks to look at. I remember going to a Soviet airfield with fighters lined up there. The Germans didn't want the aircraft and there were boys there with screwdrivers, taking everything apart. You could find ammunition, machine guns, rifles—I had a whole arsenal!

At first everything was very patriotic—it was a feeling of relief. We all, even us kids, thought 'We're free now'. The Latvian flag was everywhere. The honeymoon lasted for two or three months, before the German Party people came and that was it.

The national front was forbidden, national patriotic songs were forbidden, our anthem was forbidden. We were an occupied country again. **"**

▼ **Not all German soldiers enjoyed the rewards of a crusade well fought, as this painstakingly prepared grave to gunner Baumgarten shows.**

S.I.R.P.A./E.C.P.A. France

CHAPTER 4

BATTLE DIARY

OCTOBER 1941
2	Beginning of Operation *Taifun* (Typhoon)
6	Kleist reaches Sea of Azov
13	Vyasma pocket eliminated
14	German advance reaches Kalinin
15–16	Odessa evacuated by sea
19	Moscow evacuated but Stalin stays put

NOVEMBER
9	Germans capture Yalta
15	Assault on Moscow renewed
21	Fall of Rostov
23	Capture of Klin
24	Rostov evacuation in face of counter-attack
29	Moskva-Volga Canal crossed
30	Stalin approves counter-offensive plans

DECEMBER
5	Hitler halts drive on Moscow
6	Beginning of Russian counter-offensive
15	Soviets reoccupy Klin and Kalinin
17	German assault on Sevastopol begins
26	Russians begin counter-attack into Crimea
30	Russians recapture Tula

JANUARY 1942
7–8	New Russian offensive on northern sector
24	Russians recross River Donets
31	Soviet counter-offensive halted, except locally

FEBRUARY
24	Demyansk pocket completely sealed

MARCH
1	New Russian offensive in Crimea

APRIL
22	Relief of Demyansk pocket

MOSCOW – A MERCILESS FIGHT

On October 2, 1941, the German Army Group Center launched Operation Typhoon, the drive to capture the Soviet capital Moscow. By the 20th, the Panzer spearheads had advanced to barely 40 miles from the city, where they came to a halt. Fuel was running short, the harsh Russian winter was beginning to bite, and a new Soviet commander, General Georgi Zhukov, had arrived in the city to organize its defense. From spies in Tokyo, Zhukov learnt that the Japanese Manchurian Army had no plans to attack the Soviet Union, and the knowledge allowed him to call on fresh Siberian troops from the far eastern border.

Nevertheless, by December 5, the Germans had outflanked Soviet defenses to reach Alteryevo, a town which actually lay to the east of Moscow, but there their long advance met its highwater mark. Zhukov massed all available aircraft to protect the city as he waited for reinforcements and for the weather to worsen. The last-ditch defense succeeded: between November 16 and December 5, the Germans had lost some 85,000 men. Now Zhukov counter-attacked to the north with 100 of his fresh Siberian divisions.

The weather had worsened: as temperatures plunged to –40°F, the Germans began to fall back. Not having entered Russia equipped for a winter battle, their troops suffered badly. Many were reduced to wearing captured Russian clothing to avoid freezing to death. Vehicles and weapons became useless as fuel and lubricants froze. Zhukov's ferocious pursuit in the north cost the retreating troops 30,000 dead.

As his ambitions for taking the Soviet capital vanished, Hitler ordered his armies to stand and fight, relieving 35 generals of their commands and appointing himself Commander in Chief of the Army. His troops finally fell back to a line between Vyazma and Rzhev, which they held until March 1943. Zhukov had saved Moscow and turned back the German tide – but at the cost of 500,000 men.

A MERCILESS FIGHT

War on the eastern front was a savage, brutal affair on a scale never before conceived. Both German and Soviet fighters recall their terrible ordeal

▲The insignia of the **Russian Red Army** with hammer and sickle motif.

Feelings ran high amongst the defending Soviet troops as the Germans edged towards Moscow. Amongst the invaders, morale was teetering and falling in the appalling conditions. Had they bitten off more than they could chew?

 M E Katukov, commander of the Russian 1st Guards Tank Brigade, consisting of the excellent new T-34 tanks and some of the not-so-new KV and BT types, was intent on hampering the progress of the German troops as they launched their second attempt to take Moscow on November 16.

❝ The enemy was tearing towards Yazvishche village in order to cut off the Volokolamsk highway. The defence there consisted of a battalion of frontier guards, commanded by Samoilenko, two tanks in ambush, Afonin's and Leshchishin's, and two batteries of the anti-aircraft division, commanded by Afanesenko.

Samoilenko reported that German tanks were approaching, and the reply came, 'Use the ambush and smash them.'

The Hitlerites tried to surround Samoilenko's battalion. Four of their tanks crawled along the highway, but were set on fire by Afonin and Leshchishin. But behind them came six more tanks and a line of Hitlerite infantry amounting to a battalion.

The frontier guards could not withstand this enemy pressure and made a fighting retreat to the village of Gryadi. Afonin and Leshchishin knocked out two more tanks and,

striking the Hitlerite flank, began to crush the infantry. Some Hitlerites succeeded in climbing on to Afonin's tank from the rear and shouted, 'Russians, surrender!'

Having seen this, Leshchishin used his machine gun to clean the enemy off his friend's tank. At the same time, Afonin saw that the Hitlerites were similarly crawling on top of Leshchishin's tank and knocked them off with his machine-gun.

Our brigade was given two armoured trains, which bombarded enemy concentrations near Lystsovo. At this same time, about 30 enemy bombers attacked the station at Chismen and damaged the track.

Although no bombs hit the armoured trains, their gun platforms were put at a slant, so that the muzzles pointed into the ground. We allocated repair squads to help, but then the enemy intensified his attack. The battalion of frontier guards again went into action and our two anti-aircraft batteries fired at the enemy tanks and infantry, succeeding in beating off the attack. Soon the railway track was repaired and the armoured trains were once more fit for battle. ❞

◀ **Strange apparitions loom out of the snowscape. Red Army soldiers in winter camouflage move into action.**

▼ **Originally an anti-aircraft gun, the German 88 mm flak gun proved its worth in an anti-tank role and later became a formidable weapon in desert campaigns as well as on the Eastern Front.**

Tass News Agency

Bundesarchiv-Koblenz

Novosti Press Agency

▲ The Red Army and 'General Winter' attack the invaders.

▼ Armed with a PPD 1940G 7.62 mm sub-machine gun, a Red Army soldier calls his comrades on to attack.

Commander of the Russian 2nd Guards Cavalry Corps, I A Iliev, described a successful operation conducted by the Red Cavalry against the German troops as they advanced towards Moscow.

" At 3 o'clock all the detachments were to concentrate in a wood south of Lake Velisto, and all the commanders were to report their decisions within an hour. My voice was drowned by the roar of enemy aircraft, flying low over the wood. 'They're looking for us', observed Revin.

'We've really got them worried if they've put so many aircraft up', I heard Dovator say from behind me, as he jumped off his horse, adjusted his sword and pistol and came up to us.

The intelligence officer reported that an enemy motorised column of infantry and artillery was moving along the road from Nikulin and would cross our path. 'What does this mean? Is it a planned regrouping or is it . . .? No, if they were coming after us, they would be in battle deployment by now.' We instantly decided to destroy them.

I give the order to move off. Liaison officers hurry off to their units. Our movement slows down, the units tense.

We stop, with the road in front of us. We can hear the sound of motors, and the German commands. I look at my watch, whose luminous hands show that it is twenty minutes to midnight. The attack signal.

Grenades explode. The babel of mixed rifle and machine gun fire. The roar of motors. Like a thousand black ghosts tearing out of the night, we rush out sowing terror and death.

It's soon over. The cavalry dissolve once more in the thick mist of the wood. All that can be heard is the dull clink of harnesses, the excited breathing of horses and the occasional Cossack voice. "

◀ Snow can be fun—but only in small bursts, as these German soldiers would soon discover on long forced marches in arctic conditions.

▼ From fast-gained experience, this German infantryman knows that Russian partisans could lurk anywhere—his slow, painful advance must be carried out with the greatest caution.

M A Zashibalov, commander of the Russian 60th Infantry Division of the 23rd Reserve Army Group, recalls the part his troops played in the defence of Moscow after a speedy training as a division of the 'Peoples' Reinforcement' —a kind of rapidly recruited citizens' army.

"The enemy, having broken through the front in the Kaluga area, began to mount an offensive against Tarusa and Serpukhov. The 49th Army HQ did not have enough reserves to defend these towns and an operational 'gateway' 30-40 km wide began to form, undefended either by troops or defence obstacles.

Luckily for us, the German-fascist command was so drunk with success that it did not always carry out a proper tactical or operational reconnaissance, and therefore it had no idea of the favourable situation which was developing in this sector.

The Military Council of the Western Army Group decided that the 60th Division should be immediately transferred to the 49th Army, and by forced marches, the division moved to the Tarusa area, where its units occupied the 30-40 km sector of the defence line and busied themselves with filling the breach that was forming, so as to bar the enemy's route to Serpukhov.

With such a length to be defended, our density on the ground was not, of course, very great. We had one soldier for every 100 – 150 metres of front, and one heavy machine-gun for every three kilometres. "

As Germany continued to push through towards Moscow on land, Flight Sergeant Alfred Sticht, Observer in a Heinkel 111 of Kampfgeschwader 53 Legion Condor, was flying in to make the first bombing attack on Moscow.

"It is a Sunday afternoon—the crews are in their tents and the sun is blazing down on the Russian soil. We will be going in from the airfield at Minsk-Dubinskaya. Nobody moves from his tent—heat, dust and mosquitoes are our constant companions.

Our truck driver, Feldwebel Panizzi and Unteroffizier Methner have been standing at the same water pump for three hours, waiting in vain for a few precious drops. We have no choice but to wait.

In spite of everything, there is a solemn quiet in our 'tent-city'. The Group Commander, Oberst Leutnant Kaufmann, comes to see the flying crews in the afternoon and tells us that we will most likely be starting another raid today. My crew is sitting pensively in their tent; perhaps one or

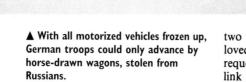

▲ With all motorized vehicles frozen up, German troops could only advance by horse-drawn wagons, stolen from Russians.
▼ 'Gross-Deutschland' Division receives its mail – a small, but welcome comfort.

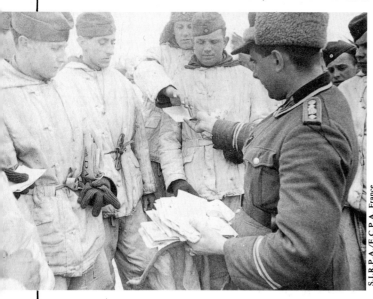

S.I.R.P.A./E.C.P.A. France

two of them are thinking of their loved ones and home. There is a request show on the radio, the one link between the front and home.

Our youngest crew member, Martin Lehner, Unteroffizier and gunner, is just writing to his mother in Vienna, telling her he'll soon be home on leave as the Unteroffizier vom Dienst announces standby III. Now there's a real commotion in the tents. The crews are getting all their equipment together. Parachutes can be seen, flying suits, helmets, maps, navigation equipment, fur boots, high-altitude breathing apparatus, and pistols strapped to belt buckles, for any emergency, particularly in case you get shot down and have to make your way through enemy territory in the dead of night. There's a more serious look on the men's faces. I look at the map and plot the flight path.

Ten minutes later, the UvD announces Standby II. We're off in about half an hour.

Once our princely meal is over, the

Staffelkapitän, Hauptmann Allmendinger returns from the combat position and calls in the crews for a meeting. We get orders—night attack with strong forces on Moscow.

Heavily loaded, our Heinkel 111 A1 + AB tears over the runway into the twilight. We fly over the radio beacon on the airfield and head off on a course east. We leave Smolensk behind us. We are flying along the taxiway leading to Moscow. We pass Vyasma. Our target is the large airfield of Moscow and the nearby aircraft factory.

Our crew is one of the longest-standing of the Squadron 53—we've done about 200 raids together. Our experience at the front has given us a certain sense of security. Nevertheless, it's a mixture of extreme alertness, conscientiousness and a large amount of soldierly luck that lets you carry out your mission.

The sun is setting. We've crossed the front—below us enemy territory. Our cannons and machine gun positions are manned, weapons are primed and ready to fire.

We've passed Gschazk. Before us, shrouded in darkness, Moscow. The glare of searchlights pierces our eyes.

The altimeter reads 1,200 metres. There is little in the way of flak. The first flashes of searchlights on the run-in to Moscow—their startled fingers grope the night sky.

The searchlights have yet to pick us out. More and more flash out, the closer we get to Moscow. I can see the runway below, threading through the landscape of Moscow. I can count 50 to 100 searchlights. Pray that all goes well. Still no sound from the flak. We were told at the stand-by meeting to expect little in the way of flak. Nevertheless, the mass of searchlights is beginning to disturb me. We are climbing cautiously, at 2 metres per second. Look! What's that ahead? Another machine is caught in the brilliant glare of a searchlight. In a flash, several other searchlights pounce on the aircraft. I can see through the telescope it's a Heinkel 111—it's one of ours. He's making frantic attempts to escape the clutches of the searchlight—in vain.

Our strategy is to pull the stick in and climb as fast as possible. Five more machines are caught in the innumerable swarm of searchlights. Meanwhile, we've climbed to 1,700 metres and have reached the outskirts of Moscow.

Süddeutscher Verlag

Novosti Press Agency

A searchlight grazes us, then loses us, but it's soon back again—and this time it catches us. We quickly put on our safety goggles and start to turn. Ordinary manoeuvres cannot shake it off. The glare of more than 30 searchlights fix on us. The flak fires from every barrel. Shells go off all around us.

There's a huge bang, then a flash of fire. Our machine is shaking— we've been hit. I prime the bombs and pull the emergency cord. There's a giant column of fire below us. We turn off towards the south-west. The altitude gauge shows that we're descending at 10 metres per second. The flight meter climbs to 500 kph. The engines are screaming. 'Is anyone wounded?' Everybody reports they're OK.

Meanwhile, we've dived down to 300 metres and we're roaring through the Metropolis of the East. The searchlights have lost us, we've left the environs of Moscow behind and are heading on a southerly course. Five minutes later we turn off and head course west. Sluggishly, our valiant wounded bird makes its way. There's hardly a word spoken and everyone is thinking the same—will the engines hold out?

They're still turning flat out and are not dropping many revs. The pilot checks the control panel every second. We breathe a sigh of relief when we reach the front. After five hours in the air, we land, battle-worn but intact, in Minsk-Dubinskaya. **77**

▲ **Although badly injured, a Communist Commissar still directs the fighting against the German advance.**

◀ **The German army in retreat – soldiers who had been fighting in summer uniforms had to improvise winter camouflage with stolen table-cloths and bed linen so as not to stand out as sitting targets for the Soviet snipers.**

From the cover of a Schutzstellung (protection position), Hauptsturmführer Dr Med. Windisch of the Small Divisional Command Staff SS Division 'Reich', watched as the battle unfolded around Moscow.

❝ It was afternoon and we were standing beside the Magistrale, protected by the woods, observing the enemy, who were circling around in tanks on the other side. A battery of 8.8 Flak had been put in position and was firing on the Russian tanks. Our grenadiers from the Regiment 'Deutschland' had broken through into the enemy's network of positions north of the Magistrale and were pushing on further, in a bitter struggle with huge losses.

Süddeutscher Verlag; Inset: Novosti Press Agency

Meanwhile, the 'firework display' began. I had never seen anything quite like it. We were standing on the hill, with three generals beside us, watching anxiously the movements of our own troops and those of the enemy.

Suddenly I heard the unmistakable noise of the Russian rocket shells, the so-called 'Stalin's organs'. They were definitely meant for us, for everybody disappeared suddenly into cover holes. Since I hadn't dug one myself, I couldn't disappear without leaving a trace. So I quickly threw

▲ Unprepared for a winter war, only a few German units had skis – and all had to make their own snow camouflage clothing. Inset: Soviet soldiers mine a railroad track.

myself behind a tree and watched the terrifyingly beautiful display of rocket shells crashing down. I will never forget the sinister black, red and violet flare from the shells.

The whole area, the air all around was full of the explosions of shells crashing down. Suddenly behind us all hell broke loose. I hadn't a clue what was going on there, and ran to my friend Mix, the Ic (third General Staff Officer) of the Division, who lay under cover, not far from me. He laughed and answered, 'That's our

multiple rocket launchers!'

You should have heard this terrible ear-shattering scream. It mixed in with the bangs of the Russian shells hitting, there was a whistling, a drone, a hissing and roaring from the firing and hits of the artillery, from machine-guns, mortars and multiple rocket launchers. The effect of the latter on the enemy must have been devastating. The battles lasted all through the night. The effects of our launchers had been a decisive influence on the battle. ❞

Unterscharführer Streng with the SS was part of the attack on Moscow which took place on 2 December 1941.

"We could only advance step by step towards our final destination—Moscow. Fierce cold all around us—and all this with poor accommodation and insufficient food for the fighting troops. The supply problems were getting worse all the time. These are the main causes of our crisis—without these problems, we would have been much nearer our destination.

Nevertheless, the troops forced through, advance after advance, with superhuman effort, and fought themselves through all kinds of adversity with incredible patience.

Many of the soldiers had managed to steal Russian overcoats and fur hats and were hardly recognisable as Germans any more. All our winter clothing had been infested with lice and was impossible to wear. To keep the engines running, we had to light fires underneath the sumps. Some of the fuel had frozen, the engine oil had thickened and we had no glysanthine to prevent the drinking water from freezing.

The already dwindling fighting strength of the units was depleted

► The Germans have succeeded in taking a small Russian town—here, Red Army men move in to win it back.

further as more and more men were picked off by the cold. The troops could not take on much more. The innumerable losses would completely destroy the fighting strength of the company.

Half-frozen German troops were fighting on in the merciless cold, which sometimes sank to below 45° below freezing, in their normal uniforms, their normal leather boots, no gloves, no overshoes, no scarves, facing a merciless winter.

With the Russian prisoners, things couldn't have been more different. They wore the best winter clothing you could imagine. Their winter uniforms were thickly lined with padding. They had felt boots, fur gloves and fur hats. To stop themselves from freezing the German soldiers took the precious winter clothing from the dead Russians.

Over the precincts of Moscow hung giant flash rockets like the stars of Venus, and tight packs of searchlight beams hurtled around the sky, went out again, then appeared, ghost-like, clawing the air again at other places, criss-crossing in giant packs of beams. Between them, the flashing pearl garlands of heavy Russian flak. The light trails from shells sent long threads of dark red

Süddeutscher Verlag

and orange into the night sky.

Moscow roared, the loud thunder piercing the December night. Heavy German bomber squadrons attacked Moscow through the night from the air, bringing death and confusion to the centre of the enemy's power base. Along the contours of the distant hills, you could see the flash from the exploding rows of bombs, until half an hour later, the night became silent.

Moscow had opened the prisons and had armed the released prisoners. In the factories, workers' brigades had been assembled. Women and children were put in to dig trenches. Fresh Siberian troops were on their way. The streets of Moscow were filled with the Red Army, marching to the front. "

▼ Known to the Red Army as the 'flying tank' and to the Germans as the 'Black Death', a Russian Ilyushin Il-2 defends the skies above Moscow.

Novosti Press Agency

CHAPTER 5

BATTLE DIARY

PEARL HARBOR – THE SWORD DESCENDS

The Japanese war with China, which had been going on since 1937, had become a struggle of attrition, which the military government in Tokyo realized could only be won with additional resources. With France and Holland occupied by the Germans, and Britain at bay, the Japanese turned their attention to the now-vulnerable European colonies in South-east Asia, which were a potential source of oil, raw materials and food. The only serious threat in the area was the United States, which had forces in the Philippines and a major base at Pearl Harbor in Hawaii.

The Japanese planned to launch a surprise attack on the US Navy and Army Air Force bases at Pearl Harbor, leaving US forces unable to intercept the invasion fleets en route to seize the Pacific islands and the Dutch and British colonies in the East Indies and Malaya. On December 7, 1941, a fleet of six aircraft carriers under Admiral Chiuchi Nagumo, with supporting battleships and cruisers, launched 360 bombers and fighters against Pearl Harbor. Although the attack came as a surprise to the garrison, the US intelligence community had already received warning through decoded Japanese diplomatic signals.

The attackers blew up the USS *Arizona*, capsized the *Oklahoma,* and sank the *West Virginia* and *California* at their moorings. Four other battleships were damaged, another 11 ships sunk or damaged. Air attacks destroyed 247 US aircraft, killed 2,330 and wounded 1,145. The two commanders on the island, Admiral Husband Kimmel and General Short, were relieved from duty. But, for all its ferocity, the attack failed to destroy the fuel storage bunkers and repair facilities at Pearl Harbor, and the Japanese aircraft were unable to locate those US carriers that were at sea on exercises. The chance to cripple the entire US fleet had gone – the carriers that survived would form the basis of the eventual American triumph against the Imperial Japanese Navy.

THE SWORD DESCENDS

For the US servicemen at Pearl Harbor it was just another quiet Sunday with the festive season ahead. But 2,403 of them would not live to see another day.

The Japanese raid on Pearl Harbor was a major turning point in the war. For the attackers and for those who survived it would be the longest Sunday morning ever.

Mitsuo Fuchida, the brilliant commander of the Hawaii assault, led the Akagi Flying Corps into the fray. He recalls his part in the first wave which struck the US base.

" The enemy ack-ack was fierce. The nearer we got, the more it concentrated on the high-level bombers. The bombs sent filthy black smoke pouring up into the sky. Then a hail of bullets closed in on me. I looked down to see where it was coming from, and could see firing coming from the main fleet in Pearl Harbor, but also here and there there were flashes from the guns on shore, sparkling and glittering. 'The shore ack-ack's joined in,' I thought. At that instant, the aircraft juddered, as if something had slammed against it. Lieutenant Mitsuo Matsuzaki, at the controls, yelled through the speaking-tube, 'Commander, have we been hit?' I didn't know, so turned round to look. The answer came from Mizuki in the seat behind, 'I think we've been hit aft by cannon fire— there's a big hole in the fuselage and

one of the control cables has been cut. I'll try to mend it, but I don't think I can reach it'.

'Can you still fly her?' I asked Matsuzaki. 'Yes, we're OK', he said.

Closing in on our objective, it was tricky adjusting the course for the bombing run. It was time to drop now. I concentrated all my attention on the pathfinder's bombs. The instant it left his aircraft, I tugged at the release and dropped ours at the same time. Thinking we were out of range, I felt a sense of relief, then the shock of an explosion passed into me through the seat. The firing came

▲ Aboard the Japanese aircraft-carrier *Akagi*, the pilots warm up the engines of their Zero fighters. Their job – to swarm over Hickam Airfield and intercept any US fighters and destroy parked planes.

▼ A last-minute briefing for a group of Japanese pilots.

◄ 'It was as dark as midnight, a dense cloud of black smoke enveloping the great battleships'. Lt-Cdr Simpson.

US Library of Congress; Inset: Topham Picture Library

▲ **Carnage at the US Naval Air base after the raid as smoke still billows from the bombed wreckage.**

closer. In one intense moment, I thought, 'Let the bombs go, quickly, now'. I glanced down, to one side. We were already into Pearl Harbor, and over Ford Island. Bits of broken cloud floated beneath us.

The pathfinder banked sharply to starboard, signalling, repeat, repeat. We were skimming over the streets of Honolulu, turning again into the bombing run. A patch of cloud had made us miss our aim at the very moment of release.

As the first squadron followed us again into a bombing run, there was a huge explosion close to our objective. A deep red flame burst up into the sky, followed by soaring dark smoke. Then white smoke, to a height of what looked like 3,000 feet. That must be the magazine! A shock like an earthquake went right through our formation and my aircraft shuddered with the force of it. It was the *Arizona* going up. **"**

◄ **A military bearing is cultivated from an early age in a group of Tokyo cadets.**

Kazuo Sakamaki was in command of a midget submarine in the Pearl Harbor attack. Hit by depth charges and with control problems, plans misfired badly.

" The compressed air and gas from the battery were leaking, and the air inside the submarine was becoming dangerously foul. We were very tired and weary.

It was near noon. We had not done anything. I was getting very restless. The two destroyers [patrolling the harbour] looked as if they were two big cats playing with a little mouse. I wanted to sink one of them with the last of my torpedoes—but my target was not such a tiny ship. I still wanted to get a big battleship—the flagship *Pennsylvania*.

Again, my ship hit a coral reef at the port entrance. Miraculously we got our ship afloat again. We lowered the ship deep and started investigating damage. We discovered a fatal injury to the torpedo-discharging mechanism. No longer was the sole weapon at our disposal useful to us. My aide asked what we were going to do. 'The only thing we can do now is to plunge right into the *Pennsylvania*'. My aide knew that it meant our self-destruction as well.

I made up my mind to do just that—but the realisation that I had failed tortured my mind and bitter tears rolled down my face.

Although the ship had lost most of its power, I still had hopes of returning to fight. We tried to run the ship faster toward the island. White smoke shot up from the batteries. They had discharged all their electricity. There was danger that the batteries might explode—but we did not fear it. Death was in front of our very eyes.

At that moment, we hit a coral reef again. We immediately thought of the explosives we were carrying as a matter of self-destruction just in cases such as this. No matter what should happen, we could not let the midget submarine fall into enemy hands. The time to destroy the submarine had come. We had made up our minds.

[The self-destruct mechanism failed and Sakamaki was taken prisoner.] "

Robert Hunt Picture Library; Inset: Topham Picture Library

特別攻撃隊の勇士へ感状

海軍省發表（昭和十七年三月六日午後三時）昭和十六年十二月八日ハワイ海戰において特殊潛航艇をもつてハワイ軍港内に突入し偉功を奏した特別攻撃隊に對し聯合艦隊司令長官より左の通り感狀を授與せられたる旨海軍大臣より奏上せり

感　狀

特別攻撃隊

昭和十六年十二月八日開戰劈頭挺身敵米國太平洋艦隊主力を布哇軍港に襲撃し友軍飛行機隊と呼應して多大の戰果を擧げ帝國海軍軍人の忠烈を克く中外に宣揚し全軍の士氣を顯揚したるはその武勳拔群なりと認む、仍て茲に感狀を授與す

昭和十七年二月十一日

聯合艦隊司令長官　山本五十六

▲ A group of young Japanese Mitsubishi A6M Zero fighter pilots. On the surface they would seem just like any other bunch of dashing airmen but beneath their smiling appearance is a fanatical, almost religious dedication which would make them an unpredictable adversary.

◄ Japanese propaganda such as this does much to explain the Eastern way of thinking to Western minds. The ethic of the Samurai still lives in the Japanese fighting men of 1941—the same values and reverence for unquestioning courage still apply.

Minoru Genda, on the staff of No 1 Air Fleet in Japan, was charged with the detailed planning of the Pearl Harbor raid—and solving the problems too.

" Fuchida was my class-mate, and Murata was a Shimbara man, a real hero. Murata was the top torpedo authority. He had been transferred to command the *Ryuga*'s Air Unit. However, when he was doing deck-landing exercises, I watched his landings and thought, 'Right, that settles it!' and I had him transferred to the command of the *Akagi*'s Air Squadron.

We were not convinced [about the use of torpedoes] but that was the time when all the senior officers were together—not one of them said it was impossible. Mind you, not one said he was certain we could bring it off.

There were unsolved problems with high-level bombing. It's unusual for carrier-borne aircraft to carry out high-level bombing against an enemy fleet on the high seas. Torpedo bombing is so much more effective. However, high-level bombing has its strong points. It simplifies a concentrated attack using a large number of planes—but its success rate is low.

However, something startling occurred. The aircraft-carrier *Akagi* was doing bombing exercises against a target moving away freely, from a height of around 9,000 feet. A formation of nine aircraft scored four hits. That's a success rate of 45%. And they did it three times running. If that could be maintained, it was far more effective than dive-bombing. So, I thought, if we can't use torpedo bombing, we can attack Pearl Harbor with high-level bombers. I was that confident. "

Ruth L Lawson, wife of Captain Richard Lawson of the 19th Infantry Regiment, stationed in Hawaii, was at home with her daughter and mother when the Japanese struck Pearl Harbor.

US National Archives

" They came down with such screaming power dives that you felt surely they were going to crash. Then came loud explosions that made the walls of our stucco bungalow seem to push in and then be sucked out. We saw the Rising Sun on the planes, but still couldn't believe it.

I put Jeannie in the inside clothes closet with her clothes, told her to dress and not come out until someone came for her . . . the bullets and shell casings were hitting so continuously on our roof, it sounded like hail.

In the midst of the attack, someone pounded on our front door. With my heart in my mouth, I went to answer

▲ Called into action unexpectedly, a US gun crew scans the sky for low-flying Japanese aircraft from the minimal shelter at an airfield.

▼ In the town of Honolulu, civilians and firemen rush to save homes and stores as the Japanese bomb attack takes its toll.

it, half expecting a Japanese soldier — but it was one of our soldiers in combat uniform. Just as he started to say something, one of the Japanese planes flew so low over the corner of our roof that I had a brief glimpse of the pilot's face. Bullets and shell casings spattered on our front walk, so close the young soldier jumped inside the door, almost knocking me down. He immediately straightened his helmet and, standing up straight said, 'As I was saying, lady, if you get dressed, I'll take you to a safer place'. It was only then that I realised I was still in my nightgown.

You think you feel very calm, at least, I did, but afterwards I realised my stomach must have dropped to my toes and my heart catapulted to my throat by the queer sensation inside, but fortunately that doesn't show on the outside. Everyone was remarkably calm and we had some good laughs afterwards at some of the silly things we did. I only saw two cases near hysteria.

That night all women and children were evacuated from Schofield by bus. It was raining and so black that I had to hold on to mother and Jeannie to keep from being separated. They used the buses belonging to the Honolulu Bus Service and several times the bright stars and a partial moon would emerge and seem to throw the whole scene into the focus of a spot light. Each felt in her heart that our buses were gleaming targets for the Japanese planes which were expected momentarily. No one can yet understand why they didn't come back and finish us off when they had knocked us to our knees.

One shell exploded in a field to our left, violently shaking our bus and showering it with coral, rocks and dirt but not a person in our crowded bus said a word.

Jeannie, who was sitting on my lap, tightened her arms around my neck and hid her face in my shoulder. None of us knew where our husbands were, whether the Japs had succeeded in landing, where we were going, or where the next bomb would fall — but there was silence during that long ride. I have been convinced more than once since that Americans — women and children too — still 'Have what it takes'. "

Topham Picture Library

Lieutenant Commander Robert Lee Simpson was Radio Officer on board USS Argonne, *when America was suddenly pitched headlong into war.*

" I was in my cabin on the main deck, having previously been awakened by our mess boy. I had just put on my white uniform coat when I suddenly heard several terrific explosions which rocked the ship.

I grabbed my cap and dashed down the passageway for the main radio room, transmitting station aft. Some men only had time to put on their shorts and shoes in their mad rush to battle stations. The uniform for the day was white shorts and undershirts, which caused many sailors to suffer severe flash burns.

Six torpedo planes had already made their runs on the *California* directly opposite us. Great clouds of smoke poured from her hull as the torpedoes tore into the ship, tearing open huge holes in the side. The *California* sank slowly as the torpedoes entered her passageways, killing crew members as they abandoned ship.

Oklahoma, only a few yards astern of *California,* was hit by six more torpedo planes. The port side armour belt of heavy steel was torn off by the exploding torpedoes, exposing a large gaping hole about 200 feet long. The watertight compartments had not been closed. The water rushed in and she immediately capsized and went down with all hands within ten minutes. Her crew were caught like rats in a trap.

Cutting torches were used at first, but had to be abandoned because the trapped men were being cremated by the flames. Air drills were then used

Topham Picture Library

to gain entry into the double bottom compartments.

The navy department announced later that indications were found inside the ship that three men had lived for 16 days. They had consumed all their emergency rations and had marked a calendar with an X for each day from December 7th to December 23rd. **"**

▲ US flying ace, Lt. George S Welch, credited with shooting down four Japanese planes.

◀ A US army Curtis P-40A at Hickam, destroyed in the bombing.

*Ensign H D Davison was aboard the USS **Arizona** on 7 December, expecting a routine Sunday, when the first Japanese dive-bombers struck.*

" It was just before colours, in fact, I had already sent the messenger down to make the 8 o'clock reports to the Captain. Then I heard a dive-bomber attack from overhead. I looked through my spyglass and saw the red dots on the wings. That made me wonder, but I still couldn't believe it until I saw some bombs falling. The first one hit up by the air station. I sounded the air raid alarm and notified the Captain. He and Lieutenant Commander Fuqua came on deck, and the Captain went on up to the bridge. About that time we took a bomb hit on the starboard side of the quarterdeck, just about abreast of Number 4 turret.

We grabbed the men available and

▶ **Huge ships are tossed around like toys – here the USS** *Oklahoma* **has capsized, and behind it is the tower of the USS** *Maryland.* **Below: civilian damage – a Chinese local in the ashes of his home.**

Keystone Collection

Topham Picture Library

started dropping the deck hatches and leading out hoses on the quarterdeck. Then the planes that had made the initial dive-bomb attack strafed the ship. Mr Fuqua and I told all hands to get in the marine compartment. It was reported to us that we had a bomb in the executive officer's office. Just after I stepped in the booth, we took another hit starboard of the quarterdeck, just about frame 88. The Boatswain's mate and I were trapped in the booth by the flames. We started out of the booth, trying to run through the flame aft on the quarterdeck. We couldn't get through, so we went over the lifeline into the water. I was conscious of the sweetish, sickening smell to the flame. After I got in the water, my first intention was to go the quay and then on to the quarterdeck or swim to the gangway and get aboard. But after I took one look at the ship, I decided that it was useless — she had settled down by the bow, and appeared broken in two. The foremast was toppled over — she was a mass of flames from the forecastle to just forward of turret 3. "

Lieutenant Colonel H H Blackwell wrote to his wife from the United States Army base at Fort Shafter, Honolulu, Hawaii, after the lightning raid by the Japanese on Pearl Harbor. His letter was returned to him by the censors.

" I was rudely awakened just before 8 o'clock by the terrific noise of bombs and cannon . . . At first I thought it was dynamite blasting in a tunnel — but when I heard the whistling sound preceding the explosion on some of the closer ones, I jumped out of bed and ran to investigate.

When I got outside I was perfectly dumbfounded. Black columns of smoke were rising from Pearl Harbor Navy yard about three miles distant and the sky was filled with puffs of black smoke from AA shells. It looked like war, but I just could not believe that Japan could make an air attack from such a distance without our navy having some warning.

The attack caught both the army and navy completely by surprise. Being Sunday morning, most

Süddeutscher Verlag

units began firing within 45 minutes from the time they were alerted. All units began firing before the attack was ended, and we shot down four or five planes. The AA fire I first saw was from the Navy . . .

. . . The other day I saw three soldiers bringing in a suspected Japanese spy which they had caught under suspicious circumstances. The Jap was sullen and slow in following directions. One soldier was behind him with his bayonet pressing against his behind, and every now and then he would give it a slight push to speed him up. On either side was a soldier with a bayonet pressed against his ribs. Whenever they wished him to change direction, the bayonet was pressed into his off side, and he would immediately respond. He could not understand English, so the soldiers resorted to this method of directing him. From the expression on the faces of these soldiers, I could see that they would have liked to have used the bayonets more violently. They were exercising extreme self-control. You need have no fear of the fighting spirit of our soldiers. **"**

◀ **Still burning, a US army truck at Hickam Field air base. The Japanese fighter pilots were ordered to blitz the airfield and destroy aircraft and buildings while the bombers dealt with the US Pacific Fleet in the harbor.**

▼ **The aftermath of the Japanese attack. With the horror still fresh in their minds, survivors attend an outdoor service for the dead of Pearl Harbor. The huge number of casualties made the sense of shock and anger all the greater in the United States.**

everyone was still in bed. Our AA guns were not in firing positions, but were parked at Shafter or other posts. We were on alert against sabotage, and in a condition of readiness which allowed three hours to go into action in case of attack. We had frequent drills on going out into battle positions and everyone had been trained thoroughly on just

what to do (thoroughly should be qualified, however, since 80% of our troops have had less than eight months' service, and the organisation of the Brigade was not completed).

We had found that this took about three hours. However, as soon as we found out that this was the real thing, we cut the preparation time in half. Speed limits were ignored. Some

Keystone Collection

CHAPTER 6

BATTLE DIARY

NOVEMBER 1941

27 Philippines garrison on full alert

DECEMBER

8 Japanese bombers destroy B-17s at Clark Field and cripple US fighter defenses

9 Start of bombing of Manila

10–12 Japanese landings at Aparri and Vigan in northern Luzon

22 Japanese landings in Lingayen Gulf. Filipino formations fall back in retreat

24 26th Filipino Cavalry initially hold Japanese near Binalonian, but are forced to withdraw after heavy losses. 7,000 Japanese infantry land in Lamon Bay and march north on Manila. General MacArthur orders retreat into Bataan peninsula and Manila Bay forts

26 MacArthur declares Manila an open city and then takes ship for Corregidor

31 Admiral Chester Nimitz assumes command of the US Pacific Fleet

JANUARY 1942

1 Japanese troops enter Manila. About 100,000 Filipinos and US defenders start to prepare their stand on Bataan

9 First Japanese offensive starts against Bataan defenses, spearheaded by 6,500 men of the 65th Infantry Brigade

22 Japanese landings by fishing boats on Pacific coast of Bataan wiped out

FEBRUARY

8 General Homma calls off first offensive against Bataan and falls back

MARCH

12 MacArthur escapes to Mindanao in southern Philippines and thence to Australia. Wainwright given command

APRIL

3 Second Japanese offensive against Bataan begins with massive air and artillery bombardment

9 Major-General King surrenders forces on Bataan, estimated at 10,000 Americans and 60,000 Filipinos

10 Bataan Death March begins. Siege of Corregidor begins

MAY

2 Powder magazine on Corregidor hit

5 Corregidor bombarded with an estimated 16,000 shells

6 Japanese land on Corregidor and, after fierce fighting, capture the island

THE PHILIPPINES – DEATH MARCH

On December 10 and 12, 1941, the Japanese landed on the main Philippine island of Luzon, with more landings on the 22nd. Though they fought hard, the island's 65,000 American and Filipino defenders were ill equipped and at the mercy of Japanese air superiority. Commanded by General Douglas MacArthur, they took up a series of blocking positions on the road to the capital Manila, but with further Japanese landings on the 24th the city was doomed. It fell on January 2, 1942.

Along with the Philippines President Manuel Quezon, MacArthur set up his headquarters on the fortified island of Corregidor, believing it could be reinforced if his forces managed to keep a toehold on the rugged Bataan Peninsula. But the strong Japanese 14th Army under General Masaharu Homma twice forced MacArthur to retreat, until finally, on March 11, President Roosevelt ordered him to leave the Philippines and go to Australia. Under General Jonathan Wainwright, the Filipinos and Americans fought on until April 8, but they were low on ammunition and food and suffering from casualties and disease. While Wainwright's 13,000 men on Corregidor hung on under devastating artillery fire for another month, on the peninsula General King had little choice but to surrender 76,000 of his 'battling bastards of Bataan', 12,000 of whom were Americans. The prisoners, exhausted from their heroic resistance, were forcemarched some 60 miles from Mariveles to San Fernando. Suffering from cruel heat, lack of food and water, and barbaric treatment from their Japanese guards, between 10,000 and 14,000 prisoners died or were murdered in what became known as the Bataan Death March.

HELL IN THE PACIFIC

The fall of the Philippines climaxed with the savage

attack on Corregidor and the infamous Bataan Death

March. Survivors tell their stories.

The terror from the Land of the Rising Sun sweeps on—behind it a trail of death and destruction, before it an almost superstitious fear of an unimaginably inhuman enemy.

Sister Louise Kroeger, a nun in the Maryknoll Order, was in a convent in Baguio. On 23 December she answered the phone to an American businessman from Baguio.

" 'Sister', he said, 'we've had a meeting here in the Pines Hotel, and I want to tell you what we're going to do. The Japanese are coming up the mountains and right now are in the outskirts of the city. We've sent a delegation out to meet them. All the troops have left Baguio and we want to surrender. I'm asking all Americans not to offer any resistance. We're civilians, and we'll seek the protection of the Geneva Convention.'

Unknown to us, the Japanese ran amok in Baguio. I remember looking back at the convent. It was one large building—the living quarters, a now deserted school and the chapel. High on a hill and with a courtyard of tough Philippine concrete, it was built to withstand a typhoon.

A bird, high in the trees above, gave a shrill cry of alarm, and then suddenly we heard howling and screeching; a horde of Japanese soldiers burst into the courtyard. We all stood quietly calm, but even though we had led sheltered lives, the intent of the soldiers was clear. Both groups stood their ground.

Our gardener and handyman, a

quiet and unassumingly devout Filipino, stepped in front of us. At that moment, the soldiers moved aside as an officer strode into the courtyard. Tall for a Japanese, and strikingly handsome, I recognised him as a stallholder from the market in Baguio—we had regularly purchased fish from him, and never been aware of his identity.

Our gardener was a brave man. He begged the officer to explain to his soldiers that nuns were not like other women, and to leave us alone. He did —but they wrecked our convent.

Nobody was sure what they were looking for, but they tore the place apart and spared nothing. Even the beautifully hand-embroidered altar front was slashed by Japanese bayonets. Our priest, a Dominican friar who came from Belgium, was savagely beaten. We could only watch as they beat him to the ground and then kicked him near to death.

The Japanese left. I helped carry the priest in and tend his wounds.

Later that evening, when we had repaired as much of the damage as possible, I went out to lock the courtyard gate. I found a Japanese soldier standing there, who asked me to take him to the priest. The soldier was humble and subdued—there was no hostility in his manner, so I took him to the bedside. The soldier knelt before the bed and begged forgiveness. I translated, and will always remember his words.

'I'm Catholic, father, and I know how I should treat a priest—but in front of the others, there was nothing for me to do but beat you as I did. I have come back to ask you pardon. If the others find out I came here, they will send me to an infantry assault company, and I will surely die—but I could not live with my conscience and not come and say I'm sorry'.

Our priest gave his blessing; we knelt and prayed. The young man wept unashamedly. "

▲ His home destroyed by Japanese bombs, a Filipino with his children and few salvaged possessions takes to the road.

◄◄ US troops on the Death March. What the US and Philippine men saw as a nightmare torture, some Japanese saw as something of a salvage operation. A Japanese war reporter opined that if they had been left as they were, the men would have been wiped out by malaria or artillery fire from the shore opposite the fortress of Corregidor, so in a sense, the name should not be 'Death March', but 'The Life March'.

◄ Japanese Zero fighters stand primed for action.

▶ Between bouts of ruthless fighting, a unit of Japanese invaders trudges on, turning a tropical paradise into a battleground. Inset: suddenly a peaceful island of great beauty is transformed into a chaotic inferno.

▼ Their place already marked in US history, Philippine soldiers lie wounded in their US camp, awaiting removal from the front line.

US National Archives

When General King surrendered on Bataan, Captain Winston Jones of the Philippine Scouts Artillery was one of the 70,000 men who trudged 57 miles to Japanese POW camps. Although he had been without food for days, he was beyond hunger. He was about to have his first experience of an unknown enemy.

Hulton Deutsch Collection

I felt very uncertain and afraid. Despite the campaign, this was the first time I had come face to face with the Japanese, and none of us knew what was expected of us as prisoners of war. There were some in our group who were very sick—we helped as best we could, but none of us was strong enough to carry anyone.

We had just come abreast of the dirt airstrip called Cabcaben Field when a battery of Jap heavy artillery opened fire on Corregidor. The island fired back, but its first rounds fell short—they burst along the road and decimated the ranks of the column ahead. Then a Japanese military policemen appeared and motioned our groups off the road into rice stubble. We were made to stand directly in front of the guns, and in plain view of Corregidor.

The Japs made us stand there for over an hour, while guns blasted Corregidor. Our boys could see us through the range-finders and did not return fire.

When the time came to move on, some of the men were too ill to move. The guards bayoneted them where they lay.

From Cabcaben the road runs north and then straight up the east coast of Bataan. There were artesian wells every kilometre along the roadside. Their pure water had been used to irrigate the rice fields. Now the ground around the wells was littered with the dead, and in some, where we stopped to drink, the Japanese guards would urinate in the water first.

The worst was when a convoy of enemy trucks came down the road in the opposite direction. The dust they created was bad enough, but Jap soldiers in the back of the vehicles thought it was great fun to knock our hats off with long bamboo poles as their trucks went past. There were many men in my column who were knocked senseless into the path of oncoming vehicles.

The columns became strung out and frequently we were out of sight of the ones behind and in front. This made our guards very edgy, and they made us march double time to catch up. Some of the men couldn't maintain the pace, so they fell back through the ranks until, alone, behind the column, they were bayoneted.

We were one of the later columns, so the road was littered with dead, who were already being picked over by carrion birds. The smell of the dead is something I shall carry with me to the day I die. "

Malcolm Champlin, 'Champ' to his friends, was a Naval Reserve Lieutenant serving in Manila, working as Aide to Rear Admiral Rockwell, when, on 10 December 1941, the Japanese bombed the Cavite Naval Yard.

" I rushed outside with a faceful of lather and looked up into the clear sky. I counted a formation of 54 bombers banking high over the base. A smoke bomb burst. Then nine 3-in anti-aircraft batteries opened up at their maximum range of some 24,000 feet. The Japs climbed above the shell bursts.

They turned for a second high-level pass over the base and another smoke canister was dropped, presumably to get the windage. On the third pass, the planes bombed in formation and with precision. It seemed that not a single bomb missed the base area, as the yard erupted into smoke and flame. The ground shook beneath my feet to the concussion of high explosives. The planes now dived into two formations, then came in at a lower level and dropped their incendiaries. Cavite burned.

I ran for a car and headed for the 'Commandancia' or headquarters building as floods of frightened Filipino workers hit my car like a tidal wave. Harassed Marine guards tried to clear a way through the mob, but it was no use, so I turned into a side road. This proved just as

Hulton Deutsch Collection

bad—fires raged and the dead lay in the streets, so I abandoned the car and pushed through on foot.

I found Admiral Rockwell—he had established a command post in front of the ammunition store. Hoses were directed on to the dump to keep the temperature down. Lieutenant Commander Whitney, Captain of the Yard, came limping up with his knee in a bandage, uniform torn and bloody, to report that some 800 gas-masks were stored in a loft above one

of the machine shops. At that moment, another report came in of fresh fires near the post office and radio station. Admiral Rockwell turned and told me that the gas-masks were my problem to solve.

I flagged down a passing four-by-four and climbed aboard. I needed a working party and quick. As the truck rounded the corner near the commissary, I chanced upon a group of sailors and shouted to them to come with me.

▲The musical efforts of a Japanese clarinet player seem to fall on stony ground—his attempt at friendliness is greeted with a mixture of amusement and utter contempt by his Philippine audience.

US National Archives

We got as close to the burning machine shop as we dared and I led four of the men up the outside staircase and into the loft to look for the masks. They were easy to find, stored in cans like small barrels, with six masks in each of the sealed cans. We rolled the barrels down and tossed them over the balcony to the ground below, where the other men piled them on to hand carts and ran them out to the truck.

We worked like fury. I remember there was a loud crack and a beam directly above split open in a shower of cascading sparks. I ordered the men out of the building. We had saved more than 700 gas-masks, ready for the day, as we believed, when the Japs would use chemical weapons against us!

We climbed on board the truck and the driver edged out into the street. Our route to safety lay between buildings which were burning on both sides. Burning debris littered our path and there were buildings caving in all round us. My driver hesitated, but I thumped him on the shoulder and urged him forward; he was only a kid, and scared to death. He crashed the gears into a low drive and the truck ground

forward over the burning timbers. The sailors behind clung on with one hand and warded falling timbers off with the other. The heat was incredible. I could feel my skin tighten and begin to blister. Then we were through the tunnel of flame and into an open area.

I stopped the truck to let the sailors down and thanked them for their efforts. One of them I remember was a bruiser of a stoker, had the sort of face that was scarred from a hundred bar-room brawls.

It seemed the stoker was the spokesman. 'I'm up for a summary court martial, lieutenant', he said. 'Will you testify for me, sir?'

I assured him that I would, whatever his crime, only to find that all the others needed the same favour. This threw me a bit, and I asked where they had all come from. It appeared they had been in the brig and released by the Marine guards when the air raid started.

There was no problem. I told them that the headquarters was a total wreck and all the courts martial records burned to a cinder. As far as the navy was concerned, the sailors had a clean slate, so we got on with the war. 🙶

▲ **Instruction in destruction—US Marines from a base on the Philippines teach a group of Filipinos how a machine gun works. Time alone would prove that no amount of small arms would stop the Japanese.**

▶ **Injured and taken prisoner in the Philippines, an American soldier walks among his Japanese captors on the way to a POW camp. Even if he survives his injuries and captivity, he is unlikely to return to full health again.**

John Spainhower, a lieutenant in the Philippine Scouts, wounded early in the campaign, had barely recovered when the garrison surrendered.

" I marched for two days without water and on the third, as our column approached Orani, the guards allowed us to drink from a small creek which stank from the decomposing remains that floated in it.

We stayed a night at Orani. The conditions were awful. We were dumped into fields and left until the morning—there was no food and no sanitary arrangements. The next day, I was questioned by a Japanese officer, who found out that I had been in a Philippine Scout battalion.

The Japs hated the Scouts, perhaps because we beat the hell out of them at the Abucay Hacienda. Anyway, they took me outside and I was forced to watch as they buried six of my Scouts alive. They made the men dig their own graves, and then had them kneel down in a pit. The guards hit them over the head with shovels to stun them and piled earth on top.

I was made to stand at attention over the graves until eventually I collapsed with sunstroke. "

▲ Crouching in a foxhole somewhere on the Bataan peninsula, a group of US troops duck the flying shrapnel as they continue the struggle.

Hulton Deutsch Collection

US National Archives

Seiichi Nishida was a Private First Class with a water purification unit in the Japanese 16th Division when the horrific 'Death March' came into view.

" Before our eyes, hundreds of prisoners of war were moving along. When I looked closer, I could see they were, in fact, stumbling along, half-naked, in broken boots. A fiery sun beat down on their heads. From mouth to mouth I could hear a babbling sound, 'Water! Water!' At first I didn't understand what they meant, then I realised what they were asking for, so I filled my mess tin lid with clear water and gave them some to drink. A US soldier, face burned red with the sun, kept repeating, 'Thank you, thank you', with tears streaming down his face. "

Hidezumi Ima was a member of the No 1 Propaganda Team with the Philippines Expeditionary Force from Japan. His view of their landing on these lush islands belies the violence to follow.

" Someone bawled out, 'Wakey, wakey, we're there!' Of course, everyone woke up. I folded my blanket and tidied it away with my life-jacket, which served as a pillow, and hurried out on deck.

The island of Luzon was green—so beautiful a green it made you want to cry out. A bright cobalt sky, like something by Fra Angelico, stretched away over receding mountain ranges which seemed to be piled up, one on top of another. By the seashore, clusters of coconut palms, between them you could make out, here and there, 'nippa huts', sprouting nippa palm leaves, the high-floored huts of fishermen. The sea was totally green, like molten jade, and utterly peaceful.

As far as the eye could reach, bright primary colours. The shore must be about 2,000 metres away, but everything seemed terribly near, as if we could quite happily swim the rest of the way. We were more used to scenery which was like a water colour swathed in mist, rather than a brilliant oil painting—but the island's vivid green was so lustrous that it dazzled.

I was overcome by its unfamiliarity, and quite forgot we were on enemy territory—but as I gazed, leaning over the railing of the starboard side, I saw the shape of a plane glide over the mountains. Then an ear-spitting roar as the AA guns from our ships began to fire.

Tracer shells described a red arc. In the distance another plane, hugging the ground, seeming to be sweeping the landing units with machine-gun fire. From another ship, more AA fire howled up into the sky. In the intervals of all this racket, you could hear bursts of rifle fire. The enemy planes did not seem to be coming for the convoy, which was moving into Lingayen Gulf, but were concen-

US National Archives

Robert Hunt Library

▲ The Japanese invaders march through the jungle. They are quite at home—this is the warfare they trained for.

◀ Just as it had in the fight for Malaya, the bicycle proved its worth for the Japanese on the Philippines— after all, why change a winning tactic?

▼ Cheerful in spite of the mayhem outside, Filipino Red Cross nurses tend a woman wounded in the bombardment of the Bataan peninsula.

trating on the landing units close into the shore. Like someone passing out lines of red tape, the tracer was cast up into the sky like so many threads trying to trap the enemy planes in their fibres. They sped away, without approaching the convoy. 'You asked for it!', shouts went up from those of us who had been watching.

With that, the battle came to an end. After the enemy planes had beat a retreat, all there was was an innocent, clear morning sky. **"**

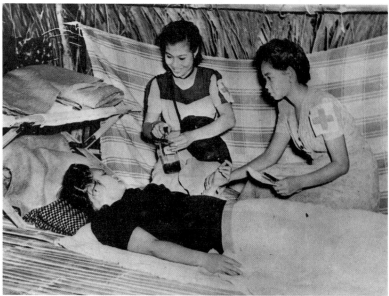

Hulton Deutsch Collection

Private First Class Kyūichirō Maeda of a Japanese Signals Unit, No 9 Infantry Regiment, became used to operating behind the US lines keeping his superiors informed about enemy moves.

❝ Our boundary was the road running across the peninsula. We used to wait for nightfall every day, then slip into the area held by the enemy. I was attached to No 3 Company, and had with me a No 6 wireless transmitter set. I was responsible for following officer patrols and reporting the reconnaissance of enemy positions. If we came across an enemy patrol from the US/Filipino army, we would hide among the trees, let the enemy pass on, then open fire and attack.

Noticing that the fire was coming from their rear, what looked like their own positions, the US/Filipino troops would flee in amazement. Another time we were going through the pitch-dark forest and the US/Filipino Army wire loomed up in front of us. Everyone kept absolutely silent as I typed out my message. ❞

Lieutenant Hirohisa Murata of III Company, 1st Battalion, 61st Infantry Regiment, and his troops began embarking in landing craft at Limay, a town on the east coast of Bataan, to attack Corregidor.

❝ Our regiment was clearly marked out as a suicide unit, the whole lot of us. Because of this, we all cut our hair and nails and left them behind as souvenirs for relatives. At 7 pm we finished embarkation. I had made up my mind that I was going to die.

Before embarking on the landing craft, we received detailed instructions. According to these, while the landing craft were on the sea, the artillery positions on Bataan would continue to pour a fierce gunfire bombardment into Corregidor. It was indicated that the landings should take place after the shelling stopped, in two or three minutes. However, things were not to pan out so gracefully. On the contrary, the too-detailed arrangements caused an unheard-of number of casualties among the first wave to land.

At the signal, 'Approaching shore', everyone dashed out of the landing craft. But they had not reached the coastline, and in the pitch-black night the men hurled themselves into the sea and were soaked to the skin. Bullets poured point-blank into them, and when they finally managed to struggle ashore, right in front of them were perpendicular cliffs about 10 metres high. They put their hands out to touch the cliffs, and felt a queer, slippery sensation. When they looked closer, they saw that the rock surface of the cliff was running with coal tar. The men closed up to the cliff and tried to tackle it with hands and feet, but all they got was a slimy, slippery sensation—it was quite impossible to climb it . . .

Preparations had been made for an assault landing, and we expected to be placed in that sort of situation. Luckily for us, as the unit came up to the rock face of the cliff, the enemy fire could not reach us. So we threw up the ropes we'd prepared for the landing and reached the cliff top by hauling ourselves up on the ropes. ❞

▲ Under the cover of darkness, Japanese troops make a stealthy landing from a small craft. Each man carries the vital equipment for survival as the invasion pushes on.

Robert Hunt Library

CHAPTER 7

BATTLE DIARY

MIDWAY AND CORAL SEA – OUT OF SIGHT

If the battle of the Coral Sea between US and Japanese naval forces on May 4–8, 1942, could be described as a draw, Midway three weeks later was the victory that wrested the initiative from the Japanese in the Pacific.

Coral Sea, fought south of the Solomon Islands, marked a new era of naval conflict: it was the first action to be fought entirely by aircraft, with no visual contact between warships. The outcome was the loss of the carrier USS *Lexington*, the fleet oiler *Neosho* and destroyer USS *Sims*. US aircraft sank the carrier *Shoho* and disabled the *Shokaku*.

The following Japanese attempt to land troops on Midway Island – home to a vital American airfield – was part of an elaborate plan involving a diversionary force being sent far to the north to land on the Aleutians. But Admiral Chester Nimitz was aware of the plan from intercepted signals – the US had cracked the Japanese codes – and maneuvered his carriers *Yorktown, Enterprise* and *Hornet* close to Midway and the approaching 165-ship Japanese force. The initial air attack on Midway caused extensive damage, but as the returning aircraft were being re-armed the Japanese carriers came under attack from dive bombers and torpedo aircraft from USS *Hornet*. Although the US aircraft suffered many losses, they delayed the Japanese long enough for dive bombers from *Yorktown* and *Enterprise* to attack and score immediate hits on *Akagi, Soryu* and *Kaga*. In response, the *Hiryu* sent two waves of aircraft to attack *Yorktown*, damaging her so badly that she was evacuated. At almost the same time, dive bombers from *Enterprise* found *Hiryu* and set her ablaze – she was scuttled the next day.

The young airmen of the United States had paid an enormous cost for victory, but Midway marked the turning point of the war in the Pacific. Victory paved the way for the landings at Guadalcanal and the entire subsequent sea and land offensive against Japan.

OUT OF SIGHT

The Pacific sea battles of Midway and Coral Sea were fought 'blind' with the enemy many miles away, an enemy seen only by the men who flew their bombing missions from the all-important carriers.

Out in the Pacific Ocean on the US and Japanese carriers, aircraft stand ready for action. Airmen and soldiers, too, wait in grim anticipation of the battle which is to come.

Rear Admiral C Wade McClusky was Air-Group Commander aboard the US carrier Enterprise *and led the initial bombing run on the Japanese carriers. A Lieutenant-Commander at the time, McClusky's leadership was crucial in the American success.*

My orders were to make a Group attack on the enemy striking force. Radio silence was to be maintained until sight contact with the enemy was made. That was the extent of my instructions. The *Hornet* Group was likewise to be launched and, although the *Hornet* Group Commander was senior, no command relationship or co-ordination was prescribed. No information was received to indicate how the *Yorktown* Group was to participate. So, with this meagre information, we manned our planes.

At 0945, by flashing light signal, I was ordered to 'proceed on mission

◀ **Survivors of the** *Yorktown* **go on board the USS** *Fulton* **from** *Portland.*

assigned'. No information was given as to why the torpedo planes and fighters were delayed. This meant we would be without fighter protection—a serious predicament.

Climbing to gain altitude, I led this small force on a south-westerly course and figured to intercept the enemy at about 1120. At our departure time they were believed to bear about 240°, distance 155 miles and heading toward Midway at 25 knots. Our Task Force was to maintain a course of 240° to close the enemy except when flight operations dictated otherwise.

Arriving at the estimated point of contact the sea was empty. Not a Jap vessel was in sight. A hurried review of my navigation convinced me that I had not erred. What was wrong?

With the clear visibility it was a certainty that we hadn't passed them unsighted. Allowing for their maximum advance of 25 knots, I was positive they couldn't be in my left semi-circle, that is, between my position and the island of Midway. Then they must be in the right semi-circle, had changed course easterly or westerly, or, most likely, reversed course. To allow for a possible westerly change of course, I decided to fly west for 35 miles, then to turn north-west in the precise reverse of the original Japanese course. After making this decision, my next concern was just how far could we go. We had climbed, heavily loaded, to a high altitude. I knew the planes following were probably using more gas than I

was. So, with another quick calculation, I decided to stay on course 315° until 1200, then turn north-eastwardly before making a final decision to terminate the hunt and return to the *Enterprise*.

Call it fate, luck or what you may, because at 1155 I spied a lone Jap cruiser scurrying under full power to the north-east. Concluding that she possibly was a liaison ship between the occupation forces and the striking force, I altered my Group's course to that of the cruiser. At 1205 that decision paid dividends.

Peering through my binoculars which were practically glued to my

▲ **The pilot emerged safely from this Wildcat which skidded on landing on the USS carrier** *Lexington,* **and now hangs from the flight deck.**

▼ **A US SBD Dauntless, with its arrestor hook used for deck landings beneath it, flies over the** *Enterprise* **as the fleet prepares for battle.**

eyes, I saw dead ahead about 35 miles distant the welcome sight of the Jap carrier striking force. They were in what appeared to be a circular disposition with four carriers in the centre, well spaced, and an outer screen of six to eight destroyers and inner support ships composed of two battleships and either four or six cruisers.

I then broke radio silence and reported the contact to the *Enterprise*. Immediately thereafter I gave attack instructions to my Group. Figuring that possibly the *Hornet* Group Commander would make the same decision that I had, it seemed best to concentrate my two squadrons on two carriers. Any greater division of the bomb-load we had might spread out the damage, but I believed would

not sink or completely put out of action more than two. Picking the two nearest carriers in the line of approach, I ordered Scouting Six to follow my section in attacking the carrier on the immediate left and Bombing Six to take the right-hand carrier. These two carriers were the largest in the formation and later were determined to be the *Kaga* and the *Akagi*. As a point for later mention, after radio silence was broken, Lt Dick Best, skipper of Bombing Six, radioed that he was having oxygen trouble, had dropped to 15,000 feet and would remain at that altitude to commence the attack. One remarkable fact stood out as we approached the diving point—not a Jap fighter plane was there to molest us. We attributed this to the Japs'

fear of the torpedo plane and the defeat they had sustained by that plane in the Coral Sea.

It was 1222 when I started the attack, rolling in a half-roll and coming to a steep 70° dive. About half-way down, anti-aircraft fire began booming around us—our approach being a complete surprise up to that point. As we neared the bomb-dropping point, another stroke of luck met our eyes. Both enemy carriers had their decks full of planes which had just returned from the attack on Midway. Later it was learned about the time we had discovered the Jap force, an enemy seaplane had detected our forces. Apparently then, the planes on deck were being refuelled and rearmed for an attack on our carriers. Supposing then, we, Air Group Six, had turned southward toward Midway, as the *Hornet* Group did—I can still vividly imagine the *Enterprise* and *Hornet* at the bottom of the sea as the *Yorktown* was some three days later.

In the meantime, our bombs began to hit home . . . I levelled off at mast-head height, picked the widest opening in their screen and dropped to deck level, figuring any anti-aircraft fire aimed at me would also be aimed at their own ships. All their ships' fire must have been pretty busy because I was well through the screen before I noted bursting shells creeping up behind. With the throttle practically pushed through the instrument panel, I was fortunate in avoiding a contact with death by slight changes of altitude and varying the getaway course to right and left.

It was quick work to figure the return course, and as I raised my head from the plotting board, a stream of tracer bullets started chopping the water around the plane. Almost immediately my gunner, W G Chochalousek, in the rear seat, opened fire. Then a Jap Zero zoomed out of range ahead of me. A hurried glance around found another Zero about 1,000 feet above, to the left and astern, about to make another attack. Remaining at 20 feet above the water, I waited until the attacking plane was well in his dive, then wrapped my plane in a steep turn towards him. This not only gave him a more difficult deflection shot, but also enabled my gunner to have free room to manoeuvre his guns. Then ensued about a 5-minute chase, first one Zero attacking from the right, then the second from the left. Each time I would wrap up towards the attacker with Chochalousek keeping up a constant fire. Suddenly a burst from a Jap seemed to envelop the

▼ Ensign George Gay sees the US victory in print as he convalesces. He is the only member of his 15-plane torpedo-bomber unit to survive the attack on the Japanese carrier *Kaga*.

Peter Newark's Western Americana

whole plane. The left side of my cockpit was shattered, and I felt my left shoulder had been hit with a sledgehammer. Naturally enough it seemed like the end, we sure were goners. After two or three seconds, I realised there was an unusual quietness except for the purring engine of the Old Dauntless. Grasping the inner phone, I yelled to Chochalousek, but no answer. It was difficult to turn with the pain in my left shoulder and arm, but I finally managed and there was the gunner, facing aft, guns at the ready and unharmed. He had shot down one of the Zeros (probably the one that had got the big burst in on us) and the other decided to call it quits. **"**

We found that our plane had been hit about 55 times.

Captain Elliott Buck-master was in command of the US carrier Yorktown *as Japanese aircraft attacked—and was witness to an astonishing victory of the US navy and aircraft against overwhelming odds, although he lost his ship.*

" The *Yorktown* joined up with other carriers in attacking Jap forces. Our group immediately hit one carrier with torpedoes and bombs. Later it was reported that this carrier sank. About this time, our fighters intercepted a large group of enemy dive-bombers and fighters. The sky was filled with falling Japanese bombers. The AA fire of the supporting ships and the *Yorktown* was magnificent. Our gunners literally chopped the enemy planes apart. Every single dive-bomber that came towards us was blown to bits, but three made hits on us before being destroyed.

By this time, our engines had stopped, but through superhuman effort our engineers got our boilers operating. A swarm of enemy torpedo planes appeared—we avoided several torpedoes, but two dropped close aboard.

I felt that the ship would capsize very soon. Reluctantly I gave the order 'Abandon ship'. The courage displayed by the officers and crew throughout the engagement is beyond my powers of expression. I believed the *Yorktown* was stricken beyond

▶ **In the quiet before the storm, US carriers** Lexington, Ranger, Yorktown **and** Enterprise—**a foursome not to be seen again after Midway.**

repair. Later, however, I returned with a small salvage party. With the help of the destroyer *Hammond* we were able to right the ship by 2°. We felt sure she would live. Then suddenly, four torpedoes fired from an enemy submarine outside our destroyer screen were sighted. We were heavily hit and the destroyer *Hammond* alongside was sunk. As our destroyers were attacking the enemy submarine, our crew was transfered to a small tug to await the arrival of salvage tugs at day-break.

▲ **Regulars, the crew of a Cataline PBY. Inset: a call to the navy for tradesmen.**

However, the next day, from a companion ship, I saw the *Yorktown* slowly sink beneath the waves. The Japanese lost 4 aircraft carriers in that engagement and many of their best aviators. In the *Yorktown*'s four short years, she destroyed more Japanese planes and ships than any other single US ship. Tonight, the *Yorktown* rests on the bottom of the Pacific. **"**

▼ **In the US too, all the nice girls love a sailor!**

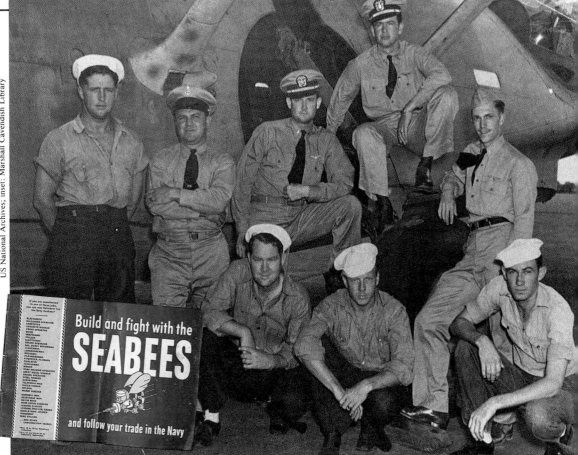

Build and fight with the SEABEES and follow your trade in the Navy

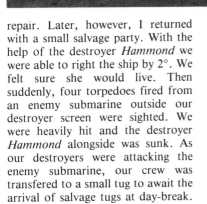

Shove Off

I haven't got a handkerchief. What else could I drop?

US National Archives; inset: Marshall Cavendish Library

Popperfoto; inset: T & V Holt Collection

Iyozō Fujita, Flight Commander on board the Japanese aircraft-carrier Sōryū, was piloting an escorting Zero fighter when the Americans attacked.

" I sighted a formation of 20 torpedo bombers—but this time they had an escort of three fighter planes. I made for the enemy fighters, to get rid of that nuisance first of all, but strangely enough, they seemed to have no stomach for a fight and made off. Without pursuing the fighters, I turned and made for the assault planes.

A shell, which I thought came up from our carrier, smacked into my plane amidships—exactly where my fuselage fuel tank was. In no time, smoke began to pore out. The cockpit began to fill with flames.

Next thing, bullets began to spatter from the 7.7 mm magazine. There was going to be no time to make a forced landing on the water, and when I looked down, I saw the cruiser *Jintsū* speeding ahead below me, so I decided to use my parachute. I opened the cockpit windshield and tried to climb out, but my head was pushed against the windshield, and I could not get out.

I heard once how a man got out of his cockpit by hanging his legs over the edge and lying athwart. I spotted the altimeter as I left the aircraft—I was at 200 feet.

I could hear the wind scream past in my ears, but the parachute refused to open. The canopy stretched out, but when I saw it was not bellying out with air, I grabbed the chute with both hands and tugged at it. As I did so, I felt a shock go through my whole body, as I entered the sea.

My body was entangled in the cords of the chute, and I tried to free myself. Finally I came to the surface. With amazement, when I looked round, I saw the *Jintsū* making full speed ahead. She hadn't seen me.

On the distant horizon I saw three columns of black smoke. The waves were calm enough, but there was a very big swell. I was carried to the top of the swell, from where I could see for about 20 miles, but when I came down to its base, all I could see was sky above my head.

At any rate, I thought, those must mean that's where our fleet is, and I began to swim towards them. The flying helmet was a nuisance, and I took it off and threw it into the sea. Next, my flying boots, my socks, gloves. Then I began to worry about sharks.

I remembered I'd heard someone say that sharks line up alongside you and measure the length of your body against theirs. If you are longer than they are, they don't go for you. So, I began to unwrap the muffler and tied it round my waist to make me look like a long object. But the back of my neck got so cold I couldn't bear it, so I wrapped it round my neck again.

I remembered my long-distance swim from Naval Academy days. I did 10 miles, going into the water at 7 o' clock and coming out at seven in the evening. Now, as I gazed at the black smoke, I could see it was 20 miles away, and if I kept swimming as I was, it would take 24 hours. I lost all appetite for swimming. In a mood of quiet despair, I spreadeagled myself in the water and lay gazing at the sky.

I saw a 96-type sea recce plane fly over. Without thinking, I waved my hands to signal to him, but he flew off without spotting me.

About four hours must have passed like this, when I heard a noise and opened my eyes. What had been the aircraft-carrier *Akagi*, still burning, had come to within 1,000 metres of where I was. Then one of her escort destroyers, came up close. Soon I became aware of some-

▲ **Main picture: a fire-fighting detail on board the stricken *Yorktown*.**

thing. From her gunwale, the muzzle of a gun was pointing at me. My hair was long in those days, and my face, burned by the sun, had turned red. 'They've taken me for an American pilot!' I realised. I trod water and began to semaphore with my arms: 'I AM AN OFFICER FROM *Sōryū*'. I don't know if they followed this on board or not, but the gun muzzle moved up. "

◀ **Buckmaster's ship, the *Yorktown*, already listing badly from damage by Japanese bombardment, starts her descent to the sea bed.**

▶ **A young pilot, resplendent with ceremonial sword, stands by his Kawasaki Ki-45 Toryu ('dragon-slayer') in a propaganda photo.**

Mitsuru Iwashita was a Japanese gunnery officer on board the battleship Kirishima, and saw for himself the destruction of Yamamoto's aircraft carriers.

" The bugle sang out the order for anti-aircraft combat readiness. An enemy plane, apparently. Far off, the sound of machine-gun fire.

Enemy torpedo-bombers came in to the attack, but our Zeros shot them all down.

Suddenly, another anti-aircraft warning. Fierce machine-gun fire. Enemy aircraft coming in to attack. They seem to be coming in quite close this time. Our anti-aircraft gunners are all keyed-up. 'Fire!' comes the command, then an appalling roar from our guns, with the MGs chattering away. Everyone makes for the shelters. When I take a look outside, I can see the sky filled with AA gun bursts and puffs of smoke. The enemy planes drop their bombs, and the roar of the explosions splits the sky apart. First one plane, then another, swoops over our ship, then skims away again.

After them come our Zeros, in hot pursuit, and a burst of AA fire hits the sky from close to me. The MGs cease fire. The enemy planes have all been hit, but there seems to be little damage on our side.

Then a signal comes in, reporting the sighting of enemy aircraft-carrier force. We all feel the tenseness of anticipation.

A voice—'Aircraft-carrier hit!'. I

US National Archives; inset left: Peter Newark's Western Americana; inset right: Marshall Cavendish Library

▼ The new expansionist policy produced a high level of national fervor – the Japanese were keen not to be seen as a race of delicate orientals, but as a vigorous fighting nation.

make it fast to where the voice is coming from, and look out from the deck. A sea of bright red flames engulfs the deck of our flagship *Akagi* which was making speed far off to port.

Then they say another carrier's gone—and gazing far astern I can see *Sōryū* turning, her decks a mass of smoke and red flame. The first

carrier to be hit, *Kaga*, is now only a distant column of black smoke.

Whether or not it was the result of induced explosions, I don't know, but the fire on *Akagi* looks frightful enough to blow her sky high. So our carrier force is reduced to one, *Hiryū*. With no more than *Hiryū*'s carrier-based planes, we mount an attack on the enemy's task force.

Enemy aircraft coming into the attack again. Now we have no fighters to go up and meet them. Apart from the random firing of the MGs and AA guns from our ship, there's nothing, but they manage to spread a curtain of fire across the sky. At length the attack begins to flag, and I can see the *Hiryū* making speed on our starboard side. Everyone is wild with joy that *Hiryū* is still in good shape. Then we notice black dots appearing in a gap in the clouds above her. Enemy dive-bombers. In an instant, the decks of the *Hiryū* are a sheet of crimson flame. That's it, then, they have had it. Our fleet is now running completely naked before the enemy task force. When night finally comes the fires are almost out on the *Hiryū*, but she can't manoeuvre and comes to a dead stop, listing. The fleet quietly watches over the blackened shapes of the ships. The Battle of Midway is over, and fortune has not been with us. 〞

▼ The Japanese battleship *Nagato*, seen in December 1941. Before Midway, the Japanese thought their fleet invincible.

海軍志願兵徴募中

青少年諸君!!
急げ!
海の空の決戦場へ!

詳細は至近最寄の町区町村役場へ
お問合せの事

● *Akira Tendo was special correspondent for the Japanese newspaper Asahi Shimbun and navy correspondent at Wake Island when US aircraft sank his ship, the Shōhō—in the Coral Sea.*

〝 I felt the ship give a shudder. What looked like blackened fragments of burned wood swept past our eyes as we stood on the bridge. Then the ship was enveloped in a great noise, like a steel curtain being hit by some great force. That can't be, I thought, nothing can have gone so wrong. 'They're bits of enemy planes', I tried to convince myself. It was no enemy plane, I soon realised, a bomb had done for our rudder.

The enemy pilots must have jumped for joy when they saw our carrier, like a man paralysed from the waist down. They came at us with renewed strength, harrying us, closing up, then dropping bombs.

On they came, sweeping over our heads. As we watched, we wondered if their attack would hurl them into the sea, then we saw them roar up into the sky again. These were not the American lushes we'd learned about in Japan!

I felt a sensation as if I'd been struck with a whip.

'So, we've had it, at last. That must be the third or fourth bomb that's hit us'. The instant I had time to think 'that's close', something

smacked into the deck, and there was the blast of an enormous explosion.

'Bastards!' I turned round in amazement at that voice, ablaze with rage, and saw a petty officer with his cheek torn away. He was holding it with both hands, and from between his fingers the blood was flowing. A sailor was standing close by, his right arm almost torn off.

He had a cloth at his waist and, taking the shrapnel fragment between his teeth, he staunched the blood from his right arm, using his left hand. Then he went into the signals cabin. His gait was steady, as if he were not seriously wounded at all. Then, with his left hand, he began to tap on the key of the W/T set.

Another sailor started to his feet, quite near me. I looked at his leg and was aghast. The flesh of his thigh was scooped away, and the white bone was clearly visible. He stood in front of the telescope, trying to support himself. He began to report what he saw. In these conditions, to collapse would be shameful.

The bombs and torpedoes kept coming. When a torpedo hits, the ship does a pitching and tossing movement. They work together, and the result is like an earthquake. The sound's dull, but it makes you feel as if your intestines are being drawn out. Suddenly I had the impression that I was wounded too. I looked down at my leg. Blood was flowing from it. Was I going to die from loss of blood? My instinct at first was to go down to the ward-room and have it treated. But what was happening around me stopped me. Men with worse wounds than mine were still at their stations. I stayed.

After a while, I noticed my wound again. I was increasingly aware that the blood was still flowing from it, but all I could see was a scratch on my kneecap. 'Is that all there is to it?' I comforted myself with that thought, and stayed on the bridge.

The ship finally began to settle into the sea, bows first. I hurried from the bridge to the bridge deck. I saw our photographer, Yoshioka, taking pictures of enemy planes coming into the attack.

'You press men, get down below, it's dangerous!' The gunnery officer was concerned for us, but we did not listen. An enemy plane released its torpedo. 'Still alive?' We shook hands. 'Let's go!' 'Yes, let's both go together!' But where did I intend to go? Perhaps my mood was, 'If we're going to die, let's die together'. The deck below was already awash, and the waves swirled in front of my eyes.

Although the ship was on the point of sinking, the men were still at their stations. As one man, they had refused to leave. The ship's bows plunged into the sea, and she came up by the stern. By now up in the air, the screw kept turning. The engine room, went on doing its job to the end.

A petty officer climbed up a mast which was beginning to go under. Someone said he was trying to keep the ship's flag flying. Then, along with the ship, he vanished from sight.

Although the ship had gone down, you could still hear the sound of machine-gun fire. It was very odd, as if the firing were coming from the sea bed itself. The gunners were all dead. What happened was that the gunnery officer—the one man left alive—went on firing until the very last. The paymaster crewmen all remained at their stations. From the portholes of the sinking ship, they waved their white caps in a gesture of farewell.

Apart from us war correspondents, there were three non-combatants on board—the barber, the cook and the laundryman. These too, stuck to their posts, moving badly wounded crew, giving medical aid. Like the sailors, they too died at their posts. 🙶🙶

大日本帝國陸奧

CHAPTER 8

BATTLE DIARY

JANUARY 1941

21–22 Australians assault and take Tobruk with 27,000 Italian prisoners

FEBRUARY

12 Rommel arrives in Tripoli

APRIL

10–17 German assaults on Tobruk repulsed. The town is isolated and bypassed

NOVEMBER

18 Beginning of Operation Crusader

20 Heavy fighting around Sidi Rezegh. Tobruk garrison begins breakout

28–30 German armor attempts to break link-up. Heavy casualties on both sides

DECEMBER

8 Rommel abandons fight with only 40 tanks left. Tobruk relieved

JANUARY 1942

21 Rommel takes Allied forces by surprise and recaptures El Agheila

29 Benghazi recaptured by Germans

MAY

26–7 Rommel outflanks Gazala Line. Heavy fighting at Bir Hacheim

29 Fierce battle around 'Knightsbridge' road junction

30 Rommel withdraws all his armor into defensive positions in 'The Cauldron'

JUNE

2 Renewed assault on Bir Hacheim repulsed by Free French

20 German assault on Tobruk, preceded by heavy air attacks, breaks through perimeter; by evening German troops reach the harbor

21 Tobruk garrison surrenders. Germans take 30,000 prisoners and stores. British troops in disorderly retreat towards Mersa Matruh

TOBRUK – DESERT FURNACE

Tobruk, a port in Italian-controlled Libya, was captured by the British on January 22, 1941. When Erwin Rommel's Afrika Korps counter-attacked across North Africa, rolling towards Egypt, the Seventh Australian Division dug in behind the abandoned Italian-built defenses. From April 1941 the city remained under ground and air siege from German and Italian forces. When the Nazi propaganda minister was goaded by the continued resistance into describing the defenders as 'rats', the Australians gleefully christened themselves 'the Rats of Tobruk'. Under the command of General Leslie Morshead, they were supplied and reinforced from the sea at night by the Royal Navy in what was known as 'the spud run'. The garrison remained a thorn in the Axis side, making continued raids into occupied territory, until, on November 29, its six-month siege was brought to an end when it was relieved by a land offensive, Operation Crusader.

In May 1942, Rommel launched a fresh offensive at Gazala, this time determined to take Tobruk. The garrison now comprised 35,000 troops, drawn largely from the South African Second Division with some British and Indian troops, under General Klopper. On June 20, Rommel attacked the port with his 15th and 21st Panzer Divisions supported by dive bombers. Within three hours the Germans had breached the defenses and reached the harbor. The following day Tobruk surrendered, and the Afrika Korps captured 33,000 men and an enormous quantity of stores. The town would remain in Axis hands until it was taken for the last time by the Eighth Army under General Bernard Montgomery following the Second Battle of El Alamein.

DESERT FURNACE

Whole armies traverse the sun-punished wastes in search of each other – yet the ordinary soldier shows the adaptability of human beings to inhuman conditions.

OLD KENT ROAD SE.15

I'LL BE THERE.
HOME SWEET HOME.

Spr Baiden
1941

◄◄ As this Tommy is only too aware, this exit road from Tobruk bears little resemblance to its namesake back in London.

◄ Enveloped in dust raised at every burst, a British 6-pounder gun crew opens fire on enemy motor transport.

▲ The 'Desert Rat' emblem of the British 7th Armoured Brigade.

Both the Allies and Axis forces were far from home—and had to deal not just with persistent onslaughts from each other, but with the relentless, wearying battering by the desert elements.

South African Sapper Wesson was with the 5th Field Engineers when, after the battle at Sidi Rezegh, the survivors of his unit were left to try to join up with any other group they could find.

❝ Our company found itself right in the thick of it, with Jerry tanks and armoured cars everywhere. The only protection we had was under our trucks.

Having spent all our ammo, trying to shoot Jerry heads as they appeared from tank turrets, we found our shallow slit trenches were of no use, as the tanks and armoured cars rode over them, firing at random.

One of our men, Andy O'Grady, was shot at point-blank range in a shell slit. The three lead bullets all hit his tin hat and bounced off. He still had the helmet months later, as evidence of his lucky escape.

Some of our men held string attached to landmines and were pulling them across from truck to truck, trying to get the Jerry tanks and armoured cars to go over them.

And, in all this, our Malay cook went about his business out in the open, making pancakes over a fire made by pouring petrol into the sand. The Jerries seemed to take no notice of him—and he brought around to each truck some of his cooking.

At dusk, an officer shouted, 'Into your trucks, and join the convoy to the east'. Most of our trucks had been destroyed, so we got on anything that moved and headed east.

I think the driver went over every shell slit in the desert that night, while we were bashed around in the back. As soon as we found the convoy we tagged on. A German armoured car came up, not certain where it was.

When they realised they were in our convoy, they opened up with everything they had, but fortunately all went high and through the canvas of our truck. Then they made the quickest getaway I have ever seen.

It was late afternoon, and we were still under our trucks, when I saw General Erwin Rommel. A line of German tanks came straight past our position. In the middle tank, with the hatch open, stood Rommel himself. The battle was over, and he knew it. He was right out of the turret, saluting to both sides. ❞

Ian Quarrie was a Sub-Lieutenant RNVR commanding an experimental boat in October 1940, when he was given an order which seemed nothing short of suicidal. It was to be the first incident in an uncanny coincidence which concluded in the sea off Tobruk.

❝ In 1940 I was a Sub-Lieutenant, commanding HMMTB 106—an experimental boat with one torpedo and a speed of over 45 knots. On a dull, cold October morning I was suddenly ordered to take her to sea to explode an enemy mine by going over it! Off Southend, a convoy was waiting to sail with cargoes desperately needed up the east coast. The Germans had just begun laying acoustic mines, and that night an aircraft had dropped one in the narrow channel the convoy had to take.

There was no known antidote and it was considered worth risking us to get the convoy away, hoping our speed would carry us clear of the explosion.

▲ A thick barrier of barbed wire marks the border as a truck-load of British troops crosses from Egypt into Libya.

▼ South African troops flush out the enemy with hand-grenades on the push towards Tobruk.

We managed to pass directly over the mine. The reaction was instant, and we were blown out of the water. The launch sent to pick us up in this eventuality had stopped and couldn't restart her engine—and we had a long swim waiting for MTB 107 to come and rescue us. Her First Lieutenant, Sub-Lieutenant Johnny Wolfe RNVR pulled me out of the water.

Four months later, my father's ship, HMS *Rosaura*, an armed boarding vessel, was also sunk by mine, close to Tobruk. A strong swimmer, he too survived.

In the spring of 1942, I also found myself in Tobruk, commanding a new boat, MTB 312. Our flotilla spent some months there, carrying out offensive sweeps up the enemy coast, landing agents behind the lines and so on. We were a well-knit, happy unit but oh, how we hated Tobruk! Stukas by day and night were bad enough, but my own pet hate was the appalling water supplied—too brackish even to brew a drinkable cup of tea. We left just before the town fell to the enemy. I hoped never to see the place again.

I was back again on 14 September, MTB 312 being part of a Combined Operation intended to hold Tobruk for a day and destroy the enemy's ammunition, fuel and other military targets. Unfortunately our operation failed, and our losses were high.

The attack was abandoned shortly after dawn, and soon after setting course for home, we were attacked by several Italian Macchi fighter planes. Despite our manoeuvrability and fire-power, augmented by the Bren guns of the soldiers we were carrying, we were eventually set alight from end to end by incendiary bullets. The boat burned long enough to enable us to take to our collapsible boats or jump into the sea and swim some distance away before our ammunition, 3,000 gallons of petrol and four torpedoes, blew up with quite a bang. And there I was, swimming for my life again.

To my relief, two MTBs came across and took us all aboard, though not all were to survive the running battle back to Alexandria. As I was hauled aboard MTB 265, her captain looked down from the bridge and said with a wry smile, 'Haven't we done this before?' His name was Lieutenant Johnny Wolfe—and I later confirmed my suspicion that we had been sunk within yards of where my father had swum for his life too, 19 months before.

▶ The fortress of Tobruk has fallen to the Germans, and in the harbor the wreckage of British ships lies deserted.

Dennis O'Brien, Petty Officer Coxswain on Motor Launch 1048, was trapped inside the port as it fell. Escape seemed less and less possible as the enemy fire grew more intense.

"One night we were on patrol off the boom when a submarine must have spotted us—our boat had a very clear silhouette. They fired at us and the torpedo must have been very, very accurate, because the ASDIC operator threw the headphones off because of the noise of this torpedo. However, being a coastal forces launch, our bottom was hardly below the surface of the water, so the torpedo missed.

We never knew our status at Tobruk. The only way we could judge our situation was by going out to sea at night and listening to the Home Service.

We could sense the situation was getting worse—you could feel it. One particular day, as we came in to the port, it seemed very serious. The enemy seemed to have made a pincer movement on the port and the air raids were very intense.

We went alongside a beached ship, awaiting orders from Navy House. Messages were delivered from the Admiralty by the despatch boat called the *Eskimo Nell*. The firing went on all day, and despatches came over telling us to go easy on the ammunition.

Towards the evening, the situation was getting very bad. There were enemy tanks appearing out of the

▶ German troops close in from the sea to lend support to the land assault on Tobruk.

▼ The unofficial insignia of the *Afrika Korps*, most probably embroidered by one of the men. Below, the official cufftitle of the *Afrika Korps*.

Roger-Viollet, Paris

Georgia, an Italian cruiser which had been sunk and was resting on the bottom. The shells were hitting the other side of her and we didn't know what to do. We turned around and proceeded back towards Navy House. Another motor launch was coming down towards us. One of the heavy shells hit it. ZAP—it was gone.

When we saw this, we decided to go back to the shelter of the *St Georgia*. We saw some sailors on the jetty in the distance. They had a large dog with them. They yelled across to us, '1048, 1048!' We replied, 'Not on your life—you swim it!' After some discussion, we moved alongside and picked them up with their dog.

It was the best thing we ever did, because among this naval group was the Boom Defence Officer, who knew a particular point where the boom dipped. All the MTBs had departed and we were the last ship there. The fire on the boom was so heavy that you couldn't have lived.

We nipped through the point that the officer knew, and as we went through, a German tank hit us in the wheelhouse. Our captain was hit in the face and suffered bad injuries.

The tank shell hit the chart box and destroyed half our chart, but God was very kind to us. The half of the chart that we didn't need had been blown off, the rest survived!

Another fairy tale happened as we went on our passage. Fog came down—which is very rare in the Mediterranean. We heard the high-revving engines of the German mopping-up craft, but we were safe in the fog. All our MTB pals had been mourning us for lost. "

➕ *Private Robert Brady was a nurse with the 22nd Field Surgical Medical Team which, when drafted out to Tobruk, was attached to the First Armoured Division. Their duty was to help the wounded, whatever their nationality.*

" My duties were general nursing work in the operating theatre, but every man did what he could. There were seven people in each medical team, but often you were under—a lot of good men got killed getting the wounded back, or when working in the operating tents.

Half the time we were level because as the enemy advanced, you couldn't keep moving backwards, so he was bound to come within range—they were advancing all the time.

I remember once, when our tents were pitched and there was some shelling—and they were ours. It carried on until they got the word that it was our hospital there.

All the members of the team used to go out and take the wounded back. If you saw a bloke go down, you would go and get him. We took the Germans in as well—a casualty is a casualty. He's just a soldier. They picked up ours—we picked up theirs.

You knew when shells were coming because you listened—and from listening you could tell whose fire it was. Ours had a sharp noise—with the Germans you could hear a sigh as the belt was going through.

We had terrible casualties—legs blown off, arms blown off, tummies opened up. We would stop the bleeding if we could, and we tried to stop infections by cleaning the wounds. We gave people morphine, if we could get it. We had medical supplies, but we were in the lines, so you couldn't always replace what you'd used. We had plasma from England, but the soldiers were giving blood for the wounded.

We laid the wounded out on stretchers. They were kept under canvas, as best we could, but there were no guarantees. If the tents were full, we laid them outside as close to the tents as we could. We did what we could for them, and then they were taken back to base hospital. Until you've been through a battle, you can't begin to understand what it was like. "

▼ **A German heavy artillery post in the desert, lightly manned while two comrades take a break.**

Bildarchiv Preussischer Kulturbesitz

sand, around the perimeter. We were called over to Navy House and went alongside *Eskimo Nell*. She was released and we were told to leave and tell a minesweeper to proceed to Alexandria and not return. We could see German tanks arriving on shore.

We delivered the message to the minesweeper. The firing was getting worse all the time, so we sheltered around the other side of the *St*

Bill Bebbington had joined the Royal Warwickshire Regiment and was in an anti-aircraft unit when, in 1941, he was drafted out to Egypt. From having a relatively quiet time at home, he was suddenly in the forefront of the battle.

❝ I'd never heard a shell fired or anything, and within two hours, we were in action—we had walked slap into the lion's den. We knew where we were going, but had no experience of it, and we arrived on a very fast minelayer and just leapt ashore. Stuff was flying everywhere—it was hair-raising.

In two hours, we were firing like hell. An air raid over there consisted of one Stuka after another, coming straight down at you, and if they were Germans flying them, they used to come down very low indeed. My Sgt. Major, Nobby Clark, had a pile of stones and he used to throw the damn things at them—they were that low. The Italians didn't like that— they used to stay a bit higher— sometimes they had Stukas too. We always knew when Germans were flying them, they used to come so low. It was bad enough seeing them coming straight at you and dropping the bombs, but later they had screamers—and they made a hell of a row.

It would start early in the morning—you'd have your morning raid, then they'd stop for breakfast. You'd have six or seven air raids a day—sometimes we never got undressed, because they made a dead attack at the AA sites, and we were protecting the place without any help from the RAF. There had been some Hurricanes there—but the two we had left couldn't do much.

It was incessant—there was no way of having a couple of days off. They did considerable damage, killing men and knocking out guns.

Süddeutscher Verlag

▲The pages of an illicit diary, kept by Bill Bebbington during the desert campaign, recall the lead-up to the relief of Tobruk.

◀ Painstakingly folded and stowed away in a belt, a silk map of the desert area could be a life-saver for any man who got separated from his unit, or for a prisoner who managed to make a lucky escape.

Roger-Viollet, Paris; inset: Bundesarchiv-Koblenz

They did tremendous damage to the town—just one church spire left. It wasn't just the damage—they denied you rest too.

My first day was 20 September, though the siege started on 11 April, 1941. I remember the first two casualties—deaths—we had. We used tiles from a bombed bathroom in the town and made a proper grave.

One day, after Tobruk was relieved, we were sitting having breakfast in my dugout. Shells started appearing out of nowhere. We thought the army was miles away—but the Germans were knocking on the door. We fled—just packed everything up and fled. I had one thing in mind, and that was that I was going to be in an Alexandria night-spot as soon as possible. We did not stop until we got to Alexandria.

The tank boys and infantrymen fought a rear-guard action all the way back—and a bloody fine one too. We were getting our equipment out of the way and on the way back, I had to do without a hat. A shell landed while I was talking to the sergeant. It didn't go off, but it hit a brick, bounced off and hit me on the head—knocked my hat off. I scarpered!

Another funny episode was when

◀ Probably none too pleased to be captured on film by a German photographer, two Tommies supporting a wounded officer and another soldier resign themselves to spending the rest of the war as prisoners.

▲ The work of some *Africa Korps* man's leisure hours, his mess tins, etched with a desert scene and the emblem of the Korps.

we had newspaper men with us. J L Hobson came, and others—Chester Wilmot stayed with me for three days in my dugout. We sat in these little holes and the mice and rats came in too—it was terrible.

This chap Wilmot was a great character. Somehow, he got hold of SRD Naval rum—special reserve something—stone-bottled. You know, I've never touched rum since. I can't even be in the same room as someone drinking it. He and I, one night, drank a complete jar of this really strong stuff. The last thing I can remember was a sentry saying to me, 'Are you all right, mate?'. I was out for the best part of 24 hours.

I remember my favourite food was Libby's corned beef. We lived on Maconochies canned stew and corned beef. We had no greens—we had ascorbic acid tablets instead.

We had Bill Bowes posted to us, the Yorkshire cricketer—and he was taken prisoner. We left him behind. I remember his last words to me, in a broad Yorkshire accent. 'Just my bloody luck, I should have kept my bloody mouth shut and stayed in Cairo'. He got taken prisoner because he couldn't run fast enough! 🙾🙾

Süddeutscher Verlag

Australian Private Bob Swanborough with the 2/3 Infantry Battalion was in the drive to take Post 57—part of the attack to take Tobruk in 1941. His job was to go in after the engineers put the 'Torpedo' charges under the wire.

◀ As fearsome and effective as they were in the drive through Western Europe, Stuka Ju-87 dive-bombers with desert camouflage scream over the wastelands. Inset: a Bf-109F of Jagdgeschwader (fighter wing) 53—with improvised sun protection.

▲ A group of Australian soldiers keep up 'business as usual' in the painting and camouflage department. The Tobruk defenders have developed into a flourishing community during their stay.

🙾🙾 We knew about land mines around there—they were like a Thermos flask, filled with fragments, obviously from a munitions factory floor—and there were four of them inside a box. They were attached by a grey cotton in among the sage brush, and the idea was that if you hit one with your foot it would set them off.

As we moved up to the start-line, we suddenly walked into a nest of these bloody things. Two sections were immediately wiped out . . . I'm on the ground and my first reaction was, 'The bastards have got my leg.' There was blood, but no feeling.

The stock of my rifle had been blown away and I was ripped, right across the front of my uniform, and had bits and pieces stuck in my webbing. I had a steel mirror stuck in my pocket and lodged in that was a piece about the size of a large coin. I found out later that my leg had a fragmentary wound which did muscular damage more than anything.

About then, the Italian bugle sounded, calling their troops to arms. Eventually I got up and used my rifle as a crutch and hobbled forward to the tank trap where the Company was. By this time, our platoon had been reduced to one section, the platoon commander had lost a leg, and my mate had been wiped out.

When the 'Torpedoes' discharged, we all went forward, what was left of us. I was limping into the show, and we hit the first position where the bugler had been—and took that. The remaining section attacked the next post. By this time it was daylight, and the brown-shirts had the idea that they would use their bayonets. Immediately, our fellows swung into line, stretched out a bit and went in with a bit of a bayonet charge . . . we took those two posts. 🙾🙾

Hauptmann Adalbert von Taysen was Company Leader of the 3rd Company Machine-Gun Battalion Tank Grenadier Regiment 104 as his men went to retake Tobruk.

" We crouched in the dark, the tension enormous. You could only detect the presence of the next man by the cigarette behind his hand.

The question was, 'Would it work this time?' We had maps of the fortress, but would we be able to spot the bunkers, machine guns and gun emplacements quickly enough?

The veterans among us remembered the fateful days of last April . . . At about 00.30 hours, the Company broke up to push forward towards the barbed wire. There was an eerie quiet in the battle zone. The peace of the night was then broken by a brief exchange of fire. The 4th Company overpowered an Indian advance group.

Time passed too slowly—it seemed like an eternity until the first glimmers of dawn appeared. A light ground mist blinded us, but the British were in the same boat.

Five minutes later there was an ear-splitting roar. Stukas flew in, dropping their bombs on the fortifications about 100 metres in front of us. The last machine had scarcely turned away when there was an almighty bombardment of shells raining down on the British positions. Before us was an almost impenetrable wall of mist, dust and smoke.

The commanders and platoon leaders gave the signal to attack. We shot up and stormed through the barbed-wire and minefields ahead.

In front of us were tank traps—we jumped in and climbed up the opposite wall. Anti-tank gunners raced through a sloping passage, intended for the British reconnaissance trucks. The men worked their way through under the protective fire of the machine guns, threw hand-grenades and took the combat positions. Then came the first British, running towards us, their hands in the air. **"**

Bildarchiv Preussischer Kulturbesitz

Pausing for a rest on the push towards Tobruk, the men of a Panzer group have removed their protective goggles and masks – to reveal strange patterns on their sand and dust-beaten faces. Inset: a German Panzer man's pocket calendar and unofficial DAK (*Africa Korps*) ring.

Bibliothek Für Zeitgeschichte

◀▼ Raising an enveloping cloud of dust, Mark III Panzers advance across the desert, giving a welcome lift to some German infantrymen.

▼ Their topees pulled well down over their eyes against the sun's glare and the swirling dust, German infantrymen armed with MG34s press on through the heat of the desert.

Hans-Dietrich Arberger was Platoon Leader/ 2nd Lieutenant of a machine-gun company with Tank Grenadier Regiment 104. His group made an attack on the Tobruk fortress in June 1942.

❝ The 3rd and 4th Companies broke through and built a bridgehead. The 1st Company, far ahead of their own artillery fire, stormed a British artillery position to find Tommies peering out, nonplussed. They hadn't expected to see the German infantry so far behind the bunker lines!

Isolated counter-attacks by British infantry were fought off. We found out they were 11th Indian Brigade. We'd probably have encountered

Süddeutscher Verlag

stronger resistance had they been New Zealanders or South Africans.

The men lay in the positions, drenched in sweat and exhausted, but still full of attacking adrenalin. 'Now the tanks can come', they were thinking—and there they were, as if summoned, coming out of the layers of dust behind them.

At the road fork on the way to El Adem, we dug in until our armoured cars arrived. We drove down the Djebel to see the town which had been so bitterly contested.

Now there were only a few dozen buildings left, mostly in ruins. In the harbour we could see masts and funnels sticking out of the water from the ships which had been sunk. On the west side of the harbour, a black wall of smoke was rising up, where the British had set fire to fuel stores. Several small ships made their way laboriously to the open sea, peppered by shells from our artillery and AA guns. Behind us the noise of battle had died out, but in the south and west, a dogged fight was still going on. That was where the core of the defensive troops were—the 2nd African Division. We got the order to turn south-west to break up the resistance.

In the evening, a British Brigadier General appeared at the battalion combat post and surrendered his troops to the Regiment Commander.

Despite the darkness, we went on booty raids. There was nothing in the way of food that the mighty stores did not have . . . The night was full of rejoicing, despite the day's efforts. Tobruk had fallen. We'd our revenge for April! ❞

Leutnant Fritz Starke of the 1st Company Machine-Gun Battalion 8, Tank Grenadier Regiment 104, was at the Gazala Line in June 1942, when some British troops tried a last-ditch break-out.

❝ A few athletically built Tommies tried to fight their way out with fisticuffs. One warning shot fired in the air ended this little sporting endeavour. A few stray Arabs appeared and led us into hiding holes and camps. In winter they had led the Tommies to our hide-outs. They applauded in April 1941, when we marched into Derna, in December they applauded the British on their march west, they rejoiced when we came into Derna again two months ago, and they would be clapping again when . . .? Who could hold it against them? After all, the Arabs were not Italian citizens!

An old Arab took Oberleutnant Pfeiffer to a wadi. In front of a cave stood an armoured truck, the engine still warm, which meant the crew could not be far away; then three Tommies came out. After we'd searched a bit more, Oberleutnant Pfeiffer and Feldwebel Sievert found three freshly bathed men sleeping, and judging by the uniforms on the ground around them, they were officers. They got quite a shock when they woke up—less because they were now being taken prisoner, but more because they were stark naked. This is not how the English gentleman likes to be seen. ❞

CHAPTER 9

BATTLE DIARY

JUNE 1942

24	Rommel begins pursuit of Eighth Army from Tobruk to Mersa Matruh
26–28	Battle of Mersa Matruh; Eighth Army pulls back to El Alamein Line
30	Beginning of First Battle of El Alamein; Rommel attacks in center

JULY

7–8	Australian raid against Ruweisat Ridge
10–11	Successful Allied counter-attack in north
13–16	German attacks repulsed with heavy losses
17	Rommel ceases attack and takes up defensive positions
21–22	Auchinleck launches unsuccessful counter-attack
26	Further Allied attack beaten back with heavy losses

AUGUST

7	Montgomery appointed commander of Eighth Army
12	Montgomery arrives in Cairo. Both sides rebuild their strength and lay minefields
31	Renewed German attack towards Alam El Halfa

SEPTEMBER

2	German attack called off
23	Rommel flies home on sick leave; Stumme takes over command

OCTOBER

6	Montgomery finalises outline for Second Battle of El Alamein
23	Second Battle of El Alamein begins in north
24	Stumme dies
25	Rommel returns, XXX Corps makes good progress against 164th Infantry Division, but elsewhere Allied attacks contained
26–29	Inconclusive fighting all along front

NOVEMBER

2	Beginning of Operation Supercharge
3–4	Rommel begins withdrawing
5	Afrika Korps pushed back from Fuka
8	Torch landings in Morocco and Algeria

EL ALAMEIN – FINAL ONSLAUGHT

In tough fighting during the first week of September, 1942, General Montgomery's Eighth Army – helped by decoded German signals which exposed the Axis plans – brought the joint German and Italian forces to a standstill close to the Alam El Halfa Ridge in Egypt. On the defensive, the Axis troops constructed a deep line of field fortifications and minefields that stretched from the Mediterranean coast west of the railroad station at El Alamein to the salt-marsh depression of Qattara, about 60 miles to the south.

Despite pressure from Churchill to take the offensive, Montgomery calmly amassed troops and equipment. By October 23 he had 150,000 men, 1,114 tanks and 2,182 guns, as well as 500 fighter aircraft and 200 bombers. At 21.40 that evening nearly 1,000 guns opened fire in a huge artillery barrage against the Axis troops along a 40-mile front. Infantry advanced during the night to clear a way through the minefields for the tanks, and by the following morning the tanks were engaged in some costly fighting. The British Ninth Armoured Brigade hit a tough anti-tank screen and lost 87 tanks, more than 75 per cent of its strength.

A fierce tank battle at Tel El Aqqaqir on November 2 resulted in estimated Axis casualties of at least 2,300 killed, 5,500 wounded and 27,900 captured. During the fighting General Stumme, acting commander in place of Rommel, who had jaundice, died of a coronary, and General Ritter von Thoma was captured. Rommel returned from sick leave to try to save the battle, but was forced to accept defeat and begin withdrawing on November 3.

The battle marked the most eastern point that Axis forces were to reach in North Africa. At the cost of 13,500 men, Montgomery had signaled the beginning of the end for the mighty Afrika Korps.

FINAL ONSLAUGHT

The constant strain and harshness of the Desert War takes its toll on both sides of the fence – and the worst is yet to come.

The Desert Rats suddenly had unlimited supplies, effective 6-pounder anti-tank guns – and a new, determined leader. The *Afrika Korps* had strong tanks – but failing supplies. The Italians had weak tanks and a number of defeats behind them. Who was going to triumph? The stage was set for the be-all and end-all of British assaults.

Brigadier George Roberts – now Major-General CB DSO, MC – was given command of the 22nd Armoured Brigade immediately before the Battle of Alam el Halfa as he returned to the action after being wounded.

❝ At the time I was commanding the Third Royal Tanks during the battles at Gazala. I got rather burned and had to recover for about four weeks.

A shell came into the tank perhaps. There was a terrific explosion and I was in the turret, with a gunner below me to my left. He got out with only his boots on – everything else had been blown off. He died – he was burned all over. I was burned on my face, arms and legs – I was wearing shorts at the time. It was a Grant tank we were in, just the two of us. I don't really know what hit us – whether a shot came in and exploded one of the shells from the inside, I don't know, but there was a terrific bang. I was lucky – I wasn't anything near as badly burned as the other chap. I went to hospital and was covered in plaster – one arm and both my legs. Cutting the stuff off was almost worse – the man took my skin off while he was doing it. I was in plaster for three weeks, so my legs got very thin in that time.

I was very surprised to find I was asked to go and command the 22nd Armoured Brigade. I'd only commanded a regiment for about six months, so I was astonished when we got up to Alam Halfa. Monty hadn't joined us then, and we were about the only armoured brigade left – everyone else was getting re-equipped. There was one regiment of Valentine tanks up in the north, otherwise it was just the 22nd Armoured Brigade.

As soon as Monty joined us, things were entirely different – he saw exactly what the situation was, and went on from there. There was a very clear view in his mind what the situation was, and how it should be handled. The whole atmosphere changed, without any doubt. Alam Halfa went satisfactorily, and so he was thought of as the chap for us – everybody was very impressed after that.

We were expecting the enemy to attack us at Alam Halfa – so everything was adjusted to that. Alam Halfa was a feature, and it was where the main battle would probably have to take place. Before Monty arrived, there were three possible plans for what we would do. When Monty arrived, there was one plan – that's all there was to it, and we put that into operation and were ready to go to certain positions when the

▲ Monty's first meeting with Brigadier Roberts (right) and Lt-General Horrocks (center).

balloon went up. We knew the Germans were going to attack – it was inevitable in order for them to get to Alexandria and Cairo. It was quite an important situation which dominated the area. He who had Alam Halfa was all right.

On the first night, the Air Force was sent over to deal with their supply situation, and they bombed them very heavily. That was pretty well the deciding factor.

All the guns and tanks had their places to go to, and on the word, we took up our situations, and there we stayed, waiting to be attacked. They came up and we were waiting for them.

The Germans had put a much bigger gun on their Mark IV tanks – they didn't have many of them, but the ones they had were much better than any of the guns we had. But, fortunately, we'd disposed our small anti-tank guns behind little hillocks, and they came on and, as they came to a hill, they had to tip up to climb – so we could hit them from below as they reached the tops.

During the attack I was in a tank a little further back, watching the battle, and telling people where to go. One regiment was almost knocked out in their first attack, and I had another in reserve, which I hurried down to take their place. **❞**

Maj-Gen Roberts, CB, DSO, MC

▲ The Army Commander watches the 22nd Armoured Brigade on maneuvers before the capture of Tripoli.

▶ Monty's message to the men may have been cliché-ridden – but it worked!

▲ From his tank, Roberts points out the German lines to Monty at Alam el Halfa. On the rear of the tank is Christopher Milner, Rifle Brigade, Intelligence Officer.

◀◀ Filling a Crusader tank – 4 gallons (18 L) at a time!

▲ At Alamein, British infantry advance towards a disabled German tank.

Ray Kennedy arrived from New Zealand with the 22nd Battalion three weeks after Dunkirk, to work in the desert. As a stretcher-bearer – 'body-snatcher' – he helped retrieve the wounded at Alamein, as the numbers of his own battalion were steadily whittled away.

▶ A blood-bank orderly dispatches precious supplies – pleas for donors met with a generous response.

▼ Relieved that his war is over, a German medic is tended by a British counterpart.

Imperial War Museum

❝War had become a way of life. New reinforcements were always horrified at the handling of the wounded, which was no better than in Nelson's day. At least then the badly injured were chucked over the side — here some had to be left to die a lonely death.

It wasn't pleasant having to decide who was going to die — we have to live with these memories now. There were never enough body-snatchers, we lacked medical skills and there was always a shortage of bandages.

There was a long walk to the start line, the stretcher being carried on the shoulders of two men, in the hope that the enemy would see it. The start line was a strip of ribbon on the desert floor. At the precise hour, the infantry started off, behind the artillery barrage.

We started collecting the wounded. The enemy made the job very difficult.

Streams of incendiary bullets floated by at chest height. Trip wires at instep level glistened in the moonlight, about 12 inches apart. Stretchers bearing the wounded had to be carried by two men, crawling crab-like, counting the wires they stepped between. Any pressure set off a booby trap, which would cause appalling injuries.

The only protection we could give the wounded were the sand bags which made up part of the machine-gun pit. The walking wounded were rounded up and sent to the rear. With no landmarks in the desert, it was difficult to tell north from south, so they were faced towards the flares that were sent up at regular intervals from base HQ. They were given water bottles and sent across the desert.

I wondered who would bury the dead. It was eighteen hours before we were able to get back to the badly wounded. I can still see the look in their eyes — they thought we had deserted them.❞

Captain W Cobb MC led a patrol of 13 Australian by night. They had moved 1,500 yards forward of their own positions, when suddenly they were challenged by a German sentry. He continues the story.

Imperial War Museum

❝Everyone knew that surprise had been lost. All talking and digging had ceased. They were waiting for us.

We crawled for about 60 yards and heard the bolt of a Spandau ripped

back, about 15 yards in front. I pitched my 69 [grenade] at him and he fired at the same time. One bullet got me through the leg, one got Munckton through the foot and one got Cooper in the body. We then followed the others into where the Spandau just fired from.

The gun was not firing, but there was movement in the fairly large trench behind it. Munckton emptied his rifle into it, then Corporal Else yelled out, 'I've got a prisoner, and all my men are safe'. The patrol withdrew to where Corporal Else and party were. Just then the prisoner had a bit of a scuffle and threw himself to the ground, shamming dead. Private Woods reminded him that he was alive with his bayonet and he moved off with us.

We had gone about ten paces when someone fired from the ground at us with a Tommy gun. I got him twice with my pistol from about ten feet, but not before he had put one into my arm and killed our prisoner. I began to realise that the bullet through the arm was going to be a different matter from that in my leg. I got Private Pickup to give me a hand along but just as we reached the Bren gunners, I blacked out and Corporal Else threw me over his shoulder.

He remarked when I told him that I could stumble along behind, that he'd carry me home even if I were bloody well dead. For about 1,000 yards, they took it in turns to carry me until some particularly close medium machine-gun fire forced us to ground. When I got to my feet I was feeling much better and was able to walk most of the way to the road where we found a stretcher and I rode home.❞

▼ The Aussies have rechristened Alamein with the unlikely name 'Heaven' – and now settle down to let the folks back home know that they are safe in their desert paradise.

Imperial War Museum

Captain Ian Quarrie's Motor Torpedo Boat set sail with a small force on the eve of the main battle. Signals would reach Rommel to lead him to believe that this force carried vital supplies for the Allies – but the force's job was that of a decoy to draw the Luftwaffe from the main assault.

Bill Bebbington

As soon as darkness fell, the Landing Craft were left plodding on, while the MTBs moved out to sea a bit and increased speed to get well behind the enemy lines before the battle began. Our aim now was to make a feint landing at Ras el Kenayis, a promontory on the African coast, just behind Fuka. The RAF would provide a smoke screen as we approached the shore and meantime it was hoped the Landing Craft would still be in a position to attract the Luftwaffe.

When we were a mile or two off Ras

▲ **The navy does its share to support the troops at Alamein. Craft armed with machine guns and (inset) motor torpedo boats such as these drew the Luftwaffe away from the main action on the eve of the great artillery bombardment.**

el Kenayis, we turned inshore and reduced speed to something under 10 knots. In the leading boat, MTB 309, I had not only Lieutenant Denis Jermain, DSC, Royal Navy, now my Flotilla Senior Officer and overall commander of this operation, but also two soldiers with equipment resembling an enlarged version of the old HMV gramophone logo (without the dog, of course!). As we slowed down, they assembled their sound machine and prepared for their part in the battle.

We began to look out and listen for our friendly aircraft to lay us a smoke screen. Temporarily we wanted to be neither seen nor heard by the enemy.

Suddenly, there the aircraft was, right overhead and dead on time. The Beaufort started laying her smoke-screen along the shore and we followed slowly with our two Pongos pointing their sound-machine shorewards, playing sound-tracks of fleets coming to anchor – depths of water being called by the navigators, then 'Stand by' and 'Let go', followed by the roar of cables rattling out through big ships' hawse-pipes, then more shouting — all this repeated as long as the smoke-screen shielded us. The MTBs to seaward were dropping depth charges to give the illusion of big guns firing.

While all this was going on, we all threw into the water a number of homemade rafts to which we had taped electric torches pointing upwards, suitably waterproofed, hoping to entice the Luftwaffe into thinking they were lights on our Landing Force, and to go on bombing and firing at them long after we had left. Finally, with the

smoke finished and our sound-machine once more below, we formed up together and bombarded the shore with our Oerlikon and .5 guns nobly assisted by our splendid Beaufort.

Then we all set off for home at something over 30 knots this time, as we wanted to make all the noise we could and show a good bright wake to those damned aircraft up top — they were meant to find us.

It appears our rafted lights were seen and not only attacked from the air, but reported from shore to the Germans. We were certainly bombed and fired on by the Luftwaffe on our way to Alexandria, although I do not remember it quite as the 'running fight lasting three hours' when 'time after time the planes roared down on the ships, blazing away with their cannon and hurling bombs' as reported by the *Egyptian Gazette* next day. To the best of my memory, only one of our MTBs suffered a little damage, and we had two ratings slightly wounded. But what had our decoy achieved?

As a result of our little jaunt, the German 90th Light Division consisting of three Panzer Grenadier Regiments, one Artillery Regiment, one Anti-Tank Battalion and a Heavy Infantry Gun Company, said in all to total some 15,000 troops, were held back from the battle for over 48 hours. I like to think it was to us that General Montgomery was referring when he signalled his 'gratitude for the valuable assistance afforded by the naval operations on D-Night', as to the best of our knowledge, there were no other naval operations in the vicinity of the battle on the opening night. "

Imperial War Museum

Henry Byrne 18, a gunner with 154th (Leicestershire Yeomanry) Field Regiment, Royal Artillery found himself among complete strangers – on the way to fight in the desert.

"Where was I going? What was I doing on this troop ship, risking my life at sea, manning a Lewis gun, watching the sky on August Bank Holiday and remembering my picnic in the Dublin Mountains only a year before?

Last year a junior salesman — now a highly trained field gunner. Is it fate or madness? My comrades must have thought the latter, since compared with these men of a pre-war yeomanry regiment, I was only a boy. Gibes abounded and for the first time in my life I felt isolated and at times near to tears. Instinct told me not to lose my individualism. I too had my culture, and my father and uncle had served in the First World War in an Irish Regiment. There must have been some English among them — so how did those poor souls feel among all the Paddys?

Young though I was, I decided to do what the Irish do best—laugh at myself — little knowing that in weeks of becoming the local comedian, the lads would seek me out to cheer them up with my jokes and a smile. Suddenly I was one of the lads. This came back to me at Alamein, remembering my solitude. Suddenly all our lives depended on each other.

Three days before the battle, our

▲ **A British gun team change the position of their gun, moving it to a new pit with all the necessary camouflage from nets already prepared.**

▼ **Even in the desert, with a limited supply of water per man, the Tommy can always find a way to make a cup of tea.**

regiment moved up to the front. With evening drawing in, the sun disappeared and we were faced with a dull, dreary and eerie scene, our faces grey with dust in an empty, cold wasteland. Here and there were the burnt-out remains of vehicles and the odd crane. The rumble of gun and machine-gun fire told us we were near the front. Suddenly we were ordered to halt. In the distance we could see Stukas dive-bombing our lines — our war had begun. We had to wait until dark to take up our positions, so we ate our 'desert chicken', otherwise known as bully beef, and waited. No fires - no tea. I shall always remember, in the dusk of that day, feeling I would never come out of this.

That evening we took up positions under light, intermittent fire which indicated that the enemy was just feeling out the ground on hearing transport movement. We dug into our holes and for the next two days it was as though not a soul was in the desert. Over a million men hidden deep in the sand, not a sound anywhere 'til sunset, when the Stukas came, followed by a repeat at sunrise.

On the afternoon of October 23, leaflets were distributed, giving Monty's eve-of-battle message. 'Fight as long as you have breath in your body'. It seemed unreal in the quiet afternoon. Where were the tanks, infantry, planes and guns?

At 21.40 hours, the desert shook like an earthquake. For as far as we could see, the sky was ablaze from the guns. Such was the deafening noise that we could see enemy shells exploding on our positions, but could not hear them. Our gaunt stares said it all — we were scared stiff, but oddly enough, not

▲ **A later picture of Gunner Henry Byrne – only 18 when he fought at Alamein.**

frightened. In the hours that followed, the tension eased. Our barrage was having the desired effect, but the infantry and engineers had it rough.

In the glare of the guns, men could be seen falling and groups being blown up by mines. Cameramen were moving forward with the infantry, but to no avail. Jerry held a strongly fortified line.

By morning we were veterans, or so it seemed. Gippy tummy reared its head, and though painful and distressing, it provided a comic relief watching each other going back and forth with a shovel to dig a loo.

We got our bottle of water in the morning and each put some in a petrol can for washing. We then got another tin, pierced holes in the bottom, put some holes in and sifted the water after every wash. After two days, one of my quips was 'It's cleaner to stay dirty'.

US Library of Congress

Henry Byrne

Imperial War Museum

WHEN IN DOUBT. BREW-UP.

Most of us went for bald heads because of the sand lice.

The cook-wagon, when it could provide a hot meal, did wonders with bully stew, bully fritters, cold bully (which melted in the tin), biscuit porridge, biscuit date pudding and good old cocoa. They were few and far between, but most welcome!

They occasionally gave us Carnation milk, tea and sugar when they couldn't cook and, thanks to the petrol can, we made the famous 'Benghazi' fire, made by cutting the can in half, filling it with sand and piercing holes in the sides. We then poured petrol on the sand and lit it. Our shirts and shorts were dropped into a petrol can, dipped, removed and dried in two minutes in the sand.

Of course the war was in full swing though static, and with all the above, the shocks of the 23rd became a bad dream. Stukas came over and we came out of our holes and fired rifles at them. Although no advance was possible yet, the whole picture of war changed. Morale was high, and as the days passed with the endless bombardment and bombers and fighters soaring above, the warning came that if we didn't break through soon, we may have to withdraw into Palestine. None of us accepted this – we had been too stirred by Monty's message.

On the tenth day, the Axis collapsed and the breakthrough came. We were on the chase, moving up and down the line of advance to give support.

Soon we caught our first glimpse of POWs. The Aussies were throwing

▼ British rations – interesting enough to warrant a German photo.

▲ A tank man lights up in the company of 'Titus', his painted mascot.

stones at a group of Italians, telling them to go back and fight. I found this to be in bad taste, though on the surface it was comical. On we went, and at the famous Knightsbridge, thousands of Hitler's supermen, dishevelled, dirty, some in stockinged feet, all thoroughly dejected and apparently starving, were taken, escorted by a handful of Scots Infantrymen. This is what we waited for – a victory for the British, finally breaching Hitler's master-race.

In the event, I couldn't hate. We stopped and watched these men pass by. I thought what heroes these men were to have withstood this bombardment from land, sea and air for ten days. I wished I could be sure I could be so brave. For a moment I imagined they were British and I was one of them. I thought of my family at home, and I'm proud to say it brought a tear to my eye. I was to see more of the Nazi element of Hitler's men in Italy, which did fill me with hatred – and a determination to destroy that evil empire.

However, remembering Alamein, and I often do, I feel there is a certain affection between the *Afrika Korps* and the Eighth Army.

It was man's war and I had become a man. We fought soldier to soldier, no civilians involved, and though we all lost friends, I feel sure we will always have a healthy respect for each other for the manner in which we conducted ourselves in that war. "

▲ The moment of impact as a Stuka crashes in flames, south of El Alamein. Inset: a Tommy ducks but enjoys only scant cover.

▼ British soldiers inspect the wreckage of a grounded Stuka.

▶ Major Tom Bird, MC, wounded in the action at Snipe, is understandably grim-faced as he signs the casualty list the day after the battle. It was an attack spectacular for deeds of bravery. Lt-Colonel Turner was awarded the VC, Lt Toms the DSO, and Sgt Calistan the DCM.

WHATEVER'S IN HIS POCKETS, YOU MAY WANT IT. INTELLIGENCE NEED IT! HAND IT OVER

▲ Both in the desert and in the towns, intelligence discipline has to be upheld. Even the smallest memento or minor detail might hold untold significance for the military.

Cathleen Violet Chidley was working in Sainsbury's before she joined up. After a few weeks with the Army Pay Corps, she found herself posted to the Provost Corps in Cairo.

Imperial War Museum

❝ I was 23 and very excited when I was told I was going. We went around the Bay of Biscay to Alexandria and the convoy was attacked by U-boats. It was most uncanny—when you looked out, you couldn't see any of the other ships, but you could hear the depth charges.

We were put on to these cattle trains almost as soon as we reached Alexandria, and sent to Cairo, where we were billetted next to an Egyptian army place. They were always cadging cigarettes. Their conditions seemed very over-crowded compared with ours. We had lovely billetting and the food was always good.

We used to patrol the streets in groups of two men and two women. We would go out at about 7.00 am and work until midday. We would work again in the evening from about 5.00 until 9.00 or 10.00. In the afternoons we used to sleep — it was so hot that you couldn't do anything else.

There were some nasty incidents when we were patrolling, but when you're young, you don't feel fear of anything. On one occasion, a knife was dropped from a window and landed inches away from me. We also heard rumours that some police who had been patrolling with us had been mixed up in a drugs deal — the incident had something to do with that.

We women would be hassled a lot by the local men when we were on patrol, and we never went out alone. King Farouk used to invite the English girls on to his yacht. I went there once, but some girls went often.

There used to be a saying you'd hear at get-togethers, that we were the 'officers' ground sheets' — but you

◀ Alexandria – for many of the men in the desert, a refuge where they might spend a few days' leave away from the battle. For the overall war effort, though, it is a vital point of supply for equipment, ammunition and food. If Alameinn is lost, Alexandria is next.

always get that sort of mentality, and it was only a minority of the men who were like that. Most of them regarded us as equals.

We were very, very naive. One of the girls was pregnant and she kept telling us she felt sick. We were all very concerned, but it didn't occur to any of us what was wrong.

Another girl I used to patrol with used to dance in a night-club. She was a Greek, and absolutely lovely. I think they knew what she was doing, and used her as a sort of spy for any information she could pick up. She was short and stocky, but when she danced, she was beautiful — I can still see her now.

It wasn't fun really, but a lot of the time we looked on it as such. We joined ENSA and used to go singing. I appeared in a play called 'The Old Mill'. In the evenings we went to places which were like beer kellers, and they were full of mainly English people. There weren't many incidents of drunkenness, although I can remember one, where I jumped on the table and started blowing my whistle **❞** to restore order.

Major Tom Bird MC commanded the six-pounder anti-tank company of the Rifle Brigade in the 'Snipe' action on October 26 and 27, earning him the DSO. Here, he tells mostly of the courage of other members of his company.

❝ The battle for Alamein had come to an impasse — neither side was winning. We, a motor battalion of three rifle companies and one anti-tank company, were instructed to carry out a night attack and take what was thought to be a ridge, some 2,000 yards in front of our line. At the point from which we were going to start there was disagreement as to where we were. The infantry holding that line were part of the Highland Division, and they were fairly confident that they knew where they were. We, on the other hand, had been in the desert for about two years and thought we knew all about navigation there – and we thought we were somewhere different.

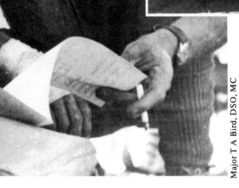

Major T A Bird, DSO, MC

◄ 'Before July '42 we had 2-pounder guns – which bounced off every enemy tank. Suddenly we'd got 6-pounders which went through every enemy tank . . . it went through all the German tanks side on at ranges up to 800–900 yards, and through the front of them at 200–300 yards – and it went through all the Italian tanks both front and sides. We started winning because we could actually knock the tanks out.'

Major Tom Bird, DSO, MC.

▼ It takes an Australian sense of humor to devise this sign.

▼▼ The tables have turned – now it is the Allies who are taking the prisoners in the desert war.

The Colonel decided we would form up as if *we* were right, and he was then going to ask the gunners to put down a round of smoke on the area which we were to attack. To our embarrassment, the Highland Division were correct, so when the smoke came down, we had to switch around in the middle of the night.

As we met almost no enemy resistance, the rifle companies' attack succeeded and the anti-tank guns were sent for and dug in during the night. But at dawn, to improve their field of fire, some had to be resited. I think probably the majority of our casualties were at that moment, and it's always one of the remarkable things in the desert, that if you were just below ground in a slit trench, you could have a fantastic amount of bombing and shelling and not come to a great deal of harm—unless they actually hit you. But if you moved about, that's when you got casualties.

All day we found ourselves under fire from our own men. As far as they were concerned, we were 2,000 yards ahead of where they thought there were any of their own troops. Added to this, during the night, various German tanks and guns had come through our positions, and we'd knocked them out. Looking through the haze from quite a long way away, all they could see were some jeeps and some enemy tanks, so they assumed that we were the enemy. Once when we were being attacked very hard indeed by our own side, our intelligence officer, Jackie Wintour got in his jeep and drove straight at them. Luckily they didn't fire. He went right up to them and stopped the leading tanks firing, but the rest went on unabated.

The most memorable occasion was when we were being attacked by nine Italian tanks—but only one of our guns could fire at them. This was manned by the Colonel, Vic Turner, the Platoon Commander, Jack Toms, and Sergeant Calistan. They'd shot six when they ran out of ammunition. Jack Toms got in his jeep and drove to one of the other guns. Tanks which were still coming on were shooting, and everyone else was shooting at us, so he drove through very heavy fire. Then he loaded the ammunition from one of the other guns on to his jeep and as he drove back, his jeep was hit and caught fire. But he managed to drive as far as the gun and he and the colonel, and Corporal Francis, unloaded the ammunition – and of course, with the fire, this was liable to go off at any moment – and managed to get the ammunition to the gun. Calistan then hit all the rest of the tanks and knocked them out. Vic Turner was wounded in the head in this action.

I was hit in the back of the head but was more or less *compos mentis*. Vic Turner and I were more or less knocked out. Two German tanks got within about 100 yards from where we were. There was one gun in a position to fire but the gun crew were in a trench a little bit away from the gun, and they couldn't get to it because every time they made the slightest movement, there was a huge burst of machine-gun fire. The platoon sergeant, Sergeant Swann, managed, by using dead ground, to creep up to the gun to shoot at the tanks. They were within such short range that one exploded, more or less. I can remember the cheer which went up—it was a very, very brave effort.

Monty came to give the battalion a talk—I suppose it was before Alamein. I remember him telling the men that they were 'a fine body of men' — which was such a cliche, if I'd said it to my company, they would have roared with laughter and they'd have known that I was pulling their leg. However, it seemed to go down quite well. It didn't seem to matter that he talked in cliches. **"**

IF GOING MUCH FURTHER PLEASE TAKE ONE ➜

▶ Heinz Erdmann (right) of the German Special Unit 288, with an ambulance 'borrowed' from the British after Tobruk and eventually returned, 'kaputt' in 1943.

 Heinz Erdmann volunteered for the 'Sonder-Stab F', a special staff unit, and set up Special Unit 288, in which he served, in the medical unit, during the early part of 1943.

Heinz Erdmann

▼ Sitting in the shadow of a petrol tank, at a desk improvised from a board and two petrol cans, an *Afrika Korps* man writes home.

" We had erected a first-aid post between the coast and the road, marked with a huge red cross and situated away from the combat troops. We had made it through the so-called 'six-day race' from August to September '42 and waited to see what would happen. As a medical unit, we had relatively little to do. Then we were woken in the night of October 23/24. We suddenly heard ahead of us at the front (some of us had started to bed down for the night) a terrible roar and rumbling and crashing over a broad area, and saw a long, wide flickering gleam of light in the background, from the sea right over into the desert. It went on and on, sometimes stronger, then less. And this rumbling went on for days and nights, sometimes further away from us, sometimes nearer.

Now we had more than enough to do from the medical point of view. The first returning vehicles and smaller units were blocking the road and tracks. It became difficult for us to get our wounded back to the post. Sometimes we had to force our way through. Once our first-aid post was bombed. The fighter/bomber attacks on the road and the tracks were very bad.

Around the 30th October, we had to up sticks and move back. Then on the 3rd November the front collapsed and we began to retreat. This was definitely the worst for us, the sand blowing in our eyes, the air and the fighter/bombers, to say nothing of the artillery and tank fire. At night the coast road and wide strips to the left and right were lit up by flares.

Everything blocked up, terrible chaos, screaming, cursing, running about, burning vehicles, rescuing the wounded between them, treating them and carrying them off, and burying the dead. All this went on for days and nights — about 10 days. Then, at the Halfaya Pass, Sollum, things got more or less back to normal (for us at least). I was, and still am, grateful that my unit and myself got through this period relatively well. "

▼ A German pack for on-the-spot dressings, complete with instructions.

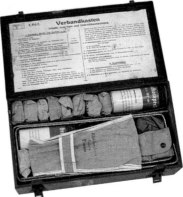

Dal McGuirk

Süddeutscher Verlag

 Lieutenant Heinz-Dietrich Arberger, with the 3rd Company of the 21st Armoured Division recalls the start of the battle, while Adelbert von Taysen, Commander of 1 Company Machine Gun Battalion 8 remembers the final stages.

" The previous evening we were playing cards and chatting. Shortly before 22.00 hours there was a rumbling and roaring, and flashes to the north of us. We stared at the horizon, which had turned a pale colour. Were the Tommies ready to attack? Around midnight it had quietened down, and we went off to sleep. The next morning the noise of fighting could be heard. Everything was quiet where we were, so we thought this couldn't be anything to worry about. The 3rd Company were enjoying their afternoon, presenting medals, roasting gazelles — there was a jovial atmosphere. Then the alarm came. 'Prepare to march!'

On the evening of October 25 we marched off, initially to the west, then in a wide arc behind north section, which had been heavily burned up by the enemy. After an extremely wearisome night march, during which night bombers inflicted heavy losses, we reached the telegraph strip south of Tell el Aqqaqir. We found an area of dunes which it was impossible to see over. This was already occupied by the enemy in unknown strength, but should have been occupied by Italians.

The commander ordered us to attack on the spot to clear out the area. There was a brief exchange of fire with British reconnaissance units, who immediately withdrew to the east. While chasing after them we came upon unoccupied Italian positions, some with primed 88mm Flak. The Italian battalion which should have been there, turned up afterwards from areas at the rear or from deep bunkers into which they had retreated.

The adjutant reported location and intentions to the Corps over the

Hans Dietrich Arberger

Dal McGuirk

▲ Lieutenant Heinz-Dietrich Arberger of the 21st Panzer Division. Inset: From 'The Soldier in Libya', identifying pictures of British ranks.

▶ Adelbert von Taysen (left), in the desert in 1941.

▼ The Tommies were tired – but not as tired as these Germans, downcast by their retreat from El Alamein.

headphones, and got a lengthy whistle back, because our intentions had been greeted with disapproval. The Corps obviously still had faith in our allies. The events of the next 24 hours were to prove them wrong.

At about 21.00 hours there was a heavy barrage from the enemy, the like of which we'd never witnessed before. Fortunately, we had been able to find useful cover in the sandy landscape. About half an hour later, the firing suddenly stopped. It was suspiciously quiet. Then suddenly voices could be heard. We released the safety catches on our guns. With loud shouts, the Italians hurtled past us to the rear, some on foot, others on overloaded trucks, like a phantom — then silence.

On the morning of the 28th, British forces were gathered in strength in front of our sector. Without bothering too much about cover, they got into position for an attack — obviously completely aware of their superiority. However, before they could take position, our heavy artillery section fired on them. The attack ceased, but it was a gruesome sight, watching the British orderlies toiling without a break to rescue their wounded and dead. In the twilight, we scoured the battlefield behind our position and came across a badly wounded captain. It was very moving to watch the efforts our men made to bandage up the unfortunate chap, who had been lying untreated for a day and a half. They gave him food and drink and carried him off.

Adelbert von Taysen describes the night of November 2/3.

A 60-minute barrage rained down in the night on our positions by the telegraph strip. At about 1 o'clock the fire stopped. A few minutes later, British soldiers stormed the 1st and 2nd Companies on foot and on carts. Six of these agile little gun carriers managed to destroy the anti-tank guns at point-blank range, then the enemy was on top of us. A battle for the cover holes

Hans Dietrich Arberger

ensued, with rifle butts, spades, hand-grenades and bare fists. All you could hear was the sound of panting, groaning and whimpering. You could just see the silhouettes of the attackers against the night sky. The best way to recognise who was friend or foe was by the flat steel helmets the Tommies wore. After a half-hour battle they disappeared eastwards. Only a few dead were left behind. By some sort of miracle, we got away with only a few wounded. **"**

▼ A German night-watchman waits to be relieved after cold hours on guard.

Süddeutscher Verlag

Süddeutscher Verlag

CHAPTER 10

BATTLE DIARY

SICILY – RUGGED TEST

Once the last Axis forces had surrendered on Cape Bon in Tunisia on May 13, 1943, North Africa was in Allied hands. The next objective, the southern Italian island of Sicily, would require the Allies' first amphibious operation of any scale in the war, directed by US General Dwight Eisenhower. The island was defended by 350,000 Axis troops – about a third of them German – under the command of General Guzzoni. Although outnumbered, the Allies enjoyed air superiority: 4,000 aircraft against 1,500.

For the landings on July 9, 1943, codenamed Husky, 160,000 men landed from 3,000 vessels, the US Seventh Army under General George Patton between Licata and Gela, the British Eighth Army under General Montgomery along the shore between Avola and Pachino, south of Syracuse. Although airborne forces were employed, they were only partially successful – the men of the 82nd Airborne Division were badly scattered and some British First Airborne gliders crashed in the sea. Nevertheless, the British captured Syracuse on July 12 and Augusta on the 14th.

Hitler sent the one-armed Eastern Front veteran, General Hans Hube, to take command of the German divisions. Axis resistance hardened, but US forces outflanked the Axis defenses with a series of small amphibious landings along the north coast. On August 17, British and American forces reached Messina, a strategic position which lay opposite the toe of Italy.

Although the Axis powers were able to evacuate troops, equipment and aircraft to the mainland, they lost 178,000 killed, wounded and captured, compared with relatively low Allied losses. With the capture of Sicily, Allied shipping could operate more freely in the Mediterranean, a substantial area of enemy territory was under Allied control, and the way to Italy was open.

A RUGGED TEST

The ancient towns and mountainous landscape of Sicily provide the backdrop to the bitter fighting which this island is about to witness

By now accustomed to the Mediterranean climate, and justifiably considering themselves veterans after surviving the North African campaigns, British forces converge on Sicily to take on Hitler's next relay of men—some just raw recruits.

Shipped out by boat from Africa, Sergeant Herbert Parkin arrived in Sicily in July 1943 with the 2nd Battalion London Irish Rifles, as part of the massive Allied assault on the island.

"We disembarked and came up the beaches. There was no opposition at the beginning, because the Germans had already landed and pushed inland.

We moved in, towards Mount Etna. The Germans were moving back, but slowly—they were good soldiers and they fought every inch of the way. They were always on the hills and we always got the middle. We had to get them off the high ground, as we called it, which involved climbing the mountains. It was amazing that we got up them.

Our tanks could only go up so far and you've got to remember that once they get up, they have to get down again. They had to be very careful, but they would come up and give as much supporting fire as they could. The crowd we had was very good.

Eventually, the Germans would withdraw off the hills, and as they withdrew, you had to prepare for them to come back, because invariably they would push a counter-attack in. They didn't just walk away.

We would have to dig in straight away, and HQ would try to push a fresh company up to strengthen our position, but it wasn't always possible because there might have been a lot of casualties. It was always very fluid until we got settled. You could take a position and then lose it. It looks nice on these pictures with the little arrows and things, but it wasn't like that. It was very hard work, especially for the infantry—they had the worst of the lot.

As we moved along we had to be careful of the mines. You couldn't just wander along. The infantry would come up first and then the engineers would go along and put notices up of where the mines were. They used to lay white tape down.

The infantry had to take pot luck, because they had to go first. A lot of people got blown up.

The mines were in little wooden boxes which were about 3 inches square. Because they were wood, you couldn't detect them. If you trod on one, it took your leg off. There were S mines too, which were like a flower pot with prongs which showed above the ground. If you trod on that it would explode like a fragmentation bomb. There were a lot of them about.

On one occasion, we were moving up with the transport at the back and we pulled up around the base of Etna. We were told to get our heads down and get some rest while we could, before we moved off again. All of a sudden, someone shouted, 'Don't move, we're in a minefield!' You could see them all over the place and every one of us had missed them. We were so lucky. The engineers came in and shifted them.

Sometimes we moved forward at night and we would get in position, waiting for the dawn, which was when the Germans were supposed to attack. Sometimes they did, sometimes they didn't.

You waited there, and you could feel the tension as everyone was wondering what was going to happen. People tended to get very bad-tempered. You could laugh and joke, and then suddenly someone would shout or swear. It was the tension.

Everybody moaned in the line, including me. This was wrong, that was wrong. One of our officers used to say, 'Oh they're happy enough. When a British soldier isn't moaning, there's something wrong'.

Once the Germans had left, we got

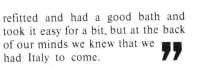

Hulton Deutsch Collection

refitted and had a good bath and took it easy for a bit, but at the back of our minds we knew that we had Italy to come. "

▲ An early call to action on board one of the landing craft which forms part of the Allied armada heading for Sicily.

◄ Men of the 51st Highland Division make good use of mules captured from the Germans.

◄◄ An incongruous sight among the bombed-out ruins and religious statues of the town of Catania—troops of the Royal Marines carry out a mopping-up operation in war-torn Sicily.

Imperial War Museum

Captain Ian Quarrie, on Motor Torpedo Boat 670, was speeding up the east coast of Sicily towards the Strait of Messina when he encountered a U-boat. His objective was to close the Strait to traffic by night and prevent interference with Allied supplies.

▼ **Pictured later in the war, Captain Ian Quarrie in Dover, 1944.**

We increased to full speed, the submarine still on the surface and guns blazing on both sides. We could only assume that our SO's signals had confused the U-boat into believing us to be an Italian unit, as never before had British forces been sighted so close to Sicily in broad daylight. The attack appeared to be unsuccessful, though.

We turned directly towards the U-boat at full speed and opened fire with every gun that would bear, striving to get alongside her before she disappeared below the surface. Her gunners, brave fellows, were still firing at us and presumably took a last-minute dive down her conning-tower hatch—or not, we would never know. Even so, they managed to score the odd hit and wounded one of my young gunners, not seriously, but quite painfully. The sea around the enemy bubbled as the air was

forced out of her ballast tanks and she disappeared below us. We dropped our four charges, set at 50 and 100 feet, close around her...and then waited.

In a hurry to press on and reach our patrol area, we could not stay long looking for signs of damage or destruction, and we saw none. Later we learned that we had, in fact, sunk the [Italian] submarine *Flutto*.

We had been told that there were two small Italian destroyers operating from Taormina, and as we took up our stations for the night, I caught sight of them in the darkness to the east. We moved into our positions for the attack—I signalled to the SO when I was beginning my stealthy run in at low speed to fire. No sooner had I begun my run in than all hell was let loose! I could just see the enemy in my torpedo sight, and my firing levers in front of me on the bridge were 'ready'. The enemy's first salvo straddled us and the second was just as accurate...not at all what we had been led to expect from a small Italian destroyer! If we were to survive to get our 'fish' away, it must be now or never. Pulling hard at my firing levers, I held my course until the torpedoes had leapt out of their tubes and away, then throttled to 'full ahead'. Wheel hard aport and with lumps of shrapnel all over the place,

◀ **Ian Quarrie, center front, on board HMMTB 106, pictured prior to sailing from Britain.**

▼ **A motor torpedo boat, typical of those in Sicily, speed 42 knots, armed with two Lewis guns and a torpedo.**

we were off on a reciprocal of the enemy's course.

At that moment, I caught sight of my First Lieutenant on his knees at the foot of the ladder leading from the bridge to the charterhouse. I asked him what the devil he was doing there and he gave me the perfect answer by showing me his tin hat, the front edge of which had been bent down vertically. 'And I think it got you on the shoulder on the way', he said. I was lucky—my shirt needed quite a bit of sewing, but the cause of the damage, a piece of metal the size of my fist, had hardly drawn blood. As the destroyers sped on their way, our SO gave us a course and speed to rejoin him and together we followed them down the coast towards Catania. It was not long before the unexpected reply came back, 'Forces being followed are friendly. Disengage immediately!'

The ships we attacked were, to the best of my memory, HMS *Aurora* and HMS *Penelope*, two of the crack gunnery cruisers in the Mediterranean Fleet. We were supposed, of course, to be patrolling well to the north of them, so they took us to be enemy. With no accurate radar available, a cruiser at 1,200 yards (the range at which they opened fire on us) looked to us very like a small destroyer at 600—our poor torpedoes must have been at their last gasp when they passed astern of their target. The next time we met one of the cruisers at sea, in broad daylight, we took great care to identify ourselves early and received the daylight reply, 'Let's be friends this time!'

Photographss courtesy of Ian Quarrie

![flag] *Petty Officer Dennis O'Brien was Coxswain on motor launch ML 1048, which played a vital role in the landings on Sicily, guiding the landing craft in to the shore.*

❝ We picked up our buoy and started patrolling. Another ML was also patrolling the beaches. There was a dogfight overhead, which a young lieutenant was watching through binoculars, when he suddenly dropped down dead. Nobody could understand what had happened, until they found a wound from a ricochet under his arm.

We went on to Syracuse harbour and went alongside the jetty, where a group of locals were standing. There was a very old lady, dressed in black, who gave us the fascist salute. The others stopped her very quickly—she didn't realise that we were on the other side!

While we were at Augusta, one of the merchant ships, an Empire boat, was bombed and sunk. We got as close as we could to pick up survivors. The sea was on fire, and there was one character swimming away from the ship still in his tin hat. Things were getting quite close, and a Geordie yelled out to him, 'Take your hat off, mate'. He yelled back, 'No fear, I want this as a bleedin' souvenir!'

One survivor stayed on the bridge—he looked very tired and kept very quiet. All he said was, 'I'm Royal Navy'. The other sailors were pouring all sorts of curses on the head of their chief engineer. Apparently he had manned four ships and he had never returned with any of them. They had all gone out from the UK and been blown up. They all blamed him for the bad luck. As I was in charge, I got permission from the captain to splice the mainbrace. I got the rum out and I offered the young navy man a drink, which he refused. We went alongside a cruiser to transfer the survivors, because they had better medical facilities than us. As we were putting them aboard, the young fellow collapsed on the deck. He had the most horrible injury in his back. He hadn't said a word about it, he had just sat there quietly. **❞**

▲ **As Allied progress on Sicily continues, British troops, tan from the African campaigns, walk through the streets of Pachino.**

▼ **Led by an ardent United Nations enthusiast, Sicilian civilians cheer for their Allied liberators as they progress towards Catania.**

▼ **As he waits for his landing craft to reach shore on Sicily, a Tommy swots up on the details of the island.**

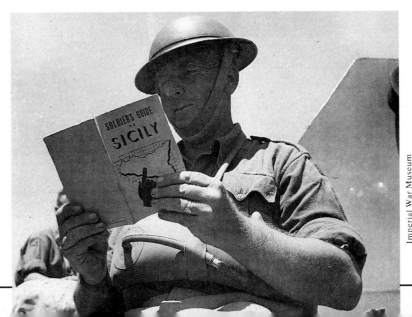

▲ Watched by a group of Sicilian locals, a US soldier wounded by shrapnel receives an on-the-spot plasma transfusion in the street.

Fred Jordan was a medic with the 217 Field Ambulance, attached to the Royal West Kent Regiment and was involved in action at Bronte in Sicily.

" We landed in Sicily in July 1943, arriving by boat from Algiers. It was a quiet landing with no opposition. We marched up towards Mount Etna, where the terrain was very hilly. The Germans were already there, dug into the hillsides. We had a lot of casualties because the Germans, being higher up than us, had the advantage, and our men had no protection. Their mortars were deadly accurate, and they were just hailing down on to the

infantry.

We were attached to the infantry, so that wherever they went, we went with them. On Sicily we were doing the attacking, so the infantry would go in first, and then we would follow up behind and pick up the men as they got wounded. We would evacuate them on stretchers to the next post down.

Out of all my experiences on Sicily, the incident I remember most vividly happened in a town called Bronte, which had been badly shelled by the Germans. They were mortaring the town and casualties were occurring. We moved up into a railway tunnel where the civilians were taking refuge.

Our Corporal was called Bill Lea—a very good man, very well liked. He

said to us, 'You stay here and I'll just go up a wee bit and see what's happening'. He went up and there was an almighty bang. We ran out, and he'd been hit. We picked him up on a stretcher and managed to get him back to the ambulance.

After the Germans had moved out, we went to the hospital that he was in and asked for him. They said, 'He's there'. There was a blanket covering him! By all accounts, the blast from the mortar bomb had burst his lungs. When you get a blast, it doesn't blow in, it sucks out, and he'd simply died.

The sad thing was that a chap that was with us was a big friend of Bill

▶ A British Brigadier talks to men of the US Paratroop Airborne Infantry. Inset: an RAF bombing map.

▲ Getting their first close-up glimpse of the island of Sicily, British troops wade ashore from their landing craft.

Lea. Whoever had covered the Corporal up had left his feet outside. It's a simple little thing, but when you cover a body up with blanket, all parts of the body should be concealed. This poor chap went absolutely berserk–almost hysterical– when this happened. 〞

◎ *Sergeant Pilot Rupert Cooling with No. 9 Squadron was flying exhaustive attacks on Pantelleria in their over-worked Wellingtons when the situation in the Mediterranean pointed to some major event taking place.*

〞 We knew something would happen soon. Axis forces had been expelled from Africa, and the bombers were switched to round-the-clock attacks on Italy's 'Malta'– the island of Pantelleria.

Our Wellingtons were doing three trips a night, the crews two one night and one the next. On our last sortie, hours before the island surrendered, we watched the man ahead go down in flames. As we left, the rear gunner called up. 'There's another on fire behind us!'. Nightfighters . . . but somehow we had slipped through undetected. The air was never silent– aircraft buzzed like a swarm of bees. We watched as drones of troop-carrying Dakotas moved like skeins of geese against the blue. Something was cooking, and when the Ops board listed every crew, we knew for certain.

Sentries stood at the entrance to the walled courtyard where we assembled for briefing. Unusually, the display was covered. 'Tonight, gentlemen', said Group Captain Powell, unveiling the maps, 'we

return to Europe. The Army is landing in Sicily at 0245 hours. Airborne forces, gliders and paratroopers will go in ahead. Our target is Syracuse and four aircraft will each carry 18 flares to be dropped exactly on time from 10,000 feet. Our troops will be on high ground waiting to move in. Bombing lines must be strictly observed.'

Many aircraft would carry flares and six 500 lb bombs. It was good to be chosen for that specialist task–to know that tonight we would make a little bit of history.

Take-off was at 2345 hours, on course at midnight. It was quiet until, ahead, pin-pricks of light then massive fire, flashes, spurts of flame. We reached the target area with twelve minutes to spare, then turned to circle just off the coast. At 0216 hours the first flares blossomed. Syracuse lay white and naked against the dark seas, like a photographic negative. Sweeping inland, Y-Yorker headed for our dropping point. Right on time, Bill's finger stabbed the release. At 0220 hours, our flares opened up, spot on schedule. Down to 7,000 feet and run in over the bay towards the inner harbour, our aiming point. There was a little flak and we were jolted once or twice by heavy bursts, then, 'Bombs gone'. I turned to starboard, out to sea and watched great pillars of smoke rise gradually to spread a white shroud over the target area. A few fountains of water erupted as an occasional bomb over or undershot into the sea. The flares died down–Syracuse once more retreated into the darkness. A few threads of light flak hosed into the night then ceased. The navigator was back at his charts whilst Bill the bomb-aimer stood beside me, thumbs up and a nod of approval. Our part in the drama was over–it hadn't been all that different from any other trip. 〞

▼ The 25-pounders of 165 Field Regiment provide artillery barrage against Vizzini, lighting up the sky.

(left margin) Robert Hunt Library

SYRACUSE (SICILY)

DATE OF PHOTOGRAPHS 14.9.42

Franz Strnad was only 18 years old when he joined the Hermann Göring Panzer Division as a recruit from a flak brigade in Vienna. His story starts when he was 'selected' and concludes with a remarkable coincidence.

▲ The Panzer Battle Badge (army version), awarded for at least three days' combat.

▼ A German looks out over the line where the Allies are attacking.

Associated Press

❝ On the way to Block 4 we bumped into NCO Müller, who had a sergeant with him. 'Who wants to go to Sicily with this sergeant? His name is Peter Romme', he said.

We were flabbergasted. We were not used to this sort of speed of events. Since neither of us said a word, he asked the sergeant, 'Which one do you want to take with you?' He weighed us both up and pointed at me. I had to report straight away to the orderly room to get my marching papers, and got myself ready for the journey. We were to set off that very evening.

The train journey went via Munich and Rome to Naples. The further south we got, the more unbearable became my blue Luftwaffe uniform. Even at the posting office for the front, where we had to wait to be taken on the rest of the journey, I still couldn't get my hands on a tropical uniform. We finally set off, this problem still unsolved. With a

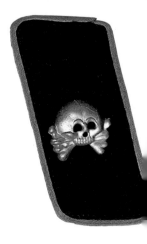

▲ A Panzer army service death's head collarpatch.

◀ General Hans Hube, German C-in-C in Sicily and reputedly one of the last Germans to leave the island.

convoy of five Opel-Blitz, loaded with tank-engines, spares and tank shells, we travelled on to Santa Maria Capua Vetere near Caserta. Our division had a base here in the Italian army barracks.

We were sent on from there and four days later arrived at Villa San Giovanni, a coastal town in the vicinity of Reggio di Calabria, right down on the toe of the 'boot'. We were then taken by ferry across the Strait of Messina to Sicily.

The first day in Sicily was my birthday, so I had to drink a bottle of Marsala with Romme and the CO, an old policeman. It was a lethal brew in the unaccustomed tropical heat. It was only when we were attacked by fighter bombers that I was able to move myself—with glazed eyes I looked at the two Spitfires, firing at us on all barrels.

While my comrades dove for cover, I stayed on the truck, which had just been loaded up with 5 cm tank shells. The two planes only launched one attack on us and nothing happened. Later, when I'd sobered up, the policeman told me that a volley of shots had hit just in front of the truck.

That night the attacks continued. When dawn was breaking, we took off into the surrounding countryside, camouflaged ourselves and lay down under the bushes for a sleep. At about midday the driver woke us, and got the truck ready to start. He explained that the Tommies would be taking a lunch break between 12.00 and 2.00, and we would have to take advantage of this interlude.

I was assigned that look-out position at the front again, and made with 'looky-looky', as we said then. Peter Romme was assigned the look-out at the rear. None of us looked at the time for ages, and when I finally checked, it was five minutes after 2.00—and as I looked up, there in the sky in front of us were two dots—

▲ **A German Tiger tank waits in the street of a Sicilian town for the order to move and attack the invading Allies.**

▶ **Dejected among the men of the 1/6th Queens Regiment as they take the town of Scafati, a prisoner from the Hermann Göring Division awaits his fate.**

▼ **Kept busy by the marauding RAF fighters and bombers, a Messerschmitt Bf-110 is given a thorough overhaul on a Sicilian airfield.**

fighter bombers heading straight at us!

I immediately bashed my fist down on the driver's cabin. We were just on the outskirts of Catania. The truck stopped and I guided it backwards into a side street. Then I jumped down, went back to the main street and watched the fighters, which, as they got close, I could just make out as Spitfires. One of the machines, whose pilot had obviously spotted me, made directly for me. I quickly leapt behind a garden wall and took cover.

It fired at me, but the wall provided enough protection. Once it had flown by, I jumped out and looked up at the plane flying away. To my horror, the two Spitfires did a huge curve and came back, firing on all barrels again. So I jumped over the wall and stood there for a few seconds. When one of the machines headed straight for me again, and I could see the pilot, I waved to him. Was this defiance of just plain bravado? Then I threw myself to the ground. I got up again once the planes were out of sight.

This little game happened twice more. Whenever a plane came straight at me, I waved and then dived for cover as quickly as I could behind the stone wall. On the fourth

occasion that they flew straight at us, they held their fire and just flew by. This time I could see the pilot of 'my' machine clearly, and this time he waved at me.

Twenty-five years later, in 1968, I was working as a porter in the big department store in Graz. One day, a Jaguar with English numberplates drove into the garage. A woman got out and went in to see the manager. The driver, meanwhile, came up to me and in the middle of the conversation asked, 'Were you in the war too?' 'Yes, I was with the Luftwaffe, with the Hermann Göring Division.'

The Englishman was startled and said, 'So you were in Sicily, as well?' I told him I was. He said he had been with the RAF in Sicily, and said what an amazing time that was. Then I asked him, 'Why did the RAF pilots only fly from 8.00 to 12.00 and from 2.00 to 6.00?' With typical dry British humour, he replied calmly, 'Oh, we already had the 48-hour week by then!'

We chatted further and I told him of my experience with the low-flyers in Catania. His eyes widened, he threw his arms around me and danced around in a circle with me. 'That was me in the Spitfire!' he was shouting. **"**

CHAPTER 11

BATTLE DIARY

DECEMBER 1942

16   Start of Russian winter counter-offensive

JANUARY 1943

12   Second phase of Russian counter-offensive begins

FEBRUARY

2   Last German units in Stalingrad surrender

8   Russians recapture Kursk

16   Russians recapture Kharkov

20   Guderian appointed Inspector General of Armored Troops

22   Manstein launches spring offensive

MARCH

15   Germans recapture Kharkov

18   Germans recapture Belgorod

MAY

4   Kursk attack plan approved

13   Last German units in Tunisia surrender

JULY

4   Manstein begins attack in southern half of Kursk salient

5   Model begins attack in northern half of Kursk salient

7   Ninth Army's advance halted

10   Allies land on Sicily

12   Major tank battle around Prokhorovka – over 1,500 armored
        vehicles involved

13   Hitler orders halt to attacks at Kursk

14   Red Army launches its counter-attack

23   All German gains around Kursk wiped out

KURSK – BEGINNING OF THE END

The winter fighting on the Eastern Front, where Field Marshal Erich von Manstein halted the Russian offensive after its victory at Stalingrad in February 1943, created a huge salient 100 miles wide and 70 miles deep, with the railroad junction city of Kursk at its center. That summer the Germans planned two simultaneous attacks from north and south to destroy the Soviet forces and stabilize the front. The operation, called Citadel, used 2,380 tanks and assault guns, 10,000 guns and 900,000 men supported by 2,500 aircraft, under the command of Field Marshall Gunther von Kluge in the north and Manstein with Army Group South. Although senior German officers had reservations about the operation, Hitler was adamant that it go ahead. But Ultra intercepts of German signals had been passed to the Soviet High Command, giving them full details of the plan. Consequently, the Red Army turned the salient into a huge fortress, laying deep and dense minefields protected by artillery, supported by 3,300 tanks and assault guns, 2,650 aircraft and 1,337,000 men.

In heavy rain and under heavy artillery fire, the German attack in the north soon became bogged down. In the south, however, tough Waffen-SS troops made headway and on July 12 at Prokhorovka, 700 German tanks of General Herman Hoth's Fourth Panzer Army clashed with 850 of Marshal Pavel Rotmistrov's Fifth Guards Tank Army. The encounter was the biggest tank battle in history.

On July 13 Soviet forces launched a counter-offensive that crushed the German salients north and south of Kursk and rolled their forces back over 150 miles. The retreating Germans lost around 1,500 tanks, 1,400 aircraft and 70,000 men; although Soviet losses were probably only slightly less, the victors had taken the tactical and strategic initiative. They would retain it all the way to Berlin.

BEGINNING OF THE END

At Kursk, over 2 million men grappled in a battle where tanks fought at close quarters, and anti-tank gunners stood to the last.

After storming through Russia, beleaguering her cities and starving her citizens, the German invaders have finally come face to face with the might of the Red Army's tanks. Under orders from Hitler to hold on and press home their attack at any cost, the Germans, worn down by the attrition of the long campaign, go into battle. They have no illusions, though—the resources of the huge Russian Bear, once called to action, must prove victorious.

◀ **Despair on the Eastern Front. A young German buries his head in his hands, his comrade dead behind him and his gun smashed beyond use.**

▶ **A German tank is towed out of a hole by a fellow Tiger, against orders to wait for recovery vehicles. If the stranded tank's engine helped, the strain on the rescuing tank would not be too great.**

▶▶ **The insignia of the Division Das Reich.**

Süddeutscher Verlag

Georg Berger was First Ordinance Officer from the SS General Command with the division Das Reich. Almost surrounded at Kharkov, they were ordered to hold the town, but commanding general Paul Hausser decided to withdraw – an initiative which proved successful.

❝ The decision to disobey an order from the *Führer* was a rare occurrence and in this case testifies to the civil courage of one of the most important commanders of the Waffen-SS.

The SS Panzer Corps with the Divisions *Leibstandarte* and *Das Reich* was virtually encircled in Kharkov. Awaiting it was the same fate as befell the Sixth Army in Stalingrad – that is, unless, at the eleventh hour, an order to withdraw and evacuate the town was issued.

On February 13 Russian tank units broke through to the outskirts of Kharkov – only the arterial road to the south west, direction Poltava, could be kept clear. As First Ordinance Officer of the SS General Command, I experienced those fateful hours before the break-out from Kharkov, and witnessed first-hand how Hausser was thrown into a terrible crisis of conscience by a senseless order from the *Führer*.

The order from the *Führer* of 13 February was curt and simple,

Tass

'Kharkov is to be held'. In a situation report to the Army Section Lanz, Hausser requested permission to evacuate the town, which was rejected, citing the order from the *Führer*. Following a number of telephone conversations with the High Commander of the Army, General Lanz, Hausser was permitted to speak personally.

I passed this conversation on in the evening of 13 February. Hausser, unfortunately, had been unable to get Manstein's consent, on the grounds that we were dealing with an explicit order from the *Führer*. However, Field Marshal von Manstein empowered Hausser to seek direct contact with the *Führer's* HQ, in order to give his own explanation of how precarious the situation was.

▼ **General Paul Hausser – the man who defied the Führer's order.**

Munin Verlag GMBH, Osnabruck

I succeeded in relaying this conversation to the *Wolfsschanze* (*Führer* HQ near Rastenburg), and the Chief of General Staff of the Army, General Zeitzler, promised Hausser that he would persuade the *Führer* to change the order during the *Lagebesprechung* (situation meeting) at 02.00 the next morning.

In the meantime, on 14 February, the orders to the Divisions *Liebstandarte* and *Das Reich*, instructing them to withdraw from Kharkov, had long since been written up, and the Ordinance Officers of the Divisions were waiting impatiently for the orders to be distributed.

▲ **German grenadiers and SS men await orders while sheltering in an anti-tank ditch made by Russians.**

▶ **An Elefant bears the legend 'We will conquer through our Tigers' – such would not be so at Kursk.**

In the late afternoon of 14 February, Paul Hausser came out of the cramped farmhouse into the shivering cold and paced up and down in silence. Turning, he said calmly, 'Give out the orders to the divisions to withdraw'. I held my breath then said, '*Obergruppenführer*, the order from the *Führer* states quite clearly . . .' Paul Hausser interrupted me, 'An old man like me is no loss, but I can't do this to the young boys out there. Give out the Corps order.'

✠ *Herbert Brunnegger was an Unterscharführer with the Totenkopf Division of the Waffen-SS in the tank battle at Kursk. He had no illusions as to the futility of the Germans' task in this merciless battle.*

❝ The most destructive battle in the history of the war had now begun. In the prelude to the battle, a matter of only hours, more shells and bombs were used up than during the whole of the French and Polish campaign.

Beside us our comrades from the *Leibstandarte* and the Division *Das Reich* were preparing to attack. We were waiting in our positions far ahead in the advancing front and at midday we watched from some kilometres away as their heavy Tiger units, guns blazing, broke through the Russian anti-tank and tank cordon. When we got the order to dismantle, they were moving up closer to our hill and were about to push past us. At around 16.30 hours we clambered into the troop carrier in what was previously the main battle-line, and we were whisked off to one of the main parts of the battle. The same evening the infantry attack began. Resistance was slight. The enemy had already withdrawn his main forces and his second and third lines were lying in wait for us.

We trudged uphill and downhill lugging the heavy equipment, under constant fire from Russian machine-guns, which were nailed to the ground. As evening fell we reached our marked destination and set up camp in the open air, while the engineers set about laying down a cordon of mines in front of us. They also took over guard of the resting troops, while we wrapped ourselves in blankets and tarpaulin. In the gathering dusk, half-asleep, I heard my name called out, and that of my comrade, Schulz. Schulz, like me, was a newly commissioned *Unterscharführer* [Second Lieutenant]. In the hope that I had been dreaming, I dozed on, until I finally had to accept that my name really was being called out. My company chief, *Obersturmführer* Schmoelz, explained to us what we had to do from his tarpaulin-covered hide-hole: we were to reconnoitre the enemy territory as far as the runway Bjelgorod-Kursk by two different

Süddeutscher Verlag

▲ The insignia of the Sixth Panzer Division.

▶ A column of German supply trucks and tanks with troops on bicycles on the Bjelgorod-Orel road.

◀ Attacking German infantry-men spring from their position to storm a Russian post, 5 July 1943.

▼ The insignia of the Third SS Division *Totenkopf*, veterans of the Eastern Front.

routes. 'Toss for who takes which', we were told. We quickly agreed on this. Schultz would take the left, and I would take the right sector.

I took half of the group with me. We took with us machine pistols, hand grenades, gas masks and bayonets, but we would be without steel helmets. Our order – to form a line of infantry, spaced out just so that the man in front was in view.

It was pitch black all round us as

▶ Two Germans inspect two shot-up Russian T-34 tanks near the most advanced German field position on the Eastern Front.

we left the *Igelstellung* (position of all-round defence). I set the bearings on my field compass. I picked out a glow of fire on the eastern horizon as a provisional marker . . . As long as it continued to glow, we wouldn't lose our way and, despite the darkness, we would be able to find our way back to our departure point.

I was at the head of the group, trying to make as little noise as possible, when suddenly we were stopped in our tracks by loud shouts from behind us: 'Stop, stop, you're standing right in the middle of a minefield!' Christ, this was too much, and we'd only just set off. One false step could mean instant death. I ordered everyone to get down on their haunches without touching the ground with their hands. Then, the last man in the line took the first step back out of the minefield along the path indicated by the engineers. We got out without losses. Once we finally got under way again

we had wasted half an hour.

We crept quietly through the darkness. Not a sound of guns or the rattling of equipment, only the breathing of the men and the soft rustle of the stiff blades of grass in the cool night. We could expect to stumble upon the enemy at any moment.

The wind carried an aroma of Machorka tobacco. We waited a while

▼ German Panzer Mark III tanks advance *en masse* across the vast unprotected wastes of Russia.

without being able to make out a thing, but we knew now that 'Ivan' was around. We were smack in the middle of the enemy lines, but we had to go on, we had to get to the runway and complete our mission to establish whether defensive preparations had been made there.

As we crept further forward the aroma of Machorka grew stronger. I had our Russian speaker brought up to the head of the line, and instructed him that should we stumble unexpectedly upon the enemy, we would quite brazenly pretend to be Russians. I told him that he was to go on ahead alone and speak to the Ivans in their own language, while we would hang back. A few minutes later I spotted a dark cluster of people lying just below my feet. As I crouched down I noticed that it was two Russians sleeping in a hide-hole behind a light machine gun. Karp raised his machine pistol, but I gestured to him to put it away. That's the last thing we needed on a nice summer evening like this. I carefully lifted the machine gun out of the hole and gave the signal to continue. . .

At about 2.00 am it dawned on me that the flame beacon I had taken for a marker had strayed a good way to the right. There was only one explanation for this: the flame was coming from a burning ship moving down a river. This could only be the upper reaches of the Don. It was clear to me now that we had lost our way, and finding the way back would be a matter of instinct rather than a compass. I ordered my men to withdraw immediately, and we wasted

no time heading back, since we had to be out of enemy territory before dawn broke. The anxiety that the greying light of dawn could prove to be our captor quickened our steps. I found the departure point with great accuracy, and thus also the guard company, who had been waiting impatiently for us to return. The shout of 'password' from their sentry relieved all the tension.

The reconnaissance unit led by Schulz had got back before us. He had strayed into a Russian minefield. Schulz was at the head of his men and had had his leg blown off up to the thigh, and his other leg was also seriously wounded. His men had risked their lives to get him out of the minefield, and had carried him

▶ Major Hans-Ulrich Rudel, top 'Panzer-cracker'. Hitler awarded him the Knight's Cross with Golden Oak-leaves, Swords and Diamonds, ordering him not to risk his life flying any more. Rudel said he could not accept if it meant being grounded – so the Führer conceded. Inset: the insignia of 4 (Pz)/Schlacht-geschwader I – the Panzer Bear.

Süddeutscher Verlag
Rinzier Dokumentationszentrum

Bibliothek für Zeitgeschichte

▲ A German field telephone operator shelters behind a wrecked plane wing near the front at Orel.

◀ Advancing German tanks in the battle at Kursk storm over Soviet opposition, laying waste to the country-side.

Bildarchiv Preussischer Kulturbesitz

back to the departure point. The ambulance driver came back an hour later with the news that my comrade had died.

Around 8.00 am we attacked without advance artillery fire, and with little resistance from the enemy we advanced swiftly and reached the runway around midday.

We'd arrived in the nick of time, because Franz was stuck fast with his light 2.2 cm anti-tank gun – a novelty. We all mucked in and pulled the tiny gun – of which the most striking feature was the hugely out-of-proportion barrel – up the slope. 'So much sweat for a little toy like this', we quipped. 'You wouldn't believe what a thing like this can do', Franz said, defending his weapon. And we'd have plenty of opportunity to find out.

We dug ourselves in in the road ditches by the runway, Franz's anti-tank gun beside us. Our task: to hold the position no matter what . . .

Right in front of us was a long line of enemy installations, still completely intact. According to statements from prisoners there was yet another carefully constructed locking installation beyond this defensive cordon. And behind this massed colonies of tanks ready to launch a massive Russian break-through offensive. I could not help thinking that the enormous mass of hardware assembled on our side was a gigantic drop in the ocean. This would only put paid to the first cordon, which, as I saw it, had been left empty or was occupied by only a few men. The second bulwark would bring us to a halt and stop us reaching the core of the enemy installations, the ultimate target of our offensive.

The night grew cold. It began to rain. Once again, I couldn't snatch even a few minutes sleep. I kept on wishing I'd be transferred to a new observer corps or fireman unit. The *Oberdeppen* (total idiots), as Franz Huber called them, brought the artillery fire down on us promptly the next morning by mucking about as usual, and one of these suicide cases strutted right past me.

► In the Kursk Bulge, during an early morning attack, a German Panzer explodes under a direct hit.

Bildarchiv Preussischer Kultubesitz

▼ Mark IV Panzers press on through the rubble of a Russian village which stood in their path. Inset: two Russian tank men examine a defunct Tiger tank.

Novosti Press Agency

▼ Ready for the attack, Russian infantrymen wait in a trench, Orel 1943.

Bibliothek für Zeitgeschichte

Ringier Dokumentationszentrum

Whenever I saw one of these characters, proudly displaying their 'heroic' coldbloodedness, I couldn't stop myself shouting to him whether he thought he was in some kind of Punch and Judy show. One of them shouted back: 'What is your name? I'll report you', which left me completely cold. I thought to myself, fat chance of that, you idiot; if you carry on like that you won't survive beyond midday. **"**

Sergeant Grigorii Sgibnev had started his career in 1941 with the Pacific Fleet, but in July 1943 was a platoon commander in the Russian 44th Guards Infantry Division. He recalls the fighting at Izyum, an action for which he received the Hero of the Soviet Union award.

" At first everything went well. After an hour's artillery preparation when, it seemed, not a single survivable place remained in the fascist positions, we dashed into the attack. So long as we were running among the trees and bushes, the Hitlerites remained quiet, but as soon as we appeared in the open in front of the fascist positions, their trenches became alive. Machine guns and automatics rattled out. Grenades also flew to meet us – one of them spun around beneath my feet.

Everyone who has been in battle knows the feeling, when it seems that one is in the space between life and death, a space, so the saying goes, that would be too narrow for a mouse to jump. One acts automatically, half consciously. I also, quite instinctively, seized this grenade without thinking and hurled it back towards the enemy trenches. It exploded as it reached them. 'Smash them with their own grenades!' I shouted.

All this happened about 20 metres from the enemy defence line. It was too close for us to get artillery or mortar support, but the fascists could not use that kind of support either,

▲ In a moment between attacks in the greatest Russo-German battle of the war, two Russians light up.

▼ A Russian anti-tank rifle crew dig themselves in, preparing for an enemy tank attack, Kursk, 1943.

▼◀ Lying low on the grassy plain, Red Army anti-tank riflemen guard the top of a shallow incline.

without risking being caught up in it. A grenade battle flared up. Moving towards their trench, we bombarded it with the same grenades that the fascists hurled at us.

Having overcome the first defence line, we moved on to the second trench on the village outskirts. We had to take this by storm also – and once again we threw back the enemy's own grenades.

I can remember that I had managed to pull off the firing ring of one of my own grenades and was preparing to throw it, when a German grenade fell at my feet. I seized it with my left hand, and it exploded. . . From hospital I went home. My father met me and said, 'You've come back alive, that's the main thing'. "

Semyon Belozvertsev, age 18, was a private in the 887th Infantry Regiment when, to capitalise on the German defeat at Kursk, his unit pushed forwards through the Ukraine. He recalls the problems of crossing the rivers which divide up the area.

" Usually, when people talk of their first battle, or of the period waiting for it, they speak of some feeling of anxiety, but at the beginning, I did not experience this. I was young, full of strength and confidence . . .

In the night of 19-20 September, our unit reached the Desna. It was the darkest of Ukrainian nights, and the river was frightening in its mysteriousness. The order arrived to force the river in darkness, using whatever was to hand – or, simply speaking, force it one way or another.

I went down to the edge, overgrown with short bushes, to feel if the water was warm or not. I bumped into a dugout canoe. Soldiers were all around. Using the seat as an oar, and baling out water continuously, three of us (the limit of the boat's capacity) managed to get across to the other side. And in the water, the whole width of the river, we could hear splashes, talk, orders, quiet swearing . . . we also heard several screams.

On the whole, the crossing was successful, helped by the presence on the bank of an abandoned village, which in a flash was converted into rafts of boards and beams.

At 11 or 12 o'clock, German aircraft came and began to bomb our crossing place. The bombs fell with a

Novosti Press Agency

terrifying scream, which at first pulled our nerves almost to breaking point and really was more psychologically effective than the acutal explosions. Having released their bombs, the aircraft began to circle and machine-gun us. Sitting in our little dugout, I watched with great interest everything that was going on around me. Soon after the aircraft came light tanks, which fired at us and began to outflank us. We came under crossfire and abandoned the village with heavy losses, because our infantry weapons had no success against the tanks.

We lost many officers, and a sergeant-major took over. He already had battle experience. He ordered us

▲ **Russian artillery push out their guns for point-blank firing, Kursk, July 1943.**

▶ **A Russian anti-aircraft gun crew let fly against close support German aircraft.**

▼ **Russian soldiers overrun a former German strongpoint, Kursk, August 1943.**

Ringier Dokumentationszentrum

to dig in and act on the defensive. We could not retreat any further, because the river was at our backs. Going away for a while, the sergeant-major came back with dozens of anti-tank grenades which he handed out to the more experienced soldiers. The village we had abandoned was now burning.

During the night, some 45 mm anti-tank guns were sent over to us. At dawn the next day we captured the burned village and pushed on. 🟊

CHAPTER 12

BATTLE DIARY

NOVEMBER 1943

12	First attack groups sail for Gilbert Islands (Operation 'Galvanic')
18–19	Makin and Tarawa 'softened-up' by carrier air strikes and naval bombardment

MAKIN (Butaritari)

20 NOVEMBER

06.10–06.30	Carrier air strike on western ('Red') beaches
06.40–08.30	Naval bombardment of Red beaches
08.32	Assault touch-down on Red beaches
10.00	Red beachhead secure. Progress inland halted
10.15	Destroyer bombardment of lagoon ('Yellow') beaches
10.40	Yellow beach landings commence
pm	Progress bogged down
21–22 NOVEMBER	Intermittent and confused progress

TARAWA (Betio)

20 NOVEMBER

05.10–05.42	Flagship *Maryland* in action against shore batteries
06.10	Dawn air strike arrives (scheduled for 05.45)
06.22–08.55	Area gunfire support from warships
09.13	Assault touch-down commences. Marines confined to beaches
11.54	'We need help. Situation bad'
13.30	'Issue in doubt'

21 NOVEMBER

06.15	Marine reserves arrive
16.00	'We are winning'
22 NOVEMBER	Marines forced back slowly
23 NOVEMBER	'Betio secured'

FEBRUARY 1944

1	Kwaljalein and Roi-Namur assaulted (Operation 'Flintlock')
2 (14.00)	'Roi-Namur secure'
4 (15.30)	'Kwajalein secure'
17	Eniwetok operations commence (Operation 'Catchpole')
22	'Eniwetok secure'

TARAWA – ISLAND GRAVEYARD

Tarawa – a coral atoll in the Gilbert archipelago – was to be the Calvary of the US Marine Corps. Earlier landings at Apamama and Makin had been achieved with relatively light casualties and, although there was limited information about the coastline at Tarawa, American planners were confident.

The landing on November 20, 1943, by 5,000 men of the Second US Marine Division under General Julian Smith marked the first tactical use of amphibious tractors. However, the landing went badly. A heavy but poorly coordinated sea and air bombardment left many Japanese positions, well constructed and camouflaged under layers of felled coconut trees, intact and able to fire at the Marines as they waded towards the beach or advanced in Amtracs, many of which were unable to cross a sea wall of coconut palms and became easy targets. By the close of the day, the Marines had only a tiny foothold in the lee of the sea wall, and the next day a second landing also incurred heavy losses.

The Marines, however, supported by artillery fire from nearby Bairiki Island, relaunched attacks on two fronts with the small number of tanks they had landed. In a final, furious *banzai* counter-attack, the Japanese threw all their remaining strength against the Marines, but were fought off. By the morning of 23 November, the atoll was declared secure.

Of the original Japanese garrison of 4,800 men, only 146 wounded prisoners were taken. The Marines suffered more than 1,000 killed and 2,100 wounded: such a scale of casualties, the heaviest yet in the Pacific conflict, would have a traumatic effect on US public opinion at home.

ISLAND GRAVEYARD

The hotly contested prize is the tiny Pacific atoll of
Tarawa. After the battle, the bodies of Marine heroes
rot in the equatorial sun.

The US forces have been sent in to take the apparently innocent-looking Pacific islands held by the Japanese – but defences are cunningly hidden. No-one from either side could have foreseen the carnage both on land and at sea, which took place in the blistering heat of the equatorial sun.

▲ Pilots of the new carrier USS *Lexington* at a briefing before an assault on the Gilberts. Inset: a US Navy pilot's log book and badge.

Lieutenant-Commander Donald J Ramsey, Captain of the destroyer **Hughes**, *was at hand with his ship when US 'jeep' carrier* **Liscome Bay** *was sunk by torpedoes from the Japanese submarine* **I-175** *off Makin Island at 5.13 am on 24 November 1943. He rescued some survivors – but 712 men perished.*

❝ Apparently bombs, torpedoes, gasoline and ammunition all went up together. The whole ship was enveloped in flames so rapidly that damage control and fire fighting appeared to be out of the question. The personnel who did manage to escape were all very badly shaken up and some of them had suffered bad burns, broken limbs and shock.

Nearly every man aboard had some bruises and cuts. One man died while the medical officer was administering blood plasma – another died in the water before being picked up by the motor whaleboat. This ship has rescued survivors from the old *Lexington*, the old *Yorktown* and the

old *Hornet*, but it was unanimously agreed that the sinking of the *Liscome Bay* and the condition of the comparatively few survivors constituted the most heart-rending disaster yet.

Inspiring is no word for the conduct displayed by the men picked up in the water, and the absolute courage of these men was electrifying. One man, who had been operated on for appendicitis just two days before not only scrambled up the life net without assistance, but on arriving on deck, asked if there was not a rubber boat handy for him to take out and assist others whom he knew needed help.

It was common comment on this ship that though the personnel losses were horrible enough as it was, it was a miracle that *anyone* managed to escape the inferno. ❞

The scene of destruction seen from the comparative safety of the battleship *New Mexico*, which lay 1,500 yards off the carrier's starboard quarter, was described by a young lieutenant as follows in his combat report.

❝ A few seconds after the first explosion, a second explosion which appeared to come from inside the *Liscome Bay*, burst upwards, hurling fragments and clearly

◀ On Tarawa, a scene of devastation surrounds the advancing US Marines.

discernible planes, 200 feet or more in the air. The entire ship seemed to explode, and almost at the same instant, her interior, except for the extreme bow and stern sections, glowed with flames like a furnace.

The ship was showered from forecastle to quarter-deck with oil particles and burning and extinguished fragments. The whole central section of her starboard hull seemed to be blown out and she immediately took on a heavy list to starboard. About a one-hundred-foot section of her flight-deck had blown clear off of the ship. One of her Helldiver aircraft, already ablaze, was also blown clear of the ship and in turn set on fire the floating oil fuel that had leaked from her shattered hull. The floating flames spread over a wide area, making rescue attempts of the survivors in the water a difficult business. **"**

US National Archive

each section. When we headed for them, they would make a violent pull-out and climb at a 60° angle. Then the next two would come at us.

We pulled into the standard protective 'thatch weave' formation, with each of our sections swinging back and forth to protect the other. It was a case of hit them with all you had, reverse, and do the same again. We were giving them everything we had with no quarter asked on either side. There wasn't time to see what happened to the Japs we hit. I would have given ten years of my life for another gun (I had only one operating, and my sight was out of commission), and for 5,000 more feet of altitude.

This continued for several minutes until one of the Jap bastards set Si Satterfield's plane on fire, shooting him on the outside of his weave. Both his wing tanks were burning, with flames reaching half way down the fuselage, apparently out of control. Why they didn't shoot us all down is more than I can figure out. Maybe they would have if they had been better gunners. **"**

Lieutenant-Commander Ed Owen, senior officer of VF5 (Fighting Five, as they were known) from the US carrier Yorktown II, *and his team took off in Hellcats as they were jumped by 18 Japanese Zeros, 4 December 1943.*

" This was a first-line team, and they knew what they were doing. Six Zeros positioned themselves on each of our two-plane sections, with two of their planes always firing on

Carl J Moore, later to become Rear Admiral, was Chief of Staff to Admiral Raymond Spruance during the campaign in the Gilbert, Marshall and Mariana islands. His view of the Tarawa assault was from aboard the cruiser Indianapolis. *From this vantage point he observed the bombardment – but later landed on Tarawa.*

▲ Hellcat and Avenger fighters on the deck of a carrier. Inset: a Landing Signal Officer signals to an incoming pilot to lift one wing.

▶ The badge of a US Navy pilot, with anchor and wings. More than ever before, naval aviators played a vital role in the Pacific.

" The particular job of the *Indianapolis* was to bombard suspected gun emplacements and ammunition dumps on the east side of Tarawa Atoll, while the rest of Harry Hill's outfit bombarded Betio, at the south end of the atoll, and while the troops disembarked from the transports. We made a run the length of Tarawa's east side and along the south coast, firing at lookout towers in the beautiful palm groves and at Japanese barges. We started a few fires, one of which burned for a couple of days.

By the time we reached Betio it looked like a shambles. It had been bombarded and bombed for two hours. Fires were burning everywhere. The coconut trees were all blasted. It

seemed that no living soul could be on the island. Then we joined with Hill's ships in the bombardment of Tarawa and the troops approached the beach. It looked like the whole affair would be a walkover.

We saw the first wave reach the beach. Then we saw the next two or three waves get stuck on the edge of the reef that fringed the island. We saw the troops disembark and advance for about 400 yards in water that was waist-deep. It was in this phase that we had our greatest losses, for with all our bombardment, the Japs had not been routed out of their beach pillboxes. For the next 24 hours they made it hell for our Marines.

The destroyers remained in close support and the big ships continued to bombard all the next day. Finally, by ingenuity and by taking advantage of the breaks, the Marines managed to beat down the opposition on the main beaches and to land on a couple

of others. By the night of the second day we felt pretty secure. The fighting continued hard, however, for a few days longer. It must have been awful tough on the men ashore and those in the boats waiting to get ashore. We couldn't see much from the flagship except the raging fires, the shells and bombs falling, and the destroyers and small boats manoeuvring about the harbour. We had to keep moving because of the threat of submarines. But the destroyers did a fine job and good luck kept us all safe from the enemy subs. Through it all we on the flagship kept in pretty close touch with what was going on and had a general picture of the situation.

One week after the first assault, our flagship entered the lagoon at Tarawa. Raymond went ashore to meet Nimitz and his party, who had come out from Pearl Harbor. Raymond got separated from them and didn't find out the things I had hoped he would. I went ashore for an hour that afternoon but had to hurry back because Raymond and I couldn't both be away for long.

The place was swarming with Marines. I had never know that men could look like they did – dirty, burned, ragged, hot, a week's growth of beard, tired, hungry, thirsty. They were about as fine a lot of men as I ever have seen. What they had been through that week! I have never seen such a shambles – coconut logs everywhere, sheet iron, guns, ammunition, smashed tanks, equipment, shot-up cars, bicycles, carts. In fact, everything that goes with war was scattered all over – pillboxes, tanks, traps, slit trenches dug up through concrete strongpoints in such numbers they couldn't be counted. Some were smashed to smithereens. Others, still good, had

◀ The airfield on Wake Island burns under heavy bombardment from Rear Admiral A E Montgomery's Task Force. A sunken ship lies off the beach in the distance.

▼ The badge of the US Marine Corps.

▼ The efficiency and speed of the US Marine fighter aircraft takes its toll. This Japanese Zero fell prey to US marksmanship on the Marshall Islands, 9 February 1944.

◀ The USS *Mississippi* bombards Makin Island in the Gilbert Islands group, seen from on board the USS *Baltimore*.

Topham Picture Library

◄ The guns of a US cruiser open up to subdue resistance on the Gilbert Islands. Inset: US Marines on shore are pinned to the beach by enemy fire.

◄ ▼The crew of a Japanese anti-aircraft gun prepare for action on an island base.

contained live Japs the day before.

When I was ashore that day, all the dead Marines had been properly buried and most of the dead Japs had been thrown into bomb craters and bulldozed over. There were many Japs lying about in an advanced stage of decomposition. I contented myself with smelling them and avoided any closer examination. Some of the strongpoints were still full of hundreds of them. No-one knew it was so thoroughly defended. ""

US National Archive;

Topham Picture Library

Tadao Onuki, a Japanese Naval Chief Petty Officer attached to No. 3 Yokosuka Special Base, found himself preparing for battle on the island of Tarawa, having asked to move to a tank unit. From a mood of confident optimism, his comrades' morale was to receive a heavy blow. The arrival of overwhelming numbers of US Marines and constant bombardment would finally take their toll and leave him stranded.

" I went back to Japan from our base at Rabaul, and in June 1943 I was transferred to Tarawa after expressing a wish to serve in a tank unit. Tarawa is the main island of the Gilbert Islands, and is surrounded by many other islands, large and small, such as Makin.

Our unit was called No. 3 Yokosuka Special Base Unit, and we spent day after day busy with constructing positions and in battle drill. Air-raids by large enemy aircraft were a daily occurrence, but they never hindered us in any way. We were once raided for 24 hours, by a combined force of fighters and bombers, but they didn't do us any harm – in fact, they very effectively raised our morale. Here and there on the island we built some really tough positions making skilful use of the natural features of the terrain. The construction went on without a break, night and day. Our tank unit was completely combat-ready and preparations for the encounter battle went ahead.

At dawn on 21st November, a great fleet of enemy ships appeared on the distant line of the horizon. So the time had finally come – the enemy's destroyers' naval guns soon began to fire simultaneously, and their shells rained down on the Japanese positions. One of the shells scored a bull's-eye on our magazine and started a huge blaze. This in turn offered a prime target to the enemy guns. In addition, bombers and air-craft from the ships attacked us from the air, setting ablaze the food dumps and other key installations, one after the other. Soon the entire island was covered in flames and black smoke.

The enemy's naval gunfire and aerial bombing went on for several hours, while we waited in the air-raid trenches like sheep in a sheep-fold, expecting the order to attack. Soon, under a full-scale covering fire, hordes of enemy landing craft approached the shore. They looked likely to swamp the Japanese forces completely.

In the face of fierce, ear-splitting small-arms fire, the enemy landing-craft began to run aground, and the US soldiers began to fall into the sea. I think we damped their ardour, but they had guts and, although they received the full impact of our small-arms fire, they crossed the shallows to the shore, and then trod over the bodies of their fallen comrades, one after the other, until they finally managed to install themselves at one end of the island.

Inside my tank, I poured out shot until the barrel of my gun was red-hot, but it was impossible not to be aware of the threat of the enemy's numbers. Our men had seen our magazine and food dumps go up in flames, and from the material point of view, they were already no match

for the Americans. But we moved here and there on the island and gave the Americans something to think about. Hunting for tanks, I burst into the enemy positions and ended up by penetrating deep into them, almost before I knew what was happening. I tried to withdraw, but for some reason, the engine refused to budge. I was frantic, and couldn't find the cause of the stoppage. There were signs from outside that enemy troops had begun to gather round the tank. I thought I'd had it, then I kicked my foot down on the axle in sheer desperation and the motor sputtered into life – to my intense joy! As if in a dream, I scattered the Americans who were swarming around my tank, knocked them out of the way and put on speed until I got back to our own position.

It wasn't long before the battle turned against us, and Major-General Shibasaki and his HQ moved from No. 1 Command Post to No. 2. Our tank unit was ordered to give them covering fire. At the time, the tank unit couldn't move, because we hadn't enough fuel, so we acted as gun platforms. When we finished that assignment, I clambered down from the tank. In that instant, shells from one of the enemy's naval guns came down with a shattering roar and burst all round us. My two comrades who were just emerging from the tank were blown to pieces in a split second.

On the 25th we separated into No. 1 and No. 2 troops and resolved to carry out one final attack. The report of our fight to the finish was sent off to Japan beforehand.

At that time, the number of US troops who had come ashore was

several hundred times greater than that of the Japanese who had survived, and bit by bit, they began to encircle us. We were no longer masters of the seas or the skies, we had no food or ammunition left, and there was no longer any hope of a force coming to relieve us. There was only one way ahead for the Japanese on Tarawa – a fight to the finish and total annihilation.

We said goodbye to No. 1 troop as they moved off for their first attack, and those of us who belonged to No. 2 troop waited in the air-raid trenches until the evening hour when the attack was expected. But in the end, we were spotted by a keen-eyed enemy pilot, who came in to the attack. In an instant, the inside of the trench was turned into an inferno

◀ US Marines who have taken the Eniwetok Atoll by storm take a coffee break on an assault transport after their ordeal.

Robert Hunt Library; inset: Topham Picture Library

▲ Wounded from the main Tarawa assault are evacuated back to the US ships offshore, strapped on to a rubber boat.

by his bombs and the explosives hurled at us by US troops – and by the flame-throwers which poured flame at us before the smoke from the bombing had cleared away. Everything was incinerated.

In that burned-out trench, where everything was totally destroyed, no human being could have survived other than by a miracle. As it happened, there was a miracle.

I don't know how long it was before I was aware I was still alive. I could not move my hands or feet freely, and my body felt as if it were being pressed by something heavy. All I was sure of was the fact that I was still alive. Then I regained consciousness completely. I was lying under a heap of blackened corpses, and around me in the trench I could see hands and feet scattered all over. It was a scene of such disaster that, without thinking, I wanted to cover my eyes, even though I was quite battle-hardened by this time.

Of the 15 of us who had sworn to live or die together, I was the only one left. There was no sign of any of the others, and my insignificant life had only been saved because I had been sheltered by the dead bodies of my comrades. I could feel there were burns on my face, but I was still not sure I was all in one piece and for a while, everything went blank.

When I came to again, I tried to crawl out of the trench. It was already dark, and all round me everything had gone uncannily quiet. Tarawa felt exactly like an island of the dead. Apart from a few lights which seemed to be in the US positions, far off, the deep blackness stretched everywhere. The sound of guns which had made the whole island shake, had completely died away.

Had the fighting come to an end? If that were the case, and I was on an island where the Japanese forces had

been completely wiped out, and I was the sole survivor, what was I to do? There was no-one to give me orders. I was unarmed, I hadn't even a rifle to fight with. There were no comrades to give me comfort or spur me on. How was I going to stay alive on this island which was filled with enemy soldiers? And supposing I stayed alive, there was absolutely no hope of ever going back to Japan. When I thought about it, an indescribable feeling of loneliness pressed in on me, the terror of it almost stifled me.

Then dawn came. If I can keep alive, then that's what I must do, I thought – and at the same time, I became aware of the gnawing emptiness in my belly. I began to go round the island from then on, looking for

▲ **An abandoned Japanese tank, used in the defense of the Marshall Islands, 8 February 1944, stands in the wreckage of the tropical island.**

▼**Smoke rises from burning Japanese installations as US Marines charge and take a Japanese pillbox on Tarawa after the beach landing.**

something to eat, prepared to take the risk of being captured by avoiding being spotted by the Americans and watching out for any signs of other Japanese. But I found nothing to eat, and there was no sign of any Japanese either. All I was left with was my empty stomach and a feeling of unbearable solitude.

One night I crossed the sea channel secretly, and moved across to a small island nearby, about half a mile away. There should have been Japanese garrison troops there too – but that island also had been occupied. Since I might be spotted by an American sentry, I hid during the day in deep foliage or under the shadow of rocks, and then at night-fall, I pottered along the shore in search of food. Small fish, prawns and crayfish which could be caught in the shallows were important articles of food. On rare occasions, there would be a feast – a coconut fallen from a palm tree.

As the days went by in this fashion, I was joined by other survivors – Japanese soldiers who began to gather in ones and twos from the other islands. In the end, there were seven of us. In a way, that gave me strength and encouragement, but the way ahead was gloomy. We thought that if we were taken prisoner we would be killed, in which case, we preferred to take our own lives. So, all seven of us tried to hang ourselves, together. But the rope was weak and it snapped, so we ended up unable to kill ourselves.

On this island, if you dug down about a foot, salt water came out, so there was no drinking water at all. I found thirst harder to bear than hunger, but I knew that if I drank the water I would pay for it. Of course, there was nothing to eat, and every day rather than look for food in order to live, we lived in order to look for food. The seven of us had come together with great difficulty, but in the end we split up and went off to different parts of the island in the search for food. In the end, I was left on my own again.

This miserable existence went on for three weeks, until one day, being unable to endure my parched throat which felt, as usual, as if it were on fire, I went out along the beach, by the water's edge, almost without knowing what I was doing. US troops on patrol found me. By that time, I had absolutely no physical or spiritual strength to resist left in me.

After they had captured me, the US troops seemed to begin a search of the whole island, every nook and cranny, and one by one, my six comrades were taken. Once again, our seven faces were brought together – but this time we were no longer free men – we were prisoners of war.

The destruction on Tarawa at an end, the seven of us who had secretly survived but were weak enough to drop, were soon transferred to a US Navy destroyer. We were helped and looked after at first, rather than interrogated, and they gave us food. However, since we had resolved that we would be killed sooner or later, when the next day dawned we said to ourselves, 'This is our last day', and then when the sun went down, we thought, 'We've lived one more day today', with some surprise. It was a complicated feeling. Although for the past three weeks we'd had no fear of dying at all, we began to think we'd been lucky, and as we continued to stay alive, life began to seem a desirable thing.

The Americans treated us with amazing politeness, giving us injections to give us strength, and masses of food to eat, which restored us. It was perhaps a bit late in the day, but we were gradually made to feel the enormous gap in combat strength between the US forces which could have enough food like this, even in the midst of a battle, and our army which depended on hard tack and dried bonito. Our weakened bodies were restored to health – but the wound in our hearts would not heal.

Afterwards, the six of us were split up and I was sent by ship to a camp in Hawaii, then to New York, then again to a camp in Wisconsin and finally one in Texas. That was where I heard the war was over. It was a pitiful defeat. But the fact that the earth of my mother country still remained was a consolation for me. If the war had gone on any longer, I might have become a man with no mother country at all. 〝

◄ Although very heavily reinforced, this Japanese dugout was not sufficient to protect the inmates from US attack. The dead lie in the debris of their shelter.

▼ Japanese POWs, naked either to prevent them concealing weapons or due to their clothes being blown off, await transfer to a prison ship.

▼ The cap badge of a non-commissioned officer of the Japanese Imperial Navy.

CHAPTER 13

BATTLE DIARY

OCTOBER 1943

1	US Fifth Army takes Naples
3	Germans retake Kos
12–15	Fifth Army forces Volturno crossings

NOVEMBER

8–30	Eighth Army crosses River Sangro but unable to make more headway
12–16	Germans retake Leros
20	British evacuate Samos

DECEMBER

2–6	Fifth Army takes Monte Camino
10	Eighth Army crosses River Moro
17	Fifth Army takes Monte Sammucro and San Pietro

JANUARY 1944

12–1	French Expeditionary Corps crosses River Rapido
17–19	X Corps attacks across River Garigliano and takes Minturno
20	II Corps starts first assault on Cassino over River Rapido
22	Anzio landings begin
30	First Anzio breakout attempt

FEBRUARY

2	Anzio attacks called off
7–11	Battle of the 'Factory' at Aprilia
13	Alexander calls off Cassino assault
15	Allied bombing of Benedictine Abbey
16–19	German counter-attack at Anzio repulsed with difficulty

MARCH

15	Allies bomb town of Cassino
15–22	Most of Cassino falls to New Zealanders and Indians

MAY

11–14	French outflank Cassino in south
17	Poles outflank Cassino in north. Kesselring orders retreat
23	Beginning of final Anzio breakout assault

JUNE

2	Germans abandon Rome
4	Allies enter Rome

CASSINO – MOUNTAIN INFERNO

The town and sixth-century Benedictine monastery of Monte Cassino were the key to the Gustav Line, or Winter Line, dominating the approaches to Rome. Here, the Tenth German Army under General Heinrich von Vietinghof made a successful stand from January to May 1944, despite direct attacks on the town and 1,700 ft mountain by the US Fifth Army under General Mark Clark and the British Eighth Army under General Oliver Leese. On January 22, in an attempt to outflank the Gustav Line, British and American forces landed at Anzio south of Rome but, despite having the advantage of surprise, were successfully contained by the Germans in a cramped and dangerous beachhead.

On February 15, the monastery was heavily bombed and immediately afterwards the Fourth Indian and Second New Zealand Divisions made limited gains. On March 15 the town was pulverized by 1,000 tons of bombs and the fire of 600 guns, and the New Zealanders captured Castle Hill after fierce fighting with the German First Parachute Division. Gurkhas of the Fourth Indian Division captured the exposed position of Hangman's Hill, but were forced to abandon it on the 24th.

A lull followed and the Allies looked for a way of breaking the deadlock. The new plan included a decoy operation to convince the Germans that there would be a breakout from Anzio and then, at 23.00 hours on May 11, 2,000 guns opened fire. The Polish II Corps isolated and captured the monastery, the British XIII Corps crossed the River Rapido, and the French and US II Corps attacked south of the Liri. The Allies' advantage of surprise won them the breakthrough but General Clark's obsession to capture Rome meant that many German troops escaped to fight on.

MOUNTAIN INFERNO

Even to soldiers used to giving their very best, the stony wastes of Monte Cassino prove to be a test far beyond normal limits.

In battles spanning the months from late 1943 to May 1944, Italian locals and British, Polish, American and German servicemen witnessed the effects of steady attrition on the town of Cassino and the razing to the ground of one of the great centres of the Christian world.

Douglas Lyne, age 20, was a gunner in the Royal Artillery, acting as Observation Post Assistant in the 57th Field Regiment, part of X Corps. To him the destruction of the Cassino Monastery had a special significance, his ancestor Father Ignatius of Llanthony having founded a Benedictine monastery in Wales based on this very edifice.

❝ Suffice it to say that by the end of January, beginning of February, no real progress had been made towards the capture of Cassino Monastery, without which it was impossible to proceed along the road to Rome. It was about this time that my own regiment of artillery was posted into the line there, in support of the 201st Guards Brigade. Monte Cassino was on the height of about 1,500 feet and we had to climb up to an observation post at about 2,500 feet.

From there we could see across the valley, whenever weather permitted, this shining monument of Cassino Monastery, which, I must say, did look in a way menacing and odd, in so far as it was the only undestroyed object in a vast waste of destruction. It was rather like seeing Buckingham Palace in the middle of Passchendaele.

On 15 February we'd been up there about a week and were feeling absolutely miserable – it was terrible weather. In the occasional breaks in the clouds we saw this monastery all the time, and it got on our nerves, to be quite frank. It became, from being a thing of beauty, a thing of monstrosity – an excrescence – and somehow it was the thing which was holding up all our lives and keeping us away from home. It became identified in an obsessional way with all the things we detested.

Remember, I had been about two years in almost continuous action,

and action is barbarising and our sensibilities were blunted.

Suddenly out of the mist of the south, on this really rather nice morning, just after breakfast at about 9.30 hours, appeared this vast armada – a huge bomber force – mainly Flying Fortresses, some 250 of them.

We were wondering where on earth this vast armada was going, when all of a sudden, the bombs started dropping out of these things, and came bashing down on the jolly old mother of monasteries of St Benedict, about ten miles away over the valley. I must confess it was a gigantically stimulating sight, to suddenly see this sort of Barnum and Bailey's kind of Brock's benefit – it must have been comparable to seeing the early Christians being eaten by lions in the Colosseum, I suppose. We all started cheering wildly and hugging each other. We went mad and everybody thought it was the greatest thing since the eruption over Pompeii. But there was, with me, a remarkable Welshman called Tom Roberts, who'd been my constant guide, philosopher and friend since the earliest days when we went around the Cape of Good Hope to get to Suez. He was a man of great spiritual merit who knew all about my connection with Father Ignatius of Llanthony. After I'd stopped trembling and the laughter and hysterical gaiety faded, he sat me down at one side and said, 'Steady on Doug – I mean, it's all very well, but are we really in this war for the business of bombing monasteries. What would old Father Ignatius think

of that?' Suddenly, I had a sort of complete bloody double-take. I thought, 'What the hell are we doing, up on this bloody hill and surrounded by destruction and mayhem, and everything gone to pot? What are we fighting for or against? Here we are, cheering the destruction of one of the great monuments of Christendom.' One's mood changed from exultation to a peculiar sort of horror and self-questioning, which was very disturbing . . . ❞

▲ **Douglas Lyne, one of many cheering the fall of the monastery – but who would later work for reconciliation and restoration.**

▼ **Polish gunners prime shells during an attack on Monte Cassino.**

◀ **Dug in well below ground level, Polish infantrymen in a mortar emplacement take aim on a German position higher up the hill.**

John Watney Photo Library/Interpress

John Watney Photo Library/Interpress

Douglas Lyne

► It may not be *haute cuisine*, but the 'chef' of the Royal West Kent Regiment makes the best of facilities in a quarry on Monastery Hill.

Imperial War Museum

Sergeant Herbert Parkin with the 2nd Battalion of the London Irish Rifles was based at a holding position high on a mountainside, facing Cassino. His company depended totally on mule trains getting through for all their supplies.

▼ Herbert Parkin of the London Irish Rifles was involved in the Cassino struggle from the early days.

Herbert Parkin

▼ Mules carry all-important food and ammunition to the troops holding positions on the hill – as a means of supply it leaves a lot to be desired.

" We landed at Taranto naval base towards the end of 1943 and we reformed just outside Taranto to move forwards through Italy. The terrain wasn't easy – it was all valleys and ridges and you couldn't advance too fast in case that you had no back-up. We came out of the line at a place called Inferno Valley, which was a mule point. Inferno Valley was the start line and from there we got into position on a mountain facing Cassino. We were well within firing distance of the enemy. The Germans were up in the monastery with a bird's eye view of everything. You couldn't move without them seeing you. The Royal Engineers used to put up smoke screens from the valley – pots and pots of smoke – but you could only blind the Germans for so long before the wind carried the smoke away.

The Germans would let the ambulances through, but everything else was shelled. They used the old moaners – we called them 'Moaning Minnies' – which were six-barrelled mortars. There were six at a time and they moaned like anything. The Germans were pretty accurate with them, and they did a lot of damage. Our mortars were with different companies at the time. I was therefore acting as infantry on the forward slope, in case the Germans came through.

Although the Germans were in the monastery, they were right the way around as well, dug in. You had no idea where they were. It was worst at night because, of course, you couldn't see anything in the dark. You had to listen and try and make out what the noise was. You couldn't start firing, though, because you didn't know if you were going to hit one of your own patrols.

Everything came up to us by mules – our water, rations, first-aid – everything. We could see the mules clearly from where we were, coming along the valley. If they got shelled or started misbehaving, they would dance about and sling their loads off their backs.

It was uncomfortable on the mountain, but we always got our meals. Our cooks were very good. They would send hot food up to us in boxes and looked after us very well. We couldn't dig in to the soil because it was too stony and scrubby. We built sangars instead from the loose rocks. Although the ground was uncomfortable, you managed to sleep. You had a blanket and a ground sheet and you just put your haversack down and pulled your blanket over you and your tin hat over your head, and tried to get down.

When the Poles came to take over from us, we picked up the rest of the battalion and marched across to Inferno Valley where we had a mug of tea and formed up to move back behind the lines. "

John Watney Photo Library/Interpress

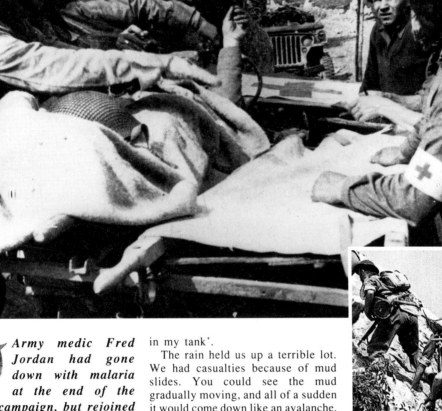

◄ **All transport on Monastery Hill is precious and the winding paths are hard to negotiate, especially when the jeeps are loaded with wounded men on stretchers.**

Army medic Fred Jordan had gone down with malaria at the end of the Sicilian campaign, but rejoined the 14th Field Ambulance who were attached to the 6th Armoured Division, dug in at the base of Monte Cassino.

❝ Anybody who was there will always remember the monastery at Monte Cassino. We were there for about two weeks before we were pulled out and the Poles took over. The Germans were in the monastery, firing down at the men on the hill. They could see all the area around, which made it very awkward to get anywhere. Our front was halfway up the hill. The medics were at the foot of the hill, evacuating the wounded as they came through, back to the roads and the general hospitals.

We dug in as best we could. There was no cover – you just made your own slit trench and stayed until you got the call for stretcher-bearers.

Italy should have been quicker, but the rains came. It was continuous rain. Nothing could move. The guns and tanks couldn't move because they were stuck in the mud.

We used the tank drivers as stretcher-bearers because we didn't have enough men. I can remember one chap saying 'I wish I was back in my tank'.

The rain held us up a terrible lot. We had casualties because of mud slides. You could see the mud gradually moving, and all of a sudden it would come down like an avalanche. People were buried underneath it and suffocated. The strangest thing was how they were stripped of their clothing – shoes and shirts missing.

The trenches filled up with water and you had to bail it out. You slept as best you could. Eventually you came to a point when you're so tired that you could sleep anywhere.

We were being attacked by Stukas. They're a really frightening plane. They dive-bomb, and they scream as they come down at you, which is terrifying.

The morale was pretty low. You can see it in a man's face – fear and quietness. It's something you can't explain. ❞

Private Harry Courcha of A Company, 1st Battalion, Royal Fusiliers, was sent as a reinforcement into the final crossing of the Rapido River at Sant' Angelo on the Cassino front. For him it was a baptism of fire.

❝ I was called up in April 1943, when I was 18 years old. After basic training I was sent to the Physical Development Centre at Richmond-on-Thames for 12 weeks as I was considered to be underdeveloped. This was probably due to the effects of malnutrition during childhood. After that I was sent to training camp on the Isle of Wight until my group was sent overseas at the end of March 1944. You weren't allowed to be sent overseas until you were 19. I had my birthday on the boat, so they were cutting it a bit fine. The voyage took two weeks as you had to try to avoid the U-boats. We arrived in Naples – Vesuvius had been active and it was still smoking. It was a tremendous sight for someone who'd previously regarded a penny trip to Hampstead

▲ **A Polish commando company tackles the ascent of the hill the hard way, heavily loaded down with their own equipment and vital supplies.**

George Rhodes, a sergeant with the 70th Field Regiment, Royal Artillery, had been through the fighting at Salerno and now found himself at Cassino. His story starts as the final attack is planned.

❝ April 20, 1944. The Germans came up with a new idea at Anzio – they started using human torpedoes. Thirty-seven were used and 24 were lost without any damage to the Yanks. I have gone round firing flashless shells and captured two German thunderflashes as thousands of troops are gathering behind my gun position. All are told to take their shoulder flashes off in case they are taken prisoner. You see, Alexander does not want the Germans to know that he is quietly building up a mighty army behind Monte Trocchio. Everything is heavily camouflaged.

Thursday, 11 May 1944. General Alexander issues order of the day, 'We are going to destroy the German armies in Italy. No armies have ever entered into battle before with a more

▲ Two British Tommies armed with a Bren gun and a Thompson sub-machine gun flush out the remaining Germans among the ruins of Cassino.

Heath as 'living it up'.

We were sent for two weeks to a training camp where we were told the most horrendous stories about the front by the old sweats. We were reinforcements, as there had been very heavy casualties in the Fusiliers. They selected which company you'd join by initials, and I was sent to A Company. All my mates had later initials and almost all of them went to B Company. They only seemed to be a few feet apart. Our objective was to force a crossing of the Rapido.

The Americans lost thousands trying a similar stunt. We moved up under the cover of darkness and when we reached a certain point, we were told to pick up these canvas boats. At a given sign the whole of our artillery erupted – every gun as far as the eye could see. They also put smoke down so we couldn't see.

We discovered that the Germans were firing on fixed lines, which meant that they'd mapped out their fields of fire beforehand. The bullets started whizzing round our heads and we just kept stumbling forward to the sound of the river. Some people were already dead.

We could hear the water a long way down in the dark, running very fast – hence 'Rapido'. Many of our blokes pitched over the bank and drowned as they had full battle-kit on. I heard a voice down below, but I couldn't see a boat. Well, I was hanging on to the bank and kicking out with my feet and someone dragged me into the boat and we went across. Many of the boats were just swept away because the river was so fast. We eventually made it and found that the fire was even heavier than before. Luckily there was a ditch there and it seemed like the whole

battalion was in it. It was rough. The German artillery was pounding away at us, but they couldn't hit the ditch. Machine guns were buzzing away. One of the hero types put his head up and got a bullet through it. We were pinned down for 24 hours until a Bailey Bridge was put across at St Angelo for the tanks to come across.

Our next objective was a heavily fortified farmhouse on a steep hill. The Germans had lined a hidden road between steep banks with machine guns on the flank. These couldn't be seen from our position. B Company had tried it first, and we were told that they'd suffered heavy casualties. They hadn't waited for tank support. I suspect it was sheer bravado on the part of the officers. As B Company had gone forward, they'd just been cut down from the side. Well, the tanks arrived and sorted the Germans in the ditch out. I was a machine gunner, and he's always the first to go in. There was I, 5ft 4in, charging up the hill with this heavy American 'Thompson', almost as big as myself. I was really expecting to die any second. Well, we got to the top and the remaining Germans surrendered. We'd stumbled over the bodies of B Company. All our friends.

After a while, when it was all over, we were ordered to bury our comrades. You have to take the identity disc and all their personal possessions and put them on a stretcher to carry them down. These were all my friends. They were the same age as me, just wanting to enjoy life. I'd been with them through training and on the boat out. Now they were dead, and I was searching them and carrying them down. I was devastated. I'd lost all my friends – I was alone. ❞

just and righteous cause'.

At exactly 11 pm, 16,000 guns opened fire. We were attacking on a 20-mile front. On my left, the two American Divisions, the 85th and the 88th, moved straight into the attack to capture Damiano Hill. Forty minutes later, the two French Divisions captured Monte Faito, which was 3,000 feet high. They were on the Yanks' right side, but my left. Five minutes after the French, the 8th Indian and the 4th British Divisions on the French right side, splashed into the fast-flowing Rapido river, into a hailstorm of German machine-gun fire. At 1 o'clock both divisions of the Polish Corps swept up to Monte Cassino. Two hours after we had opened up, the entire front for 20 miles was now locked in combat.

The Poles on my right were doing fine. Their commander, General Anders, had studied our previous three attempts and he decided to attack everything in his path at once and no mercy to be shown to the Germans. However, as daylight came, the Germans picked them off one by one, so he had to withdraw to his start line.

The planes, 3,000 of them, came

over during the day in 2,750 sorties. It was hell on earth. The Germans, even so, launched a fierce counter-attack along the Gustav Line. What a day – my gun was red hot!

Sunday 14 May. The French break through at Monti Aurunci. The 8th Indian, the 4th British, the 1st Infantry, the 5th Canadian Armoured and the 78th British Divisions all moved in for the kill.

General Juin let his hawk-faced Moroccan Goumiers loose. Their job was to climb mountains and come on to the Germans from their rear. They did not use rifles – only knives – and many lopped off the German's ears and put them into sandbags.

Tuesday, 16 May. This morning, in a beautiful classic attack, the 78th, the 6th Armoured and the 1st Canadian Divisions broke through. All we wanted now was for the Poles to deliver the coup-de-grace. Everything is going well and to plan. I am being kept informed every half hour as more gunfire is called for and of course, after five years, the War Office had decided that Hitler's blitzkrieg is the best method of attack. So now we have RAF officers in our observation post, and when the Infantry call for an air strike, it can be delivered within minutes. The Germans used this method with their tanks – it certainly works.

Wednesday, 24 May. The Poles attack Piedimonte. They did very well, even though they had lost 281

officers and 3,503 other ranks and 102 missing. They were all buried on the slopes of the hillside that we knew as Point 593, behind the Monastery Hill as you come from the south. On their memorial, these words are printed.

We Polish soldiers,
For our freedom and yours,
Have given our souls to God,
Our bodies to the soil of Italy,
And our hearts to Poland. ”

Polish Institute/General Sikorski Museum, London

▲A pair of Tommies lie low as they watch the barrage of shells on a nearby hill.

◄ German prisoners, under escort, trudge past a Sherman tank in a battle-torn landscape.

◄ Captioned as follows, 'When they call us D-Day Dodgers – which D-Day do they mean, old man?' the cartoon by 'Jon' referred to Lady Astor's jibe that those in Italy were dodging D-Day. In fact, they had already seen bitter action at all the D-Days detailed on their jeep. Needless to say, the men felt justly indignant.

Topham

Bibliothek für Zeitgeschichte

evening after. The bombers came and 300-400 people, still waiting to leave, were killed and buried alive.

When we were transferred from Terelle to Montforte by the SS, who wanted all civilians well away from the front lines, we witnessed a dog-fight between an English and a German aircraft. Due to the sun it was very difficult to tell which was which, but all of a sudden, one caught fire and started to plummet to the ground. We saw the pilots jump out with their parachutes. Then we noticed that the remaining aircraft did not go away, but turned steeply and shot the two flyers in the air. This has to be the most horrific thing I have ever seen. We were under the misapprehension that there was a certain camaraderie among even opposing pilots. The flyers fell from the skies to crash against the rocks below – I will never forget the sound of these poor flyers as they screamed 〞 and shouted.

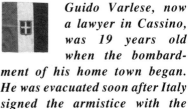 *Guido Varlese, now a lawyer in Cassino, was 19 years old when the bombardment of his home town began. He was evacuated soon after Italy signed the armistice with the Allies, after the first bombs had fallen on Cassino.*

❝ The first bombs fell at 9.00 in the morning. We were not expecting this at all, due to the fact that the armistice was already in effect. For us, we thought that the war was over.

I was in the piazza with a friend when we saw Flying Fortresses, going towards Rome from Naples, which unloaded their bombs on the outskirts of the town. We were all amazed at these marvellous flying machines, when we realised what was happening.

This first bombardment caused enormous damage and killed many, many people. I took refuge in the shop where I usually had my hair cut. While in there, in came a German soldier with his ear shot to pieces by shrapnel. I put a towel, the first thing I could see – around his head to stop the blood pouring from his ear. He certainly would have died otherwise.

There were two more bombardments that day, the first was down by the station, the other was on the outskirts of the town, destroying mostly the road to Rome from Naples. They had spotted retreating German columns and decided to attack these.

▲Their homes destroyed by the heavy bombing, Italian civilians from Cassino sit, listless, in a Red Cross camp, awaiting the end of the bombing.

After this, my sister and my sister-in-law decided to retreat to the mountains, just under Monte Cairo. Here we thought we would be safe, as the road came to an abrupt end.

We were wrong. We found ourselves near the front lines of the German Army. This was the position of the German Alpini troops who had been fighting around this location during the winter months when several attacks were centred on Cassino. Due to the bad weather, the terrain was very muddy and the attack in December by the Allies was staved off. Tanks just got stuck in the mud and were unable to cross the fast-flowing river. The Germans had blown up all the bridges.

15 March was the total bombardment of Cassino, which I watched from a nearby village. The abbey was destroyed on February 15.

The day before the bombardment, the Allies dropped leaflets telling everybody to leave the church and that they would be bombing the area. The Germans at this time were not inside the church – they were outside, around it. Freyberg, the Allied commander on the spot, was worried about the Germans using the abbey as a stronghold, at which point the Allies would be confronted with a huge task to get past that point.

A German lieutenant decided to tell everybody that they would not be able to leave the abbey until the

Imperial War Museum

Kazimeircz Gurbiel was 26 and a Lieutenant with the 4th Platoon, 1st Squadron, 12th Podolski Lancers, 3rd Carpathian Rifle Division, when he led the first Polish troops into the ruins of the monastery.

❝ Point 593 was captured, over-run at about 7.00 or 7.30 am on May 18. Maybe an hour later, I was sent out on patrol with 13 men. I left some men on guard at the foot of the monastery and took half the men with me towards the ruins. There was no shooting and we had heard that the Germans had gone.

Everywhere you looked among the rocks were poppies, blood-red poppies.

It must have been about 9.30 when we entered the abbey ruins. I had a Silesian with me who spoke very good German. I told him to call out that 'it was not in our minds to kill them' – after all, today, they are prisoner – tomorrow it may be me.

The commander of the Germans, a cadet officer, came out. He asked for a half hour's time to get ready to become a prisoner with dignity. One minute before time is up, he comes to me and says it is time for us to go. In that time, one of my lancers said, 'Lieutenant, here is a hole'. I said, 'Come on, boys', and took about six or seven men to St Benedict's crypt. I look in and there were three wounded boys lying there.

What I see in their eyes is fear. I said, through my Silesian, 'Don't worry, boys, nothing will happen to you'. There were 17 or 18 Germans, and enough food to feed an army.

We raised our flag, made out of bits and pieces, at about 10.00 am – after all that fighting, all those months, the monastery was captured without a shot being fired. ❞

◀ **Becoming accustomed to house-to-house fighting as the Italian campaign continues, a Tommy advances through the rubble. Inset: a Polish unit works out its battle strategy on a model of the local landscape.**

 Corporal Cadet Officer Zbigniew Fleszar with 3 Co, 1st Bat. 1st Brig, 3rd Carpathian Division, 'deserted' from a temporary post in a rear echelon to join his own company at the front line to see some action.

❝ We knew Cassino would be a very significant battle. We simply didn't want to miss it. After breaking relations with the Polish Government, Stalin accused us Poles of not wanting to fight the Germans, so, however small our contribution, we had to be there. The victory at Monte Cassino was to be our gift to Poland.

We were assigned the task to take the Gorge. My company was to reach the slope over it and protect the march and attack of the following company. We were loaded with equipment and already hot. I don't think we were scared – just apprehensive.

The company left the Big Bowl immediately after dark, passed the Small Bowl and slowly progressed over the rocks and bushes. Then a whistling shell flew low overhead – and another, and another. I felt as if a bridge of iron was being erected overhead, and wondered how it was that shells did not collide. Over a thousand guns were firing. The noise reverberated over the mountains. One could pick out whistles, crying and sobbing and roaring of shells. Then it all changed. The Phantom Hill in front of us was suddenly on fire. There was an explosion every split second. The mountain trembled.

Sweat running down our eyes, battledress wet, chests like smithies' bellows, we pushed forward on the slope. Then all hell broke loose. We did not expect it. The heavy shells started breaking among us. At first we thought it was our own artillery firing short. The code for this was 'Oranges'. This went out over the wireless – but the explosions were not oranges. This was German artillery. The explosions sounded like an enormous giant clearing his throat. I had an extraordinary wish – to be one of the smallest pebbles under one of the biggest rocks.

▲ **Zbigniew Fleszar (right) salutes as his unit marches through Italy. For him and many Poles like him, it was a point of honor to be part of the action at Cassino and to get their revenge on the Germans who violated their homeland.**

Zbigniew Fleszar

Polish Institute/General Sikorski Museum, London

My company was lucky. The barrage caught only our tail. The following companies were not so lucky. As a result of this first shelling, the first battalion lost almost half of its complement killed, wounded and shocked. We chased away some of the advanced German posts and sat just over the Gorge, waiting for the following company to pass over.

Towards the evening of 12 May, the Corps Commander decided that the attack must be called off. The taken ground was evacuated. Somehow it was left to me and a few others to perform the final action. Our 3 Platoon, together with the company commander, for some reason did not receive the order to withdraw. They sat on the edge of the Gorge the following night and throughout the next day. My platoon commander, looking me straight in the eye, informed me that volunteers were needed to fetch them.

A small group of us was formed with a lieutenant, second in command of the company. 'You going for a cross?' someone said. 'Yes – maybe a wooden one!' I replied. We went back and found the missing men. On the way back the lieutenant was killed and a few were wounded.

Now, on the Calvary mountain, on marble tablets, there are the names of the fallen soldiers of the 3rd Carpathian – 1045 graves facing the Abbey. At the centre of a podium, a huge carved cross of Virtuti Militari, the highest Polish battle honour, has at its centre an eternal flame. Around the circle is written, 'Passer-by, tell Poland that we fell faithful in her service'.

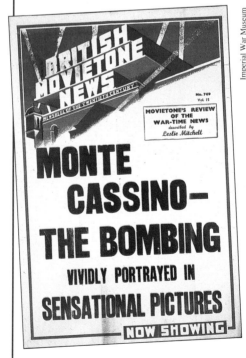
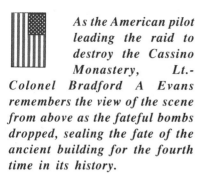

As the American pilot leading the raid to destroy the Cassino Monastery, Lt.-Colonel Bradford A Evans remembers the view of the scene from above as the fateful bombs dropped, sealing the fate of the ancient building for the fourth time in its history.

" The monastery of Monte Cassino unquestionably looms ahead. Sitting 1,500 feet above the valley floor directly above the town of Cassino, the abbey is a welcome sight – welcome in the military sense that the pilot, navigator and bombardier are assured that they have the correct target in sight.

In seconds the 96th Red Devils, led by 'the Beast', 666, will unleash the start of the bombing that will turn out to be the largest ever directed at a single building in World War II.

666 suddenly lurches upward and the proverbial 'bombs away' was heard over the intercom system . . .

Snapping on a portable sausage-like oxygen bottle, the commander worked his way back to the bomb bay section from where he could observe the initial impact of the ship's 12 bombs, and those of the following aircraft a fraction of a second later. Suddenly a small puff appeared in the south-western portion of the monastery, which was the explosion of the 12 bombs, and then a gigantic blast occurred which covered the entire abbey. In another fraction of a second the bombs from the other squadrons of the 2nd Group added their weight to the fatal blow, but by now the smoke, dust and debris were so heavy that they covered Monastery Hill, precluding further observation.

At the same moment an act of providence took place in the monastery where the Entrance Cloister and the Cloister of Bramante were joined by an archway, for here was the impact point of the bombs.

Moments before, a refugee, 24-year-old Oslavia Pignatelli, her parents and another family from Cassino were secluded in the small post office (now the gift shop) at one end of the Entrance Cloister. When they realised that danger was just around the corner, they wanted to descend into the depths of the monastery for better protection, but they were prevented from doing so because the passageway doors were

Imperial War Museum

locked. When the first 12 bombs from 666 exploded, the blast blew open the locked doors and the refugees fled to the lower levels of the abbey during the 15-minute lull between the first and second wave of bombers. Also at the time of the first bomb impact, Abbot Diamare and eleven of his monks sat helplessly, reciting the prayers of the divine office, in a long and narrow room in the bottom level below the monastery's college.

Imperial War Museum

John Watney Photo Library/Polish Institute

▲A scene of destruction greets German troops as they enter the monastery.

▼A few moments' heavy bombing destroys the monastery.

It was an act of providence that some of them had not ventured to other parts of the monastery.

Nearby, German soldiers scattered to places of seclusion to escape the blasts. They looked on in disbelief, wondering, 'Why are they bombing the monastery – it is not being used for military purposes?'

Allied soldiers hooted and hollered when they saw the first explosions. To them, those observing eyes of the enemy in the abbey would be prying no more. **"**

Paratrooper Robert Frettlohr with 15th Company 4th Regiment 1st Division Fallschirmjägerpionier (Paratroop Engineers) recalls the final moments of the battle for Monte Cassino and his capture in the ruins of the monastery on 18 May 1944.

" The 4th Regiment was in reserve when the monastery was bombed in February and many civilians were killed. Then on March 15 it was Cassino's turn and 470 bombers dropped many tons of bombs, but I remember seeing the bombers going over, wave after wave.

There must have been several hundred or so. It was the first time that a front line has been bombed like that.

On April 1, I was posted to the Rocco Janula (Castle Hill) and I was up there until the order came to retreat.

They were shelling us all the time as we were going up. As a young man of 20 years old, it was impossible to know what you felt. They kept telling you you had to fight for your country. Forget it. You fight for self-survival. If anyone gets killed you say, 'It's not me'. Anyone who says they weren't scared is lying – 'cos you were scared – all the time.

After we'd rested, we waited to time the shells – one . . . two . . . then two of us – always by two – would go. Off . . . gone. Then it was my turn. We waited for two shells – always the two – and we were off.

Then there was a flash close by and my left leg . . . I don't known, I must have been stunned . . . I passed out. When I woke up it was like a balloon. I was off again. I crawled up to the monastery – literally crawled – and I got to the first-aid post which was in the old Roman part, where St Benedict was buried. The doctor there put a bandage round my leg and said, 'That's it, you're not going back'. If there had been a road and I'd had a stick, I would have tried to get back – but there was no road, only rock.

It was 10 o'clock in the morning when the Poles came into the monastery. Lieutenant Gurbiel came in with some men. I don't know what we were expecting – a grenade to be tossed in, maybe. There were three of us wounded and 14 men trying to

▲ **German parachute troops bring vital supplies of ammunition and much-needed surgical equipment to their men on the hill at Monte Cassino.**

take us back, but that didn't materialise. Anyway, one of the Poles with Gurbiel spoke very good German to me, and I remember him saying, 'Are there any mines?' I said, 'There are no mines. This is a first-aid post'.

We talked, in German, about this and that, and about midday the 14 were taken down to the command post, Gurbiel said. There was no massacre as had been reported – I wasn't there. Later, all these reporters arrived. You can imagine a soldier who has been fighting for weeks, dirty, filthy, unshaven, full of lice. We must have looked a terrible sight.

Later on we were taken down the hill to a Polish first-aid post, where a British ambulance took us to a big Yankee tent hospital, six or seven miles behind the line. We were treated there, but I don't know what happened to the third badly wounded man. A few days later we were transferred to a POW hospital camp at Aversa near Naples. **"**

▲ **Bob Frettlohr, now a Yorkshireman, remembers his 20th birthday in Italy. 'I remember I was got paralytically drunk by my mates. We were drunk much of the time – it didn't hurt so much if you got wounded'.**

CHAPTER 14

BATTLE DIARY

NOVEMBER 1943
30   Directives for Overlord issued

DECEMBER
6   Eisenhower appointed to command landings in France

JANUARY 1944
17   Supreme Headquarters, Allied Expeditionary Force established in London

FEBRUARY
1   Revised Overlord plan, Neptune, issued

APRIL
18   Allied air forces begin preparatory bombing of France

MAY
8   D–Day date named, 5 June

JUNE
4   D-Day postponed for 24 hours due to weather
5   **21.30**   First aircraft take off from British airfields
6   **00.15**   Pathfinders start arriving in Normandy
            00.50   Bridges over Orne in hands of 6th Airborne division
            01.15–02.51 Main airborne landings take place
            04.00   British paratroops control Ranville
            05.00   Merville battery knocked out. US 82nd Airborne Division
                           captures Ste Mere-Eglise
            07.30   Us 101st Airborne secures exits 3 and 4 off Utah beach
            11.00   101st and US Fourth Infantry Division link up at Pouppeville
            13.00   British Commandos reach Orne bridges
            19.00   Merderet crossing at Chef du Pont controlled by 82nd Airborne
                           Division

OVERLORD — FALLING INTO FRANCE

Planning for eventual landings in occupied Europe began soon after Dunkirk, but it was only when the full resources of the American shipyards became available to the Allied war effort that an invasion became realistic, as large numbers of ships and landing craft were needed to cross the Channel. Of the potential targets, the coast of Normandy was selected because it was less well defended than the Pas de Calais, and its large shelving beaches would allow landing craft to beach and offload troops and vehicles. The Germans, under the leadership of Field Marshal Rommel, built bunkers and obstacles to defend the beaches, while coastal batteries were installed under thick concrete protection.

Allied planners decided that the best time to land was at half tide, when many of the obstacles would be exposed. From west to east, the designated beaches were codenamed Utah and Omaha for the US Army, and Gold, Juno and Sword for the British and Canadians. As the tide would rise up the Channel from west to east, Montgomery's British troops would be landing later than the Americans, so in order to compensate for the loss of surprise he lengthened the offshore bombardment of German bunkers. The Germans had flooded the land behind Utah, so paratroops of the 82nd and 101st Airborne divisions would land to secure the causeway exits from the beach. In the weeks before the planned landing, Allied aircraft attacked the road and railroad links to Normandy to prevent the Germans moving men and equipment to the area.

British paratroops of the Sixth Airborne Division would land at the eastern edge of the beachheads to secure or demolish the bridges that gave access eastwards and prevent German reinforcements attacking the beachhead. Bad weather prevented the operation, codenamed Overlord, from taking place on June 5, but in the early hours of June 6 paratroops and glider-borne soldiers began to land in the darkened French countryside.

FALLING INTO FRANCE

Men are called from all over the world to prepare for
D-Day. Some have seen the sun set on many
battlefields – others will be blooded in Normandy.

Back from Africa and Italy, British servicemen, home for the first time for years, go into training for something big. A landing of some sort — but where? As the mystery 'D-Day' approaches, not only those due to participate but also those defending the 'Atlantic Wall' have the feeling of something afoot. At last, the US 101st and 82nd Airborne Divisions go into action, dropping into Nazi-occupied Normandy. The invaders, the spearhead assault troops and the defenders recall the run-up to D-Day.

◉ *Sergeant Pilot Rupert Cooling, after flying support missions for the Sicily invasion from bases in Africa, returned to England to train for the big invasion. With 516 (Combined Ops) Squadron he found himself in Western Scotland.*

❝ Our squadron was equipped with a motley mixture of machines – Mustangs, Hurricanes, Blenheims, Ansons, two Lysanders, a Miles Master and a Tiger Moth which we flew mainly for fun.

Exercises simulated both air support and attack during practice assault landings. Blenheims carried cardboard case bombs with the blast and noise effect of a 250-pounder. We dropped sticks of four ahead of the troops as they hit the beach. Care was needed – these could kill at seven yards. Mustangs and Hurricanes strafed the shore with cannon.

One Blenheim was fitted with a siren which howled like a banshee as one dived to attack – its purpose was to put the vertical breeze up any brown or blue jobs below. For an encore, we laid smoke. As the landing craft headed for the beach, we would level out at some 50 feet and head straight across their bows. Press the bomb-release tit and a long, dense white sausage of smoke would blot out the view all around. It was hazardous, but we were away in the clean, clear air above – except once.

Loch Fyne forks at its eastern end. The shorter spur thrusts into high hills which plunge down almost to the water's edge. The target beach lay in the lee of this high ground.

Approach from the west was barred by these 2,500 foot plus mountains. No way could a Blenheim clear those – it had to be a run in from the east. By the time I was down to 50 feet, the aircraft was travelling at about 250 mph. I throttled back to kill

▲ **Around Britain practice landings take place before the big day. Here smoke pots on the beach obliterate the harbor as US trucks land.**

▶ **Sergeant Pilot Cooling, seen here in North Africa, is one of many in training.**

excess speed then pressed the firing button which blew the seals on the smoke cylinders in the belly. What happened next is uncertain, but the effect was cataclysmic. The cockpit, instruments, flying controls, even my hands on the stick disappeared from sight within a brilliant dense white cloud. I sat and waited to die as the aircraft plunged into the water or exploded in a ball of flame upon the surrounding hillside. After an aeon, perhaps three or four minutes, suddenly the smoke cleared. The Blenheim was in a gentle climb ten miles from the target, flying at 1,500 feet down the centreline of the loch. High ground lay on either side. After landing, I went first to the medical section for treatment, and then to the Padre – it seemed appropriate.

We lost three pilots, four aircraft on various exercises. Not many in the total cost of that mighty enterprise, but they were just as much casualties of the D-Day operation as those who died on, off or above the Normandy beaches. ❞

◀ **In a practice landing, bazooka teams take up positions below the sand dunes. The soldiers wear US Navy life belts as a precaution.**

◀◀ **The landing in France is a reality at last - and not an unwelcome one, as these villagers show as they go about their daily round, unworried.**

Lt-Colonel Michael Forrester DSO, MC, was serving with his Regiment in Palestine when war broke out. Joining the 7th Armoured Div., he fought through Greece, Crete, the Western Desert and the Italian invasion before returning with the 'Desert Rats' to train for the European invasion.

" We didn't know, of course, when D-Day was going to be – in fact we knew very little about anything. We were given training directives and facilities in Norfolk at that time were quite good. But there were things other than training to be dealt with. Everyone had been abroad for a very long time. Leave was the first thing. I remember we got as many people as we possibly could away on leave. I forget how long they had now, but this was the first time they had seen their families for a long time.

One other aspect which I'd like to mention is the fact that we were back in England again for the first time after a considerable number of years, and this meant being at home as opposed to being in the desert where there were virtually no inhabitants, so all needed reminding of the importance of local public relations, which in our case included the people of Kings Lynn and the villages around it which we would be passing through for training. We were trying to weld ourselves into the community and become part of it, although we knew we weren't going to be there for very long. The people of that part of England were open-hearted and kindness itself and they gave us a

marvellous welcome – they could not have made us more at home.

There was also a memorable day which General Erskine, our divisional commander, arranged specially for the division, and that was an investiture at the Palace, when every member of the Division who was due to receive a medal, won during the previous months and years abroad, was included, so it was very much a family affair at Buckingham Palace. All these things, including the visits, tended to raise our spirits and morale, and made us feel we were in for something very important.

Training directives indicated that we were going to be fighting in fairly close country, and in the event, when we got to Normandy, we found the so-called *bocage* country there even more restricting and close than even we had anticipated. It was, because of its nature, almost as great a change from Italy as the desert had been to Italy, because the fields were so very, very small, with high banks with hedges on top of them dividing up the fields, making fields of view and tank movement very, very difficult indeed. Of course, the Germans had the advantage over us there – they were familiar with it.

Of course we were aware from the start that we were going to take part in the invasion of Europe, but we didn't know where we were going, and I remember very late on, all the officers had to assemble at some cinema somewhere, and the Army Commander, General Miles Dempsey, was to address us. I had served under him for a short time when he was commanding XIII Corps with his headquarters in Syria.

He very kindly spotted me in the audience, and had a few words with

▲ Although the fight for Italy still goes on, these men, back from the Italian front, are destined for more action on the Second Front as soon as D-Day's landings start.

Topham Picture Library: Inset Maj-Gen Michael Forrester

me, and something I said must have caused him to say, 'But surely you know you're going to ...' and he got 'Nor' out, and then he checked himself. He said, 'Didn't you know?' He had stopped at 'Nor', so I thought Norway. Then he realised we didn't know – weren't supposed to know – so he deftly changed the subject. I went round in a haze for the next day or so, wondering if we were going to Norway or Normandy!

So it was as closely kept a secret as that, right up to the end, and when our time came to get ready finally, we moved out of our areas in Norfolk down to camps, very sparse, primitive tented camps – but perfectly adequate for the purpose, in Essex. It was there that our camps were sealed, or we were sealed into them, and we were briefed properly, and allowed to brief right down to soldier level – but up 'till then, no-one had known.

It's very relevant to talk about fear.

▲ **Lt Colonel Michael Forrester DSO, MC, - now Major-General CB, CBE, DSO, MC - CO of 1/6th Queens.**

◄ **Lt-Colonel Michael Forrester (center) introduces Lt Paddy Toolan (left, who was awarded the MM in Palestine, but was sadly killed in France at Briquessard) and Maj-Gen Erskine to King George VI, on a visit to 131 (Queen's) Brigade in Norfolk. Here the king inspects 1/6th Queens.**

Maj-Gen Michael Forrester

▲ Flight Lieutenant David Warner, navigator for D-Day glider drops.

⊙ *Flight Lieutenant David Warner, a navigator with 296 Squadron, had returned from North Africa late in 1943, and started to train in towing gliders, dropping paratroops and supplies in accurate zones, and using Gee radar. All this was in preparation for the D-Day assault.*

❝ In between training and the invasion we were sent out to France to drop supplies to the Maquis. That also gave us training for map-reading at night. A typical exercise was to go to somewhere where the mountains start, in the middle of France, where the Resistance were.

We would fly over from England to Fécamp, and then gradually reduce our height from about 6,000 to 2,000 feet and descend to about 1,000. I used to aim for three little islands in the middle of the Loire, which always reflected in the moonlight and gave me the confidence of having a pinpoint, then we would come down to 500 feet.

All the searchlights would be out looking for something, but at 500 feet they couldn't get you, because as they came down, they would go out, and you could duck underneath the lot. Usually we would be over the top of the flak before they could get organised, but there would be quite a lot of things shooting behind. Then you would come to the rendezvous and the dropping zone, where there would be the reception party.

We would go round and ac-

The unknown, which we were going into, meant uncertainty. You don't know, and uncertainty very naturally leads to apprehension, and so the adrenalin is flowing, quite rightly.

I don't think fear actually comes into one's thoughts until one is confronted with something dangerous, but the apprehension is there all the time. I would say I felt really frightened on several occasions. I think too, that the definition of war (which is anonymous, though someone may lay claim to it) that 'War consists of long periods of intense boredom, punctuated by short periods of intense fright', is a good one. I think it was coined for the First War, it was very relevant for the Second War too.

Once confronted with a situation, there are certain sorts of fear. I think the predominant sort of fear, in the case of some, is 'Am I going to be up to this myself?' I think it's awfully important to recognise that – it takes a certain amount of personal drive to overcome it, and to say, 'Yes, I am'.

Certainly, while people were very frightened, they went on because they felt they couldn't possibly *not* go on. *Esprit de corps* is very important for morale because you drive yourself to meet the challenge, and you know other people are meeting it too, and you are going to be in it with them. ❞

▼ Part of the reconnaissance view showing the bridge where his gliders were to land, which David Warner would learn by heart during his training.

knowledge the fact that we were there, then we would lower the flaps and the wheels, reduce speed to about 80 or 90 mph and go 600-800 feet above the line of torches to drop the goods. Then up again, go around, flap our wings, wish them good luck and away.

When it came to D-Day we were given lots of pictures of the French coastline. I had to look at this panorama all day long. I had it in my room, when I woke up in the morning with my cup of tea – I tried to memorise it. What we had to do was to take a glider over there.

On D-Day we had to fly somewhere up to Newcastle to start with, because that take-off was between two and three minutes, and you had 40 to do, so it's quite a long time. We had to go up north for about 50 minutes, come back over the airfield and by then the rest of the gliders were airborne to go across together.

When we got there there was nothing happening. We saw the area and we had a wire through the tow rope to talk telephonically to the glider pilot without going through the air. We circled over the area and asked the glider pilot if he could recognise his landing zone and he said he could. So we asked him to let us know when we should release them. He said, 'It's OK, you can release us right now.'

This was at about 2.00 or 3.00 in the morning that the drop took place, some eight or nine miles inland.

There was a battery three or four miles up the coast, of heavy German 'Atlantic Wall' stuff, and that was being bombed very heavily by about 80 Wellingtons.

It wasn't until three or four in the morning, when you saw the dawn,

▶ An Armstrong Whitworth Albemarle of 296 Squadron. Although first built as bombers, Albemarles were used in the D-Day landings as glider-tugs and for dropping paratroopers.

David Warner

▲ As an Albermarle taxis along the runway to take off, its glider becomes airborne behind it. Inset: the insignia of 296 Squadron of the RAF, based at Brize Norton during the Normandy invasion.

SQUADRON
296 296
ROYAL AIR FORCE
PREPARED FOR ALL THINGS

RAF Museum

▶ In the early hours of 6 June 1944, British paratroopers board an Albemarle bound for Normandy.

that you could see the fantastic sight. It was like a tail-back on the M25! The air was full of aircraft going in every direction. I've never seen so many aeroplanes in all my life. Of course at night, when you were flying, you never thought of that. You just took your course and went ahead.

I wasn't aware of anything at sea until the return journey, when dawn broke, and the pilot said, 'Come up and look at this,' and you saw all these ships coming in, the bombing and the fighting.

I have to say the operation didn't worry me at all – you get used to it, don't you? It's like driving a new car you've never driven before but after you've had it for about six months it becomes second nature. I went to the Loire so many times, looking for these three islands, that I knew what was going to happen. The only thing that would have been frightening would have been if we had lost an engine – then we'd have problems. There again, I planned for all exigencies. I used to pack everything up in my room in case I didn't come back, and I used to take with me all sorts of things. Just before I left the mess, I used to tear the front page off the Daily Mail and stuff it in my back pocket. This was because if I had to land in France, the Germans were setting up decoys to pretend they were British airmen trying to escape, to try to find out the French families who were helping them, then rounding them up and

shooting them. So to let anybody know I am a British airman, I would have that day's date on a newspaper.

I thought of everything for survival – I carried yards of string and had razor blades stitched into my trousers. They gave us one or two pieces of survival equipment – a handkerchief with a map of France on it, some French money. I had a pipe which had a compass built into the bowl, and that sort of thing, and I also took a pair of shoes, because if you baled out, I'd heard people say that they lost their flying boots. Most of this was my idea. But on D-Day I didn't do anything at all. I felt it was a mass organisation and we'd all be back in five minutes. It didn't worry me one little bit.

Imperial War Museum

AIRBORNE *Lieutenant Sumpter Blackmon was leader of First Platoon, Company A, First Battalion, 501st Parachute Infantry Regiment. He recalls his part in the 101st Airborne's D-Day drop into France. Their aim was to seize bridges and main road junctions to prevent the Germans from flooding the estuary area behind the beaches and to nip any counterattack in the bud.*

It was 10 o'clock in the evening of June 5, and it was nearly time to go. The officers and men of our First Platoon joined hands and prayed that God guide us. I took my 'stick' of 18 men on to the aircraft. Our equipment was so abundant and binding that we could scarcely move.

We took off just after 10.30 that night, and all the planes circled above the airfield and waited, then began forming up in Vs. It took us an hour to get into formation. The V was so perfect that I could have pitched a grenade at the plane just outside the open cargo door of the C-47. Then

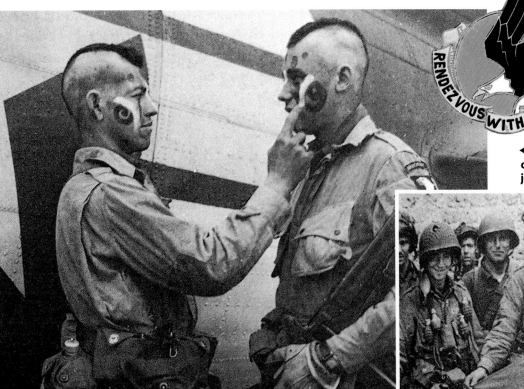

US Army photo

◄ The crest of the US 101st Airborne Division.

◄ For Privates Ware (left) and Plaudo of the 101st Airborne, their dangerous job excuses an unconventional look.

▲ Triumphant members of the 101st Airborne Division hold up a trophy taken at St Marcouf following the Normandy assault.

our formation turned inland and the sky erupted in fireworks – flak.

All around my plane the others were jinking and diving, but my pilot – I never did learn his name – flew the course without a tremor. He flew directly into a fogbank, and all the other planes disappeared. When we came out of the fog, we were all alone.

I stood at the cargo door with the equipment bundle of machine gun and ammunition, ready to kick it out when the jump light came on. I saw the proper landmarks come up, but felt no tap from the No 2 jumper, Private Thurman Day, or from Sergeant Adams. Then I saw the ground disappear and then whitecaps – we were back over the sea.

Private Day pulled me back from the door and shouted that the pilot wanted to see me. He looked worried. 'Lieutenant', he said, 'we missed the drop zone and are over the Channel, headed back to England. What shall we do?', I told him to take us to land and we'd get out.

The pilot dived, came around and headed for the French shore again. He took us down just above the waves to evade the flak, and as the plane reached the shoreline, he put it into a climb so steep that it threw several men off their feet.

I decided it was now or never. I pushed out the equipment bundle, hooked up my chute ring and followed. I was jerked by the ring and my parachute opened automatical-

ly just before I hit the ground.

After I landed hard, I cut myself loose from the parachute. I found the equipment chute in a low tree, a part of one of the Normandy hedgerows — thick, nearly impenetrable lines of trees and bushes. I pulled the red light attached to the pack, which was showing clearly, and pulled it down and turned it off. Then I pulled out my carbine. I crawled into a hedgerow and waited and listened. Finally Private Day came up.

We had no idea where we were. I pulled out my flashlight and map. I studied the map but could not find any points of terrain that matched – we'd obviously jumped off the map.

We waited some time, but no-one else showed up and we decided we'd better take the machine gun and two boxes of ammunition out of the bundle and head south. After about half a mile, we were exhausted, and had to stash the gun and ammo.

Finally we met up with some other troopers and I really felt as if I had an army, with the 34 men I collected. Soon we approached a village and saw a light in a house on the outskirts. The others surrounded the house while I went to the door and knocked.

A woman came to the door and as she opened it, I could see another woman sitting at a table in the kitchen, three empty chairs, bread on the table and two bottles of wine.

The woman was not very friendly and she seemed monstrously stupid,

but she told me we were in Foucarville, near the fourth causeway that led the beach road – about three miles from Utah beach and about ten miles northwest of St Come-du-Mont, where I thought I could find some of my battalion. I asked the woman the way and she didn't understand, or said she didn't. I repeated my question. She became sullen, and when I told her I was an American paratrooper, her eyes widened, and she shouted something and tried to run out the door. I stuck my carbine in her belly and she stopped.

I didn't know if she was a German collaborator, or just frightened. I told her to sit down at the table, and when she did not, I went out, closed the door firmly and motioned to the men to come with me, back to the road. We had just rounded the bend when we ran into our first enemy fire. Had there been men in the farmhouse, and had they run off to warn the Germans? A burst from a German light machine gun swept over the road. It sounded like someone tearing paper. We

US Army photo

► Pictured on a night training maneuver, Col Howard Johnson is every inch a conventional paratrooper.

Süddeutscher Verlag

dropped and crawled off the road to the left and moved into a field of grain. The noise started up again.

I got up and started to run. I saw a ditch ahead and got ready to jump it. Just then, a German soldier stood up in the ditch and raised his hands. I could not understand what he was saying. Private Nick Denovchik came up and said the German was speaking Polish, which he understood. They began to talk, and the firing suddenly stopped. They must have decided that we had moved on.

The Polish German told Denovchik that he and his buddy were manning an aircraft listening station. He shouted and his buddy stood up about 50 yards away. After some more talk, they led us to a pillbox buried underground in a grove of trees, in which was a big radio set and enough ammo to withstand a minor siege.

The two prisoners helped us destroy the listening device, four large instruments perfectly camouflaged in the trees. We blew up the ammo dump and wrecked the radio. We accepted these two soldiers as our allies, and they showed us the way to the causeway. We were still a long way from our assigned objective, the locks of the Douves. It was nearly time for the troops to be landing on Utah Beach, I could only hope and pray that someone else had taken the locks at La Barquette.

They had, and a vast armada of ships were in the English Channel – the invasion of Normandy was on. **"**

Bildarchiv Preussischer Kulturbesitz

▲ Rommel had been shocked at the inadequacy of field-gun emplacements to defend the much vaunted 'Atlantic Wall'. The heavy fire from the offshore armada would prove his concern to be well founded.

Corporal Hans-Rudolf Thiel, in the Regimental platoon of 6th Para-troop Regiment, recalls how it was left to him to sound the alarm for the airborne invasion of the Allies over Cherbourg, on 6 June 1944.

" The invasion alarm of the previous day and last night has been lifted. The storm has abated and it has stopped raining. The sun is even shining today, as if it wants to compensate us for the unbearable

tension of the last 24 hours.

The rumour is going round that the Allies have ordered their invasion fleet to turn back because of the poor weather. This can only help us – a stay of execution.

Today no *Rommelspargel* ['Rommel's asparagus'– anti-glider obstacles] are planted, instead of this we have machine-gun exercises in the field. We march out to the surrounding meadows and move into cover positions. Sergeant Major Geiss, our platoon commander, allows us to catch up on the sleep we missed last night. As well as we can, we all seek out a place with good cover in the hedges, or sunbathe.

At high altitude above us one enemy bomber squadron after another flies into the hinterland, and from there we can hear a terrible thundering. The daily reconnaissance plane does his rounds and now and then a few fighter-bombers buzz by like hornets. Our morale is good, but the old front veterans have 'something in their water'. They don't trust the overall aura of peace.

Arthur Volker, my bunker comrade, has indigestion. He says he always feels like this when something's afoot. Even I can't conceal a sense of unease. After the relative calm of the last few weeks I turn my thoughts to the massive bombardments of the hinterland. Something is going to come down on us.

The food today was wretched once again – a lot of groats and no meat – a lot of jam and no sausage. Hopefully it will remain quiet tonight, and we're all hoping that there won't be another 'false alarm'.

Arthur and I are assigned the task

◀ Field Marshal Erwin Rommel (right) pauses on a Channel coast inspection, 1943. Doubts already show on the Desert Fox's face.

▼ The cloth badge worn above the right breast pocket of German Luftwaffe servicemen.

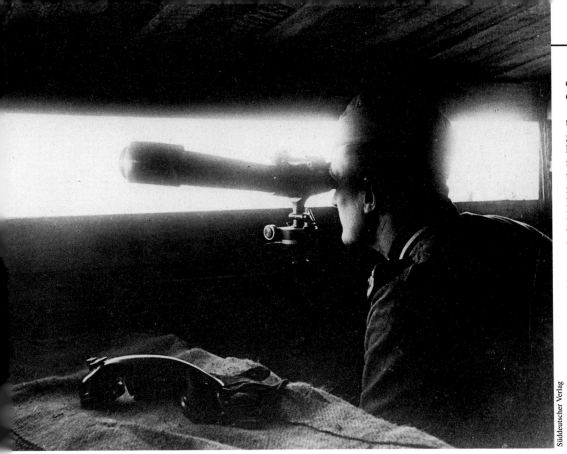

Süddeutscher Verlag

of 'high-chair watch'. This is a very exposed and windy job. There's a stiff breeze coming in from the sea, the moon shines brightly now and again through the gaps in the clouds. It is not cold – just chilly – and up on the high-chair in the poplars you get a real shaking.

At midnight I have to take over from Arthur, and until then I try to get a few winks of sleep. No chance. I just can't get to sleep. I'm getting more restless with every hour that passes. I try to read with only the Hindenburg light, but I can't concentrate. What the devil is going on?

The night is so quiet, no sound of engines. Only the wind rustling through the poplars. I have to take over from Arthur soon.

Since I can't get any sleep anyway, I take over from him earlier. I get dressed, fasten my belt, check my machine pistol and magazine and crawl out of the bunker. The fresh air suddenly makes me shudder and I look around in the darkness. Strange – this peace is just not normal. I have the feeling that there's something lying in wait for us.

I go up to the high-chair tree and call out, 'Arthur, come down. I can't sleep, I'm going to take over now'. Arthur climbs down the ladder and says, 'Bloody wind. It's damned cold, and there's absolutely nothing to report,' and he disappears into the night.

I climb up to the high chair and look at my watch. Still 10 minutes

Bildarchiv Preussischer Kulturbesitz

before midnight. I hang my binoculars round my neck, load my machine pistol and put the catch on, then I sit down and make myself comfortable. A few minutes later I can hear the familiar but distant sound of aircraft engines. 'Bloody hell', I think to myself, 'there's more than a few – I hope they're not going to drop their bombs on us.' I look at my watch again, and take a look through the binoculars.

It was seven minutes after midnight when I saw masses of red and bright white lights in a north-westerly direction. To every soldier with any

▲ **A German look-out scans the horizon over Omaha beach - he would soon be rewarded with sight of the invasion fleet.**

▼ **Alone on the Channel coast in Normandy, a German anti-aircraft gunner mans his post ... and waits.**

experience at all this could mean only one thing – ENEMY ATTACK! ! !

My common sense told me 'this is the invasion'. After the first shock I grabbed the telephone connecting the high-chair position with the regimental command post and turned the handle like a madman. At the regimental command post: 'Duty clerk here, Corporal?' I told him what I had seen. In the meantime the sound of the engines could be heard over our position.

Duty clerk: 'One moment, I'll get the adjutant'. Regimental command post: 'Lieutenant Peiser! What's going on? Report!' I give the report: 'Corporal Thiel here, platoon, direction north-west, Cherbourg, red and white lights sighted, loud aircraft noise. The enemy is attacking!'

As the receiver was not put down at the command post I could hear Lieutenant Peiser give the duty clerk the order to fetch the Major straight away. Then I could hear the major rushing up and could pick out a few scraps of the conversation – 'this afternoon' – Frenchmen' – 'damn' – 'why no alarm?' – (a word I couldn't understand). Major: 'Platoon, report!' Me: 'Corporal Thiel here, platoon. Mass of lights direction of the coast and Cherbourg. Enemy attacking. This is the invasion, Herr Major, should I sound the alarm?' I look at my watch – it's 11 minutes after midnight.

Major: 'Sound the alarm! Sergeant Major Geiss to me immediately.' The receiver is put down.

I put down the receiver and shout out as loud as I can: 'Alarm, alarm!' Again and again I shout 'Invasion!, Invasion!' and fire off two machine-pistol magazines... **"**

CHAPTER 15

BATTLE DIARY

6 JUNE 1944

05.30	Bombardment of beaches begins. US troops land on St Marcouf
06.00	German Seventh Army HQ informed of bombardment
06.30	H-Hour on Utah and Omaha
07.00	First landing wave pinned down on Omaha. US Rangers begin scaling Pointe du Hoc
07.30	H-Hour on Gold and Sword
07.45	US troops advance inland from Utah. H-Hour on Juno
08.00	US troops on Omaha begin ascending bluffs
09.00	German 84th Corps informed of seaborne landings
09.30	Announcement of Overlord made to press. British troops one mile inland from Gold. British capture Hermanville
10.00	US troops reach clifftops overlooking Omaha
10.30	21st Panzer Division ordered to attack between Caen and Bayeux
11.00	US soldiers enter Vierville
11.15	St Aubin falls to Canadians
12.03	Commandos link up with Airborne troops at Orne bridges
12.15	German tanks reported north of Caen
12.30	British 185 Brigade moves inland from Sword
13.00	US Fourth Infantry Division links up with 101st Airborne at Pouppeville
13.30	US troops move inland from Omaha
13.35	German 352nd Division reported to have thrown the enemy back into the sea from Omaha
14.00	Fighting on Periers Ridge overlooking Sword. Hitler holds his first meeting about landings
16.00	British and Germans clash between Villiers-le-Sec and Bazenville. US tanks begin moving inland from Omaha. 12th SS Panzer and Panzer Lehr Divisions released from reserve
16.30	21st Panzer Division attacks Sword beachhead
18.00	British advance on Caen halted
20.00	Colleville-sur-Mer secured by British
20.10	Taillerville captured by Canadians
21.00	Gilders carrying reinforcements land behind Utah and east of the Orne

D-DAY – STRUGGLING ASHORE

The invasion force was composed of 4,000 ships carrying 176,000 troops and their equipment, escorted by a fleet of 600 warships. The defenses along the coast had been softened up by 2,500 heavy bombers, which dropped 10,000 tons of bombs, while 7,000 fighters and fighter bombers swept the skies.

After a rough and nauseous Channel crossing British and American troops landed on the Normandy coast. At Utah the US Fourth Division had surprisingly few casualties and by 13.00 was in contact with the advance paratroops; by the end of the day it had secured a beachhead 4 miles wide and 9 miles deep. Meanwhile, on Omaha, the US First and 29th Divisions suffered over 3,000 casualties and had penetrated only 1½ miles inland by the end of the day. A combination of factors had worked against the Americans at Omaha: the shore bombardment had not hit the coast but had landed further inland, and the defenders of the beach were a freshly arrived well-trained German unit.

On the British and Canadian beaches, longer naval bombardments and specially developed tanks and armored vehicles for breaching the coastal defenses kept casualty levels lower. At Gold Beach, the 50th Division captured Arromanches and by midnight had reached the outskirts of Bayeux, which fell the following day. The Canadian Third Division, which landed at Juno pushed 7 miles inland. On Sword, the British Third Division linked up with the Sixth Airborne and advanced to within sight of Caen.

Though the German High Command was slow to react, individual units such the 21st Panzer Division were quick to counter-attack the invaders. Nevertheless, the end of D-Day saw 57,500 American and 75,000 British and Canadian forces ashore. They had suffered losses of 2,500 killed and 8,500 wounded: but, with a bridgehead established in Europe, the Allies were at last in a position to begin to push the Germans back.

STRUGGLING ASHORE

Having suffered the cramped conditions inside their landing craft, most of the Allied attack force are ready to face the hazards of an enemy-held coast.

As morning light grows over the Normandy beaches, British commandos wade through the shallows to join the tanks which have already landed.

◄ Richard Todd leaves behind his paratrooper's uniform in a post-war film, *Portrait of Clare* – a far cry from his real life army career.

Hulton-Deutsch Collection

Kobal Collection

▲ In the Darryl F Zanuck film of D-Day, *The Longest Day*, Richard Todd (center) stars as Major John Howard in the action at the Orne River Bridge. On the left, Peter Lawford plays Lord Lovat.

Training was at an end – this, from now on, was the real thing. British and Allied troops who had trained for months would see the first action on the Second Front – and German nightmares would become real.

Richard Todd, possibly better known for his acting role in The Longest Day *than for his real-life action on D-Day, went through officer training at Sandhurst and after a varied career in the Army joined the 6th Airborne Division. His battalion was to be the first in on D-Day.*

" I was to be in aircraft 33. We had very carefully worked out our load tables for the aircraft in terms of who should be in there first, who would have such and such weapons and who would have other things with them. On that particular night, first of all we were in a *laager* on Salisbury Plain, wired in for about a week, even our supplies and food were just dumped outside the wire gates, and our own chaps went out and brought it in, because we weren't allowed to talk to anybody. We were being briefed, a week or so before D-Day, we knew where, when, how and everything about it. We had no communication at all with the outside world, except me one day, because I was Assistant Adjutant, and I was sent to Southern Command Headquarters. I was terri-

fied. I thought, 'Oh, my God, I hope I don't open my mouth'.

We knew the whole thing, all the planning. We knew our own particular thing – we had sand-table models of the area we were dropping in and we knew every tree and every house intimately. We had maps galore and every day we had a fresh batch of aerial photographs for our intelligence officer to interpret.

We were getting worried because we saw a lot of little holes being dug and we found out that it was posts being put in with wire between them as anti-glider defences. We also saw large areas flooded – we wondered if the whole thing had been blown.

That night of D-Day, or the night before, at about 11 o'clock, we drove round the airfield perimeter, each stick of paratroopers in a three-ton truck, and each truck stopped by its numbered aircraft. Mine stopped at aircraft number 33, as that was the one I was to be in – and I was going out first from the aircraft.

The pilot and crew were lined up beside the aircraft – they shook hands and wished us luck and all the rest of it. The pilot was a very senior officer, an Air Commodore or something. He said to me, quite blithely, 'As I'm the senior officer going in tonight, I'm going in first, because we've got the gem crew'.

I thought, 'Oh Christ – I'm going to be the first out of the first air-

▶ John Leopard recalled his nightmare voyage across the Channel, 'I had never sailed in a tank landing craft before in such ugly conditions – it seemed to me that it climbed the waves' front left-hand corner first, and slithered down into the trough right-hand corner first!'

▶ Men of the 27th Beach Brigade and 13/18th Hussars wait to land with their Sherman tanks. Inset: Landing Craft Infantry come close in to the shore to allow British commandos to land.

craft,' but I couldn't argue with them because he was senior to me, and I couldn't say, 'Look, this will upset our load tables.' It wasn't the time.

So I got in – and that actually saved my life. I'll tell you why in a minute. I think people thought I was very cool because I fell asleep on the way – but that's a thing of mine. If I'm very worried or really down about something, my tendency is to be like an old ostrich, and put my head in the sand and go to sleep – and I was very worried and had lots of stress on me that night.

I was wakened up – we lined up and hooked up. The old green light came on and out we went, with me in the lead. Incidentally, it was a very big hole in the bottom of the Stirling, with enough room for two men to straddle it, and on the word 'go' pull their legs together and drop out through the hole. The man behind me had to hang on to me because the aircraft was jinking a bit. I could easily have fallen out – in fact a few people did fall out over the sea – because I hadn't a hand to hold on with as I had kit bags on each of my legs. One kit bag was full of a rubber dinghy, and the other had picks and shovels for digging in. They were fixed to your legs – you pulled the rip-cord when you were out of the aircraft and they dropped 20 feet below you and then dangled below on a rope. I was having to hold these things to my leg. Out I went.

We dropped from 400 feet, which didn't give you much time in the air – about seven seconds. In the flurry of all this, I let the bloody kitbag on my

right side slip instead of letting it out hand over hand. That gave me a very nasty burn all down my right hand. Then I thumped down.

We had got in with the element of surprise. A certain amount of light flak came up and we could see tracer, floating by us. But nothing hit us – the big stuff hadn't really started, and as I was getting out of my 'chute on the ground, looking up at the other aircraft, they started getting shot down. By that time, the ground defences had wakened up to what was happening and the ack-ack guns had gone into action. The aircraft round about the numbers 30 were the ones that all got shot down, and it was just my luck that I went in first. ”

◆ *John Leopard commanded a troop of four 95 mm howitzers, mounted in Centaur tanks – part of a 100-strong tank unit, formed specially to give close support for the assaulting infantry. The Royal Artillery and tank boys had bowed out — this job fell to the Royal Marine Armoured Support Group.*

❝ I was woken before dawn on what was to be one of the most significant days of my life. After having slept but fitfully with violent motions of the boat adding to my inner strain, I went through all the automatic preparations for any ordinary day. I tidied myself up, checking my few possessions, and stowed away my supply of just two ounces of tobacco. It was an absurdly small amount, but I felt I might be tempting fate if I took a sensible supply!

I stepped out on to the spray-blown, wind-swept tank deck. In the half light of near dawn, the tanks stood up in the dark silhouette, straining against their rasping chains. One of my lads was lying on the water-swept deck, being too sick to care. I hoisted him to his feet and bundled him into the mess deck. I then climbed up to the wheel house and, circling round it to the narrow after deck, I paused to look at the vague shapes of the vessels which were following us. Our wake carried a quite brilliant display of multicoloured phosphorescent lights which seemed singularly inappropriate in a setting, and on a day when beauty was the last thing one might expect. It was there, completely alone, that I found I had to fight down a feeling of near panic which made me want to dive overboard and swim home. I just could not accept the situation I had made for myself.

I made my way into the Mess Deck where the Colour Sergeant had already assembled the men, washed, dressed and in all respects ready to face the day. We lined them up and

the Sergeant issued the grog. It is a strange thing that when troops are facing a particularly perilous situation, they become noisy, tell outrageous jokes – at which they roar with laughter, and generally behave as if life was one big party. On this occasion, when we could not even guess our chances of survival, everyone – including me – was unbelievably cheerful.

We were now close enough for those fearsome rocket-launching craft which operated from not far astern of us to send their warheads over our heads towards the beach. Each of these vessels carried 1,000 rockets which were released in a series of volleys. To have released them all at one time would have threatened the fabric of the vessel itself. We had always disliked these rockets, they passed all too close above our heads in an erratic cloud. We feared a mid-air collision over our heads, or a drop-out in our direction. On this, the only 'for real' occasion, a swarm of these things was flying towards an area also the target of one of our diving aircraft. I foresaw the tragedy ten seconds before it happened. The aircraft exploded in a ball of fire.

Before we too went into the water, the tank jarred violently. I knew we had been hit. I checked that nothing untoward had happened in the driver's compartment, so assumed that nothing too serious had happened. Later I found a scar on the turret about a foot long and one inch deep in the middle. Had the anti-tank solid shot which had bitten so deeply into the steel of the turret struck us at a slightly less acute angle, it would have been curtains for us.

The plan had been for the first wave to land below the first of the

obstacles so that the Royal Engineers could tackle their clearance problems before the rising tide put later arrivals at risk from obstacles which would then be under water and capable of doing considerable damage. It occurred to me that had there been an experienced yachtsman on the planning committee, he would have recognised that with the heavy westerly winds which had been storming up the Channel for some days, tides would have been earlier than stated in the tide tables and have brought H-Hour forward.

Still dodging these obstructions, I was concerned to hear some erratic noises from our engines. At the same time, the driver reported that he was up to his ankles in water — but somehow we made the waterline to join the two Centaurs and I ordered the drain cocks to be opened. A glance back showed me what I suspected. Our air and exhaust extensions were pitted with bullet holes.

We were now in our required

▲ **Much equipment for the D-Day landings had been updated and made more technical, but the trusty bike remained a standard transport for the infantrymen. Inset: looking more like hikers out for a ramble, infantry with bikes land on Queen Sector – part of Sword Beach.**

▶ Although some men have turned toward the camera as the crowded infantry crouch on the Normandy beach to avoid the shells passing overhead, most are more anxious to keep their heads down before the advance.

All photographs Imperial War Museum

◀ For dispatch rider Bill Williams, D-Day was his first venture out of Britain — a massive culture shock for a 19-year-old from a sheltered background!

▶ Concealed in a dug-out in the beach area, a Tommy finds a German 'Goliath' tank. These were first used at the Anzio beachhead.

position and were joined by the other two Centaurs which landed only shortly after we did. We could now settle down to keeping as many German heads down as possible to ease the lot of the Queens Own Rifles of Canada, who were now beginning to come ashore. We had no more open sight targets in view. We could only wait for indirect fire instructions from the advancing troops, or await our orders to move off the beach to our first normal gun position. With devastation all about us I could scarcely belive that my five tanks were largely undamaged and we had no casualties.

During the lull, I ordered all tank crews to dismount to clear the bodies which had been washed up against our tracks. I could not move the tanks further up the beach while they were still there, in case any were still alive. **"**

At the age of only 19, Bill Williams joined the RASC, seconded to the 3rd Canadian Division for supplies. Having led, by his own admission, a sheltered life until then, his first foray abroad on D-Day was a voyage of discovery.

" It was around midnight on June 5 when we became aware that we were moving. One could sense tension rising. At last the order came for us to don our equipment and prepare to move down to the vehicle deck. Nothing could be heard except the drone of the ship's engines, and it was 6 am when we sensed that we had stopped.

Once outside, we found we were at least two miles out from the coast, which we could just see from our low position. The sea was full of ships of all shapes and sizes. Naval destroyers were firing over our heads towards the coast. All this time we were plodding forward, so slowly it seemed at times we were not moving. A DUKW's normal speed is about 4 knots in calm water, but loaded and in a heavy swell, our speed was more like 2 knots.

I suppose one could describe the scene on the beach as organised chaos. A boat had been sent out to guide us in and the engineers had

done a fantastic job in clearing areas of the beach enforcements, which were all piled in huge heaps. I can't say how many landing craft were on the beach at that time – a number of them were burning and had obviously been struck by shells. But apart from the spasmodic shell coming over on to the beach, there didn't appear at that time to be very much danger. We understood that the Canadians had moved inland some half, three quarters of a mile. One

was still conscious of a lot of gunfire – in other words, ships were still firing inland to various points, but basically we were very tensed up about it, and one could say it was organised confusion.

The beach itself was cluttered with debris, a number of landing craft were burning on the water's edge.

My first shock was spotting the first dead body. I'd never seen a dead body in my life before. This particular chap was so immaculate – just as though he had been stood to attention, with his small pack and his webbing all beautifully blancoed. There he was, and we had to stop for a moment right beside him. It was if he had been standing then just gone flat down on his face. It absolutely shattered me – I couldn't take my eyes off him. We saw quite a lot of other bodies lying around, but what the Medical Corps had done was to set about treating the wounded and get them away, and then take care of the bodies afterwards.

There was a sniper in the church tower and we had to wait for them to be cleared. We passed into the centre of this small town – not even a square – then we turned into an open field.

Looking over the fence, the best part of a herd of cows had been slaughtered by the shell fire and were lying around with their feet in the air – which rather upset me, coming as I did from the country.

After that we dismounted and unloaded the ammunition into heaps and were escorted back down through Courseulles, along the causeway, to the outskirts of Bernières-sur-Mer. We turned into a fantastic driveway of a château which had hardly been damaged at all. We drew round the back where orchards were laid out and were told to disperse around the perimeter there. There was a lot of noise going on there, but one felt quite remote from it. We were very delighted to have got there in one piece.

We got together and dug one hell of a big trench then constructed a ledge half way down so we could sit, and covered the top with apple branches which had been knocked down by the shells. We covered over with groundsheets and had a hot meal of stew – we did nothing else but smoke and talk about the events of that day. **"**

As a Tank Commander with the 24th Lancers, Charles Wilmot landed with his men at Arromanches beach. After months of training for the actual landing, they did not expect that their tank would be put out of action so quickly.

" Prior to D-Day we had done lots of training manoeuvres — we knew exactly what we were going to do. We were all formed up, in and around Fordingbridge, waiting to go.

We were crewed up, gunned up and, what's more, sealed up. We had fitted various chutes on the tanks so that they could take what they called a six-foot wave. We had spent weeks and weeks filling each crevice with plastic stuff which was similar to plasticine. Wherever there was a join, it had to be filled and the guns and gun turrets had to be closed and sealed. They called it 'feathering'.

In preparation, we had been issued with Rhinos. They were huge platforms fitted with engines to control them. The idea was that we

▼ **A Crusader anti-aircraft tank of the 22 Armoured Brigade, 7th Armoured Division, leaves its landing ship to make for the beaches of Arromanches.**

HINDENBURG UNDER NEW MANAGEMENT

Sgt. SAVAGE AND HIS CHINDITS

▲ **Victory written all over their faces, a Bofors gun crew enjoy possession of the Hindenburg Bastion – a huge concrete emplacement with an adjoining radar station and trench communications.**

▶ **Before the furore and sudden call to action occasioned by the arrival of the invasion fleet, life for a German soldier on the 'Atlantic Wall' is a leisurely affair. Here a group of soldiers enjoy the sun outside their bunker.**

would come off the LST and then get on to the Rhino. This was in case the LST couldn't get close enough to the beach. We had to practise driving up the ramps and on to the middle of the Rhino and stopping there. It wasn't easy, as you can imagine, because these Rhinos would tip up in the water. None of the tanks fell off them, but they nearly did.

As it happened, we lost the Rhinos on the way over. They broke away from the tow. There they were, floating in the Channel. I've no idea where ours went. Fortunately, we didn't need it, our ship went inshore as far as it could, where the water was just a couple of feet deep.

We were all ready to go on the 5th, but the weather was bad, so it was cancelled. We were completely fed up. Then the message came across 'Advance' – and it was a wonderful sight. There were ships coming up here, ships going up there, all in arrow-head formations, heading towards specific beaches.

As we went over, the Navy were running up and down the beaches with their rocket ships, clearing the beaches for us before the landings. I noticed a hospital ship – she looked lovely at night because of all the Red Cross lights. We were under air attack – they would keep nipping in – but they didn't bomb her at all.

When we got in on the beaches, the Beachmasters shepherded us off the LST and then up the beach. We had a little bit of an explosive charge to unseal the equipment, and after

that we could operate the guns. The beaches were all mined and we had to follow the white tapes showing where they had been cleared – but the worst thing was the snipers.

Anyway, I didn't last very long. An 8-pound mortar came over and hit the top of the tank and, of course, we all got blown to the bottom of it. It was all down with sympathetic detonation, which means that the power with which we were hit set the ammunition off around the tank. There was a round up the gun, and the pressure set that off. I was in the way of the recoil which came back and smashed my arm up.

We managed to crawl out and the medical people were soon with us in a half-track. They brought us up forwards of the beach where all the medical tents were.

They put me in the compound where I was waiting for about a day and a half before they got me on to the hospital ship. There were quite a few young Germans on the ship – two of them refused to be attended to, and died. **"**

Friedrich August Freiherr von der Heydte was CO of Parachute Regiment 6, part of the 2nd Parachute Division under Commanding General Ramcke, which fought at the French coast from 6 June onwards. In 1941 he secretly conspired against Hitler.

" I was in the north of Périers, just in the middle of the peninsula, the most westward part of Normandy, covering Utah Beach. The funny thing was that the Germans were expecting a landing north of where the landing actually occurred, west of Ste Mére-Eglise. One the first day I received no orders. I was my own boss. Most of the divisional commanders had been called to Rennes for an operational exercise. I tried to get through to the corps commander General Marcks.

The only contact was by the normal French phone network. The Germans were forbidden to use this, officially, because of the spies. But I couldn't get through on our own network, because the French Resistance had prepared well for the invasion, sabotaging the phone lines.

I first saw what was happening when I arrived in St Come du Mont. I had come across an old church tower, had got hold of the key, and went up there to take a look out over the coast. I knew that I had to tell General Marcks what I had seen. I wanted to tell him that in my opinion the forces we had were not in a position to offer vigorous resistance to the invading forces. At every mile along the coastline was a German bunker and, of the three that I could see, only one was actually firing at the Americans. All the bunkers were manned, of course, but only one was

firing. In my opinion, they feared for their lives, considering that they would be easily wiped out by the invading Americans. Only one bunker did its duty, forcing the Americans to spread out.

I felt that my troops were very vulnerable with no artillery assistance. We had our heavy company with 12 cm mortars. I gave the order for them to get forward quickly and fire.

When I saw the invading troops, I gave the order by radio to the regiment, but I didn't dare use the same route back to the Command Post. I made a detour, and on this detour I came across a German battery which had been totally deserted. This was the second line of defence, the artillery line, about six guns in the battery, totally unmanned, but all ready to fire, the ammunition boxes open on the left side of each gun. I don't know what had happened to the gunners, but it was my opinion that they had deserted, though it is possible that they had received a new order. But all the Americans had to do was turn the guns round and fire them at our men. I had no artillery men with me, so I could do nothing with the guns. When I finally contacted Marcks I reported what I had seen.

I told him I had to try to defend the line north of St Come du Mont, and he agreed. But then I had to leave the place for two reasons. First, because someone, I don't know who, had given the order to the engineers to blow up all the bridges. So we had no way to fall back from St Come du Mont to Carentan. Then, there was a funny thing. It was on the second or third day, and all the forces who had been north of Carentan, including the Regimental Staff, had been given the order to withdraw to the south, because we were afraid that we would be surrounded. The Americans attacked to the west, and this attack would have led them to the south and behind me, and so I said, no, it's nonsense to stay in St Come du Mont, we should defend Carentan instead, because in my opinion Carentan was more important. But how the hell could we get to Carentan? All the bridges had been blown up. So, nearly all parts of my regiment, a reinforced battalion, had to cross the water. It was up to our chests and we had all our heavy guns with us. But we had to do it. And thank goodness the Americans didn't spot this. They continued to attack St Come du Mont. Two of my soldiers drowned. One of them was a Jew who had signed up for the German Army using a false name. I had two Jews in my regiment. Both had used false names. One was the nephew of Albert Schweitzer, the famous German doctor and the other was the son of a German aristocrat whose mother was Jewish.

At Carentan I had parts of the 2nd and parts of the 3rd Battalion with me, and some regimental units, intelligence troops etc. Then I was given a reinforcement battalion of Russians, Georgians, in fact. These were anti-Communist Russians fighting on the German side. They fought very well, but they couldn't stand the bombing from the air. The American bombers attacked my regiment near Carentan the whole day, and after the attack the Russians deserted.

The heaviest fighting was at the north-west part of the town. The Americans had managed to get over the flooded area by the railway bridge, which my 2nd Battalion had used. The only way of destroying this bridge would have been by bombing it from the air, but the German Luftwaffe was held back by the superiority of the American air force. I did not see one German fighter plane. As we said then: 'We have the ground but the sky belongs to the Americans'.

So, in my opinion, the crucial factor was American air superiority — and second, the lack of unity among the German forces. 〞

▲ The leisurely atmosphere does not mean that the German defenders were entirely without preparation for any Allied invasion. Here men rush to their posts in an exercise – in case there should be an attack from the sea . . .

▲ Friedrich von der Heydte, 37 at the time of D-Day, came from an old aristocratic family. After the war he became a member of the Bavarian state parliament.

CHAPTER 16

BATTLE DIARY

1	Patton's Third Army activated
7	Operation Totalize begins
8	Phase two of Totalize begins. US Eighth Air Force bombs Allied troops by mistake
9	German withdrawal from Paris begins. Totalize bogged down in German defenses
10	Railroaders go on strike in Paris
11	Totalize called off
13	Elements of US XV Corps reach Argentan, Falaise 'Pocket' starts to form
14	Operation Tractable launched against German forces around Falaise
15	Paris police force goes on strike. Allied forces land in the South of France
17	Falaise falls
19	Members of the Resistance seize the Prefecture. General insurrection called for
21	Falaise gap closed. German garrison in Paris retires to strongpoints in the center of the city
22	Fighting ends in the Falaise Pocket. Second French Armored Division is ordered to advance on Paris
23	Severe street fighting in Paris. French troops under Gen. Leclerc rush towards city
24	Leclerc orders reconnaissance column to enter Paris. Column reaches the Hôtel de Ville late in the evening to ecstatic reception
25	German commander in Paris, von Choltitz, surrenders during the afternoon. Fighting continues until next morning
26	De Gaulle makes triumphal progress through Paris. Luftwaffe bombs Paris during the night
28	French Resistance forces dissolved

NORMANDY – THE ROAD TO PARIS

As the Allies worked hard to expand their beachhead, the Germans rushed reinforcements from the Pas de Calais to try and drive them back to the sea. The terrain of the Norman *bocage* – small fields separated by thick hedges – was ideal for defenders, and the German Waffen-SS Panzer units were effectively able to slow and delay the British advance inland in the east. Meanwhile, the US VII Corps swung north up the Cotentin peninsula to liberate Cherbourg on June 27.

The tide was turning for Hitler. As his troops struggled against the Allies, he came under serious threat closer to home. On July 20, a timebomb planted by a group of disenchanted German officers and civilians exploded at his headquarters, but failed to kill him.

As the British and Canadians battered away at German forces around Caen, the Americans regrouped and prepared for a breakout and a drive inland. On July 25, Operation Cobra was heralded by a heavy air attack that dumped 4,200 tons of explosive on the German positions. General 'Lightning Joe' Collin's VII Corps led the main effort and, after advancing through tough resistance at Coutance, broke the German defenses at Avranches. General Patton's Third Army punched through the hole into open country. The final German counter-attack, at Avranches, was foiled by Allied air support responding to Ultra signals interception.

The way to the French capital of Paris lay open. In a huge sweeping maneuver, American forces linked up with British near Falais, trapping or killing 60,000 German troops. On August 23, as Resistance forces rose against the city's German garrison, the US Fifth Corps, headed by the Second Free French Armored Division, made a drive for the city. It reached it on the 25th, liberating the French capital after four years of German occupation.

THE ROAD TO PARIS

With massive air support and the help of Allied SAS and underground teams, liberating troops move towards the French capital to seize control from the German occupiers.

Vicious fighting and attrition have laid waste the Normandy countryside, leaving it strewn with bodies and wreckage – but at last the Allies reach the capital and, judging by the ecstatic welcome they receive, all the carnage is somehow justified. Men who paved the way to Paris and those in the city recall the liberation.

Dropped into Central France, Gordon Davidson and his stick of eight SAS men were to make strikes against German transport columns retreating from Nantes and other U-boat bases on the west coast. As their Halifax transport turned back towards England, the men prepared for the job in hand.

❝ For all of us, this was our first experience of the Continent. What would the reception committee be like? Were they FFI or FTP? No idle question. A week or two before half the Squadron had dropped at Châteauroux, to the north west in the same area just south of the Loire. They had been met by FTP (communists), betrayed to the *Milice* and shot out of hand.

The group of figures approached. '*Vous êtes les bienvenus*', called out one taller than the rest, and there was a mutual pumping of hands before we hurried to some cars and along the mysterious darkness of a country road to a farmhouse. Once inside the large warm kitchen, we could take stock of our hosts and load up with omelettes, bread, cheese and wine.

Chief of the reception committee of the local *maquis* was the tall, thin Commandant Duret, whose appearance and manner were strikingly similar to that of de Gaulle. Definitely FFI, so, all things being equal, we shouldn't risk another Châteauroux. There were four or five other *maquisards* besides the farmer, his wife and two daughters. The atmosphere was friendly, even jovial, and we were indeed welcome – perhaps not so much for our military skills, as the assurance we represented of arms and supplies.

With the busy German supply route from Bourges to Nevers only a few kilometres away, we were guided into the adjoining woods for the night. *Milice* patrols were a hazard and the farmer and his family could not be compromised.

Dawn came and went unnoticed, and by midday it was time to take stock of the situation. In any case, no action could be taken until cover of night, and it was a good time to assess resources and tasks now that we were safely in position on the chess board. Arms and ammunition were sufficient for several small strikes until the next supply drop.

What of the men? We were a stick of eight. The sergeant, a cheerful, solid man from Glasgow. Like almost all of us, he was new to the SAS and his approach was that of a regimental soldier. His battalion had recently been dispersed and he was more fortunate than his comrades sent to the Glider Regiment, who had come to grief in Normandy.

There were two corporals. One from Norfolk had been with the SAS in North Africa, where he had earned the MM. He was small, lively, quick-witted and a demolition expert. A natural 'jelly' man, and ideal for this mission. The other, a small, saturnine man from Dorset, who had apparently run donkey rides on the sands at Weymouth. Perhaps he had been a stable-lad in happier times, for he exuded a sort of horsiness and, as he cheerfully carried a Bren gun, it could have been a saddle in Lambourn Yard.

Like him, three others were from the west. Two from Swindon, a butcher and a railwayman. The third, a Swansea lad, was quick to make his mark with the farmer's teenage daughter.

All four, Weymouth, Swindon and Swansea, had come from Auxiliary Units, set up earlier in the war for defensive guerrilla operations in south-west England in the event of a German landing. They were trained to live rough and were familiar with the night attack techniques.

The remaining two came from London. A tall, youngish, rather academic-looking man who, it transpired, was an actor who had recently worked at Stratford. I am not sure how he came to the Unit, but he was a good and reliable man. A cockney medical orderly of uncertain background, but certain humour, made up the number.

Like the sergeant, my own experience had been with another Highland regiment and, after working at Airborne Forces HQ as SAS liaison officer, I got a transfer to B Squadron at Fairford.

In August 1944 the military situation was fluid, to say the least. The main Allied forces moved towards Paris and Brussels and the pattern of conflict was reasonably clear. However, in central France, no Allied forces came nearer to us than Orléans, some 100 miles to the north, where Patton and his armoured divisions paused briefly in the drive to the Belfort Gap. Meanwhile, the Germans withdrawing from their naval bases had to pass

▼ At the end of a major operation in central France, Gordon Davidson (center) and men of his stick of SAS paratroopers (left to right) Hanford, Beckford, Blandford and Youngman MM, relax for a 'team photo'. Inset: the 'wings' which denote that the wearer is SAS trained.

Gordon Davidson

from Bourges in the central Sologne to Nevers or La Charité – both with bridges over the Loire – and make for the Belfort Gap before Patton could close it.

It is useful to 'paint the picture', as Monty had said, because the odds in our case were 20 SAS to cover an area half the size of Surrey against a constant flow of Germans moving east and culminating in the von Elster column of 20,000 men, halted at Bourges on 5 September.

Our mission, to harass German columns, would have been quite impossible without the wholehearted cooperation of the *maquis* and local population.

A typical operation meant leaving at nightfall in a couple of ancient cars, and a drive of 10-15 miles to a point where enemy transport was most vulnerable.

Sten and Bren guns with precious grenades were our weapons against the highly armed Germans, so that our attacks would be met by a hail of Schmeisser automatic fire, and as their bullets whistled all around us, we gave inward thanks for the camouflage of trees and darkness.

In one engagement, the hail of Schmeisser fire was so intense that it claimed an inevitable victim and my corporal (the actor) was shot in the head beside me. Taken to a *maquis* 'hospital', he was given every attention, but lack of supplies meant that he could not be saved.

We carried out eight or nine missions of this kind and, in addition, the blowing up of railway bridges which halted a couple of German armoured trains.

These were small operations compared to what was occurring elsewhere in the campaign at that time, but the pressure on the ordinary soldier in extraordinary conditions was considerable. Apart from the adrenalin of battle, he had to cope with the uncertainty of who was on our side – who gets a bullet in his back from a traitor? How were we going to eat? It is here that regimental discipline, training and a bit of humour show their true value.

The large German column, under General von Elster, halted at Bourges, would not surrender to the *maquis* (half of them communists), but was persuaded to move north to Orléans and surrender to Patton on 10 September. It was good to see Allied troops again. After our meeting, a visit to his Ordnance Park for supplies. A sergeant asked me to choose from one of 15 menus. Chicken Maryland never tasted so good. **"**

▶ The insignia of 183 Squadron of the RAF, one of the Typhoon squadrons of the Second Tactical Air Force based in France during the Allied invasion.

▶ Flying Officer Philip Murton with his aircraft 'Claire IV', a Typhoon (F) IB, photographed at Merville, France, in September 1944.

Flying Officer Philip Murton was with 183 Squadron of the RAF, based at a makeshift airfield just outside Caen. Flying rocket-armed Typhoons, it was his job to clear obstructions from the Allies' way and hunt down the retreating Germans.

" On any operations there would be, say, a section of four going out looking for anything – anything German. We had the bomb-line marked on our maps that we flew with, so anything beyond that which was moving – guns, artillery, dispatch riders – was fair game. Depending on what it was, the leader decided whether to use cannon or rockets, or whether it warranted a second attack.

This was simply freelance stuff, any anything you found, you just attacked it. The leader tried to make a note of where it was so he could report the exact position when he got back. But sometimes we'd go to do a rocket attack on a gun somewhere, and that was probably the army that had called us up, given us a map reference and said, 'There are guns here which are holding up the advance in one part on the front' – then you would go and knock them out. Very often the army would fire red smoke on to the target which gave us an extra guide – until the Germans learned this and of course, they would fire red smoke in the hope that they would confuse us.

A lot of the time it was cheating in

a way because there was nothing firing back at us. It was almost like a practice, though obviously the tanks and troops on the ground *would* fire back. Later on, when the Germans increased their flak everywhere, you could be attacking something and there would be no flak at all. Then, as soon as you got in a dive, they would open up and you would have to go through the lot. Actually, the attacking, once you had gone into echelon and peeled off to go into the attack, you were so busy trying to get

RAF Museum, Hendon

Philip Murton

the sight on what you were attacking and looking at your turn and slip indicator to try and get the skid out, allowing for wind, that really, unless the flak was quite intense and the balls were whipping past you, you were concentrating only on what you were doing.

We had complete air superiority, so we never had to bother about looking for German aeroplanes. In fact, apart from chasing two Focke-Wulfs over the Channel after they had bombed Brighton, I never saw a German aeroplane in the air through the whole of my tour.

The Falaise Gap was an absolute shambles. There was a pocket of hundreds of tanks, vehicles and goodness knows what, and there was this gap which wasn't closed. Montgomery didn't make the right decision and thousands of troops got away through it. They reckon that if the gap had been closed three or four days earlier, then we would never have had the Ardennes offensive or Bastogne, because all those German troops were seasoned men and they

went back and reformed.

Falaise was horrible because it was absolute carnage. There were dead bodies and horses and cows all over the place, and after three or four days, you could actually smell rotting bodies at 2,000 feet. The smell actually came into your cockpit. An awful lot of the local French people (because of the ground battle going on) were down in cellars but at one stage, when our flight was standing down, our army liaison officer said, 'Come on you chaps', and we piled into an army three-tonner to go and look around. There were still bodies lying around and the cows and horses all tended to lie, goodness knows why, with their legs up in the air, and they were all bloated and swollen. There were vehicles everywhere too – everything left behind by a retreating army.

When we went in on an attack I honestly don't think we had any feelings about it. We were young, and you tended to enjoy things. Over the years you tended to forget the horrible things, and shooting up

a whole lot of troops on the road was a lot of fun. It was very impersonal. I know you were killing people, but it wasn't like the army who went in hand-to-hand fighting. You were just letting loose at a whole lot of people on the ground and you would see them fall over like nine-pins and not think an awful lot about it.

We were doing it because it was a job to do. We didn't hate the Germans – possibly not as much as I hated them after the war after Belsen and all the atrocities came out. We were fighting to knock out Nazism really, and I think a lot of the army boys who were involved in hand-to-hand fighting and the tank boys who were literally blowing up people 100 yards away, were revolted by it. But eventually you got very hard. You got hard too because you saw one of your chums shot down or crash – and it was no good getting all soppy and sentimental about it, so you built a shell. In fact, about five or so years ago, I started having the most God-awful nightmares about being shot down, shooting up troops, planes, and goodness knows what. I mentioned it to my doctor and he said that it was a natural reaction. All the nasty stuff is stored away in the back of your mind and now it is starting to come out.

We all had the feeling it wasn't going to happen to us. **"**

▲ **As the Allies press on through Normandy, an RAF Typhoon rocket attack hits a German communications post. At the bottom of the photograph a rocket scores a direct hit on a railroad track.**

◄ **With only make-shift landing strips from which to operate, the Second Tactical Airforce live rough in tents and vehicles on a diet of bully beef and biscuits. Here, at one such landing strip, ground crew arm up a Typhoon with rockets for its forthcoming mission.**

Jack Clark, an air gunner with an Albemarle crew in 297 Squadron, 38 Group, based at Brize Norton, was not due to be flying on 20 August, 1944 – but a friend approached him to fly with his crew on a trip to drop supplies to the French SAS in Brittany.

" The Albemarle had been designed just before the start of the war as one of the answers to the question, 'What shall we make aeroplanes out of when there is no more aluminium?'

The Mosquito, built from balsa wood, had been the correct answer. The Albemarle, constructed from mild steel, was the other solution. It had been passed on to 38 Group to replace the Whitley after being turned down by Bomber Command, and even those sent to the Russian Air Force had been melted down, and only the engines were used by our hard-up allies.

Apart from being very heavy for its size (because, of course, mild steel is heavier than aluminium) it had also been designed with the tail wheel at the front of the aeroplane, so that the landings were usually bumpier because the drivers had been trained on aeroplanes that had the tail wheel under the tail. This meant that the electrical system wiring was constantly affected by the shocks and vibration, and until the landing had been made, we were often not sure that the undercarriage would actually lock as we hit the deck, or whether we would be coming in on a belly landing. Actually those were not the problems that were worrying my friend Bert Moss. After all, we had learned to live with those little bits of excitement.

When the Albemarle was first produced, the Air Gunner used to strut around a small open platform in the centre of the fuselage, waving a couple of Vickers K guns that ran on a ball race around the rim of a hole in the top of the fuselage, hopefully in the direction of the enemy. By this stage in the war, the gun ring had been replaced by a power-operated Boulton Paul gun turret, fitted with four Browning 303 MGs – which brings us to my friend Bert's problem.

Neither the Air Gunner, the Pilot, the Navigator, the Bomb Aimer (we didn't carry bombs but to ensure the pinpoint accuracy that was needed of crews dropping supplies to the resistance groups, the pilot was directed for the final stages of the drop by a Bomb Aimer – an expert mapreader), nor the Wireless Operator could see if anything approached from behind and below.

Because of this blind spot, one of the *Luftwaffe*'s fighter techniques was to attack from below and behind any unfortunate Albemarle they were lucky enough to find. They

Robert Hunt Library

were also much faster, better armed and infinitely more manoeuvrable.

However, there was a little window at the bottom rear end of the fuselage and just sufficient room for one intrepid, not-too-tall airman to lie down and peer through this window to observe if indeed an enemy was approaching from below and behind.

Yes, you've guessed, Bert wanted me to come with him and his 'sprog' crew, and look out of the window.

Some hours later I had tidied my kit, cleaned my boots, written my last letters, envelopes addressed and sealed, but not stamped. We had just flown over the French coast through a welcoming barrage of flak from some trigger-happy Americans – we always blamed them. They probably blamed our ack-ack gunners too.

I say light flak now, but a few years ago I was looking through some papers in the Public Records Office where the combat reports are now held, and the descriptions of the flak varied from 'light' (Bert) to 'heavy' (guess who). Anyway, as we weaved through this red hot hostile metal, I realised we were being pursued.

In the best traditional cool British manner, I switched on the intercom

▼ Air Gunner Jack Clark (second from right) with his crew, left to right: Danny Julien, Wireless Op, Mal Jones, Navigator, Alan Davis, Pilot, and George Page, Bomb Aimer.

Jack Clark

astern was a Dornier 217.

This time it took only moments to get the pilot into a corkscrew and direct Bert just where to aim his four Brownings. I watched him pour tracer into the Dornier starboard wing and engine at a rate of about 80 bullets a second, and saw it fluttering and spinning down out of sight into the cloud below.

We had been flying just above the cloud so we could use its cover, but soon it was time to descend through this shelter. We were due to drop a load of supplies (petrol and ammunition were part of the normal cargo, although one tried not to think about it), to the French SAS who were fighting for control of Brittany, assisted by a very active and courageous local *maquis*.

We flew over the Dropping Zone.

▼ In the center of Paris, FFI and 2nd French Armored Division go into action against German snipers. The French vehicle bearing the legend 'death to the Boches' is parked among German vehicles captured by the *maquis*.

▲ In Chartres, 48 miles (77 km) from Paris, men of the French Forces of the Interior (FFI) march through the city after its liberation by American forces, August 1944.

Popperfoto

and spoke in cool, calm, modulated soft tones to the pilot. 'Tail to pilot. Stand by corkscrew starboard – corkscrew starboard. GO.' And nothing happened.

The pilot should immediately have slung the several tons of mild steel, Browning machine guns and assorted air crew down into a right-hand dive, maintained that for several seconds, climbed up to the left for a few seconds, dived again to the right, climbed again to the left, thus maintaining the same direction.

Nothing happened for several moments. In a slightly authoritative, but still cool and gentle tone, I repeated, 'Corkscrew starboard. GO!'

Nothing happened... Then, with all the authority and command I could summon to my voice, shouted down the intercom, 'Corkscrew starboard. GO!'

The voices of Bert, plus the navigator, the bomb aimer and the wireless operator joined in. This heavenly choir awoke the pilot from his reverie. He threw his quivering Albemarle into violent evasive action.

Both engines cut out... then the starboard engine picked up and the port began to purr and roar again. The same pursuer was still in the

same relative position, astern and slightly below. 'No,' I thought, 'it's impossible'.

And then I realised, it had to be part of our own aeroplane. It was, of course, the tow bar to which gliders were attached when the Albemarle was used as a tug.

I ordered the pilot to cease these dangerous aerial acrobatics, telling him that we had shaken off our pursuer, and we settled back, bodies and minds alive with adrenalin. I was a little angry with myself, but glad that I had learned the only way to ensure instant urgency in battle with that particular pilot. A lesson some five minutes later I was able to apply, for coming up from below and

There was a battle going on and it seemed sensible to fly on and return a little later as the DZ party were a bit too busy to be flashing recognition letters and colours and collecting panniers and so on.

As we flashed past, at treetop height over the coast, I could see a priest, cassock flapping in the wind, with his parishioners, beating out a fire in a tiny village. Perhaps they too were involved in the same immediate strife as the SAS soldiers to the north. I don't know.

We flew back to the dropping zone, but everybody on the ground was still 'too busy' – so reluctantly back to Brize Norton, cargo intact, to fly again. **”**

William Spray had served in a Friends' Ambulance Unit in Morocco until the invasion of France, when his unit became attached to a tank column of the USA Third Army.

" We had no idea of the shape of the war. The Falaise Gap got closed and we stopped fighting, then the buzz got round that it was Paris. This was terrific. On August 25th, we went, a mixture of fêting and fighting on the way, into Paris.

It was unbelievable. I don't think I'd ever attached any particular meaning to the word 'liberation' until now. Certainly I can't ever now see or use the word 'liberation' without thinking of the experience of that day, rolling into Paris.

We were bang behind the tanks. People were out on the streets, throwing flowers, hugging every soldier they could see, and suddenly discovering we were English, and transferring their affections to us, quite as much as to the French.

I have pages in my diary about this – most of them concern particular young ladies whom we met and gave a lift to until a German sniper would open up, at which point, tin hats had to go on and we had to go into action in case there were wounded. There weren't really any wounded we met until we got right into Paris itself.

There was this enormous outpouring of joy and relief and everything else fell into what seemed the right perspective – that is as unimportant. I suppose on that day, it was.

So we drove in slowly. I remember going across the Pont du Sèvres, rolling into the Place Victor Hugo, down into the Avenue Raymond Point Calais, and there we stopped and a lovely lady handed out *vin rouge* from her sitting room window.

Snipers opened up. We had wounded in the Church of the Place Victor Hugo, and we had to evacuate them to the nearest hospital. We slept, that night, in the street, in our ambulances, with the local Parisians absolutely marvellous in their welcome and hospitality.

We were the first lot in, apart from British Secret Service. I'm sure there were lots of British in Paris before, but we were the first – and only – ones to make a public entry. So it was the French and these 30 conscientious objectors, rolling into Paris. Indeed, the very next day, (in one of the local French papers (one of our chaps was called Marcus Dukes and the other was Raymond Mann) they had conflated the two and the great headline was 'Duke Man first Englishman in Paris'.

There was not a lot of resistance going through. What had happened was, I think, that the hardened Nazis were clearly going to die fighting and they were some of the snipers, I've no doubt...

Paris looked just like any other town. Certain bits of it were obviously damaged, but it was difficult to know when. My memory is mainly of people – great crowds of people cheering. Where the French ladies had got their lovely dresses from on this sunny morning, I don't know, but there they were, looking simply magnificent – the young ones. Then there were the old ones and widows in their black, being motherly. It was a great occasion for the human spirit. It was astonishing, really, that it required a war to produce it. "

▼ At the Quai d'Orsay, Paris, in the midst of burning buildings and advancing tanks, two French ambulance staff rush a casualty to a first aid center under the protection of the Red Cross flag.

USIS/Andre Laubier

► In the Place de l'Etoile, an ecstatic crowd gathers to greet the liberating French forces – at last they see an end to the nightmare of occupation.

Popperfoto

Robert Hunt Library

◄ Cornered in a building taken over by the occupying administration, German soldiers surrender in face of the Parisians whose city they had seized – a case of 'the biter bit!'

![Nazi flag with swastika] Herbert Eckelmann was an official in the Reich Ministry of Economic Affairs when he was suddenly drafted into the army as Germany built up her military power before the war. August 1944 found him living in Paris's Hotel Raphael, the Stadtkommissar, responsible for the economic running of occupied Paris.

" My new – and last – commanding officer, von Choltitz, received his scorched-earth orders that Paris was to be destroyed – gas, electricity, power stations, Métro, the lot. Choltitz summoned me to hear my opinion, and I answered that on military grounds such destruction was pointless.

On August 17th, Abetz came to Choltitz to explain that he was removing the Vichy regime. With Choltitz I inspected the fortified blockhouses (Stutzpunkte) we had built, and saw how they were manned by dear old daddies. As luck would have it, nobody bothered them. On the 20th, we agreed it was too late in the day for any destruction. Had we simply marched out of Paris along with the rest, however, we would certainly have been condemned to death by a military tribunal. So we remained at our post in the Meurice. Jay asked Choltitz what orders he had to give, for the soldiers could not be expected to continue fighting after their senior officers had been captured. Choltitz replied that he had no new orders to give.

Choltitz' bedroom and sitting room were on the fourth floor, and he and Colonel von Unger and Jay and I and a few orderlies had retired up there. Then in came an older man in a German uniform with the insignia of the Resistance on it, and a hammer and sickle on his helmet. He manipulated the bolt of his Sten gun, and that was too much for Choltitz, who told him to rip off his badges. At that point there came a French lieutenant who saluted and asked whether he had the honour to be speaking to General von Choltitz. The Frenchman said, 'Will you give the order for a cease-fire?' Choltitz answered, 'Since you are in my bedroom, it's a little late for it.'

We were led off to Leclerc. Out in the street a huge mob had already assembled, and they screamed and spat at us, which was none too good. A French Red Cross van then drove us through Paris to the Préfecture de Police, where I was preparing myself to be sentenced to death. Instead, the behaviour was perfectly correct. About ten of us German officers were driven to the Gare Montparnasse, and on the way the Resistance men were polite. De Gaulle had arrived, and was with other officers, when Leclerc and Choltitz turned up. They agreed that fighting at the Stutzpunkte should be broken off. It fell to me and an escorting French officer to make the arrangements.

We drove out towards Vincennes, which was where I knew there were German troops. I told the Frenchman that he might be shot at and should therefore wave a white handkerchief. We crossed into the German lines and there my French officer was held prisoner, though really he had come under a flag of truce. My conscience still bothers me a little about this. But I was free. I had been in the hands of the French only one day. And I'd lived through the occupation of Paris from the first day to the last. "

▼ As the jubilant Parisians turn out the Nazi trappings from occupied buildings, a pair of civilians pose in a symbolic gesture of defiance and hatred in front of the Führer's portrait.

US National Archives

CHAPTER 17

BATTLE DIARY

DECEMBER 1943

26   MacArthur invades New Britain

FEBRUARY 1944

5   MacArthur takes Kwajalein in the Marshall Islands

10–18   US carriers launch attack on Truk in the Carolines. Japanese abandon Truk as fleet base

21   Nimitz' forces takes Eniwetok (Marshall Islands)

APRIL

3   After February attack, MacArthur takes Admiralty Islands

26   MacArthur takes Hollandia (New Guinea)

MAY

27   MacArthur invades Biak Island, which is reinforced by the Japanese

JUNE

3–9   US carrier-based aircraft attack Japanese bases on Palau, Peleliu, Truk and Yap

11–13   US carriers attack Guam, Saipan and Tinian in the Marianas

13   Ozawa sails from Borneo and Ugaki from Bataan and rendezvous in the Philippine Sea

15   Nimitz invades Saipan

19–20   Battle of the Philippine Sea

JULY

9   Saipan taken

AUGUST

1   Tinian taken by Nimitz

10   Nimitz advances and takes Guam

THE MARIANAS – TURKEY SHOOT

The islands of the Marianas chain point like an arrow at the heart of Japan. When the Americans landed on Saipan on June 15, 1944, the stage was set for a major sea battle in the Philippine Sea. In a two-day action, Admiral Marc Mitscher's fast-carrier strike-force, Task Force 58, tangled with Admiral Jisaburo Ozawa's First Mobile Fleet. With nine carriers in two groups, the Japanese planned to trap the US fleet between the hammer of their naval air power and the anvil of shore-based aircraft from the island of Guam. But, unbeknown to Ozawa, air attacks on Guam had destroyed almost all the Japanese planes, and the 300-plane Japanese strike force was matched by a total of around 1,000 US aircraft. The first Japanese wave on 19 June 1944 was intercepted about 50 miles from the fleet – only 20 aircraft penetrated the superior American Hellcat fighters to inflict damage on US warships. By the end of the day, 240 Japanese planes had been shot down, and two carriers sunk, including Ozawa's flagship *Taiho*. American tactics and intelligence, combined with numerical superiority and the poor training of new Japanese pilots, made the exercise so straightforward that it became known as 'The Great Marianas Turkey Shoot'.

At around 16.00 the following afternoon, Mitscher's planes discovered the position of the Japanese fleet. Taking a calculated risk – the fleets were 300 miles apart and the US planes would not return before dark – he launched a 216-plane attack, which sank the carrier *Hiyo,* damaged *Zuikaku* and *Chiyoda* and the battleship *Haruna,* and sank two oilers. Although it would make the ships vulnerable to attack, Mitscher ordered his carriers to switch on their landing lights to assist his returning pilots. The gamble worked: although 80 aircraft were lost in crashes, most of the pilots and crew were recovered. Ozawa's force was decisively beaten and defeat left the Japanese Combined Fleet ill equipped to stop the invasion of the Philippines four months later.

TURKEYS AND SHOOTERS

Buoyed up by a string of successes and reassured by their superiority of numbers, US morale is high. The Japanese are battle weary – but imperial pride forbids them to give up.

June 1944 would prove unforgettable for the land- and carrier-based pilots of America and Japan. The scene is set in the tropical heat of the Pacific Ocean for a confrontation between them.

Two accounts by pilots, one from each side, reveal how similar emotions went through their minds.

Commander David McCampbell was Commander of Air Group 15, the three fighting squadrons of the US carrier **Essex** *which took part in the battle against the Japanese Combined Fleet. He later became the most celebrated of US naval airmen and was awarded the Medal of Honor.*

" June 12, 1944, Admiral Raymond Spruance had led the 5th US Fleet to the Philippine Sea, preparing to invade Saipan and the other major islands of the Marianas chain, which were needed as air bases for the B-29 bombers to strike Japan. My carrier, the USS *Essex*, was part of the fleet's Task Group 58.4, which comprised three carriers, three cruisers and twelve destroyers. The other carriers were the *Langley* and the *Cowpens*. Rear Admiral W K Harrill was the officer in command. Altogether there were 15 carriers now with the 5th Fleet.

Our first task was to soften up the air defences of Saipan and the smaller island of Pagan which was important because it housed an airfield

with one small runway, and a number of barracks and shops. Saipan was the first objective. The job – destroy enemy aircraft.

Just before one o'clock on the afternoon of 11 June, we had the order to launch the planes. I led the air strike, which consisted of 15 fighters from the *Essex* and two dive-bombers along with a dozen fighters from the *Cowpens* and a dozen from the *Langley*. The two dive-bombers were rescue planes, equipped with extra life-rafts and other survival gear to drop to downed pilots. Later an amphibian or a submarine or a destroyer would pick the pilots up.

Seven of our F6F fighters carried 350-pound demolition bombs, and they dived from 12,000 feet and bombed at 2,500 feet, and then formed a strafing line and strafed the island from east to west. The other eight fighters stayed above flying cover until the bombing runs ended, and then they went down to strafe. For an hour and a half they concentrated on strafing runs on Saipan's airfields and seaplane bases.

The Japanese drew first blood. On the way in over Tanapag Harbour, Lieutenant Kenney's fighter was hit by flak. He was diving but he just continued to dive straight down to

◀ **Dauntless SBD dive-bombers fly in formation over the coast of Saipan, as landing barges wait offshore.**

▼ **On board the carrier USS Essex, F6F Hellcats of Commander David McCampbell's Air Group 15 are prepared for action, May 1944.**

the water and splashed. Lieutenant-Commander Brewer led the fighter attack on the harbour seaplane ramp. I saw his bomb strike in the middle of three seaplanes parked neatly on the ramp, and destroy all three.

Brewer then strafed, came around and headed out to sea. Five miles out at sea, northwest of Marpi Point, Brewer and Ensign R E Fowler Junior spotted a dark green Kawanishi flying boat called an Emily, with the dull red circles. They attacked. As they came up, several other fighters were shooting at the Emily. Brewer attacked from above on the side of the plane – he said he saw his bullets hit the Emily's number two engine and the port wing. Ensign Fowler reported that he attacked the cockpit and noticed that the plane was smoking. Twenty seconds later the flying boat turned over on one wing, dropped with engine aflame and smoke coming from the fuselage, and struck the water. It exploded in a geyser of smoke, water and flame.

Lieutenant-Commander Brewer turned west of the town of Garapan and saw three Zero fighters, but by the time he arrived on the scene, they had all been shot down by other American fighters.

This was our first encounter as an air group with enemy aircraft. We had heard a great deal about the Zero fighter. I was pleased to note that the F6F could stay with the Zero in turns, climbs and dives – particularly at altitudes above 12,000 feet, where most of the air action took place. I noted two deficiencies of the Zero – its lack of armour and its unprotected gas tanks. All but one of the Zeros I saw shot down that day went down in flames.

At about 2.30 I was flying 'mattress' (low air cover) and observing the attack. Suddenly a Zero came down from above our fighters and pulled up in a high wingover on my port beam. I turned into the Zero and gave it a short burst from close up – not more than 250 yards. The Zero turned over on its left wing. I followed and got in another short burst, got on the tail and gave the Zero another burst. The pilot made another wingover, but he was already going down. The plane fell off on the right wing and spiralled toward the sea. Another F6F followed the Zero down, firing. I remained in position. The Zero hit the water without burning and sank. No head appeared.

On 19 June Admiral Ozawa launched his first strike against the

▲ A group of US bomber pilots wait for the call to action, tension showing clearly on their faces as Captain Stuart Ingersol (left) prepares his men for the assault on Saipan.

▶ An F6F Hellcat comes in to land on the deck of Vice-Admiral Mitscher's ship, the carrier USS *Lexington*. Not all returning aircraft could be guaranteed such a clear landing deck as the battle heated up.

American fleet, beginning from Guam. At 10 o'clock our radar picked up a large force of 'bogies' approaching, distance 150 miles. At that point Commander Brewer was already in the air, in command of the combat air patrol, and he was ordered to take his planes up to 24,000 feet. We heard Brewer shout 'Tallyho! 24 rats, 16 hawks, no fish at 18,000' (24 fighters, 16 dive-bombers and no torpedo planes at 18,000 feet).

He then spotted 15 Judys (Aichi dive-bombers) at 18,000 in tight formation with four Zeros on each flank – and 1,000 feet above and behind, 16 more Zeros.

Brewer selected the leading dive-bomber and came up to 800 feet from the plane. The Judy exploded so quickly it was unbelievable. He flew through the debris and attacked another. This one blew up too, half the wing fell off and the plane cartwheeled into the sea.

Two minutes after Brewer's 'Tallyho', my fighter was launched, and I led 12 fighters to join in fighting off the attackers – but by the time my fighters were organised, the fighter controller announced that another raid was coming in – 50 planes travelling 150 knots, 45 miles

to the east. I was to intercept and stop them.

I took them up to 25,000. Two were affected by the altitude and their engines began to cut out, so I ordered them to orbit over the carrier. We had altitude and speed and when we reached the enemy formation, were able to make a high-speed run, leaving four planes above for protection.

My first target was a Judy (dive-bomber) on the left flank and approximately halfway back in the formation. It was my intention after completing the run on the plane, to pass under it, retire across the formation and take under fire a plane on the right flank with a low side attack. The plans became upset when the first plane I fired at blew up practically in my face, and caused a pullout above the entire formation. I remember being unable to get to the other side fast enough, feeling as though every rear gunner had his fire directed at me.

My second attack was made on a Judy on the right flank of the formation, which burned favourably on one pass and fell away from the formation out of control – a rather long burst from above rear to tail position. Retirement was made below and ahead.

My efforts were directed to retaining as much speed as possible and working myself ahead into position for an attack on the leader. A third pass was made from below rear on a Judy which was hit and smoking as he pulled out and down from the formation.

After my first pass on the leader with no visible damage observed, pullout was made below and to the left. Deciding that it would be easier to concentrate on the port wingman than on the leader, my next pass was an above-rear from seven o'clock, causing the wingman to explode in an envelope of flames. Breaking away down and to the left placed me in a position for a below rear run on the leader from six o'clock, after which I worked on his tail and continued to fire until he burned furiously and spiralled down out of control. During the last bursts on the leader, gun stoppages occurred. Both port and starboard guns were charged in an attempt to clear before firing again. I decided I must be out of ammunition and started back for the carrier. **"**

▲ Vital in the softening-up attacks on the island of Saipan, TBF Avenger torpedo-bombers warm up for action on the deck of a US carrier.

Yoshida Katsuyoshi was a naval warrant officer in the Japanese 202 Air Group when the Americans showed signs of moving against Biak Island. The Group transferred to the Island of Yap and then to the Solong base to make preliminary arrangements for operations.

" On 3 June, we were ordered to attack the enemy landing points on Biak. Apart from us, there were Army Hayabusa fighters, and Suisei (Comet) carrier-borne aircraft of 503 Air Group. We set off in high spirits.

When the carrier-borne planes had finished their attack, we dived down and strafed the enemy positions, firing at will. The skies over Biak were not the clear skies of the south – they were leaden and overcast, and I took off my tinted flying goggles during the attack. It was more important to improve, however slightly, my field of vision, though it added to the dangers. Ahead of me, and below, the carrier-borne bombers waggled their stubby wings and went into a dive, showing their bellies as they went down. Brave chaps. I watched them, but I also kept my eyes peeled for enemy aircraft coming suddenly in to the attack, but no enemy planes showed up – and, oddly enough, there didn't seem to be much flak either.

Then four planes of Sakaguchi's section, in front and to our left, went into a dive and disappeared from view. A short pause while I checked above and behind, then I signalled to my wing planes and we too went into a dive. So far, we had concentrated on what was happening in the sky, but as we went into our dive, I noticed the angle to the objective was pretty steep. Still, I could see a fair amount of supplies, tanks and ammunition had accumulated along the sandy beaches of the shoreline. I had the prize in front of my eyes and I could hardly change my goal now.

As I approached, the ack-ack fire was more intense than I had bargained for – the enemy was putting up a determined defence. I wasn't too clear about where the carrier-borne units were, or the section which had dived before, but I pounded the shore at close range. I could see enemy troops running away into the sea, as I strafed the stores, but I did not aim at them. I mean, from my experience so far, it was difficult to hit a running man.

The diving angle was poor, so I pulled out sooner than usual, but perhaps because I'd gone over the terminal velocity, my plane gave a protesting scream. When I looked round, I saw my wing plane climbing and almost at a stroke we had climbed to 10,000 feet. I drew breath, a sigh of relief, and looked

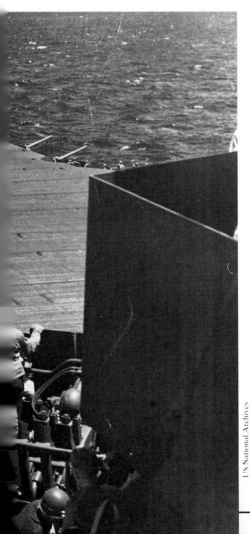

▲ The badge worn by fighter pilots of the Japanese Navy.

around. My wing man was keeping tight close behind me. I could not make out what was happening on the ground, apart from a few glimpses snatched here and there between the clouds. I wondered whether to dive again, and put her nose down, then, as I looked in the direction of New Guinea, I could see, far ahead in front, a dog-fight in progress. I flew straight towards it, and saw our planes were latching on to a four-engined PB2Y flying boat. I joined in. As our aircraft closed in for the

In a still shot from a captured Japanese newsreel, a Zero fighter takes off from the deck of a carrier to take on the massive naval air power of the United States.

attack, a door opened in the enemy plane and a W/T set and some heavy objects were thrust out. This was to enable him to increase speed a little – he was doing his best to escape. He was too low for me to fire at him from below, his weak spot, so I attacked right in front, and as he did a slow right turn and came within range, my shells passed by him on the left. I had already used up a fair amount of ammunition in the land strafing, and in this frontal attack I ran out of 20 mm ammunition.

Surely I must have scored some hits? I looked for some time, I felt sure he was going to go down – but he kept hanging on. I wanted to try one more attack, but I was out of ammunition, so there was no point. I turned towards Babo Base without being able to check the outcome.

On the west of New Guinea, Babo

▶ Deck crew on a US carrier watch as, right next to a sister ship, a Japanese fighter disappears into the sea — another victim of the US marksmen.

was in a marshy zone, which, seen from above, looked like solid earth. In fact it was only like that near the airfield. Further out there was jungle and swamp up to your waist, a place of oil gushers. When I looked down from above on the L-shaped runway, I had the feeling something was wrong, and when I landed, I heard that Captain Takao and WO Furuya of 603 Air Group had gone up to meet an attack by P38s some time before, and had been killed.

On 9 June, army reinforcements were being sent to Biak where the situation had gone against us. They were being taken in six destroyers and close escort was being provided by army and navy planes, taking it in turns. I Section, Captain Kagami, CPO Okano, PO Miyagaki, and II Section, myself and CPO Mishimoto and CPO Omori, made for Man-okwari. We found the six destroyers steaming eastward full speed ahead and, judging from their wake, they must have been doing something like 40 knots.

About 6,000 feet above them, as they zig-zagged, flew several B-24 bombers, carrying out horizontal bombing attacks. Our six Zeros instantly flew into the midst of the enemy bombers. Unfortunately, the ack-ack fire from our destroyers kept coming up to us, uncomfortably close. In such a situation, all we

could do was put our fate in Heaven's hands. Accurate aiming was not necessary, and we pressed the enemy close from the side, with one attack after the other. Then, when I took a glance in front and above, I saw those hated P38s sneaking up on us. There must have been more than 20 or 30 planes. We were too low to challenge them to aerial combat and there was no time to take up a position of advantage. We sailed right into the middle of them, a confused *mêlée*, and blazed away. Accurate aiming was out of the question, and all we could do was dodge their fire. I spotted my chance, I came out of the *mêlée*. I'd been hit two or three times, and with my wing tanks shot through I was likely to turn into a ball of flame at any minute. But I got back to Ekman Island base. PO Miyagaki failed to return.

On 17 June, I was transferred from Kau to Peleliu. It was the night before what was called afterwards 'The Battle of the Marianas' (the Battle of the Philippine Sea). In discussions, it was decided that 202 Air Group was to fill up the bomber gap. All our planes were to be fitted out with 60 kg bombs. We would become a fighter-bomber unit, and attack enemy forces landing on Saipan.

The next day, 18 June, reveille

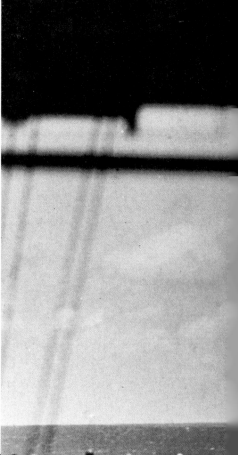

US National Archives

was at 3.30 am, and we set off, breathing in great lungfuls of the bracing air of Peleliu. After one and a half hours, we landed at the airfield on Yap. The ground crews bustled to and fro, filling us up with ammunition, bombs and fuel. At the control station, the Z-flag flew, as it had traditionally since the Battle of the Japan Sea, as if to stress the crucial importance of this battle for our country. I squatted down beside the runway to smoke a cigarette, and Furumura came up. He had been in the same reserve training unit as me. He was just as I remembered him, quite unchanged, the same thick black bushy eyebrows. We hadn't seen each other for a long time and there was a lot to talk about. From what he said, we were to set off together, as decoy planes, with the Suisei carrier-borne bombers. We slapped each other on the back and said we'd see who was the more skilful pilot of the two. I don't know whether it was a joke, or whether he was being serious, but he said 'I'll show you a good place to die'. That's how it ended.

We set out at 12 noon, a large formation of about 200 aircraft, and made a big detour east of Guam. The plan was to attack enemy ships at sea south-east of Saipan. When you fly for three hours with a load of two 60 kg bombs, the hand grasping the joystick gets tired. I felt tense just after setting off, but after an hour had gone by, then two hours, I felt pains in my legs and bottom in the narrow seat, and dull-spirited.

We were flying in a bomber role, so other fighter units were in formation in front of us and behind, and below and above us, acting as escort. Soon the southern shore of Guam came up on our left, and we came out over the eastern sea. About 30 minutes later, we were in enemy skies. I had been wounded two years before, and my neck was still not in good shape, so in order to be able to keep a lookout to the rear, I unfastened my shoulder seat belt. Flying upside down had to be done with one lap-belt.

I turned my head left, then right, then tried to move so that I could see to my rear. I worked the 7.7 mm gun and, as a precaution, went through the loading procedure again. The foremost interceptor unit was a fair way ahead, with its accompanying

◀ The naval battle may well have been a 'turkey shoot', but for many men who landed on Saipan, it was their last day. On a troop transport, the chaplain reads the service before a burial at sea.

▼ A twin-engined Japanese fighter, burning fiercely, plummets towards the sea as the American marksmen claim another victim.

▼ The waiting is over — a US pilot hurries to his torpedo-bomber as a strike is made on the airfields and Japanese aircraft based there on the island of Guam.

escort flying above it. I noticed they were flying ahead of our bombing unit, but perhaps because of the clouds I could not make out where they were making for.

After a while the bomber unit command plane began to lose altitude. Finally it seemed to be dodging between the clouds to go into a bombing run. I changed over the fuel cock on the wing tanks and took off my glasses. In an emergency I had the habit of removing my glasses, since I felt them to be a nuisance.

High overhead, our escort unit and the enemy fighters were already engaged in dog-fights. Today, whatever happened, we were going to introduce the enemy to our 60 kg bombs, but below the clouds our field of vision was not too good, and apart from ten transport ships up ahead, no warships could be seen.

Suddenly a bunch of fighters, ours and the enemy's, came falling down through the sky ahead, to my right. At the same time there was an uproar on all sides, and little time to take aim at a target. Even for objectives close to, the distance was too great for the height. The instant I became aware of this, the ack-ack fire from below became more intense than anything I'd experienced so far. A pillar of flame, as if from a dozen heavy ack-ack machine guns, roared past like an express train.

I felt a long time had elapsed up to the time I burst through, and I took a quick glance above and below, but whether or not our bombing unit had spread out, what entered my field of vision was about 20 or 30 aircraft, apparently suspended over a 5,000-ton transport, but the angle was too narrow for horizontal bombing. Partly from impatience to return to my true role as a fighter, I dropped my bombs from both wings.

An enemy fighter came in to attack me from the right as I tried to confirm what had happened below me, and I switched to the right to dodge him. The joystick had stiffened, and I put some force into it

and finally came out on top of the clouds, where both sides were engaged in dog-fights.

Some distance off, a number of aircraft were locked in combat and tracer shells flew to and fro. My wing plane was no longer behind me. I must have come out in the opposite direction of the cloud after dropping my bombs.

Then I tangled with a Grumman flying in the opposite direction. I made as if to climb and just an instant before colliding with him, I pulled the trigger from about 400 yards away. I'd meant to aim in front, but it shot past him to the right and behind. The cloud was thin, and I came out at once below it. The instant I was out, I could see I was somewhere off Saipan, I didn't know where, but I could see what looked like a military position and an enormous number of landing-craft.

I decided to dive straight down and strafe them. Aiming at a spot on the shoreline, I suddenly put her nose down. Once again, intense ack-ack fire came up at me. What ship was aiming at my plane? It seemed to be even fiercer than the ack-ack fire on shore. After glancing behind and above, I took aim at the enemy position which had come into my sights and squeezed the trigger. I felt terrific and let out a roar as if my 20 mm and 7.7 mm guns were bursting through at the landing craft which were touching down on the

▶ The bombing strikes are effective — Aslito airfield and its hangars lie in ruins, littered with devastated Zeros, after an American raid. These fighters, at least, would no longer challenge the US carriers.

◀ In the back of a jeep on a captured airfield on Saipan, Lt-Gen Holland M Smith takes stock of American progress.

▲ The naval aviation collar patch of the Japanese Navy.

▼ 'Come out now, the game's up.' Resigned to captivity and defeat, a Japanese prisoner at Marpi Point tells his comrades hidden in local caves to come out.

sandy strip of shore. The aircraft's nose juddered as I aimed and fired.

No flames burst out, so it wasn't very satisfactory, and I thought, let's put the finishing touches to it, but then I realised all my 20 mm ammunition had gone, so I climbed out through the middle of the dog-fight and turned the plane's nose towards Guam. As I looked around, I could see several streamers of black smoke on the surface of the sea, and in the sky, far off, distant aircraft looking like rubber balls.

A great many aircraft had returned to Guam by the time I came down. PO Kawada's big body was shaking and alive with gestures as he explained how he had shot down a Grumman. Below my flying cap, I was soaked in sweat.

Night came – 202 Air Group confirmed all its aircraft had returned, and gradually our spirits rose. But we had no quarters, and the evening meal was eaten sitting near our aircraft. We slept beneath the wings, using our life-jackets for pillows.

The next day, 19 June, we were attacked in the course of the morning by enemy fighter-bombers. Fierce encounter battles took place in the skies above the airfield, and we suffered casualties – a total of four pilots killed. In the evening the carrier-borne planes of 2 Air Flotilla were attacked by Grummans in the sky over the base, just as they came in to land. Half of them were shot to

pieces before they even knew what was happening.

On 20 June, reinforcements for 202 Air Group flew in from Yap and went up to meet the Grummans as they came in again for the attack. They shot down a fair number, but CPO Saito of 301 Flying Unit was hit – his engine conked out and he had to make a forced landing just outside the town. He was injured by the impact, but even so he returned ahead of us in good spirits.

Day by day, the situation on Saipan grew steadily worse and here on Guam, we fighter units lost nearly all our usable machines from combat actions and the ceaseless night and day bombing by the enemy.

I was selected to go and see the situation on Saipan on 22 June, because no news had come through. We had had no spare time for repairs on Guam, and by this time there were only two Zeros left. They were guarded the way a tiger guards its cubs. It was considered a great honour for me to be picked out of so many scores of aircrew, and I set off with PO Yamashita of 603 Flying Unit at 3 am, coming out west of Rota Island. The sea was so covered with huge numbers of enemy ships that it was hard to know where you were. There were also dozens of scout planes above them, but they did not come near us. Down below were two or three large carriers.

On the way back, we flew at a

height of around 21,000 feet and came into Guam from the north-east. We recced the situation on land for some time, and after confirming there was no danger, we landed.

We were attacked again, many times, on 23 June, but by this time we had no planes at all to send up against the enemy. When night came, reinforcements came in from 202 Air Group, making a marvellous landing in the darkness.

With the worst possible timing, my fever – malaria – broke out again on the 24th. Guam seemed to be done for, if the naval bombardment was anything to go by. Enemy landings couldn't be far off, I thought, but what could we do? We hadn't a single aircraft to send up against them. Nonetheless, I had a stroke of luck the following night. I think it was about 11 pm, a Type-1 Army Attack plane from Yokohama Air Group was on its way from Iwo Jima to make a night attack on Saipan. Its left engine conked out, and it had to make a forced landing. There were only a few people at the airfield, and after the engine was repaired, we asked the young aircraft commander, a captain, to take us with him. He agreed.

I don't recall clearly, I'm afraid, but I think that around seven of our eight men succeeded in escaping from Guam before the surrender.

Early next morning, we set foot on Peleliu. For the first time, I be-came aware how hungry I was. 🟄🟄

CHAPTER 18

BATTLE DIARY

DECEMBER 1941

14   Japanese Uno Force takes Victoria Point

JANUARY 1942

16   Japanese invade Burma

FEBRUARY

23   Battle of Sittang Bridge

MARCH

8   Rangoon falls

JUNE

17   Japanese reach Sumprabum (limit of advance)

DECEMBER

17   Lloyd's 14th Division launches First Arakan

FEBRUARY 1943

13   First Wingate group crosses Chindwin. Expedition ends early June

MAY

14   Maungdaw retaken by japanes. End of British Arakan offensive

AUGUST

1   Japanese proclaim Burmese independence

26   Formation of SEAC under Lord Mountbatten

OCTOBER

15   Slim becomes commander of Fourteenth Army

MARCH 1944

5   Fly-in of Second Wingate expedition

24   Wingate killed in air crash

JUNE

16   Kamaing taken

AUGUST

1   Myitkyina falls

27   Last Chindits leave Burma

BURMA – JUNGLE NIGHTMARE

Following the fall of Malaya and Singapore in early 1942, the Japanese enjoyed a reputation among British, Australian and Indian troops as invincible jungle fighters. By the spring, they had managed to push British and Chinese troops back to the western borders of Burma and into India. There, following the tough but indecisive Arakan campaign, the British and Indian forces were to win decisive battles at Kohima and Imphal in April 1944 and pave the way for the liberation of Burma. The first Allied successes, however, came from special forces operating behind Japanese lines.

Commanded by their founder, General Orde Wingate, the 77th Brigade, later known as Chindits – the name came from the *chinthe,* a mythical Burmese animal – marched into Burma to cut the Mandalay–Myitkyina and Mandalay–Lashio railroads. The first operation, between February and April 1943, was costly, with losses of 1,000 men, or about a third of the force. In terms of morale, however, the action was a great success: for the first time, the British had gone onto the offensive against their reputedly invincible adversaries. The following spring, the second Chindits expedition used the US Army Air Force to transport and support five brigades into bases in north-central Burma. Although the Chindits succeeded in cutting communications behind Japanese lines, they had a difficult working relationship with the US General 'Vinegar Joe' Stilwell, commanding Chinese forces to the north. The Chindits' own leader, the controversial Wingate, perished early in the campaign in an air crash.

Between April and July 1944, the Japanese 15th Army at Kohima and Imphal surrounded 50,000 British and Indian troops of IV Corps. During an 88-day siege, they failed to dislodge the defenders, until, starved of supplies and suffering from the monsoon, the Japanese were themselves defeated when the XXXIII Corps fought through to relieve Kohima and Imphal. Of the 65,000 Japanese dead, around half had died from starvation and disease.

JUNGLE NIGHTMARE

In monsoons and parching heat, plagued by diseases, insects and hunger, the British and Japanese hack through impenetrable jungle to confront each other

A lmost as if the fighting alone was not enough, the men in Burma were subjected to appalling conditions and shortages. Their home lives long since abandoned – but not forgotten – they would soon learn that nothing was as normal. Good health could not be taken for granted, supplies were just as unreliable . . . and for some, the very weapons they depended on were alarmingly unpredictable.

Martin McLane was Company Sergeant-Major of C Company, 2nd Battalion of the Durham Light Infantry. His story begins as his men are on a tropical island, training before the Arakan offensive. They have just received new guns.

" As CSM, I was scheduled to have one of these new Thompson sub-machine guns. We had received them without any instructions whatever.

The Company Commander came over to me and said, 'Bring my Thompson sub-machine gun – I want to shoot it'. Everybody wanted to shoot them – they were such an outstanding weapon.

The CC went on to the beach with me. He picks up the gun and fires one round. I said, 'Stop, sir. Wait. Wait'. He says, 'What's the matter?' 'I don't like the sound of that shot'. I was watching to see if I could see the streak of the round on the water.

'You're over-cautious. I'm going to fire'. He fired, and BANG. I looked round at this explosion, and I grabbed him – he was falling to the ground. I looked for wounds – but I couldn't find anything.

I was blaming myself – but it was not my fault really. The first round he'd fired hadn't cleared the barrel – so I would never have seen it on the sea. The second shot hadn't had a clear passage through the barrel, jammed and blew the gun to bits. Now that's just an example for what follows on later.

Eventually they decided to put us in by land, and we took over the positions from the Indian battalion which had been there for a few days. They had been having really jitter shoots-up. Now, jitters means that the Japanese, when they found anyone on defence, would fire crackers or spring grenades at you, hoping you would start firing and shooting them up. Or they would shout at you, trying to get you to fire, so they

could pinpoint your positions. We were told on no account to fire until we saw the whites of their eyes and, being English lads, we all obeyed.

It was decided, after a few days, to put in an attack on their four strong positions. Now, we were near the sea on the right, but there was flat land where we were. We were in the jungle and partially out in the open. The water, when the monsoons came, used to sweep down from the ridge and gouge out rivers in the soft soil on the seaward side.

There were three dried river beds and we had to attack over them. My company was to attack two points where the Japanese had been for some time. They used slave labour to dig a deep hole in the ground. They'd criss cross it with tree trunks to get a two-tiered bunker, solid

Martin McLane

against all sorts of shooting up.

Before we were due to attack, someone in a high observation post had seen a carrying party of Japs coming up with ammunition for these bunkers of a night-time.

They decided to send our guerrilla platoon, a group of our own men, trained like commandos, to do special stunts. Lieutenant Wilson was to take them across the *chung* (a water or tidal river), down by the beach and keeping them under cover, down to Fall Point, with an intent to ambush the Japanese carrying party. They all had Thompson sub-machine guns, rifles and grenades. They were dressed up commando-style, with blackened faces.

When they were due to put the attack in, I was on stand-by at our observation post, listening for the Thompson sub-machine guns firing – and I never heard them. But I heard grenades bumping. All of a sudden, up come running these lads, the guerrilla platoon, cursing and blinding – their Thompson sub-machine guns had blown up, the same as ours.

They should have had an enquiry on mine to find out the cause of the thing blowing up – but they didn't. Being wartime, they just accepted it as maybe a dirty barrel – but I had just cleaned the thing.

They decided that the American ammunition mustn't be waterproof. The propellant charge had got damp and wasn't driving the round out

▲ Company Sergeant-Major Martin McLane. After the disastrous action at Arakan, he stayed with his battalion until wounded at Kohima.

◀ Soldiers of the Tripura Rifles, armed with a Thompson sub-machine gun, prepare an ambush at Arakan.

◀ Troops of B Battalion, 5307 Composite Unit (Provisional) Merrill's Marauders – cross the Chindwin in northern Burma using a hastily constructed bridge.

Right and Left: US National Archives

US National Archives

with sufficient force to send it out of the barrel. The second round followed on because it was an automatic action, and blew the gun up.

Fortunately no-one was hurt. They withdrew my company out of the line altogether and decided to change all our ammunition.

The next day we went back down to our positions for the attack. We set off very early in the morning, in the dark, and filed our way down to a dried river bed. We lined up there for the attack. The artillery pounded the area in front with three-inch shells. They made quite a din.

It was just breaking daylight and over the top we went, with two platoons, 10 and 11, and Company Headquarters. Another platoon was detached to attack the other positions. My orders were to move the men from the first dried-up river bed and into the second – then wait. The other two platoons were to push on and go into the attack from there. Now they had to go to the third river bed, so I halted my men.

The CC didn't come up, and I decided to move up to the next river bed. As I went up to the next one, I saw a Japanese in a fox-hole. I didn't know how many were in there. I got my Thompson sub-machine gun up – and it wouldn't fire.

You've got grenades, but if you fling them in close proximity you'd kill your own men.

Anyway, we came back to where we were supposed to meet the CC – I wouldn't commit them to get injured if I could help it.

The attack went in – you could hear the shooting. The CO came on the set and asked what was happening. 'I've been on attacks before, sir, but this is a strange one to me. I can't hear any of our weapons firing, and they should be full blast as they went in – grenades and bren guns as they charged the bunkers. There were no rifle shots coming from the front'.

He told me to get the men moving, so I went out and found the CC. He was wounded, and I dragged him back. Then I went to the officer commanding A Company. Again I was told to get the men moving, so I run forward. The other river bed was insurmountable. The rain had gouged the earth out and it was like a steep cliff. We were carrying 76 lb of kit and couldn't get up there.

I looked for the platoon I was supposed to follow – but they had gone round to the right and come in at a lower part – so I ran round there. I was determined to get the men running and the attack moving.

I ran around a corner and there's the platoon commander, lying on a stretcher with 20 pieces of shrapnel in him. He said the attack had gone in and he'd lost a lot of men. I run round the next corner and there's a pile of dead men. The remainder of them were lying on the ground.

I said, 'Right, come on lads. We're going in to the attack'. One of the corporals shouted, 'Wait a minute,

Associated Press/Topham

Sergeant. Wait! The guns won't fire.

I tried a bren gun and a rifle – all the weapons we had. 'Hold it', I said. 'We're not going on the attack'. I run back to the set and tell the CO that the guns won't fire. Well, there's no man in his right mind would believe you!

The sergeant said, 'Let's go in with grenades' – a very brave man. They didn't have a lot of grenades, so I was to go to 9 Platoon and get all of theirs. These six men went in with grenades. They all got killed.

I ran round again through Japanese territory to where the other platoon was, and when I saw them, I nearly cried. Young National Servicemen who were brought up from Dunkirk, taught and made good soldiers – and they were lying on this river bed, devastated. They'd got in this steep trench and the Japs had just poured grenades on them.

I knew they couldn't do an attack because the body of the men had gone. The men couldn't get up the side, so I put two bren gunners up (they didn't know their guns wouldn't fire because they'd never had a chance to use them). I put both these men in for a gallantry award and both got immediate MMs.

◄ A domestic scene on the Arakan front as some British Tommies peel potatoes in a small jungle clearing.

▼ The insignia of the British 36th Infantry Division.

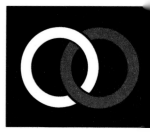

▼ Crewmen from a landing strip on the Ledo Road, Burma, conceal an L-4 Cub liaison aircraft used by the US Army, wheeling it into the jungle.

A terrific bang went off just above my head – it must have been a Japanese shell or one of our own dropped short – and it left me semi-conscious. When I recovered, I went on the set and explained to the CO that there were no men to go in and that it was foolhardy to go in with bren guns and rifles that wouldn't fire. I didn't know at the time that both of my eyes had turned brick red. The pupils were all right, but the irises were bleeding. I had a fuzzy head too, and the major sent me to the dressing station.

All the lads who were National Servicemen were a great credit to this country – great young men, great soldiers – and with hardly any training. They fought like heroes.

In a later attack, the CC says, 'We're in a serious state – have a look up there'. All this hill, right the way round, was covered with positions where the Japs could fire on to us. On a barren place at the front, the Japanese were digging in.

You could see them and tied in the middle there was a person in white and another one about five or six yards further down, tied to another tree. We assumed they were tied. It was only our brigadier, Cavendish, and the brigade major.

Now there's no way you can fire at them unless you're hitting the brigade commander and brigade major. They sited them right in the middle of this area where they were digging in. They were standing up, the Japs, and you would have loved to get a bren gun or a three-inch mortar – but we couldn't because we'd kill our own officers. They had to make a decision. If the Japs got dug in there, they would completely stop any evacuation we were going to try along the beach later. Eventually the Lieutenant-Colonel said, 'We've got to knock that position out'.

He let me look through his binoculars. They started firing, knocking the Japs out, and of course, the lumps of shrapnel killed the brigadier and the brigade major.

Now according to the Japanese story, the brigadier wasn't tied to a tree – he was found dead way behind the positions, dead with a piece of British shrapnel in him, and also the Japanese escort was dead with British shrapnel. That was a plant. I saw them and I'd swear on any Bible that I saw these two men slump. They were tied to trees and in a position where we had to fire on them. They were killed by our own 99 Field Battery. Contrary to all the history books you read, Arakan was a shambles. **"**

Private Ernest Faulkner was 23 when he was drafted out to the Far East. Although in the same regiment as Jim Howard (next page), his reminiscences are from the men's, not the officers', point of view.

▲ A group of Chindits, many with pants removed for the crossing, negotiate their way over one of the smaller rivers in Japanese-occupied Burma.

Ernest Faulkner

" We went through all the proper training for jungle warfare – marching and walking, sleeping out in the wild. We used to go on tea and rubber plantations, and of a night you could hear the beaters keeping the animals away. There were quite a lot of wild animals around – elephants and leopards.

We had scorpions and centipedes too. The chaps used to dig a pit and take a scorpion and a centipede and let them fight it out, taking a bet on it. Then they'd get a little snake and put it in too. The centipedes were five or six inches long.

We relied a lot on air drops of food and we used to look forward to them. A couple of times we ran out of rations. Once, one of our officers said to a chap, after we'd left one area, 'Go back and get the potato peelings'. We'd buried them in paper (we used to bury things like that). This chap had a tin of jam, so we dipped the peelings in it.

We were on half rations sometimes in Burma. Once I put these white panels out so that the aircraft could see where we were so food could be dropped. As it happened, we had to move on, and we went off so fast, I don't know what the result

was – but I did hear a story that they dropped rubber dinghies instead of food!

We were mainly on the defensive. In Burma they were building these roads right down to the Chindwin and as the roads progressed, we moved down to the Chindwin itself.

While they were building these roads, the army was preparing all these defences on the hills – trenches, so that when we did withdraw, it was already dug and all we had to do was wait for the Japs.

It was good thinking. It must have been about 50 miles we withdrew, from the Chindwin up into these hills. We went into prepared positions all the time, so we had an advantage on the hills. You only dug trenches when you were advancing. On the Ukhrul road, when we went round to the back of the Japs, we built our own trenches then.

We would just lie in wait for them in these trenches and they'd arrive – swarms of them. We were really

▲ Ernest Faulkner, pictured at the end of the war on a stopover in Doolally, India, where troops were gathered prior to repatriation.

outnumbered and on each hill we had a small number of men. Sometimes on a hill you'd just have a section of chaps – another might have a platoon, another one a company. The Japanese would capture one hill, then bypass the next one.

I wasn't actually on Nippon Hill, but I was on the next one. The Japs would attack Nippon Hill, but at the same time bypass it, working round, then capture another small hill. We were on Crete Hill, and they went around that one and captured this little pimple – Lynch's Pimple, we

US National Archives

500 yards. You never heard them – it was just SHOOSH.

When we got off that hill one night – we were just running across the road as they opened up their machine guns. You know we only lost one bloke. We were running through them and they were firing in the dark. We got just round a bend then, and saw the wounded Gurkhas, all bandaged up after they'd put in their counterattack during the night.

The Japs were really vicious – they'd fight to the end. They were so

◄ **A Japanese captured on the Arakan front is given tea and a cigarette by his Indian captors.**

▼ **Evacuation of wounded poses a problem in the jungle – but native craft make useful ambulances.**

good at camouflage and getting underground, they couldn't be seen by aircraft. The artillery would bombard them, but they were still there.

We, on the other hand, would attack during the day. We never got any peace or sleep at night. Half the night they'd shell you, then half an hour would go by – and then another attack. They'd do the same thing again, the Japs. On Nippon Hill they had barbed wire and left a gap, and you could see them there – they'd be shot down and a little while later another mob would come in. In the morning they had 60 to 70 bodies lying by the wire. They had no brains to alter their tactics.

The Company Commander used to shoot the Very light, and you could see and just sling the grenades at them. They seemed doped!

It was a job to get hold of any prisoners, but we started getting more on the Ukhrul road. They all had their hair shaved off. They were only kids, a lot of them. Maybe it was shock – or it could be they were brain-washed. They knew their officers would mow them down with their swords if they failed them.

On several occasions we found these Japs, not a mark on them, with

US National Archives

had only a section of men there and they overran them.

They did manage to cut us off by this tactic eventually, but the Gurkhas went in on the last night and put in a counterattack. They didn't completely get rid of the Japs – they had so many men – but somehow we got ourselves and the wounded down.

The Japs' main attacks were by night – daytimes there was just shelling with mortars. They had these 105s and 75s, and you could tell what they were by the noise. With a 105 you knew you had a few more seconds – you got used to it. They had a 72, and when they used to come over you had to get down quick. They were nearer – didn't fire so far away. The worst ones were these whizzbangs – little things on wheels – cannons deadly at about

In the monsoons you were never dry. You got used to it and plonked down where you were in the mud. The gas cape was your only protection. We were on the move and it would take all day to get up one hill, slipping and sliding in the mud with these mules – they went through hell. We had elephants too, on some hills. We fed them on special rations which came on the air drops and they ate grass and bamboo too. Boys would give them biscuits – mouldy stuff from their rations. The corned beef was really corned mutton and when it was hot you'd open the tin and it would come out liquid. Horrible. It was rotten, but we'd boil it up as a stew. I think it was the First War rations – some of them had 1918 on the bottom. We had some Canadian rations too – Quaker Oats – and they were full of weevils. You just put them in the pot too.

Eventually we knew the Japs were taking hell of a beating and withdrawing all the time. The men were pushing the Japs back on to us. It was a nightmare for them. You should have seen the graves. Bones and arms sticking out – they couldn't bury them. We knew we were winning. 🙶

deadly with a mortar – and the first thing you know about a mortar is that you've got a bomb among you.

We developed an attitude of crawling about the jungle – we stalking them and them stalking us. We had a Gurkha battalion with us and a Sikh battalion and we all learned from each other. We got acclimatised to the jungle. You'd get people in high command saying, 'It's only seven miles – ought to be able to do that in a couple of hours'. Seven miles in thorn jungle in Ceylon takes you *five days*. You learned that sort of thing. More important, the officers and commanders learned too. The generals knew what to expect. If some idiot from Corps HQ said, 'It's only seven miles – do it in a couple of days', a general would say, 'Don't be silly, it's going to take them a fortnight.'

In Ceylon we picked up about seven to ten casualties a week with malaria. It was recognised that you couldn't expect to operate in that sort of country without doing something about it – so they got top scientists from the UK and they brought out malarial suppressants. It took a month to get anywhere, and by that time 40 per cent were down

▲ American Second Lieutenant William Murray, leader of the Khaki Combat Team 5307, collects his K rations for a long route march with Merrill's Marauders.

▶ Easter Sunday 1943, the RAF comes to the rescue of a group of British raiders, many of whom are sick and wounded, and all running out of supplies, with a drop of vital food and equipment.

skin like a new-born baby. They must have been killed by the blast. We found bodies stone dead without a mark on them. They couldn't have known a thing about it. They used to have these Jap flags tied around their waists – when they captured a hill, they'd put the flag up. A lot of them had flags – it was an honour to get there first.

On another hill at Tamu there was an outbreak of scrub typhus – we lost a lot of blokes through that. We were on this hill and, one night when I was on guard, there was a sort of earth-tremor. I sort of went up in the air and the ground shook. We heard it was an earthquake along the Brahmaputra. After that, everyone was going down with typhus. The order came that we had to scrape all the green vegetation off the hill and burn it. They reckoned these ticks were living on it.

We did this patrol for six or seven weeks and no-one was allowed to shave – in fact, our CSM did shave, and they busted him down to a sergeant. It was in case they cut themselves and got an infection. We ended up like a load of tramps.

Fleas – don't talk to me of fleas. We went up on this hill and there were head-hunters' huts. When you came out of them, you were running alive – scratching.

Jim Howard was Second Lieutenant with the 1st Battalion of the Devonshire Regiment – otherwise known as 'the 11th of Foot' or 'the Bloody Eleventh'. The name was coined by the Duke of Wellington in 1811 due to the frequency of their getting decimated . . .

🙸 We got put on a ship – no-one knows why – and sailed up to Karachi. Nobody knew what the hell we'd come for, so we spent six or seven weeks there, until someone said we were expected in Ceylon.

There was me with these bright little gold pips and 20 years of age. I don't think that any of my men had served less than six months in jail, but they looked after me like a child. They were in command – I wasn't. We joined the battalion in May 1942 then did some really first-class 100 per cent training. It was good – awful but absolutely first-class.

One thing that was a great comfort – and was always true – is that the Japs are a lousy shot. If he gets a machine gun, he'll tear hell out of the trees above your head, and with reasonable luck he'll get nowhere near you at all. But he's absolutely

with malaria. In action, if someone came down with malaria, they'd be taken off. Later in '44, the Americans were there with these tiny light aircraft and they'd take you away.

We would wander around in the jungle singing – in the most unmelodious sense – *You are my Sunshine* – in the pitch dark. Wherever the Devons went you'd hear this converging through the jungle. We always had scouts out in front making a single track through the jungle. If you've got mules with you you've got to cut it twice as wide and it takes you twice as long. Something happens – and you can hear it. Everybody just scatters – the whole column disappears, because you're all mobile. You've got nothing – everything you've got is with you, on your mule or on your back.

It was a very relaxed war for the Devons. I said to my sergeant one day, 'Look, somebody reckons there are some Japs down there'. He replied, 'Ooh ar. I should leave them alone, sir. They ain't doing you no harm'. That's what we did.

In Ceylon there's either a Russell's viper or a yellow-banded krait – deadly little bootlace snakes. They were so miserable in the monsoon that they snuggled up inside our monsoon capes with us to keep warm. I remember a chap came in and asked 'What's this?' with a deadly krait in his hand.

In battle you knew what would

happen if you were captured – so you didn't surrender. *They* didn't surrender. There was no heroism involved – it just wasn't one of the options open to you. We lost one officer as a prisoner – we were pretty sure he was killed, and I'm sure we didn't lose anybody as prisoners. Nobody thought of surrendering any more than the Jap did.

Surrender wasn't an option, which makes it a lot easier for a young officer. When you fought a reasonably civilised enemy like the Germans (not including Buchenwald) you've got a chance of being treated decently as a prisoner – but not with the Japs.

A young officer was never under pressure to surrender to save unnecessary casualties. It takes a load off your mind. The troops never wanted that either – it was a different fighting ethic from any other circumstances. You just fight on to the logical conclusion. It reduces your options – it was win or die, and that was it. **"**

![rising sun flag] *Toshio Hamachi was a section commander in No 3 Platoon, Sakazawa Company of Takemura Battalion. After months in Burma, the battalion commander, Takemura, assembled all his companies to plan an attack on the Chindits towards Katha.*

▲ **US Corporal Bernard Martin of the 5307 Composite Unit compares weaponry with an Indian soldier – but all their rifles are united in the same purpose in the end.**

▶ **Major-General T Wynford Rees, leader of the 19th Indian 'Dagger' Division, gives cigarettes to Gurkha troops who are about to make an attack.**

" I got the job of recceing the enemy situation. I was to give a burst of rapid fire if I met the enemy, then leave at once.

With a feeling, 'This is it', we gripped our bayonets and felt the hot blood coursing through our veins. 'Fix bayonets!' I gave the order. The men whipped their bayonets from their scabbards and fixed them firmly on the end of their rifles. The yellow gold sun began to glow on the horizon. Suddenly, through a gap in the clouds, a US Mustang hurled itself on us. Someone screamed, 'They've spotted us! Scatter!' Then there was the metallic scream of the aircraft diving low, raking the ground with machine-gun bullets.

I heard someone panting up behind me. It was Lance Corporal Toshio Hakobe. 'Section leader, it's the enemy!' He pointed. 'That house there – they're coming this way!'

Lance Corporal Iwama, Corporal Moriyama, PFCs Fujii, Kato and Inaba vanished into the trees, keeping an eye open for the enemy.

As they moved off – can it have been about 800 metres away? – eight enemy soldiers carrying rifles came into view. 'Kato, watch out for enemy on our flank, now!' I warned him. 'Yes, sergeant. I can see three

more men'.

Moriyama stood beside him, tense, and hissed to Hakobe, 'You've got the LMG – shoot them down!' I controlled them. 'Wait! It's too soon to fire'. Meanwhile, the enemy, quite unawares, came along the path towards us. Moriyama said to me, 'Let's do something.'

As he urged me on, I watched the enemy come up, step by step, then gave the order. 'Right, let the bastards have it. Kill the lot!'

They were about 500–600 metres away. Hakobe had quite a reputation as a marksman with the LMG – 100 shots, 100 bull's-eyes. I was confident he would deal with the enemy, and left it to him. I saw the khaki uniforms coming closer. '300 metres, FIRE!'

Their rifles spat fire, the bullets tore into the enemy soldiers. They were obviously taken completely by surprise, but at once they began to return our fire. Four of them were hit as they ran forward. Brave chaps, even though they're the enemy. On the edge of the group one of them was hit by a burst from the LMG and fell to the ground, soaked in blood and moaning in pain.

'Corporal Hakobe, you're firing high! 250 metres, fire lower!' I

yelled. He gripped the LMG and cut a swath with it from left to right. Three of the enemy dropped. They were down on the ground now, crawling forward – but when they saw one of their men fall in front of their very eyes, they panicked. 'Cease fire! Take the enemy alive'.

I searched the blood-soaked corpse of one of them. Cigarettes, chewing-gum, tins – and distributed it round the section.

We continued to sweep north in pursuit of the disappearing phantom enemy airborne troops, cutting our way through the thorny creepers. The men moved slowly forward further and further into the interior, 2 km, 3 km. A mood of disquiet and unease began to come over the men. The path was a series of hills covered in deep forest – it was simply an endless track, covered in weeds.

We broke off the search and returned to our unit. At the time, the enemy force was reputed to have increased to 10,000 men.

The main body of the company kept recceing the area, but the airborne troops were forever changing their ground and never showed up.

Two days before Sakazawa Unit arrived at Katha, a British airborne unit tried to cross the Irrawaddy in

broad daylight. They were seen by one man of the Japanese garrison unit who was bewildered and paralysed with fear when he saw them. The garrison put together two sections in charge of an NCO and hid behind the embankment to observe the enemy on the opposite bank. The marksman of the group, LMG already aimed at the enemy, nervously fingered the grip as he waited impatiently for the command.

The enemy was crowded on to wooden rafts, their weapons and ammunition piled up, with mules to complete the load. It looked to be only 80 metres across at this point, as the raft left the river bank.

The LMG chattered and spat flame, breaking the peace and calm of the river. The enemy troops, crowded and bunched together on the raft, were mown down with no chance of returning our fire.

In the smoke, the screams of the British troops in their agony were drowned by the din of the rifles and the LMG. You could hear the mules whinnying as the bullets found their mark. It was as if the enemy were so many blood-sacrifices. The bullets sang in the midst of the scattering spray of water. 'Got you! Die, you hairy bastards!' our men shouted.

Those British troops who were still alive dived into the water, only to sink into the weeds at the river bottom. In the eddies you could see the profuse bright blood of the British troops. It was the work of a moment, and we had knocked the heart out of the astounded airborne troops. **"**

▲ **A British Howitzer crew, concealed with jungle camouflage, go to work in the scorching heat and hostile conditions of a unique theater of war.**

CHAPTER 19

BATTLE DIARY

SEPTEMBER 1944

1	Eisenhower takes command of Allied ground forces. Montgomery promoted to Field Marshal
3	Brussels liberated
4	Antwerp liberated: Montgomery proposes 'full-blooded thrust' to Eisenhower
10	Montgomery and Eisenhower meet in Burssels. Market Garden is given go-ahead. US troops cross German border
17	Air borne landings take place around Arnhem, Nijmegen and Eindhoven. British XXX Corps attacks towards Eindhoven. 2 Para captures north end of Arnhem bridge
18	XXX Corps links up with 101st Airborne Division near Eindhoven
19	XXX Corps and 82nd Airborne link up at Nijmegen
20	Bridge at Nijmegen captured
21	2 Para surrenders north end of Arnhem bridge. Attempt by XXX Corps to break out from Nijmegen fails. First Airborne pinned by Germans around Oosterbeek
22	Polish tropps dropped around Driel. German counter-attack cuts off road to Arnhem north of Veghel
23	Attempt by Poles and XXX Corps to cross Lower Rhine and reinforce First Airborne fails
24	Second attempt to reach First Airborne fails
25	British First Airborne withdraws over Lower Rhine

ARNHEM – NO GARDEN PARTY

As the Allies in Europe turned their attention to the German homeland, Field Marshal Montgomery proposed operation Market Garden, a plan intended to outflank German defenses on the River Rhine. In Market, US airborne divisions would capture vital bridges across the Wilhelmina Canal and the Maas, the British First Airborne Division the bridge at Arnhem on the Neder Rhine. In Garden, meanwhile, the British XXX Corps would drive north from Belgium to link up the bridgeheads.

The initial landings took place on September 17, 1944, and by the evening of the next day the XXX Corps had linked up with the 101st at their bridges at Zon and Veghel. The British reached the 82nd Airborne at Grave by 08.20 and in a joint operation captured the bridge at Nijmegen on the 20th. The Germans responded with vigorous counter-attacks which at times succeeded in cutting the 64-mile-long road linking the bridges with British forces in Belgium.

At Arnhem, however, the British paratroops landed in an area in which the Second Waffen-SS Panzer Corps was refitting: the Germans reacted quickly. Signals equipment did not work correctly and bad weather prevented the Allied air forces flying in close support. Despite the setbacks, the Second Batallion Parachute Regiment reached the northern bank of the road bridge and, under heavy attack, held it for several days. The rest of First Airborne were meanwhile trapped in the suburb of Oosterbeek.

On September 21 the Polish First Airborne Brigade was dropped at Driel on the south bank of the Neder Rhine in an attempt to reinforce the British survivors. They were joined by 43rd Wessex Division, which had fought its way overland, but on September 25 Montgomery decided that the First Airborne would have to be evacuated. The failed operation had cost 1,130 dead and 6,000 captured.

NO GARDEN PARTY

As Operation Market Garden progresses and as new problems emerge to thwart Allied plans, the men on the ground discover that the enemy is by no means throwing in the towel.

After all the false alarms, 1st Airborne Division was in action at last. The operation was designed to bring about peace by Christmas – but that was without the quick, violent German retaliation which met them. From the battle that ensued, airborne officers would always remember the extraordinary spirit and morale which saw their men through merciless close fighting.

Brigadier J W Hackett DSO, MBE, MC (now General Sir John, GCB) was commander of the 4th Parachute Brigade. Injured after six days' furious fighting, he discovered the extraordinary compassion and determination of the Dutch Resistance workers as he made his recovery.

" It was really a major error not to open the port of Antwerp before this operation. I'd add to this, that it was really very important to get the 1st British Airborne Division into action.

This Division was really the cream of the British Army at the time. These were very highly motivated, highly trained men, who had been much mucked about. They had something like 15 abortive operations, on three of which we were already in aeroplanes with our parachutes on ready for take-off, all our letters to our loved ones posted. Then somebody would come round, open the aircraft door and say, 'It's all cancelled, everybody gets three days' leave.' You can't go on doing that without irreparably damaging the morale of a first-rate, highly strung, wonderfully trained, admirably chosen and officer-manned division – without its going very badly downhill. Even though the omens were not good, it was important to go.

The best commander of an airborne formation in the whole war, Jim Gavin of the 82nd American Airborne Division, said: 'If you are going to put down an airborne force some way away from the objective, you ought to reconsider the plan – and perhaps even cancel it – because unless you put them down close on it, even with casualties which you have got to be prepared to take, you would probably fail.' You see, what they did to us was put us down six to eight miles from the objective. They feared the flak defences of Deelen Airfield which, when we got up to them, proved to be far less formidable than expected.

There is the added complication that airborne operations depend very largely on surprise. The 17th September was the day on which Market Garden opened, and when the first lift of the 1st Airborne Division went in. I commanded the second lift the next day, when surprise had gone, and instead of brandy and bonhomie, we met a whole lot of angry Germans.

The loss of surprise was really very painful, and this distance from the object was of critical importance. You see, my orders were to take the 4th Parachute Brigade in and defend the northern outskirts of Arnhem town, which would be the bridgehead around the crossing, seized by the 1st Parachute Brigade under Gerald Lathbury – Johnny Frost commanding the 2nd Parachute Battalion and putting up that magnificent performance at the bridge.

People who hadn't fought the Germans enough generally thought everything was a piece of cake, but the thing about the Germans was that they were the finest professional army fighting in World War II, and whatever there was on the ground that was weak, as soon as you threatened something vital, the German response would be swift and violent. We were told, on the intelligence available, that there were only a few Mark I tanks on the Corps front, and units of trainee cadets with a battalion of broken-down old men they called the 'stomach battalion' (men who were unfit for much more than garrison guard duties) were all we would find. That is what XXX Corps and 21st Army Group told us.

I was asked, 30 years after the war, 'When did you first realise that this operation was, if not doomed to failure, at least, not very likely to succeed?' I said, 'Before it began,' and recounted my own experience.

I had a final briefing with all the officers of the Brigade and key personnel – about 100 people. I went through, in meticulous detail, what we were to do, down to platoons, in the occupation of the northern defences of Arnhem town, to form the bridgehead around 1st Brigade's seizure of the bridge. When it was all over, I dismissed everyone but the

▲ 'Shan' Hackett, 'a remarkable little man with a pugilist's nose, sharp alert eyes and a personality which can only be called vivid . . . a wonderful leader and as gallant as any man I have ever met' (Gen. Roy Urquhart). Hackett's 4th Parachute Brigade arrived on the second day of the operation.

◄◄ From the cover of a damaged house in the Oosterbeek area, a British paratrooper keeps watch over the grounds for retaliation by enemy snipers.

◄ In the words of Lieut. Hardy, 'It was not easy for our pilot to pick a stretch of turf to make his landing that did not have a glider wing sticking into it from either the right or left side – but he managed it. There were gliders everywhere.'

All photographs: Imperial War Museum

▲ Not all, apparently, cast into deep despair by being captured, German prisoners are marched to the tennis courts of the Hartenstein Hotel where they will be allowed to dig themselves trenches in which to shelter from their own forces' shellfire.

▶ British troops guard their own Company HQ from a slit trench. It was partly due to the heavy forest which covered the area that radio contact between units broke down, causing untold problems of co-ordination and planning.

three Battalion Commanders and key personnel and said, 'Now, you can forget all that. Your hardest fighting and worst casualties will not be in the defence of the northern perimeter of Arnhem town, but in trying to get there.' We never did.

We now come to Ultra. We didn't have Ultra – it didn't come down to divisional level. It only came down cooked in the form of coded interpolations in intelligence summaries. It certainly didn't come down to Corps, let alone Division – and as for Brigade, that would have been laughable.

Brian Urquhart – not Roy – was G2 Intelligence in Boy Browning's Corps HQ, 1st British Airborne Corps, and had some inkling that there might be German armour in the area. He might have had some sort of spill-over from Ultra, but Brian had tacked on to a fighter sweep going over the area two days before some oblique reconnaissance photography. There was clearly some armour there, and it wasn't old Mark Is at all – in fact, as we knew later, and as the outcome says, they were the 9th and 10th SS Panzer Divisions, going to refit in Germany. They were not fit to go into battle as armoured divisions, but they did have a few tanks and some SP guns, and it wasn't difficult to rustle up some more along the railway line within 24 hours.

On the 18th they were too much for us. I did what I was intended to – I tried to move in, but it was quite impossible because of the tanks. What can lightly armed airbornes do against even a trace of heavy armour?

The tragic thing – and this relates to the whole battle – was that General Urquhart, who was a splendid battlefield commander – the best battle-fighting general I ever served under, a great, imperturbable, courageous fighting Scot, and a marvellous man – went forward to see for himself what was happening at the bridge, owing to the fact that signals communication was not of the best and, indeed, failed on the very first day. He got pinned by the enemy there and couldn't get out.

There he was, incommunicado, for about 36 hours at a really crucial stage of the battle. Had he been back in command and in touch, he would have called off the 4th Parachute Brigade from this abortive attempt against hopeless opposition to the northern end of the town, and put it into the reinforcement of Frost and the perimeter the Division had established around Oosterbeek.

Pip Hicks, the brigadier commanding the 1st Airlanding Brigade of glider-borne infantry, had been designated by Roy to take command of the division in the event that he, Roy, was a casualty, and his chosen successor, Gerald Lathbury, was also a casualty. Then the only brigadier who was a dyed-in-the-wool infantry soldier, Pip Hicks (Roy used to refer to me as 'my broken-down cavalryman'), was going to take over. But nobody told me of this, so when I got into the Division on the night of the 18th, having had some pretty stiffish fighting that day and prepared for much worse on the day to come, I found that Pip Hicks was in charge, and they really were in a state of confusion. It was a mon-

strously tangled situation. The idea was that I should go on doing what I had originally been intended to do, but I said, 'I want some orders about this.' Nobody was in a position to give any orders, so I said, 'This is a simple, staff duties exercise – let's treat it as such. I need to know my objectives. I need to agree with you phase lines – a central thrust line. I want to know who is on my right, who is on my left – what the boundaries are, and inclusive to whom, what support I am going to have.' But nobody had thought these things out.

Finally I had a bit of a showdown with Pip Hicks and said, 'Look, you're senior to me in the army, but I'm senior to you as a Brigadier commanding brigades in this division. I have it in mind to exert the authority this gives me to take command of this division, and give myself the orders I need. I will then go back to the 4th Para Brigade, hand the division back to you, and carry out the orders I have just received.' So I did – it was simply a very tidy way to resolve it. I wrote my own orders and took them away – but they were impossible because of the opposition which was building up in front of us.

Why did the Guards Armoured Division never arrive to relieve the 2nd Para Battalion? There were some good reasons for this. One was, I believe, XXX Corps planning. There was a euphoria that hovered over everyone after this dash from Normandy to Holland – a wonderful, thunderous advance of a victorious army against an enemy defeated, but not destroyed and still formidable.

They were so cockahoop they thought it was all a bit easy. Then there was the choice of the single road from Nijmegen to Arnhem – that really was a great mistake. This road is about 60 km long, and built on an embankment running across low-level fields. You couldn't everywhere get tanks off the road because very often the fields on either side were too wet and boggy – and it was very easily interrupted by well-placed anti-tank guns. As I later

discovered, when the Dutch Staff College used to do exercises on an approach to Arnhem from Nijmegen, anybody who moved straight up that single road got no marks!

Urquhart withdrew into the perimeter around Oosterbeek about the 20th, and I was brought in, my brigade very ragged, but splendid – this lot were absolutely first-class. They'd had a terrible time, and suffered a reduction from about 1,000 to 300, and that didn't do their morale any good, but they were absolutely on top of the world. Urquhart divided the last bridgehead of the 1st Airborne Division into two halves, one commanded by Brigadier Hicks, the other righthand half commanded by me.

I was wounded on the 23rd and was carted off to St Elisabeth's Hospital in Arnhem. I got a splinter in the stomach and spent four and a half months in Holland, hiding.

My dear wife knew that I was alive, but in poor shape – this thing inside had carved ten perforations and two sections in the lower intes-

tine – and one perforation is lethal! A miraculous operation was done on me by a British airborne surgeon.

I had made myself a Lance Corporal – I didn't want them to know they had a parachute brigadier because they might want to add me to their butterfly collection, and it was my intention that they shouldn't do that. Then, because the last of my three Battalion Commanders was dying there, and I wanted to get from him accounts of recommendations for honours and awards, I promoted myself to Major, so I could share his room until he died.

I was helped out of the hospital by the Dutch underground and spent the next four months, hidden, nursed, cherished, fed, loved, by a Dutch family – four elderly ladies

▼ Firing from open ground towards German positions in the distant trees, a paratrooper mans a 75 mm howitzer. Without radio communication to keep the companies informed of German movements, the men needed to be on constant alert.

and the son and daughter of one of them. That's why my book is called, as it is, *I was a Stranger* – it's a thinly disguised sermon on a text in St Matthew – but it's interesting stuff.

In the house where I was hidden, I was put up in the loft or down in the cellar when the house was searched. I read – one of the aunts had trained as an English teacher and she had a bunch of books in the house – the authorised version of *The Bible* (I must be one of few people who has read the whole of *The Bible*, straight through). That was how I occupied myself – I read the *Complete Shakespeare* too. I would read a tragedy in the morning and two comedies in the afternoon. I had a Greek testament as well, and one or two other books – *A Thousand and One Gems of English Poetry* – but

▶ With a German SP gun only about 80 yards away, a team of British paras man a six-pounder anti-tank gun in the cover of trees. Perhaps it is a gloomy portent that their gun bears the name 'Gallipoli' – scene of an earlier massacre of Australian troops.

what I really pined for was Thackeray and *Paradise Lost*.

I learned some Dutch and I was our military correspondent for a Dutch underground newspaper. We used to have a little wireless under the floor and we'd listen to the odd broadcast. Then I would write a column called *Notes on the War in the West* by our military correspondent, in English. It only went to three editions because the *Gestapo* got on to it, and they had to move me somewhere else less dangerous.

It is remarkable, the degree of adaptability in the human constitution. You live a life which you consider to be normal, and suddenly you are thrust into something quite different. It's astonishing how soon that becomes the norm, and you live that life as if you had always lived it. It is when you come back that it's difficult to adjust.

When I got better I'd be allowed to come downstairs. My presence was a very closely guarded secret – and of course, friends used to come and call. It would be December and dark early and I'd be coming down to the *Huiskamer* (parlour) and, before coming in, the door would be just ajar and I would touch it with my foot so it swung slightly as it would from a draught. One of the old ladies would get up and excuse herself to come out. If there was nobody there, or if there was nobody it would be dangerous to have see me, they'd invite me in. Otherwise I'd be told to wait upstairs.

When I got home, I couldn't, for weeks and weeks, go down to my own drawing room without just touching the door first. That was the norm – how I lived. **"**

▼ A group of Germans use rifles and a machine gun to cover an area of open ground beside a tree-lined road. Much of the fighting in this terrain was between small groups of infantry.

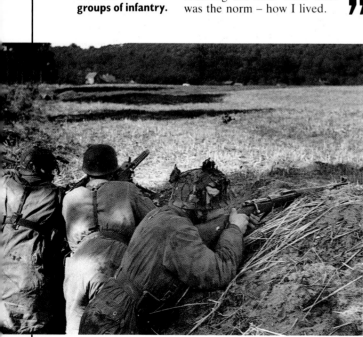

Bundesarchiv-Koblenz

 Lieutenant Joseph Hardy of the Border Regiment landed outside Arnhem. His actions under fire and, as the recommendation for his MC stated, 'his vigour and contempt for danger', were largely responsible for the successful withdrawal of B Company to the main Battalion position.

" My unit had been cut about in the Sicily and Italy affairs, so that a lot of our men were very young, and quite new to this fighting business. I thought that I had seen it all before, until I reached a point possibly half way towards the area where we were to congregate. Here I found two young lads, so delighted to be back on to *terra firma*, that they decided to get their gear off and brew up a cup of tea. I screamed at them so long and loud that I might have been heard five miles away, reminding them that this was war, not some sort of bloody picnic – but it was extremely hard to keep a straight face. Within seconds I had them back into their gear and travelling towards the forming up area at a very healthy pace, probably muttering to themselves that Joe Hardy was a rotten old b . . . . . .

Our duty was to hold the landing strips until the second lift came in, but the weather broke down in England and things started to go wrong. We eventually took up our positions to cover the western side of a defence circle, and found that it was much more heavily wooded country than we had expected it to be. At the time, all our communications were by wireless, and in the wooded country, reception of signal was very, very, poor. We were able to make contact with A, C and D Companies, but B Company, who had been sent right out to the western edge of the defence perimeter, were completely out of touch. It was considered that they would be the first to be hit by any enemy force advancing from the west, so it became imperative that, as their wireless link was screened out, the next best thing was to run a telephone line out to them.

The only two persons who had no specific duty other than to supervise, were myself and Signals Sergeant, Jock McClusky. Off the pair of us went, hell for leather, down the Utrecht Road to the village of Renkum. We arrived there just on dark, tested the line and it worked like a dream. No problems at all.

I had expected that B Company

Imperial War Museum

would be sitting astride the Utrecht/Arnhem road, so that when the enemy came along, they would be able to surprise them then, as enemy weight increased, they would be able to disengage and move back to the outer perimeter of the battalion position. However, the company had reached the village of Renkum then turned left down a lane towards the river. It did not strike me as being a good position – but I had them back in touch with the telephone.

Jock and I jumped into the jeep, me in the passenger seat, with a Sten automatic laid across my knee, and we made our way up the lane to the main road. Just before the lane joined the main road, there was a fairly steep rise in the ground and as we neared the road junction, I saw the outline of two soldiers, heading towards Arnhem. The Company Commander had not told me that he had any men this far up the lane – they were not B Company men at all – they were Germans.

Jock slammed the brakes on, and I half leapt and was half thrown over the bonnet of the jeep. I landed at the feet of the two German boys with my automatic pointed at their guts, and the only stupid thing that I could think of to say was, 'How's about it, chum'. I honestly believe that they

cycle and sidecar drove into the HQ and all the soldiers rushed over, no doubt to ask what was going on. It is hard to estimate how many there were – but there were a lot, and I had them covered with about three Bren guns at about 200 yards' range.

I had no thought of them being exactly the same sort of lads as my own fellows – no thought that they had parents, wives or children – no thought of the fact that some of the same sort of people had killed my brother before Dunkirk. They represented a target, and I gave the order to open fire. War is a dreadful, disgusting, horrible waste!

It took the enemy some time to recover from what we had inflicted on them, during which time I had a look round the area. The water level in the Rhine was about 10-12 feet below the ground level and it appeared that, with a bit of luck, it might be possible to get our troops, obscured from the enemy by the house that was the Company HQ, down to the water's edge. From here they could advance in single file

but it became clear that all the enemy fire was directed at us, the rearguard, and that the men dropping down the riverbank were getting away with it.

I gave them time to travel a couple of hundred yards, then had my own fellows sneak away a few at a time. The scheme worked to an almost unbelievable degree. We had to leave our dead there, of course, and the two German prisoners were killed by their own fire.

The Germans continued to lay a tremendous amount of fire on the place – they must have had an odd sort of feeling when they put their attack in to take the position, only to find that we had gone.

We were greeted back at HQ as conquering heroes. We had killed a great number of the enemy and had virtually walked through an enemy that was perhaps five or six times stronger than we were. The citation for gallantry paints a rosy picture of what went on that day – it makes no mention at all of Lady Luck – *she* had been gallant in the extreme.

were just the slightest little bit more frightened than I was. They dropped their Schmeissers, we picked them up, bundled the two Germans into the jeep and turned back into B Company lines.

Two Dutch interpreters questioned the Germans, and they told us that they were part of a unit that was marching along the Utrecht/Arnhem road, that they had been the connecting file between the companies in front of and behind them. This meant, of course, that there was at least one company – perhaps two or three – of enemy troops on the road that I had been going to take back to my HQ. The B Company Commander told me that his second-in-command's glider had gone astray and suggested that I take over as second-in-command. I reported the situation to HQ. There was little we could do until dawn, and then the instruction came that we were to fight our way out.

So, we discussed how we might do a break-out job, and while we were doing so, it became obvious that the enemy had decided to make their HQ straight opposite the edge of the lane, about 200 yards directly in front of us – and they still didn't know that we were there.

Soon after dawn, a German motor

Airborne Forces Museum

▲ **With radio links between the scattered companies and HQ blocked by trees, the British have to rely on jeeps to drive quickly from one position to another to relay intelligence and instructions.**

perhaps half a mile towards Arnhem, and then break out into the open to deal with anything between us and the Battalion position. I suggested to the CC that he led the company out, and I would do a rearguard job with one platoon.

The enemy now started to throw everything they had at us, and proved our theory that there were an awful lot of them. Our position quickly became a very unhealthy sort of place to be. A sergeant lying next to me was hit and killed instantly,

Jock and I went back to HQ. The enemy, presumably having taken Renkum, closed in on the battalion position and started to make life quite difficult for us.

The enemy were in the open ground to the west. There was plenty of cover for them and they came in quite close – bayonet-close on a number of occasions – but they were beaten back time after time.

On the third or fourth day, I had a message over the wireless from one of my Signals Corporals, attached to

Bundesarchiv-Koblenz

Imperial War Museum

▲ **Herded into a small area in an open field, a mixed group of British puts a brave face on captivity – maybe in the hope that it would not last very long.**

▼ **Sgts Whawell and Turrell of the Glider Pilot Regiment search the ruins of a Dutch school for snipers as furious house-to-house fighting closes in around them.**

D Company. I shall never forget it. He said, with not the slightest quiver in his voice, 'There is a flame-thrower coming in to our HQ now sir. Goodbye and good luck.' Corporal Larry Cowan must have been killed within seconds of sending the message. D Company as a fighting unit had ceased to exist – a few may have been taken prisoner, but most of them were killed.

I had taken two homing pigeons with me. I had not very much faith in them, but taking them was a way of ensuring that I was carrying as heavy a load as any of my men, and there was always a chance that they could be useful. I released the first one with a message from a senior airforce officer to Air Defence Great Britain. A couple of days later I ran out of pigeon food and realised that if the bird was weakened through being starved, it would stand no chance of

getting home at all. I requested permission to release it. I sent the following message – which amounted to a load of nonsense:

'From Lieut JSD Hardy: Have to release birds owing to shortage of food and water. About eight tanks laying about in sub unit areas, very untidy but not causing us any trouble. Now using as many German weapons as we have British. MGs most effective when aiming towards Germany. Dutch people grand, but Dutch tobacco rather stringy. Great beard-growing competition on in our unit, but no time to check up on the winner.'

The bird miraculously arrived back at Corps HQ and the newsmen got hold of the message. It made headlines in the English papers the next day and was given such a degree of importance that it ended up in the War Museum, classified as one of the epic messages from a field of battle.

Come the fourth, fifth and sixth days, the men were becoming terribly tired. There was no sleep, they were down to their last scraps of food, they were haggard, weary almost to the point of collapse. There were continual rumours of disaster, but through it all, the men were steadfast, confident and could still raise a smile.

A patrol was sent out at one time, and they had no sooner left, than the NCO returned with the news that they had been hit by shellfire. I went out to see what could be done, and found a young lad, just barely 18, with a gaping hole in his back. He was beyond help, but still conscious, with only seconds to live. Try as I might, I shall never forget the look in the lad's eyes. Try as I might, I could

never explain it.

I think it was somewhere around the sixth day that our Artillery Officer was killed, and that left me, as Signals Officer, to take over his job. I asked for shellfire on a few occasions, but the best they could do was a few rounds. On the eighth or ninth day, I again had to ask for shellfire, and was answered by a very, very American voice that told me he represented a regiment of 'Long Toms', and asked how much do I need. I asked him what the danger area was from his type of shellfire. He explained and I told him that I wanted him to plaster an area so that the inner edge of his danger area was within a few yards of our troops. I took it that he was firing from 10 to 12 miles away. It was very effective.

As each day came along, we were all quite sure that this would be the day that the Second Army would reach us. We had become used to the hunger, but the shortage of water was punishment indeed. We were short of ammunition – the men had to make every shot count.

Finally the message came through that we were to pull out. We had to observe absolute silence, and to add to our misery, it was pouring with rain. It was a journey through hell, but finally we made it. **"**

Imperial War Museum

Willi Renner was a sergeant in the 2nd Battalion of the German 6th Parachute Regiment and was involved in fierce house-to-house fighting in the town of Reusel, south of Eindhoven, as Operation Market Garden began.

" Hand-grenades were thrown up or down, and our raiding group, which consisted of about 15 men, was given the task of fighting clear one street's worth of houses. That meant clearing the enemy out using whatever means possible. The best method, of course, is to make them run away, to avoid having to shoot them. Of course, if they don't run away, you have to use force – and to use force, in a war context, means to shoot them. So we had to shoot at them or throw hand-grenades, and there were, of course, losses on both sides.

On the way back, while clearing the houses, we came upon an Englishman who had been shot in the stomach. I assumed that the man had been hit by someone from the street or something like that, and that his own men had left him lying there in the house – they couldn't take him with them.

I came towards the house and, while we ran, shots came out of the cellar window. A few metres to the left of me, one of our men was hit in the throat. Blood came pouring from his throat – it was terrible. Another comrade of mine was hit in the chest. In his wallet he had a picture of his girlfriend, and the bullet went straight through the photo.

Another comrade of ours was shot through the thigh. These were the three casualties that we could see at this stage, and of course, we now knew that there were people still in the house, shooting at us from the cellar. We took cover to the right and ran round to the other side of

the house.

We moved so that we couldn't be seen by the English soldiers in the house, and kicked in one of the cellar windows. We threw in a hand-grenade – whether it was one or a few, I can't remember exactly. There was a terrible explosion.

It's a terrible thing when a grenade explodes in such a small space – I had experienced this myself. The English emerged – a few of them were wounded and some inside must have been dead. Four of them came out and I took them back with me.

Just before this, we shot at some English who had tried to run away across a turnip field. They had been trained how to run in this situation – lie down, jump up, run, throw yourself down again, and so on.

So, the direct fighting was now over, and we searched the house to check whether anyone else was there – and now we had to take care of the wounded and dead men.

We took from the dead men all their papers, all their valuables, their watch and identity tag and packed this all away. Then the dead were buried and the wounded taken to the main field hospital. I was given the job of taking the four prisoners back.

Everything was going smoothly until at one point I could see that the prisoners had become afraid. The first thing that came to mind was that these men were afraid that they were going to be shot. Then things relaxed a little. We exchanged cigarettes. These were only young men and they were suffering from the psychological effects of the house fighting – the guilt that they might have killed someone; the shock from the exploding grenades. "

▲ Everyday life in Arnhem town is turned upside down as debris and bodies litter the streets and German armor rumbles under the trees.

◄ Willi Renner of the 2nd German Parachute Battalion.

◄ As Brigadier Hackett's note to General Urquhart after the battle stated, 'Thank you for the party. It didn't go quite as we hoped and got a bit rougher than expected, but speaking for myself, I'd take it on again any time, and so, I'm sure would everyone else.' Looking at these men, you could believe it.

CHAPTER 20

BATTLE DIARY

AUGUST 1944
19 Hitler first conceives plan for autumn counter-offensive

SEPTEMBER
4 Allies capture Antwerp

5 US forces cross the Muse

13 Beginning of operation to clear Scheldt estuary

17–25 Operation 'Market Garden'

27 Third Army commences attack on Metz

OCTOBER
2 Renewal of First Army offensive at Aachen

6 Beginning of battle for the Breskens pocket

21 Fall of Aachen

27–29 Battle of Beveland

NOVEMBER
1 Commandos land on Walcheren island

2 Allies capture Zeebrugge. End of the battle for the Breskens pocket

8 Walcheren garrison surrenders

22 Fall of Metz

DECEMBER
3 Third Army establishes bridgeheads over the Saar

16 Start of German Ardennes offensive

17 Malmedy massacre

18 Kampfgruppe Peiper captures Stavemont

23 Allies pull back from St Vith

24 Peiper orders retreat. Second Panzer Division reaches the Meuse

26 Siege of Bastogne lifted

JANUARY 1945
16 US First and Third Armies meet at Houffalize

23 St Vith recaptured

31 End of 'Battle of the Bulge'

BATTLE OF THE BULGE – COLD XMAS

Although the Germans had suffered heavy losses on both the Eastern and Western Fronts, new units called Volksgrenadiers were raised and equipped under the forceful leadership of Goebbels and Production Minister Albert Speer. Using these units, Hitler was keen to launch a counter-attack in the west to split the British and American armies with a drive from the Ardennes to Antwerp. The German High Command had more limited but practical ideas that a large local counter-attack would cut off an American Corps.

Hitler prevailed, and on December 16 Operation *Wacht on Rhein* was launched. The attacking forces – the Fifth and Sixth Panzer Armies and the Seventh Army – were to hit the US VIII Corps, a quiet sector of the US First Army. By Christmas Eve, German reconnaissance units were heading an advance about 5 miles from the Meuse at Dinant. The German commanders had made very little use of radio communications, so the Allies had no intelligence to warn them of the attack, and English-speaking troops wearing US Army uniforms in Jeeps penetrated the American lines and disrupted communications and conducted sabotage operations. Despite the considerable German success, however, their fuel supplies were running very low and they had been blocked at Bastogne, where the 101st Airborne Division under General Anthony McAuliffe was surrounded but fighting hard.

The weather improved, allowing the Allied air forces into the attack, and General Patton's Third Army swung north to relieve Bastogne on December 26. On January 3, 1945, the Allies went on the offensive and eliminated the German salient in what became known as the Battle of the Bulge. Both sides lost about 800 tanks, the US Army suffered 81,000 casualties, the British 1,400 and the Germans 100,000. Overall, the attack had achieved only a six-week respite for Germany and squandered its last tank and air resources.

COLD CHRISTMAS FRONT

With a crisp coating of snow and frost, the Ardennes front looks like a scene on a Christmas card. So the shock when the German offensive erupts is profound.

The Allied advance has come up against a major German counteroffensive in the wintry Ardennes. Ill-equipped against the cold, with supplies of food and ammunition running perilously low, every confrontation could make the difference between survival and defeat. Every gain or loss is vital. Combatants of the 'Bulge' recall the desperate days of December 1944.

 Flight Lieutenant Maurice Garton of 103 Squadron flew on bombing missions over Germany as part of the Allied softening up process of the enemy's homeland. One such mission ended in an extraordinary close squeak – others were lessons in pin-pointed mass destruction.

ly there was a terrific roar as another aircraft passed very close underneath. The red light the Engineer saw was no control tower – it was the red port navigation light on the wing tip of another aircraft!

After the shock, we settled down again, thinking that a near miss was as good as a mile. We proceeded to land safely.

The next day, when we went out to the aircraft for another raid on Cologne, the flight sergeant in charge of the ground crew came over and asked what had happened the previous night, and asked us to come and have a look at the state of our starboard tail fin.

Lo and behold, there was a big dent about 18 inches long where the aerial of the other aircraft had caught us.

In the first heavy bomber raid on the *Reich* in daylight, a Lanc of 103 Squadron was hit in the fuel tank on

the way home. On fire and in a steep glide, all seven of the crew bailed out. As the pilot came out last man, the plane exploded and then the German ack-ack opened up at the parachutes, killing the men as they plummeted down.

On another raid, however, on Emmerich am Rhein, 340 Lancasters and 10 Mosquitoes dropped 4,000 lb bombs and incendiaries. In a very accurate attack, the total damage was 2,424 buildings destroyed, 689 buildings damaged, 680,000 cubic metres of rubble, 641 civilians and 96 soliders killed. "

◀◀ A German soldier pauses by a disabled American half track in the Ardennes, December 1944. His pose is heroic yet in vain, for reality did not match this propaganda shot.

◀ Maurice Garton of 103 Squadron of Lancasters. The motto, 'Do not touch me', seems uncannily apt for his story.

◀ As Allied men push on through the wintry landscape of the Ardennes, the RAF directs its long-range Lancaster bombers against German targets to destroy their war production. Inset: a Lancaster over Heinsberg on a daylight attack, 17 December 1994.

" October 30, 1944. On returning from a night raid on Cologne, we were over England, flying north for Elsham and looking for the three Sandra lights coned over the aerodrome.

The Wireless Op came up with a message saying that German night fighters were about and so all lights on aerodromes had been extinguished – so also must be our navigation lights.

We continued to travel north on a compass bearing, waiting for the all-clear to come through from the Wireless Op.

'All clear'. We started looking for Elsham again. Suddenly, Jock Kinnear, my Engineer, staring out of the starboard window, shouted, 'There is an aerodrome – and the red light on the control tower', when sudden-

▶ Private Alfred Jenkins of the Argyll and Sutherland Highlanders. The cruel cold of the Ardennes and the constant contact with death would soon harden young recruits.

Private Alfred Jenkins of A Company of the 2nd Battalion of the Argyll and Sutherland Highlanders, was training in Holland for the forthcoming Reichswald offensive, when the Germans launched their all-out attack in the Ardennes.

Alfred Jenkins

" When the Germans broke through, all the available troops were rushed south and as I remember it for the first few days, we seemed to be going all over the place in Belgium.

Imperial War Museum

We finally wound up at a place near Maastricht, near the German border, and that was just before Christmas. It looked as if we were going to be there for a few days, so they had a sit-down Christmas dinner planned for us. Well, what happened was, on Christmas morning we were put on a half hour stand-by which meant we had to be ready to move at a moment's notice. That meant that we had our Christmas dinner out of mess tins and standing up in the open. We finally moved at 8 o'clock that night.

From there we went to a suburb of Liège. When we went into the house where we were billetted, the owners of the house were a middle-aged couple with a young daughter, and it was obvious that the daughter had been suffering from the food shortages, but they had this banner across the living room 'Welcome to our liberators – welcome to brave British soldiers'. We were there a few days, then we moved over to the other side

▶ Almost incredulous, an American soldier checks for himself the damage done to a US tank by a German 88 gun, 16 January 1994. It takes a massive gun to inflict this sort of damage on heavy armor.

of Liège, where we actually did guard a bridge at Amay. It was while we were there that we captured what we thought was a German spy. One of our section came in one day with a chap he had met, dressed in American uniform. He shook hands all round – which made us a bit suspicious, because this is a Continental, not a British or American habit. So we had difficulty understanding him and asked him if he spoke English. He said no, but he said he spoke American. We noticed that he was only wearing the liner of his steel helmet, which we knew had been forbidden by the US command. Then when he told us he had come from Paris that day, we thought 'Aha, what have we got here?', because we knew that all movement between Paris and the front had been stopped, because it was at that time they had the scare that there was an assassination team out looking for Eisenhower. We handed him over to the American Military Police. Whether he was a spy or not, I don't know.

We were there over the New Year, and it was about this time that it really started snowing. Up until then it had been fairly cold, but not the sort of snow you usually associate with the Ardennes.

I always remember, we were billetted a section to a house, and we had been there for about a week, and the lady of the house had formed a sort of attachment for us. She had baked a special cake for us on the day when we had to move. She couldn't see why we had to go, only to be replaced by more British troops. The last we saw of her, she was standing in the doorway of her house, barring the seaforths.

On the 7th January we spent the night travelling in an absolute blizzard and arrived the next day at Bertogne and then they decided the roads were unfit for vehicles and we had to take to our feet. We went on to a place where the East Lancs had had a battle – we found several of their bodies lying around there.

We got a warning that there were some German tanks and infantry approaching, so we stood to, but all that happened was we captured one prisoner, who said he was a Polish deserter. It was funny, you usually found in the German Army that there were no Germans – they were all Poles or Russians. When we got into Germany, we never found anybody who supported Hitler. They were all members of the 20th July bomb plot! You had to wonder where he got all his troops from!

We had to march back to Bertogne. I remember that march. It wasn't exactly cross-country, but the roads were fairly indistinguishable, and the shelling had brought down a lot of branches of trees – and they

are nearly all fir trees down there. There must have been a slight thaw, then it had refrozen, and each individual needle on these trees was coated in ice, so trying to march over that in hob-nailed boots was rather like walking over ball bearings.

We had as many layers of clothes as we could, Balaclava helmets, greatcoats, leather jerkins – at that point we didn't have snow suits. They didn't think of issuing them until it was all over. It was so cold there that we had to wipe all the oil off our weapons. Usually you had to keep the moving parts of your weapon slightly oiled, but we had to wipe it off because it was freezing.

Each section had a Bren gun – I had the Bren gun in our section. The rest were armed with rifles, apart from the corporal who had either a Sten gun, or, if he was lucky, he looted a Schmeisser machine pistol – this was preferable to a Sten gun because they were notedly very unreliable weapons. At one point earlier in the year after a couple of accidents, anyone who had Sten guns in their battalion was told to remove the magazines from them when travelling in transport, because more than one had been dropped and gone off. Bren guns were different – they were using them in the British Army up until the 1960s, because they said it was so accurate that you could shoot through its bullet-holes.

Next day the Black Watch were going to take Laroche, and we had to move through them. We were travelling in transport and we got

held up because the Black Watch were delayed. It was night time, and the three-tonner that we were in skidded off the road and landed on its side. There was an entire platoon in there – about 30 men – and how none of us got injured with all the equipment flying all over the place, I don't know.

En route from Lavaux we stopped at a sort of barn at a crossroads. We could see the road ahead of us went down into a valley and up again – and just at the bottom of this valley was some sort of small hut. The leading section started off and it just reached this hut. There was this burst of machine-gun and shell fire from the ridge ahead of us. It caught them all in the open – there was no cover there, and it took several hours for them to get back.

There was one chap in that section, he had his younger brother with him, and he saw him killed right in front of his eyes. They told us afterwards that they had to hold him back because he wanted to take off after these Germans by himself. Then another section had a go. The same thing happened. We could see what was going to happen. They would just get down to this hut, and the Germans were waiting for them. Then it was our turn to go. As you can imagine, everyone was trying to be last out of this barn where we were sheltering.

It was at that point that Major Samwell, the Company Commander, decided that he'd come down with us. He called up a troop of

▲ Corporal John F Zinser (left) and Private William C Mullins, Military Police in charge of German prisoners, size up their young charges. In their scanty uniforms, defeat etched on their faces, the two SS boys look unlikely to pose any great threat.

◄ US Third Army tanks assemble on a snow-covered slope outside Bastogne to launch the final drive to relieve American forces in the town. In the background, smoke from US artillery fire rises from blasted enemy installations.

▶ Lieutenant Virgil Lary, a survivor of the infamous Malmédy massacre, points out Georg Fleps, the man whom he saw fire the first shot, at a war crimes trial at Landsberg, May 1946.

Sherman tanks we had there, and we started off down. He walked behind one of the tanks to use the phone on the back of it – it was for communications with the infantry. He just walked behind this, and the tank was hit by either an armour-piercing shell or a shell – but my main memory of that was a cloud of shrapnel and dust flying everywhere. I saw Major Samwell fall there. We beat it back to the barn.

They decided, after all this, that it really was a waste of time trying to get round that road. According to the records, there were something like 28 casualties.

Fighting there had come to a stop and the Americans were just sweeping up. What happened was that we were at the tip of our movement forward, and we were pinched out by the Americans coming in from each side of us. 〞

Lieutenant Virgil Lary was with Battery B of the US 7th Armored Division's 285th Field Artillery Observation Battalion. On 17 December, he was ordered to move up to reinforce the slender American line at St Vith.

▼ American infantrymen with the Third US Army's 4th Armored Division wait while a column of armored vehicles advances towards Bastogne.

〝 The battery was on the road that morning, and by noon had reached a point three miles south of Malmédy on the St Vith road. Some 300 yards behind the crossroads of the cutoff for St Vith, the column was suddenly stopped by German machine-gun and mortar fire. We jumped down from our vehicles and took cover in the ditches on the sides of the road.

The German unit was an element of Colonel Peiper's 1st SS Panzer Division. They had stopped at the crossroads, surprised the MP who was directing traffic there (and who had escaped behind a house), turned the signs around to confuse us and then opened fire on the convoy.

I jumped down from my truck and crawled to a small stream 40 feet from the road. I covered myself with grass and mud and headed for that house. A captain from my battery followed – but a tank came up the road and I put up my hands. A German officer stuck his head out of the turret of the tank and aimed his pistol at me. I ducked and the shot missed. The German then aimed at the captain and fired again. He missed. I jumped into a ditch.

By this time, three more tanks had come up the road. They were all Tiger tanks of the newest German design. They moved along the road, spewing fire at the ditches. One German tank shot up an American ambulance. Other German tanks knocked out 24 American vehicles of the convoy. Colonel Peiper then beckoned his task force onwards, and left the mopping up to the parachute infantry troops accompanying them.

The German infantrymen came down the road, examining the ditches. I surrendered again and soon found myself in a field with about 150 other POWs, guarded by the paratroops.

The Germans searched the Americans and took wallets, gloves, rings, cigarettes – and all weapons. They ordered us, then, into a field south of the crossroads, and I noticed that they had set up machine guns surrounding the field. We were told to raise our hands above our heads. Tanks at the two ends of the field along the road covered them. A German command car drew up and ran on. An officer spoke.

'You will go across the Siegfried Line, will you, you dirty swine'?

The officer took aim at an American doctor and fired his pistol. The medical officer fell. The German fired again, and another American dropped. Then the two tanks and the machine guns in the field began firing.

I dropped. I was hit in the arm and the foot. I lay, bleeding – as if dead. German soldiers came along the line of bodies and shot some of the wounded and bayonetted some and bashed the heads of others with rifle butts. (When the bodies were found later, the eyes of some of the soldiers had been gouged out.)

The Germans came up to me.

'Is he dead?' asked one.

Something diverted his attention and he moved away. I lay perfectly still, my eyes closed, but I could hear the sound of pistols firing and the noise of rifle butts against skulls.

After about an hour, the German column formed up and moved off, leaving the field silent. Several survivors decided to make a break for it and got up and ran for the house on the road – including me. The Germans opened fire. Several men dropped, but I made it to the house and lay doggo. A German officer came

◄ **The center of the town of Bastogne lies in ruins, littered with broken vehicles, rubble and, in the foreground, a body, hastily covered with a GI's blanket.**

▼ **A German tank blasted by US fire near Bastogne is one of some 400 knocked out in the first 15 days of the German counter-offensive in the Ardennes. Even a gentle dusting of snow does nothing to soften the violence of the scene.**

through Marche, where they found an American Infantry Division, whose commander said that he was proposing to hold on there, and that the US 2nd Armored Division was due to come down from the northeast on the left flank of the 3rd Royal Tank regimental group.

This clarified the position somewhat, but at the same time, raised further complications, because the Germans were using American equipment and uniforms and consequently the task of telling friend from foe was extremely tricky.

The situation now was that there were endless good positions to the south, north, south-east and north-east of the main Dinant-Sorinne road, from which any attack could be dealt with — but for such a small force, it was impossible to go too far east, otherwise the enemy could have outflanked the group either to the south or to the north, and reached the bridge without making contact.

The most dangerous flank was the south-east, in the direction of Celles and, as I did not wish to become engaged too far out in this direction, the reconnaissance troop was sent to this area and ordered to take up a position of observation. This was done and as a result, it was found that there were some enemy in Celles — but this was not known until the evening of 22 December.

The morning of the 23rd December dawned foggy and visibility was

along, saw us, but did not fire at us – then went away. The German armoured column began to pass and for two hours, tanks and half-tracks ran down the road to St Vith. When they seemed to be gone, two of us ran down the road towards Malmédy. From the crossroads the Germans began to fire at us, but they didn't hit us and we ran on for two miles. Then a jeep came along and picked us up, and took us into Malmédy and safety. A few days later, I learned that of the 150 Americans in the field, only 43 survived, and three quarters of *them* were wounded. **"**

Lieutenant-Colonel A W Brown (later Brigadier, CBE, DSO, MC) with the 3rd Royal Tank Regiment, was at Dinant, north-west of Bastogne as Christmas approached in the Ardennes.

" During the morning, A Squadron made contact with a Belgian officer who had led the *Maquis* throughout the war. This officer is now the Baron de Sorinne. He stayed with the regiment throughout the action and was invaluable because of his local knowledge of the country.

The Regimental Group remained in these positions for the whole of the 22nd and the night 22nd/23rd,

but at night, the forward squadrons closed up into a tight leaguer mounting only guard tanks around them. Except in Dinant, there were no infantry with the tank squadrons.

During the night 22nd/23rd December, C Squadron Commander and his SSM (Signals Sergeant-Major) did a further reconnaissance

Imperial War Museum

◄ An American column arrives in the small Ardennes town of Dochamps, whose battered church bears witness to considerable bombardment in the struggle to hold this key area.

almost nil. Regimental Tactical Headquarters established itself in the château of Sorinne with A Squadron. Apart from the arrival of a British Air Liaison officer and an American officer from US 2nd Armored Division, very little occurred on this day.

Acting on information received from the American Officer, I sent a liaison officer from 3 RTR up to Celles to try and contact Headquarters of the 2nd US Armored Division. After some delay, he succeeded in doing this and remained there as a liaison officer throughout the period of the action.

It was on this day also that an apparently American jeep drove through one of the road blocks approaching the bridge at Dinant on the east side of the river. This road block, as were all the others, was manned by the 8 RBs, who had established a movable barrier and arranged for mines to be pulled across the road should any vehicle break through the barrier without stopping. As we were by now in contact with the Americans, this jeep was not fired on, but as it refused to stop, the mines were drawn across the road and it was blown up. It was found to contain three German SS – two were killed and one taken prisoner.

On the evening of the 23rd, it was confirmed from local information that German infantry and some tanks or half-tracked vehicles had got into the village of Conneux. In fact, their vehicles could be heard moving about just as light was failing. As there was still no infantry with the tank squadron east of the river, it was not deemed possible to

take any action that night. Therefore the squadrons went into leaguer in their respective positions, but gun tanks were posted to cover the road approaches. In the case of the main road leading through Sorinne, an RAC officer was placed out with a wireless set 400 yards forward of the edge of the village. This officer established himself in the upper storey of a cottage, from which he obtained a good field of view down the road. The mist had lifted by this time, and it was a clear, moonlight

night, so that he would be able to give warning of enemy vehicles approaching.

He had only been there for a short while when he found that German infantry had, undetected by him, moved into the ground floor of the same house. The enemy were not aware of his presence.

He was able to give warning of their presence, and also escape on foot back to Regimental Headquarters at Sorinne. As the enemy infantry were now only some 400 yards from Regimental Headquarters and A Squadron were 'stood to' for the remainder of the night, no attack was made. 〞

Sergeant Willi Renner of the German 6th Parachute Regiment was at Obermarbach, near the Belgian border with Germany, at Christmas. His story begins as he makes a check on the company's foxholes and emplacements.

〝 I heard a noise. I turned to the right and there I saw a black soldier right in front of me, and from where I was standing, about 30 or 40 metres away, he had a very warlike look. He had wrapped himself up against the cold – it was freezing in

▼ This US soldier from a cavalry reconnaissance squadron checks his 0.3-caliber machine gun as an increasing cover of snow threatens the smooth running of the moving parts of weaponry.

US National Archives

197934-5

have been one who spoke German. He shouted over to me, 'komm 'rüber' (come over). I'll never forget those two words as long as I live. I remember then, what I did. Just to gain some time, I shouted back, 'I cannot walk'. Then the other thought came over me all of a sudden. I could have given myself up, and of course, there's always the possibility that you are accused of deserting to the other side. It can happen that way. I thought there was no way I could let that happen – my family might suffer as a result. The only other thought that came into my head at that moment was that I should try to save myself by throwing myself behind the hedge, but of course, they could have come along

▲ ▲ A far cry from the victorious Allied surge through France and the Low Countries, the Ardennes campaign is a long, hard slog, with only minimal daily gains.

▲ Strafing Allied aircraft take their toll on a German demolition squad truck. Precious equipment lies strewn over a snowy road near Givroulle, Belgium.

the hedge with a machine gun and I'd be hit somehow.

Of course, I didn't really have the time to think these thoughts through. I just threw myself aside. I crawled on my elbows for a while, then flung myself into the bush. Anyway, there was a lot of firing, but they had lost sight of which direction I was heading in, and I managed to scramble away and get back to my comrades. One of them got hold of me and wanted to start carrying me off, like a sack of coal, back to the company combat post. He began to run, hauling me along across a turnip field. I don't think he realised how heavy I was, and he stumbled while he was running and did his knee in. Now we both had one leg out of action, but we carried on and eventually reached the company combat post.

the Eifel at that time. He had a long scarf around his neck and there he stood in front of me, this huge guy, a lot taller than me, a spade in his hand.

If I remember correctly he laughed when he spotted me, but in a situation like this, you remember your training – he who shoots first lives longer. I had a machine pistol and I was about to shoot – but because of the cold and the poor conditions of the last few days, I was only able to get one shot out of it. It was jammed. Anyway, I was more or less sure that I'd dismissed him, and he appeared to be in the hedge.

I got back to my duties and hardly even thought about the incident. It was only later that it occurred to me that it was a mistake to leave the man there – not to run back and report him – to tell the commander that the enemy had got so far.

Eventually I got to the last position, which was a machine-gun position, the guns pointed at the valley where the Americans were on the other side. I was a bit puzzled, everything was so quiet, then suddenly someone shouted out to me, 'What the hell are doing? Take cover. You'll be blasted out of sight'. Anyway, shots rang out and I dived for cover, but I didn't do this properly. My legs should have lain flat along the ground, but I had dived behind the mound of earth behind

which the machine-guns were, and my legs were sticking over the top.

I felt a sudden thump. It's a really strange feeling – a dull thud as if someone has just hit you with a heavy club. I'd been shot in the leg, in the left calf. I scrambled in panic into the machine-gun hole and my comrades tore up some pieces of bed sheets which they had picked up from the houses they had been holed up in. They wrapped them round my leg as an emergency dressing. I lay there for an hour, just waiting, but after a while the pain was too much, and I told my comrades that I couldn't wait around any longer – I'd bleed to death. But if I tried to run out, I'd probably get blasted again.

We discussed it among ourselves. One of them thought I should stay there – others said they would leave it up to me. Anyway, I decided I should make a run for it. I took a piece of the white rag that they had used to bandage my leg, tied it to the end of my machine pistol and held that out above the mound.

Nothing happened for a while. All quiet. Eventually I popped my head out. There was nothing heroic – I had no choice but to chance it.

I managed to scramble out up to my stomach, and eventually the whole of me was out, lying flat on my stomach. A few seconds passed, then there was a noise in the bushes and I heard one of the Americans – it must

CHAPTER 21

BATTLE DIARY

NOVEMBER 1942
19   Sir Max Horton appointed Commander Western Approaches

DECEMBER
13   British break German U-boat code
31   Battle of the Barents Sea

JANUARY 1943
30   Dönitz replaces Raeder as Commander in Chief, German Navy

MARCH
16–19   Battle around convoys SC122 and HX229. Heavy Allied losses

MAY
6   ONS2 battle ends with a victory for Britain
24   Dönitz order U-boats temporarily home from main Atlantic convoy routes

SEPTEMBER
20–23   Wolf-pack campaign reopens with attack on ON202 and ONS18
22   Three X-craft cripple German battleship *Tirpitz*

OCTOBER
16–17   U-boats suffer heavy losses attacking ONS20

DECEMBER
26   *Scharnhorst* sunk by Home Fleet in last major gunnery duel in Royal Navy's history

MARCH 1944
22   Dönitz recalls wolf packs

APRIL
3   *Tirpitz* heavily damaged by carrier air strike

SEPTEMBER
15   First 'Tallboy' bomber attack on *Tirpitz*
23   Evacuation of Biscay U-boat bases completed

NOVEMBER
12   *Tirpitz* finally sunk by 'Tallboy' bombs

MAY 1945
4   U-boats ordered to cease hostilities and return to base to surrender

ATLANTIC VICTORY

Drawing on his experience as a U-boat commander in World War I, Admiral Karl Dönitz proposed that submarine war be waged against the merchant ships supplying Britain with food, weapons and equipment, using 'Wolf Packs' – groups of U-boats – to attack convoys. Although ships were attacked as far afield as the Indian Ocean, the main area of operations was the North Atlantic and the sea lanes between the United States and Britain.

The longest campaign of World War II began on September 3, 1939, with the sinking of the SS *Athenia* and ended with the German surrender on May 7, 1945. During that time, German success was concentrated in two 'Happy Times'. Between July and October 1940 they sank 217 ships for the loss of two U-boats, and in 1942, when the United States entered the war, U-boats moved in close to the eastern shore of the USA and Gulf of Mexico, sinking 65 ships in February, 86 in March, 69 in April and 111 in May.

Meanwhile, the Allies complemented Ultra intelligence and a range of technology with well-proven tactics like escorted convoys to combat the U-boats. Eventually they had enough escorts, including small carriers, that they could start actively hunting the U-boats. Long-range B-24 Liberator bombers armed with depth bombs ranged deep into the North Atlantic. The battle reached its climax in April 1943, when, after early U-boat successes, Convoy ONS2 was attacked by 51 U-boats. Under the vigorous leadership of Commander Peter Greeton RN, the convoy fought back and, although 13 of his ships were sunk, a total of seven submarines were destroyed in the process. By July, US shipyards were building more ships than were being sunk, and 62 convoys had crossed the Atlantic without loss. A year later, the German navy had lost its French bases. By the close of the war, 781 U-boats had been destroyed by Allied aircraft and ships with the loss of 32,000 German sailors. In return, U-boats had sunk 2,575 Allied and neutral ships, about three-quarters of them British.

MASTERS OF THE ATLANTIC

It is now down to the men of the Merchant and Royal Navies to hammer home their advantage in the Atlantic – but the Kriegsmarine and the U-boats are not going to give up that easily.

S afe on land, scientists vied to equip their navies with the most advanced technology – but out at sea, it was luck, judgement and quick reactions as much as any scientific breakthroughs, which made the difference between life and death. Deep below the icy North Atlantic, buffeted by its merciless waves or flying above its grey, forbidding waters, men of the British and German marine forces pit their wits against each other in the battle to rule the seas.

◄ **As U-boat torpedo rating Hans Lemke said, 'It's a totally unique experience in war to be constantly bolted up in this little space.'**

they were breaking our codes, which we didn't know – they kept it a very good secret – but we were steered clear of danger as much as possible by relayed information.

Another feature of that time was the support group. This was a group of frigates or destroyers, which roamed the Atlantic, looking for

which were especially to pick up survivors from merchant ships. The first bad convoy I had was HX231, end of March 1943, and we hadn't got a rescue ship – a lot of men lost their lives as a result. If a ship stopped to pick up survivors, they had to leave the convoy – then they were sitting ducks. It was a terrible

 Commander Peter Gretton, (now Admiral Sir Peter, KCB, DSO, OBE, DSC) was senior officer of Escort Group B7, based at Londonderry. The Western Approaches was not the quiet backwater it had been made out to be, and was witness to fierce U-boat wolf-pack attacks.

❝ At the beginning of January '43, we had three convoys without any attack at all, then in March and April 1943 we had three convoys in succession in which we had heavy attacks. The idea was, if under attack, to keep the convoy together but the weather was very bad for some of the convoys and it scattered us to a certain extent.

By May 1943, when we had our last battle, we were easily on top. There were 17 U-boats in the opposition, and altogether five of them were sunk – two by aircraft and three by surface ships.

One of the most important things was the breaking of German codes – we were breaking them during the winter of '42–43. And, incidentally,

▲ **The crew of an X-craft midget submarine catch a breath of air on the surface. So well guarded a secret were these craft that the Germans genuinely had no idea what hit them.**

▲ **Commander Peter Gretton (center), captain of the *Duncan* during the eventful Atlantic convoys of spring 1943.**

trouble. They would be called in to support any close escort which was being attacked. They would be out for a month on end, just topping up with oil from tankers in the convoys.

Every day we got a U-boat situation report, based on Ultra – though of course, we didn't know that. I would be given a convoy route, but I had to act on my own initiative. The Convoy Commodore did what he was told – he was very often a retired naval officer – and he was responsible for keeping the convoy in the right formation. The Senior Officer Escorts would be responsible too, for any alteration of course which the convoy needed to keep clear of U-boats. You always tried to keep away – you weren't looking for them.

Some convoys had rescue ships

quandary whether to stop the ship to pick up and save a few men – or lose a lot of men by deserting the convoy.

One of the secrets of successful convoy escort work, was good liaison with the Air Force and Coastal Command. Bulloch was extremely good – he was a most efficient man who trained his men up to a very high standard. Some others were terrible, and in some cases we had to make signals to the aircraft – in code, of course – because they couldn't find us. Bulloch could *always* find us without signals – he was the best.

I was frightened, of course, but you couldn't just go on being frightened. During the first two convoys when I realised we were going to be attacked, I had this sinking feeling – but by the third eventful trip, we felt we were prepared to take the attack

Royal Navy Submarine Museum

John Norton was an apprentice pattern maker with Marshall and Sons and Co in Gainsborough, Lincolnshire. During the war the company's production centred mainly on weaponry – and the top-secret X-craft submarines.

" We Lincolnshire people, born and bred, are, by nature, *clunch*. I don't know if it's a Norse derivative – this is a very Norse area. There's a lot of reticence in the village areas. You'll not get a lot of information out of people – not because they want to be unhelpful or unsociable. There was never any thought of anyone blowing the gaff on the secret.

It was a well-kept secret – not many people, other than the men building them, knew. I made blocks and dies for the bolt plates on the submarines. They were constructed there until completion, then they had all the oil put in, the diesel, the batteries topped up – everything with the exception of the explosive charges, which were fitted at the operational port.

The idea was to drag the submarine out, towed by a large sub-

▲ The operational crew of X21 climb from the 'Wet and Dry' hatch. A fresh 'passage' crew would man the sub as it was towed to and from operations.

to the U-boats. We had confidence from the exercises we did. We'd have an indoor battle so that the captains of other ships were sure they understood my signals, then we'd exercise at sea with the submarines in safe waters.

One of the most important of our instruments was the HF/DF – High Frequency Direction Finding. We could pick up the Germans making signals and get a bearing on them. We'd try to get two ships in the convoy escort to get a bearing on the submarine – and where they crossed, you knew there was a submarine. This was very useful, and the more ships that had HF/DF, the more accurate our locating of the enemy would be.

Once you'd pinpointed a U-boat, you would send a ship out to attack her. One of the nearest ones would split off – if possible a destroyer (we had two destroyers in the group), because they could go faster than the corvettes. Once a submarine was down, they couldn't communicate with other submarines, so you would try to keep them under for as long as

possible – most German submarines still had to surface to recharge their batteries right to the end of the war.

The Germans had some equipment – but they hadn't High Frequency – they had MF – Middle Frequency. We made all our signals on HF. The Germans didn't realise that we had this.

At the end of '43 the Germans brought out the *schnorkel* – and this was a great step forward, and made things very difficult for us. They could then remain submerged for days at a time – they could recharge their batteries through the *schnorkel*. They also had the acoustic torpedo which homed on to the noise of propellers, and unless you reduced the speed in a big way and stopped the noise, the torpedo got you.

We developed a thing called a Foxer, which you towed astern. It made a noise which you hoped would deceive the acoustic torpedo – they had considerable success.

We also developed a new method of attacking the submarines other than the depth charge – it was called a Hedgehog. You threw explosives ahead of the ship and, you hoped, hit the submarine on its way to the bottom. You could track the submarine more " accurately that way.

Right and below: John Norton

▶ John Norton (left and inset), with other Civil Defence volunteer wardens. If not building X-craft, they were always kept busy on other war work.

marine or a depot ship, and release them 100 miles or so short of the target. They would then operate as a normal submarine, with a diesel engine to drive them. There were batteries in the forward compartment for silent running underwater – and they were really a complete submarine, but in miniature. They were about 50 tons in weight – 50 foot in length, and they would sail in underneath the nets, if possible (if they couldn't get under the nets, the diving compartment was used, and the diver went out and cut a hole to

being improved all along the line.

When the submarines were ready we had to transport them out in secret. Marshalls made a big diesel tractor and we had some long truck bogeys on big bogey wheels – big heavy things. They used to lower the submarine with a crane, on to a cradle. Then it was covered in a cage and sheeted down, and two diesel tractors towed right up on to the railway side. There were special trucks there, and the big crane would load it on. Then on a Sunday, a locomotive came, towed it out and

early days the RAF didn't have a bomb which would touch the armour on those – so all they could do was damage them a bit. We had to get under them and really give them some bumps.

The old limpet mine on the two-man torpedoes would not have gone through the armour, so they had the idea of a two-ton amatol charge, laid on the sea bed. When it blew up, it wasn't the explosion but the displacement it caused, which lifted the boat. With the *Tirpitz* it broke it in half, I think. 〞

Sub-Lieutenant Frank Ogden (later MBE) was among those who volunteered for special service. Having no idea what this might entail, he found himself in a four-man X-craft submarine, X 24 – Britain's new weapon against the German threat in the Atlantic.

〝 It was uncomfortable, and it was very cramped – of course, if you were going to be in the boat for a week or more you had to have stores and by the time you had stored ship and got a couple of sleeping bags in, it was crowded.

Operation Guidance – well, the intention was that we should go and sink a floating dock in Bergen harbour. This floating dock – the *Laksuaag* dock – also controlled the pumping for two other small floating docks, and it was the only floating dock in Norway which would take a large capital ship. In other words any large German ship which had to be repaired in Norway went there.

We went from our base in North Scotland, towed by the submarine *Sceptre*, until we were just off the Norwegian coast. There are about 35 miles of fjord, and we had to pass through two minefields with swept channels in between them and pass searchlight positions. There was one place where it was very, very narrow, and the searchlights were playing across the channel. This was at night and we were on the surface. The X-craft has a very small draught – about 18 inches – so we stayed on the surface. Max Shean, the skipper – the only one on deck – lay flat, and we went through like that.

We continued on the surface until about 4 o'clock in the morning, then we had to dive because it was getting light. We then had to go through the second minefield dived. The difficulty was the swept channel was a dog-ieg, so we had to get up to a point, then turn to starboard. The

Royal Navy Submarine Museum

let the sub through), then sailed on to the target. They identified the target by the size of its keel – this was measured by a stop watch, and the distance from the bows to the stern was timed at a certain speed.

Under the target, the two charges were released, time-set, and then the sub returned back to its parent ship.

In the film *Above us the Waves* – which was very accurate (and not all films are), one sub lost its periscope by being hit by a patrol boat, and it was therefore put out of action. When we started to build X-24, we put in two periscopes – an attack periscope and a standard one, in case this happened. The prototype was

took it to its destination. It had to be a Sunday, because it overhung the other line – they had to do it when they could shut sections of the line.

Now the Germans are good engineers – we always respected them for that – and those pocket battleships were very well built, and very fast, and very heavily gunned. They were better than ours, in that sense. We knew that. They were built to raid the convoys. Now, to get one of those ships, with its supply ship, and another cruiser probably, out on the Atlantic approaches, was a very dangerous thing indeed.

So we had to keep them tied up where they were in the ports. In the biggest difficulty was that there was so much traffic. There were Norwegian coasters, fishing vessels, German merchantmen, a German patrol vessel. This made it extremely hard for us to stay up at periscope depth for any length of time, so we were going fairly deep – 60–70 feet down – on dead reckoning, coming up periodically to have a look.

In doing this at one point we definitely got outside the swept channel, because there were no vessels passing over the top of us, and we also heard one of the mine mooring wires scraping our side.

At one stage we had a near brush with a German E-boat which went over the top of us. Max put the periscope up and all he could see was the stern of the boat with the cox-

be the floating dock. In fact, it turned out to be the SS *Barenfels*, which was a German merchant ship, moored about 150 feet from the dock. It was the same length as the dock within about 10 feet – and of course, thinking we were under the dock, we laid our charges, one towards the stern and one towards the front. We had put our charges under the wrong target, which was a great disappointment to us, but the Navy were quite pleased with us – we had sunk the *Barenfels*.

I wouldn't say that we weren't frightened, but we weren't so frightened that we couldn't do our jobs. We were a bit apprehensive – but we had been well trained for this. We had known from quite a long time before what sort of thing we could

Bundesarchiv-Koblenz

thought it was a big fish. We zigzagged to avoid it, and this was where we got out of the swept channel and into the mines.

These boats had fresh air for about six hours, and we were going to be dived for longer than six hours, and so we had fresh compressed oxygen on board which we could syphon off to freshen the air. We also had an air purifying system which recirculated the air in the boat through a carbon dioxide absorbent. This Protasorb absorbed the carbon dioxide, but after a time, even with all these things working, the air in the boat gets very foul and stale. We were dived for 23 hours and it was getting very oppressive. When we finally surfaced, we were quite sick when we started breathing fresh air. **"**

▲ A U-boat submariner sits at his post in U-373. Apart from feelings of claustrophobia, there was always the discomfort of the cramped space, the lack of fresh air and any food which was not from a tin – and on top of all this, there was the boredom!

Frank Ogden

swain's fur-lined boot standing on the back of the boat. By this stage it was nearly nine o'clock and we were getting towards the harbour. There was a lot of traffic in the harbour, and this was one of the tricky things because we couldn't run at periscope depth to get in as close as we would have liked to do to the floating dock. So we had to run into the floating dock blind or something like it, for three-quarters of a mile, and in doing this, we knew we were off-set. We went out and came back in. This time we were still off-set, but we didn't realise that we were. We got underneath a target. We checked it for length and checked it for approximate depth – it appeared to

expect, and we had even practised getting through nets – though in the event we didn't have to. It was, perhaps a little bit scary with all the boats going up above us, because that was a danger – being rammed. But you can hear boats coming from quite a long way away.

We knew that they had ASDIC. This E-boat did, in fact, pick us up. They sent out an impulse to bounce off you, and when it's bouncing off you, you can hear it. It was rather like a drip of water going into an enamel basin. We heard it that time, but bear in mind, they wouldn't be expecting a midget submarine, and they could get impulses back from all sorts of things. They probably

◄ Frank Ogden (right) with, left to right, Brooks, Shean and Coles, on the bridge of HMS/M *Sceptre*, on the way back from their mission as operations crew of X24 to blow up the floating dock at Bergen. Since they hit the wrong target, it was another X-craft crew which finally destroyed the Bergen dock.

Chief Officer Robert Leonard, on the Merchant Navy's heavy-lift ship, Fort Halkett, *had seen action in the icy North Atlantic, then his ship was 'rewarded' with an easy trip to South America, to pick up troops.*

❝ It was August Bank Holiday, 1943, that we caught a torpedo in number two hold, that sunk us, 680 miles off the coast of Brazil.

One of the lifeboats was destroyed, so I took one of the 18-foot bridge boats, and my crew – of which I was the second oldest, and I wasn't yet 21.

At that time, when you were moving independently, you had an envelope with a number of letters in it – ABCD – these were points, at random, in the ocean, and in order to keep the ships apart, so it would be more difficult to sink a number of them, you set off for a point and just before you got there, you would get a radio message in code, telling you where the next point was. We were knocked off on one of these turning points. We changed course at ten past four in the morning, and at twenty to five, BANG. A submarine was sitting waiting at our turning point. It was clear that the code books had been acquired.

I was in my bunk and had come off the eight to twelve, and I woke (I'm a light sleeper) – there was this tremendous thump. The stench of cordite showed that it wasn't just someone dropping a bucket or some clumsy bastard falling over his feet. My wardrobe gently tipped away from my bulkhead.

A chap called Stuart Beale, who I had become very friendly with, had his room on the other side of the officers' block, and I ran round there. I always went to bed dressed ready for action, more or less. His door was ajar. He was very difficult to wake but he was just going to get out of his bunk – there was a great big hole where his floor should have been. I just managed to screech at him in time to stay where he was until he was properly awake. Fortunately his whole bunk and the rest didn't go straight down into the South Atlantic. The torpedo had hit just forward of his room. She was an

taking the water, food and sails out of the lifeboats and leaving the men there. So it was with mixed feelings that we saw him get upended.

By the end of 1940, with the desperate shortage of shipping, they lifted the load-line a foot – which might mean getting on for between 700 and a 1,000 tons extra per ship. This is great fun if you are sitting in an office, but if you are running a ship in a North Atlantic hurricane, it's a joke in doubtful taste, I may tell you. The ship's like a half-tied rock, and we lost, killed and injured and drowned, a significant number of men washed off these grievously

excellent ship with a tremendous captain – Willie Walker – the first DSO of the Merchant Navy. For a merchant ship, she was very much a fighting ship – and even with the loss of one boat, we got everybody off in an orderly fashion – nobody was hurt in a serious way – and the U-boat came alongside us. They asked if we knew where we were, which we did – and was anybody injured, which they weren't.

He was sunk that night by two American Hudson bombers who had heard our SOS from naval control in Brazil. There was something about other mariners being done for by aircraft – it doesn't matter what side you are on. With the German submariners there wasn't that ferocious antipathy that there was with the Japanese submariners, who were hated and loathed and feared because of the horrendous things they did. Not just killing off people – but

overloaded ships. The more overloaded the ship, the more difficult she is to handle in heavy weather.

I developed quite a cynicism about 'experts'. People aren't what they think they are, and what they know is sometimes only what they think they know. 'Don't confuse me with the facts, my mind's made up.'

When you get an enormous stretch of bad weather in the North Atlantic, even the most experienced have a constant air of disquiet. You don't sleep properly and you get bumped about and you physically get knocked about. You are covered in bruises and you can't eat properly because the galley can't operate. On the way to Narvik, we came out of the fjord and took a huge sea which knocked all the pots off the stove – over the galley boy who was grievously scalded. And this could go on and on. The physical work went on for all hands, putting things

▼ Bob Leonard (back row, second from left) with crew from one of the merchant ships on which he sailed before the disastrous voyage on the *Fort Halkett* made on the annual legal holiday, August 1943. Behind the men, smoke floats stand ready for use.

◀ After sailing towards Recife on the coast of Brazil in their rescue boat, men from the *Fort Halkett*, a heavy-lift ship of the Merchant Navy, get a welcome tow into land from a group of local fishermen. By the later stages of the war lifesaving facilities were good and crews could survive for long spells until rescued.

together that were breaking off all the time. You are turning the watch out two or three times a night. It was very corroding to morale to listen to ships broadcasting that they can't launch their boats and that they were sinking. You could lose a man in the length of this room, then he would be gone. You'd have 40 men watching for him – then you'd spot him again – and then you'd lose him.

One of the big advances in how we improved the survival rate was with the lifeboats – how the water was stored and the food. Before, there used to be hard biscuits, which men with false teeth couldn't eat – instead there were proper pemmicans.

There were survival suits like wet suits which kept the wet, and more importantly, the wind, off you. That used to cause havoc – the older men and the younger ones used to die tremendously quickly. If you were not picked up that night, your chances of survival, if you were under 22 or over 50, faded very fast. **"**

F.Lt. Geoffrey A Sleigh-Pettit

◄ **Flt-Lt Geoffrey Sleigh-Pettit of 502 Squadron of Coastal Command. After patrols in Tiger Moths, his squadron moved to the more modern Whitleys.**

▼ **The insignia of 502 Squadron of Coastal Command. The motto, 'I fear nothing' was a tribute to the squadron's work.**

RAF Museum, Hendon

Royal Navy Submarine Museum

Flight-Lieutenant Geoffrey Sleigh-Pettit was with 502 Squadron, based at Aldergrove on the edge of Lough Neagh. Converted to flying Whitleys, he and his crew flew throughout the war, protecting the convoys from U-boat attack.

▲ **The skipper of X-craft *Xema* emerges from his surfaced ship. Although not officially named, the X-craft were given names by their makers and crew, most of which began Ex or X.**

" Our job was one of these humdrum things. You'd go on and on. I knew some first-class chaps in 502 who never saw anything –

which struck me as bad luck. You just went out – maybe a submarine saw you and you were a deterrent.

Twice at night, we picked up echoes which *had* to be periscopes, because the moment we turned off and got them on our forward aerial, they disappeared. They must have been picking us up as well. I suppose we were of some use. One likes to think that all those hours flying weren't for nothing.

We never failed to find the convoy when we had to meet them – I think our navigation was amazingly good. One didn't necessarily find the convoy straight off. If you got out to the position on the chart where the convoy should be, there was a chance that the convoy might be off-course – and you might not be spot-on yourself after flying over nothing but water and relying on getting your position by taking drifts on smoke floats or flame floats.

I don't mind telling you that the thought of all that sea did give me the shivers. I don't know if it affected other people similarly, but one never talked about it. One said, 'Christ, I'm frightened to death', but it was more as a joke.

I hated the damned sea – really hated it. The sea was almost our greatest enemy, because if you did come down, your chances of surviving were very remote.

Then there was the Navy – they were so trigger-happy, but you can't blame them. I had a set-to with the

Navy in the Bay of Biscay once. We were coming back in very misty conditions, but I saw these two wakes. They turned out to be cruisers – and we didn't know anything about them (you were normally *always* briefed about your own ships).

I went in fairly close to see if we could identify the ships. We were firing off the colours of the day, hoping to get an answer from them, and flashing them the letter of the day with an Aldis.

Eventually we made out that they were cruisers – and by that time we were within range. You don't need to be close to be in range of a cruiser! They had obviously been drawing a bead on us. I suppose they assumed that our letters of the day were known by the enemy. Anyway, they weren't going to take any chances, and they pressed the button.

I've been shot at before from the French coast, but never have I been in flak like that. Everything exploded all round us, and the whole cabin was full of smoke.

I dived and levelled out just above the sea, weaving all the time. It might all be in a day's work to a bomber pilot, but it wasn't to us! **"**

Hans Lemke from Potsdam was just 20 when he set out on his first U-boat, U-1229, in August 1944. Its sinking off Newfoundland sent him as a POW to America, then England. He finally married an English girl and settled in Yorkshire where he lives today.

" The journey across the Atlantic was two or three weeks – I can't remember exactly – constantly underwater, because of the *schnorkel*. This wasn't the best of experiences, because when there were heavy seas, the float valve would shut off the *schnorkel* to stop water coming in. So every time that happened, the diesel still needed the air, which it sucked out from the inside of the boat.

It was very boring down there in the torpedo room. I was in charge of the stern section of the torpedoes, so I was on my own. All I had to do was make sure that the pressure and all that other stuff was kept up. I had no other job – I had to be at the ready all the time, in case we had to fire.

We had to sleep down there as well – on bunks fixed between two rails. You would spend your time polishing or checking something – waiting, reading, sleeping, talking.

There were about ten of us down there, in a space measuring about 10 feet by 30 feet. Some of them, the ordinary seamen, would go up on to the bridge to do their watch, and

when they came back they would sleep. Of course, I knew them all, they had all gone through the same training with me, and so we talked a lot. I never remember us quarrelling, really – and what did we talk about? Well, the usual sort of thing. Wouldn't it be nice to have a woman and that sort of stuff . . . philosophy, crosswords.

We talked about what each thought about the universe, God and all that. We were still pretty optimistic then, and nobody was anti-Nazi.

We had a ration of about 15 cigarettes a day – no alcohol on a mission like this. I suppose we had to keep a clear head. Except for the captain who, I believe, did have some spirits with him. The food was very basic – all tinned stuff – but it wasn't too bad. We didn't make many demands in those days.

So, on the 20th August, we were off Newfoundland, and for some reason, the captain decided he would bring the submarine to the surface. I don't know why he ordered us up. Nobody could find out, because he was killed – maybe he wanted a breath of fresh air.

We had absolutely no idea that there were ships in the area and that aircraft were engaged against us. As far as I knew, everything was quiet. But as soon as we went up, we had to dive down very fast again. Alarm!

I don't think we had dived down 10 feet when a bomb hit us. A lot of damage – some of the men overboard. After about 20 minutes to

▼ **Hans Lemke, 'I remember when I was in the water, thinking what a shock it would be to my mother' – but he survived being sunk.**

▼▼ **Deep in the torpedo room of U-1229, Hans Lemke (center) and crew-mates while away the long hours under the Atlantic.**

half an hour, we couldn't hold ourselves any longer – we had to surface. Before we even got to the top, they started to shoot. So we had to go up, and the captain shouted, 'Everyone overboard! Save yourselves!' I was the furthest back, so I was the last one to the conning tower. When I came out I saw them all dead there on the deck. Nine aircraft were strafing us.

I dived straight into the water, and I didn't come up until I was yards away. I was in the water for about four hours. I didn't even have a life-jacket on – in fact, we had stripped off completely to make us as

light as possible. The aircraft kept firing and quite a few of us got shot in the water. There was no need for that, because it was quite obvious that we had abandoned ship. I've never forgiven them for that.

We got as far as we could from the sub, because we weren't quite sure whether it was going to blow or what, and after five or ten minutes, the sub suddenly reared up and the propellers came out of the water, still turning slowly. Then she just slowly went down. As she went down, we gave her a big cheer – strange – why were we cheering?

After a few minutes, she blew up – I think because of the pressure – and this nearly ripped our insides out. It was then four hours until we were picked up by a destroyer.

We were absolutely shattered – frozen stiff – and we had to climb up rope ladders to get on to the destroyer. We were numb at that stage and one of us, the wireless operator, dropped dead from exhaustion after climbing up **"** on to the destroyer.

Left and above: Hans Lemke

CHAPTER 22

BATTLE DIARY

OCTOBER 1944

20 Leyte Gulf landings

NOVEMBER

2 Carigara taken

5–15 Battle of Breakneck Ridge on Leyte

DECEMBER

15 Invasion of Mindoro

22 Ormoc Valley secured (Leyte)

JANUARY 1945

9 Lingayen Gulf landing, central Luzon

FEBRUARY

3 Battle of Manila begins

28 Invasion of Palaawan

MARCH

2 Corregidor recaptured

3 Manila secured

31 US capture Zamboanga peninsula on Mindanao

APRIL

28 Central Visayan islands cleared of Japanese

MAY

1 First Australian landings on Borneo

JUNE

15 Sulu Archipelago secured

30 Eastern Mindanao secured

AUGUST

15 Japanese surrender

LEYTE GULF – LAST-DITCH ATTACK

When it was clear that the Americans would land on Leyte in the Philippine islands, the Japanese launched on October 17, 1944, a complex naval operation codenamed *Sho,* or Victory. A decoy force would draw the US fleet to the north and so allow two forces from the west and south to attack the US Seventh Fleet Fleet near Leyte.

The ensuing battle fell into four main actions. The first came in the Sibuyan Sea between October 23 and 24, when a US submarine sank the cruiser *Atago,* and the battleship *Musashi* was sunk by carrier aircraft. The Japanese sank the light carrier USS *Princeton* and damaged the cruiser USS *Birmingham.* Then, in Surigao Strait between October 24 and 25, the Japanese lost the battleship *Fuso* and two destroyers to PT boats; the Japanese then ran into six US battleships which wrecked the battleship *Yamashiro.* Only *Mogami,* a cruiser and destroyer survived.

On the 25th off Samar the Japanese plan nearly succeeded. In a fast-moving gun battle the Japanese lost two destroyers, with two more crippled by air attack. Japanese gunfire badly damaged the carrier USS *Gambier Bay* and the destroyers USS *Johnston* and *Roberts* were sunk, with the USS *Dennis* seriously damaged. *Gambier Bay* sank at at 09.07. But although the Japanese could now have gone on to destroy the US escort carrier group, the aggressive American tactics convinced Admiral Kurita he was fighting a superior force and he withdrew.

To the north off Cape Engano on the same day the decoy force of Japanese battleships came under aggressive air attack from US Task Force 38. By the end of the day the Japanese force had lost all its carriers, a cruiser and three destroyers.

Leyte Gulf finished the Japanese Imperial Fleet – it lost three battleships, four carriers, ten cruisers, 11 destroyers and a submarine. In addition 500 aircraft were lost and personnel casualties were 10,500 seamen and pilots.

LAST-DITCH ATTACK

The Japanese planners have it in mind to deliver a final blow to the US Fleet, but plans based on misguided information can go disastrously wrong.

The Battle of Leyte Gulf was an engagement with many moves – tactics, intelligence, speculation and strategy all played their part in dictating the course of the conflict. But for individuals the main concern was their immediate actions under pressure and, for many, courage when all hope seemed lost.

Lieutenant B D Morris, known popularly in the late 30s and early 40s as Wayne Morris, a Hollywood actor, was manning one of the F6Fs of the Essex's Air Group 15 as the Americans tried to intercept the Japanese attack.

"I took off at 10.15 in the morning with eight other planes, when the fighting was getting hot. One fighter's engine began to miss and that pilot went back to the carrier, but the rest of us went in. We circled over the Task Force, giving special attention to the damaged *Princeton* which was already pouring out smoke, having been hit on the flight deck by a 550-pound bomb from one of the Japanese bombers in the clouds.

There were about 30 Japanese planes. When they saw us, the dive bombers and torpedo bombers broke off and ducked away while the 'rats' [the fighters] formed a Lufberry circle above and went around, nose to tail. I noted they were all Zeroes this time. They stayed high and the bombers were breaking off to go it alone. I decided to go after the lead of one Zero section. I made a high run and saw four bursts strike him. It flamed up and crashed. My wingman broke off just then to chase one of the four bombers that slipped out of the Lufberry circle, shot it down and then rejoined us.

I then made a pass at a pair of Zeroes coming at me. I missed on the first pass and turned to find the Zeroes turning with me and firing shots that were hitting my plane. I tried to run with the Zeroes for a few seconds but then I saw I was not going to win that way so I ducked into a cloud. Once inside the cloud I made a 360 degree turn and came back out where I had gone in. The two Zeroes were circling out towards the other side where they expected me to come out. I got on the tail of one and, in a few seconds, shot it down. But I knew my plane had been hit plenty. The engine began to cough and the cockpit was filling up with hydraulic fluid. I broke off the action and headed back to the carrier."

◄ The gun camera on a Hellcat captures the effects of the pilot's attack on a Japanese Zero fighter. The direct hit would probably result in the destruction of one of the few remaining Japanese aircraft.

▲ Ensign Brauer, wounded during a strike on the Japanese fleet on 25 October, is helped from the cockpit of his F6F which has crashed through a barrier on USS *Lexington*.

Lieutenant L Odum, the Aerology Officer of the 'baby flattop' carrier, **Gambier Bay,** *was on the starboard catwalk as, his devastated ship's decks covered with dead and wounded, the order came to abandon the stricken ship.*

❝ I didn't relish the idea of going off the high side, so I started walking to the passageway in the centre of the ship, down the stairs by my room, heading for the port side. Near my room there was an explosion and I was thrown against the bulkhead. Shell fragments were ricocheting around me but I wasn't hit. I reached my stateroom and found my bunkmate collecting survival gear. I picked up a palm-sized mirror and stuffed it and an unopened pack of cigarettes in my shirt pocket.

I got to the port side, unlaced my shoes, dropped my helmet and sidearm and holster and slid down a heavy rope. First I was dragged under by the weight of my shoes but I kicked them off and started swimming away from the ship. I spotted a raft and swam to it. About 30 men were aboard. Suddenly I found I was in charge. The leader of the group had sunk into a stupor. I got the uninjured men off the raft and had them cling to the ropes on the sides.

We were so close still that we could see the American fighters and bombers attacking the Japanese cruisers and destroyers as they were heading north. We could only wait until someone came to find us.

That night in the water we all had one biscuit the size of a Ritz cracker with a piece of Spam. There was no fresh water. One by one some of the men just drifted away from the raft

▲ **US escort carrier** *Gambier Bay* **lays a smoke screen against attack. On 24 October the eight-inch guns of three Japanese cruisers finally destroyed the ship, its crew abandoning it to take their chances in the water.**

and were not seen again.

Somehow we got through the night. In the morning we had another bite of biscuit and a malted milk tablet. Sharks began to appear round the raft. Some of the men began drinking sea water and they became delirious.

The second day the sun was hot and the men were dispirited as they saw planes flying overhead which didn't see us. I swam over to the raft next to ours. The men here were in as bad shape as we were, without

food and water. The night was full of terrors. Men who had drunk the sea water began hallucinating. Some of them thought they could swim to Samar, and went into the water and had to be dragged back. Some did not come back.

Most of the men had given up hope. I was sure that we would be rescued if we waited. Flares were sent up every hour in hope. At one o'clock the next morning, hope arrived.

A crew member on *PC 623* called out to us 'What ship are you from?' None of us would answer. What if these were Japanese rescuers? Then the patrol boat snapped on its searchlights and began probing us. Suddenly, as with one voice we all yelled, 'Yes, yes, we are Americans. *Gambier Bay*.' By now we could see the big number 623 on the patrol craft. It slowed down and sailors began lowering nets over the side for our men to climb. I started swimming over and was overrun and nearly drowned by some men as the boat pulled in towards the rafts. Men were crawling over me to get to the boat. I shook myself free and climbed to the deck, lay down on that cold steel and wept and thanked God for His deliverance. **❞**

US National Archives

Robert Hunt Library

wait for the results of the attack on the enemy's mobile force by our aircraft, avoiding for a while bearing the brunt of the attack – also, I think there was the chance that he would mislead the enemy.

So there's not the slightest justification for thinking he was going to abandon the breakthrough into Leyte. I think this was sufficiently clarified by the second reverse course after 5 pm, because of the receipt of the signal from Combined Fleet C-in-C Toyota, 'Heaven is on our side. Attack with all forces', was made about 7 pm.

Kurita realised that the breakthrough into Leyte Gulf would be delayed – he wouldn't reach it until dawn on the 25th. I remember we were anxious about adjusting with Nishimura Force how we should go about it.

But there was a more urgent problem – the passage through San Bernardino Strait. I mean, we were worried that we might be ambushed at the exit from the strait.

At any rate, because we'd taken a fair hiding from the submarines the day before, we would be in a real fix if we became a target at the exit from the strait, when we would have no freedom of manoeuvre. However,

US National Archives

the enemy seems to have judged our previous reverse course to be a withdrawal, and made no provision.

Our getting out of the strait safely didn't depend on the enemy or ourselves – of course we didn't know it at the time, but the enemy had finally become aware of Ozawa Force. The enemy had no reason to think that Ozawa Force was a decoy,

▲ Exhausted and soaked in oil, a Japanese survivor is hauled from the waters of the Surigao Strait by crew of the American Patrol Torpedo Boat 321, October 1944.

Torao Suematsu had climbed through the ranks of the Japanese Imperial Navy since 1939 and, by late 1944 was Staff Officer, Number 1 Special Attack Forces. He recalls the events in the Sibuyan Sea, 24 October.

❝ At about 2 pm, *Musashi*, battered on all sides, and already the victim of at least ten torpedoes and countless bombs, was ordered to make for Manila, and we sailed on leaving her behind. She had her escort vessels, of course – however, air attacks by enemy ship-borne aircraft increased in ferocity as time went on, and as the damage we had sustained was not insignificant, we needed to turn back and take stock. At about 3.30 pm, C-in-C Kurita changed fleet course westward.

He judged that if we continued to advance as we were, we would sustain far greater damage (besides, *Musashi*, and the flagship of No 5 Squadron, *Myoko*, had been torpedoed and had fallen out of line, and both *Yamato* and *Nagato* had been damaged by bombing), since the enemy assault planes had increased in number. He decided to

▶ After two days in the sea with no fresh water and minimal food, survivors of the *Gambier Bay*, *Hoel*, *Johnston* and *Samuel B Roberts* are rescued by a patrol boat. Thirst, the effect of drinking sea water, exhaustion and, not least, sharks took a heavy toll on the men in the sea.

◀ A cruiser comes alongside the badly bombed USS *Princeton* to give rescue workers a chance to quench the flames on board. Fatally crippled, the *Princeton* was later finished off and sunk.

US National Archives

and the fact that it was, unlike us, an air fleet must have meant they felt it to be a threat. So there seemed to be no need to pay attention to Kurita Force, which had changed course.

At any rate, that night we were able to pass uneventfully through San Bernardino Strait. Even if there were no submarines, we expected to find the enemy fleet lying in wait for us. We had to pass through the strait in a single column. At the exit, if it had come to a gunnery engagement, the enemy in line abreast, we wouldn't have stood a chance.

The loss due to the reverse course alone was about three hours, but besides that there was considerable delay due to the air attacks by enemy aircraft, so that when we came out of the strait, it was just past midnight – deep night. And at exactly that time, Nishimura Force was approaching Surigao Strait. They came down on the 25th, and when our force re-formed into a ring for night sailing, the enemy aircraft carrier units suddenly came into view. I was on the bridge at the time, and I was astounded – it was something we had not considered.

For an instant we had a bit of a scene on the bridge – of shock, surprise, quite unheard of. Ordinarily you'd never consider such an encounter. Clearly the enemy had not properly interpreted our movements. In this situation, the advantage was with us. It is the Chief of Staff who issues a fleet movement order in such a case – after, of course, obtaining the consent of the C-in-C. But if the Chief of Staff says

to the C-in-C, 'We'll do it!' the C-in-C replies yes or no. If he differs from the Chief of Staff's opinion, he can say, 'No, let's do something else', but I don't think the chief of staff was on the bridge at this time. For what seemed a long interval, although it can't have been more than a minute, no-one said a word. But I was impatient, being afraid we might let slip a thousand-to-one chance, and in the end I couldn't stand it any longer. I said, 'C-in-C, we must move towards the enemy.' 'Yes,' he answered, and then gave the order, 'Column unit turn, let's go!' looking at the compass. We raised the flag, 'column unit turn', on a bearing to contain the enemy – it must have been 110. (The order means the fleet changes direction completely as one unit, not just as individual ships.)

Because the enemy were a force of aircraft carriers and destroyers, they could not open fire on us at once with their guns. So as soon as we had completed 'column unit turn', *Yamato* began to fire. However, when she'd fired four or five rounds, enemy destroyers advanced at speed and spread a smoke screen.

This was the first time *Yamato* had opened fire with her main guns on an enemy fleet. She had only fired her AA guns before that. So everybody shouted, 'We've sunk her!' – but in fact it wasn't possible to confirm whether we'd sunk a ship or not, because of the smoke screen. Passing close by later, we saw an enemy aircraft carrier up to the deck in water, so we can only have sunk one

▶ Huge jets of water surround a stricken Japanese ship as it comes under bombardment by US aircraft. In spite of all the Japanese optimism, the American superiority in numbers was bound to win out.

▼ Even though the crew of this US submarine have the element of surprise in their favor as they move in on their quarry, the apprehension is clear on the faces of the torpedo-room men.

US National Archives

Hulton-Deutsch Collection

◀ With no air cover for her remaining ships, Japan can do nothing to stop the US landings at Leyte. Three days after the first landings, cargo vessels pour supplies ashore to the liberating forces and provide much-needed food for the Filipinos.

ship for certain. Nearby, half-naked crew members were drifting on rafts.

As far as the sunk aircraft carrier is concerned, it's anyone's guess whether she was hit by a torpedo or by gunfire. She was an escort carrier, so the enemy was not a large force. At the time we thought they were standard carriers. At any rate, we made an all-out attack. Then, un-luckily, when we were getting a thorough pasting from enemy bombers, a squall came up between us and the enemy.

How can I describe it? When we were going into the attack, a squall

Robert Hunt Library

► The cap badge of an officer of the Imperial Japanese Navy – by the end of October 1944, a symbol of a spent force.

▼ At the time one of the largest battleships ever built, *Yamato* becomes Admiral Kurita's flag-ship after the loss of his ship *Atago* to US submarines on 23 October.

comes up – how about that?

We spent about two hours searching for them, but we too had been the victims of torpedo attacks from the enemy's destroyers. In order to dodge these torpedoes, *Yamato* had to run in the opposite direction from the enemy. We ran for about ten minutes, but that was a lot of time to lose. But because visibility was poor due to the squall, it was impossible to estimate what our situation was in relation to one another. Fleet high command was possibly no better off.

Estimating was out of the question, so we had to consider our fuel situation. To control the battle line, we ordered the fleet to concentrate. The basic course in this case was north, and that was a problem. On that course, we were increasing our distance from Leyte. Moreover, all units were pretty scattered – it took a fair amount of time to concentrate them, but then we made course once more for Leyte and ran for about two hours.

The enemy bombed us the entire time. They bombed us for three days during this sea battle, without a break, and it felt as if your head was being pressed down into your shoulders – but when we ourselves went into the attack, it was exhilarating.

What kind of psychology is that,

US National Archives

US National Archives

But we needed to find out what was happening at Leyte, at all costs. We couldn't discover a thing. At about 3 am, the signal came in that Nishimura Force had been annihilated in Surigao Strait.

A signal came in, based on aircraft intelligence, to the effect that an enemy mobile task force was in a position comparatively close to our force. And just at that time, on the northern horizon, several enemy aircraft appeared, looking as if they were about to land on a deck. Aboard *Yamato*, we discussed this and judged that there must be an aircraft carrier over there. Taking what we had seen and the fact of that signal, we felt that the enemy mobile task force was really there.

Nishimura Force must have had it! Even if we charged ahead into Leyte Gulf, it was already two pm. We wondered whether to have a go at the aircraft carrier instead, but we felt we couldn't be sure of taking her. Battlefield psychology, you could say.

Yamamoto heard what I had to say, and assembled everyone to pass on my opinion. I went back to the bridge, and after about ten minutes, the order was issued, 'Reverse course to annihilate enemy mobile task force', but in the end we never managed to catch the enemy aircraft carriers.

Although we didn't break into Leyte Gulf, and reversed course, we did not catch the mobile task force

eh? The air might have been hot and humid, but we felt as if we were under blue skies. When we pursued the enemy, even when they were bombing us, we weren't worried. There's a big difference between defence and attack.

Kurita Force ended up not charging into Leyte Gulf – in fact, we withdrew northwards – and I bear some responsibility for it. I've had misgivings about it, even in post-war days. Was I the cause of an appalling failure? That's been my worry. Because I was the one who brought about the occasion by which Kurita Force reversed course. I was on the bridge, but I had no idea what was happening in Leyte Gulf.

Yamato was carrying her shipborne aircraft, so I said to the C-in-C, since I wanted to know what was going on at Leyte, 'I'm sending off an aircraft to find out the situation at Leyte'. He agreed readily, and the aircraft took off – but it was a float-plane, and the enemy had complete air supremacy, so we couldn't carry out the recce as wished. All we could do was use cloud as much as possible and catch glimpses through breaks in the cloud, and we did not, as I recall, get any useful information. We sent off two aircraft from *Yamato* but they were ordered to go to their seaplane base once their duty was finished.

▲ **An F6F Hellcat fighter prepares for take-off from the deck of a US carrier as the deck crew signal to the pilot to give him the all-clear.**

▶ **The huge carrier deck of the *Zuiho*, as seen by the camera in a fighter from the USS *Enterprise* going in for the attack. Six air strikes sank the *Zuiho* and three other carriers before being sent to support the US ships near Samar.**

▶▶ **His arm held in a makeshift splint and strapped into a cradle, a US survivor acknowledges the friendly hand extended from his rescuers' ship.**

we aimed at – the whole thing was a flop. That happened as a result of my expressing an opinion.

I suppose a fair amount of time had passed since the enemy group had gone into Leyte Gulf, and we probably thought the enemy transports were empty, and indeed, might already have gone. At any rate, we knew nothing of what was going on at Leyte. Nishimura Force had already ceased to exist, and to go into the attack in the middle of the day, under conditions of enemy air supremacy, was not how we had planned it. We wanted to have a go

► In a still from captured Japanese newsreel, a fighter takes off from a Japanese carrier on a last operation.

US National Archives

Robert Hunt Library

at this new mobile task force.

But we couldn't catch them. I felt terribly depressed. I can remember worrying about this, even when the war was over. I learned later that the enemy thought the situation at that juncture was serious, that Japanese aircraft carriers were present to the north in great strength, and were moving south. So if we *had* gone into Leyte Gulf, we might certainly have put paid to the transport ships, but I don't think we'd have come out of it alive ourselves. However, since then, I've seen the question asked in a number of books, 'Why did Admiral Kurita reverse course at that time? Didn't he miss the opportunity he was hoping for?' When I read these things, I wonder if I was wrong.

I'm afraid, from start to finish, we had no luck at all. In particular, there was that squall. If that hadn't happened, perhaps the whole course of battle might have been different. Moreover, I wonder whether the effect of the enemy's smoke screen would have been so great if there had been a squall *then*. If there'd been no squall, we might have destroyed the enemy at that moment. Again, might we not have been able to go smoothly into Leyte Gulf without spending time concentrating the force?

As evening began to draw in, and as we'd not been able to catch the enemy carriers, we withdrew through San Bernardino Strait. The next day, during the morning, we

took a pretty fair bashing from enemy aircraft. Finally, the enemy's base air units joined in.

We weren't in despair, however. By this time we had already had some experience of being knocked about. I don't think there was any feeling that things were desperate. We felt worse after Saipan.

You could say this was the last decisive fleet battle. We needed total air back-up – and we would have preferred the opposition to be warships, not aircraft. **"**

US National Archives

CHAPTER 23

BATTLE DIARY

FEBRUARY 1945

8 First Canadian Army attacks east of Nijmegen: Operation Veritable

13–14 Dresden destroyed in a 'firestorm' bombing raid

23 US Ninth Army attacks toward the Rhine: Operation Grenade

28 US 12th Army Group attacks toward Cologne-Koblenz: Operation Lumberjack

MARCH

3 Veritable and Grenade link up

7 US seizure of the Ludendorff railroad bridge across the Rhine at Remagen

13 US Third and Seventh Armies attack toward the Rhine: Operation Undertone

22–23 Patton crosses the Rhine at Nierstein and Oppenheim

23–24 21st Army Group crosses the Rhine in the north: Operation Plunder

24 Allied airborne drop to the east of the Rhine: Operation Varsity

28 Eisenhower's decision to attack into central Germany rather than Berlin

APRIL

2 Allied forces encircle the Ruhr

18 Field Marshal Model commits suicide as Ruhr pocket collapses

25 US and Soviet forces link up at Torgau on the Elbe

30 Hitler commits suicide in Berlin

MAY

4 Surrender of German forces in Holland, Denmark and northern Germany to Montgomery at Luneburg Heath

7 German unconditional surrender at Eisenhower's HQ at Rheims

8 VE (Victory in Europe) Day

9 German surrender ratified in Berlin. The war in Europe is officially over

RHINE CROSSING – OPERATION VARSITY

The psychological and physical barrier of the Rhine, stretching 825 miles from Switzerland to the North Sea, had been a source of concern to Allied planners since before the D-Day landings in June 1944. The river was the major obstacle to the defeat of Germany, a natural defensive line behind which Hitler could reorganize his forces. Crossing the Rhine was vital for the Allies' progress.

General Eisenhower's 'broad-front' approach involved all three Allied Army Groups advancing in unison. In the north, British and Canadian troops under Field Marshal Montgomery overcame fierce German resistance and heavy rain to combine with the US Ninth Army and establish control over the Rhine's west bank; further south the American troops unexpectedly captured an intact bridge across the river at Remagen during Operation Lumberjack, which drove back the overstretched German Seventh Army. Now the river was all that stood in the way of an Allied advance.

Montgomery's carefully planned Operation Plunder involved 1,250,000 men in a main thrust across the Rhine between the towns of Wesel and Emmerich. Under cover from a heavy artillery bombardment, the crossing began at 21.00 on March 23; by dawn the next day five bridgeheads had been established on the east bank with minimal casualties. At 10.00, in a supporting operation codenamed Varsity, the British Sixth and US 17th Airborne Divisions landed by parachute and glider near Wesel to reinforce the ground units in establishing a 40-mile-long bridgehead from which to push eastward to the Rhur, the industrial heart of Germany. Beyond the way lay open into the heart of the Reich.

OPERATION
VARSITY

*The scene is set for a massive airborne
invasion. Both airborne and ground-based
troops anticipate a prestigious victory – but
the Germans will still not give up the fight.*

Believing that the Germans were on their last legs, the Allied feeling seemed to be that Varsity would be a very prestigious (and not too strongly opposed) airdrop to carry off. However, the Germans were seeing their homeland under threat, and they were prepared to fight to the death to protect the Allies' goal – the Fatherland – from conquest. From that battle would come experiences and images which would stay with the men – and women – forever.

ployed in positions as close to the river as possible. Artificial moonlight to provide reasonable visibility was produced by a long line of searchlights, with their beams reflected from the clouds into the area of activity. The reason for bringing the guns so far forward was that they would still be in range of more distant targets without the need for time-wasting redeployment during the early stages of the advance beyond the Rhine. When our move was completed, I went forward with

◀ **A Horsa glider takes off, towed by a Halifax. Air Chief Marshal Sir Arthur Tedder briefed the crews taking part in Operation Varsity that the majority of the enemy aircraft were out of action and the flak was reduced – but not eliminated.**

◀ **Advancing through the wake of destruction left by the preliminary bombardment, Tommies file across the border into Germany at Breedeweg.**

At night, there was a cautious movement of men and equipment between my dam and the river. Came the hour, and the world exploded. The noise was ear-splitting and got worse as the German guns hit our side of the river. Terrified stampeding cattle, some of whom thundered along the top of my dam, presented a far greater danger to us in our slit trench than enemy shells.

Some of our shells just fell in the river – this I knew was incorrect, so I went through the motions of making adjustments. To be honest, it would have been pure, blind chance had any of them been accurate, but at least it kept us busy. At one point, out of the corner of my eye, I saw the signaller duck. Like any old soldier, I followed him a split second later.

Eventually the devastating shelling ended and our advance troops made a triumphant crossing and established a bridgehead from which the advance proceeded. The dawn came up and everything was relatively peaceful. I questioned my signaller about his ducking during the night. He indicated a shell hole a few yards from our trench. He saw the shell burst – I did not.

Our questionable night's work concluded, I looked with admiration

🪂 *John Leopard, formerly Staff Captain with the artillery of 6th Airborne Division, was transferred to the 10th City of Glasgow Field Regiment, Royal Artillery, and witnessed what was, reportedly, the heaviest artillery bombardment in military history, covering the Rhine crossing.*

❝ The plan was to so damage the opposing forces that our assault troops could gain the enemy shore with the minimum casualties.

The main crossings were to be made by the 15th and 51st Divisions, just north of Xanten. We in the 52nd were among those in close support.

For days before the attack, shells and masses of equipment for the crossing were brought well forward under the cloak of continuous smoke screens. On the night before the action, all the field guns were de-

my signaller to a pre-planned observation post on top of a flood barrier, some 50 yards back from the river bank. Here we dug a slit trench from which I would have a clear view of the German-held side of the river. Cunningly, we were very close to a forward aid post. We'd be assured of endless hot sweet tea during the coming battle.

I had a map showing the scores of target areas and the artillery units responsible for each of them. It was my unenviable task to assess the accuracy of the fall of shot and to signal back such corrections as I deemed proper. How I was supposed to accomplish this during the night, lit only by the light of thousands of exploding shells, I had not the least idea. In the event, the light from the many fires started helped a bit.

Our guns in their vulnerable positions remained silent all day. There was quite a lot of random fire from the Germans, no doubt in the hope of an informative response.

▲ **John Leopard, from his strategic point overlooking the Rhine, was witness to the spectacular bombardment which heralded the river crossings north of Xanten.**

at the long tank-carrying Bailey bridge the Royal Engineers had built.

At a forward aid post, I saw a well-bandaged German officer inside. At the same time, the 6th Airborne Division, with its scores of aircraft and gliders, was passing overhead to stiffen our forward troops. I pointed upwards. The German looked pretty glum, but said in passable English, 'Zee var ees ofer'. ❞

Flying Officer Rosemary Britten, unbeknown to her uncle, Ian Toler (see next account), had bartered and bluffed her way into a place on the Rhine landings operation. The only woman on the flight, her story is a unique one.

"All the night before, my conscience pricked me horribly, and I was like a cat on hot bricks, knowing I should have let one of the men go. However, too many people knew I was going, although I had been very careful not to tell a soul, so I couldn't back out, even had I wanted to!

Having got Ops to ring me in the Waafery at 0345, I was at breakfast at 0415, having emptied my pockets in the approved manner. Contents were now comb, £2, escape kit and powder and lipstick (which I didn't use the whole time – at first, because I wanted to look like a German girl in case of baling out, and afterwards because I was too dirty to make any difference!).

A bad moment was when Uncle Ian [Ian Toler] came up to say goodbye and asked me to come and see take-off. An even worse one was when I found myself getting into the crew bus alongside a Canadian war correspondent. He started to interrogate me about being the only woman on ops, and being in quite a panic anyway, I told him my name. Afterwards I appealed to his better nature and, I think, persuaded him to leave it out until after the war.

Holland was a shattering sight – some of the fields were flooded, others had been and were now dryer – a bit black and quite dead. I don't think I saw a single sign of life in the part of Holland that we crossed,

▶ **Rosemary Britten's Halifax, D-Dog, bears the scars of the eventful return from the Rhine. Only miraculous handling landed the plane intact.**

▼ **An operational photo, taken from D-Dog, on 24 March shows the huge expanse of the Rhine as the airborne drop begins in apparent calm.**

Right and below: Crown Copyright

▼ **Flying Officer Rosemary Britten, the only woman on Operation Varsity, had as good as given herself and her crew up for dead when their plane was badly hit after the glider drop.**

Rosemary Cavendish Morton

every little village was gutted.

I was surprised to find I could recognise the country from the briefing photographs, and saw the wood near Hamminkeln, although the actual LZ was out of sight in a very effective smoke screen. We wished our glider good luck and he was gone – down into the smoke with the hundreds of others.

We did a violent turn to port, miraculously avoiding other aircraft, for there were black puffs of flak coming up ahead, and a Halifax went down in flames with only three parachutes, one of which went into the crash, and a Hamilcar disintegrated, spitting out its tank and crew.

The flak seemed to be singling out our aircraft, and Ron took some pretty violent evasive action – but not violent enough, as there was suddenly an almighty crack, and D-Dog shook all over, and various parts of the controls began quite obviously not to connect.

We crossed back over the Rhine, which was one great comfort anyway, as at least we should not have to bale out into the battle – but it became very apparent that we should have to bale out somewhere,

as more and more things became conspicuous by their absence. Ron was holding the stick with his knees and couldn't take his hands off for a moment.

Then the intercom went u/s [unserviceable], but the wireless operator did something to Ron's helmet which improved matters spasmodically – though it was difficult getting it back on his head, as he couldn't spare his hands. I did a small amount of shouting messages, but it's hopeless when you can hardly hear yourself speak.

The control column was hanging together by a quarter inch of metal, so, of course, everything depended on whether it snapped or whether it didn't. Fred tied a hammer on to it as a kind of splint, which saved the situation – luckily, I didn't see it, but only knew from the frantic activity that things were NOT WORKING.

I then remembered the crew had said, on getting into the aircraft, that they didn't bother to do their parachutes up properly, so, not wanting to be a sissy, I didn't either. That took me a few minutes fumbling and so I got hot and bothered and oily. Mac opened the escape hatch and told me what to do. I was afraid they would not trust me to jump of my own free will and give me a push when I wasn't expecting it. Holland looked even more dead and desolate than on the outward journey. By that time I knew I was going to be either killed or court-martialled, and was amazed to find I didn't really mind either. I remember thinking that now I wouldn't have to live to a

NA 698

dreary old age, which was a good thing. But I could do with another year or two, now it had come to the point. It all seemed too extraordinary to be true – but very interesting.

Harry worked out the distance home and, as it still seemed to be getting on for 200 miles, and a stretch of sea, it was decided we couldn't make it, as any minute the column might break altogether.

The compasses were u/s, so we didn't really know where we were. The hydraulics were u/s, so there was the problem of whether to bale out or crash land – I had a slight leaning to baling out, myself, as I hate being chopped about by metal and I had visions of the Caterpillar Club.

Ron decided to land, having found a suitable looking airfield. He asked

itions, with the escape hatches open above and below, and the wind blowing through what had been the door. I couldn't help thinking what a horrible mess we three would make.

George went back to the turret to get his hat, so I got mine too, just in case we survived, in which event, one might as well put up as good a show as possible. Then a fountain of evil-smelling hydraulic oil came up all over us. We had the option of moving from our crash positions, or sitting in the spray – so we sat in it.

Then Fred performed some amazing technical feat with the hydraulics and got the undercarriage down. We landed perfectly, but I felt rather sick when I saw what had been the control column – a direct hit had burst inside the fuselage, blowing the

LG for lame ducks. A circle of Yanks and gaping French surrounded us.

After a good deal of waiting and questioning, we were finally flown back to our base. I would have done anything to have gone to bed as I had a ghastly headache, but rather than it should be thought I couldn't take it, I took a few aspirins and went up to the mess with Ron, where we were greeted as if returned from the dead. Apparently four crews had reported D-Dog shot down.

I felt rather bad about turning up after all, and decided to acquire an operational twitch at least! **"**

◀ **Its old engine decidedly the worse for wear, a Dakota is fitted with a reconditioned motor before taking part in the operation to drop gliders for the Rhine crossing at Wesel.**

▶▲ **The insignia of No 296 Squadron, based at Earls Colne. With sister squadron 297, 296 provided many of the pilots for Operation Varsity.**

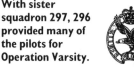

Ian Toler, a member of the Army's Glider Pilot Regiment, trained by the RAF, was part of the airborne armada which reinforced the ground troops' crossing of the Rhine. A survivor of the Arnhem landing, he was well prepared for events.

" As we approached the Rhine, a great pall of smoke appeared on the far side, covering our objective. There were several crashed Dakotas on our side of the Rhine and my tug pilot told me later, 'I saw a lot of very frightened Daks streaking out of the smoke like bats out of hell, and I said to the crew, "This is it, chaps".'

On my landing zone there was a very prominent feature – a small wood, codenamed Bunty. This was completely obscured, but luckily our run-in release point was clear. Over the release point I released the tow rope and flew towards the railway, which I could just see. We were then flying completely blind in the smoke.

US National Archives

me what would happen if I turned up on the Continent, which I thought very considerate of him. Quite immaterial, though, as I had no hope of being in a state to try and explain when we did reach the ground, as I thought we'd all be mixed up with bits of aircraft.

George, Harry and I sat on the floor in the rear bay in crash pos-

door away and pepperating the aircraft all round, cutting a lot of vital parts – but it missed the petrol tanks and the crew.

There wasn't a door, but there were so many jagged edges that one couldn't get through it, so we had to jump through the escape hatch.

We found ourselves on Strip B53, Merville, near Lille – an American

Major T.I.J. Toler

I followed my planned flight path from the release point. At about 200 feet I saw the tops of some high-tension power lines, and knew I was going in the right direction. However, just as I was preparing to land, I saw some low-tension cables or telephone wires on posts below me. There was no time to avoid them, so I ploughed straight into them, hoping they would break – which they did, but in so doing, caused me to stall about 20 feet up, so that we landed heavily and the front of the glider was damaged – but no-one was injured. As the smoke cleared, I was able to identify Bunty, which was only 100 yards away, and I found I was within 50 yards of where I should have been.

We now had to unload the glider, and as the nose had been damaged, we were not able to use the new method of nose unloading, so had to remove the tail. We were lucky not to be under fire – if we had landed further forward, I should probably not be telling this story.

Having unloaded the jeep and stores, the gunners moved to their headquarters. I moved to a farmhouse which I had selected as our HQ at the briefing, and we found that we had about 200 prisoners to deal with. We put the farmhouse in a state of defence and collected food and water – remembering how important this was at Arnhem. We put the occupants in one room and set up a guard, as they didn't seem very cooperative. One of my pilots came to me and said there were a number of pigeons in the farm, and he

thought they might be carriers to take information to the enemy. I went to have a look, and a small boy, with tears in his eyes, indicated, as he had no English, that we must not shoot them – they were his pets. I thought he was right, and we didn't.

The Division had taken all objectives within four hours of landing.

Next day, looking around the landing zone, it appeared to be a mass of crashed and broken gliders. Many had been attacked on the ground as soon as they landed. I tried to assess my casualties, which seemed to be pretty high. Captain

US National Archives

▲ Men of the 15th Scottish Division, crew of a DUKW, take a rest on the road near Hamminkeln after their early Rhine crossing and link-up with airborne troops. A salvaged top hat lends an odd holiday feel to the occasion.

▶ Ian Toler, as seen by one of his pilots, Mike Stringer, who later became an artist of some repute.

Rex Norton had been killed – the only officer of the squadron apart from myself to return from the Arnhem battle. I went to where he had been killed by a mortar burst, and saw him buried in a temporary grave. I reckoned my casualties were about 20 per cent.

The following morning, we heard the thunder of approaching tanks and shortly a whole regiment of the Guards Armoured Division with their Sherman tanks drove through our positions on their way into Germany. What a lovely sight – and one I shall never forget. This was the third day after landing and, as far as we were concerned, the party was over. I have recollections of going back through the woods with hundreds of German prisoners shepherded by an American (surely a cowboy) riding bareback on a commandeered horse.

So ended the last airborne operation of the war. Historians will argue whether it was necessary to use such a large and expensive force to take ground which would probably have been taken by the ground forces, or if it was right to send highly vulnerable gliders and parachute aircraft into an area where the anti-aircraft guns were still active. Casualties were heavy – but perhaps not as heavy as would have been those of the ground forces, had we not been there. Objectives were achieved, and that is what counts. **"**

Major T.I.J. Toler

◀ Glider Pilot Ian Toler. As he described the air lift, 'All around us was the great armada of aircraft, as far as the eye could see in all directions, with squadrons of fighter aircraft weaving about above and below us'.

▶▲ Glider Pilot David Brook, whose Horsa was towed from Birch Airfield, near Colchester. As he recalls the landing, 'I would not have been a passenger in the back for twice our flying pay!'

▶ A Horsa glider in flight. Pilots were briefed to land them slowly so as not to smash the nose and hamper unloading – but not all pilots had the luxury of this option on the day!

Glider Pilot David Brook's Dakota-towed Horsa made a hurried landing amid heavy fire, close to the Rhine village of Hamminkeln. He then faced a hostile reception from the German forces on the ground.

❝ The Horsa came to a halt in soft soil, warm with the early spring morning. Suddenly a rather persistent MG34 turned its undivided attention on our Horsa. Its much faster rate of fire than our Bren was unmistakable, and I recall the captain of the small group of Ox and Bucks Light Infantry that we were carrying, who had recently won the MC at Arnhem, saying, as they struggled to open an uncooperative door, 'This is f****** terrible'. Realising I was still wearing my flying helmet, I dived back into the cockpit to dress properly for the occasion by fastening on my round pudding basin of an airborne helmet. As I made back for the doorway, a steady stream of bullets banged through it. I dropped down behind large crates of stew which were stored under the troop seats and watched, fascinated, as the machine gunner slowly raked the glider back and forth from stem to stern.

The noise of battle outside my plywood coffin was overwhelming in its intensity and I barely heard a voice shouting my name and urging me to get out if I was still there, as German tanks were coming. There was a pause in the machine-gun fire and I made a headlong dive, landing on the soft soil some four and a half feet below. I lay behind the portside main wheel in the furrow it had made and watched the first of several German anti-airborne troops roaring down the road on the half-tracks which they had designed specially for the opposition of unwelcome visitors.

My role when I reached the ground safely, which I had at last now achieved, was as PIAT man. This weapon was still with the rest of the gear in the Horsa, and all I had on me was my personal 9 mm automatic which I proceeded to fire in earnest at the men seated on the half track and the motor cyclist following them, all of whom had the unmistakable mien of people who were no more wishing to find themselves just at that moment where they were, than we did. At any rate, they did not stop and mop us up, but disappeared down the road. Then I noticed that noise was coming from

another battery of light anti-aircraft guns to my right on the side of the railway track. Evidently they had temporarily tired of knocking our gliders out of the sky. I could see dead men lying everywhere, each a pathetic little heap, and only two live ones some distance off firing back from behind the wheel of their glider. I then found that the captain and the rest of the men were sheltering in a small weapon pit recently vacated by the first Germans I had seen.

Meanwhile, the battery had turned its three guns down low angle and were firing at my Horsa. I felt a blow as if a hammer hit me on the right shoulder. The shells were bursting just above me and unknown to me, in the heat of the moment, I now had a piece of one in my shoulder.

The captain was obviously feeling much better since he had got out of the Horsa and, unrestricted, proceeded to lead an attack on the gun position. We had to run directly at it, and as I ran I had what proved to be my last look at the Horsa which had carried us here so well. A shell hit the glazed nose of the machine, which was also the closed cockpit, and from a nice shining office, it instantly collapsed in drooping

L. David Brook

Museum of Army Flying

pieces. Had I been able to maintain my glance, I would have seen her go up in flames, destroying everything in her, including the three bodies in the back, one of which, I was told days later by a seasoned veteran, was one of the worst he had seen on any battlefield. Apparently his charred remains stuck in the ground upside

down with the iron tips on his boots being all that remained of his uniform, stuck to his heels.

We had landed close by a small farmhouse and I and another man ran up to it. A large barn-like door was closed and I fired some bullets through it before bursting it open. We ran in to find a room at the side with a large pile of turnips and hay on the floor. The Ox and Bucks captain, his face red and perspiring with nervous and physical effort, ran up, pushing a tough-looking young German paratrooper ahead of him.

'Here, glider pilot, you've been wounded – stay here and guard this prisoner until we come back'. I pushed my prisoner back into the house and sat him down on the heap of turnips, telling him to keep his hands over his head.

Later the Ox and Bucks captain returned and told me to take the prisoner up to join the others at the railway station. He assured me that the station was ours, so I left the house and set off with my charge up the railway line. The chaos was indescribable. Trucks were overturned and the huge broken remains of a couple of Horsas lay across the tracks. Men were lying alongside the rails as if to shelter from the small-arms fire which was still banging about my ears.

I handed my prisoner over and went into the station house. Shattered bodies lay everywhere on the floors, their camouflage smocks torn and blasted by shot, grenade or mortar and stained with the mixture of earth and blood. I recognised a fellow pilot who was in great pain, having received a bullet through the bottom of his foot, which had continued up into his leg.

A medic poured sulphonamide powder in my wound and applied a field dressing. It was to be a week later in England before the piece of shrapnel was removed.

The walking wounded were told to get themselves to a large country house about half a mile away, where, exhausted, I lay down on the floorboards of a large downstairs room. I dozed fitfully and later was aware of a trooper in an adjoining small room which had the door open, gasping in

if they knew where we were and where to stop.

Outside, the machine guns started up again as the promised counter-attack developed. Close fighting was taking place in the orchard around the house and the woods beyond. Our Ox and Bucks, Devons and RURs were defending our position while the barrage lifted again so that it must only be half a mile away – or so it seemed. The noise increased until it filled everything. The building was now shaking and I could not believe that we were going to live through it. Suddenly it stopped. The silence that followed for a minute or so was uncanny, and I realised that something was missing. As the barrage had stopped, so had the struggle for life of the wounded trooper. 〞

Jack Taylor, a Driver with 227 Company RASC, VIII Corps, Second Army, had landed with the invasion force in June 1944. Having fought through the Netherlands, his Company faced the Rhine crossing. The following are excerpts from a closely guarded secret diary he kept at the time.

Right: US National Archives; inset: Jack Taylor

Will Fowler

a terrible way at about 120 to the minute. He had fearful chest injuries, and had been injected with morphine. They had turned him over on what remained of his chest and left him.

For some time now the heavy rumble of Monty's artillery on the other side of the Rhine had been growing in intensity and the house was beginning to vibrate. 'A creeping barrage', I thought. I wondered

〝 Wednesday March 28. Arrived back with my Company in Geldern after being on a course for training as a Driver/Wireless Operator in a Tank Crew, using Morse Code. White flags are hanging outside all the houses and we are not allowed to speak to civvies. Moving to Wesel over the Rhine tomorrow, so went on the scrounge in civvy houses and found hundreds of notes in German Marks in the rafters of a

roof of a house, but they were 50s,100s and 1,000s and of no use.

March 29. Moving to Reesfeld across the Rhine, moved off early and arrived at Wesel. The Rhine is some river, and we crossed on a pontoon bridge built by the 7th Armoured Division. It was a fantastic job – I will never forget it. The roads are choked with vehicles and troops. On the left side of the road I could see scores of dead paras hanging from trees and in the fields, dead horses still in their harnesses, dead cows and a lot of dead Germans.

It was utter confusion. All kinds of nationalities were here – Poles, French, Dutch Resistance – all giving themselves up, and also quite a few SS who had been betrayed by the people they had forced to fight for them – the tattoo mark under their left arm gave them away.

We commandeered a house for a guard room and prison and that night it was hell on earth. The confusion was endless – no-one slept

▲ Driver Jack Taylor with the RASC. Their advance into Germany was met with unqualified surrender by a cowed civilian population.

◄ Hamminkeln near Wesel – a major target for Operation Varsity – becomes a reality for the conquering Allies after heavy local fighting.

a wink and wholesale looting went on all night by the freed labour force, and we didn't stop it. Quite a few of us spent the night burying the dead British Paras in our sector.

March 30. Set off for Borkan, arrived and billeted in a German factory. The town is a terrible wreck and wholesale looting is still going on – by both sides.

Thursday April 5. Moved again to Bissendorf, some 20 miles north-east of Münster, and billeted on a farm. It was a bad journey through seas of mud, the vehicles bogged down.

April 6. Moved again to Utche at 1800 hours – it's about 25 miles. What a life. Arrived at 2000 hours and billeted in a grand German house. We were the first troops in the town – the main body had passed it by for some reason. I and a pal of mine – a Driver Howells – went into the main Post Office. The staff were still working – all middle-aged women, so we cleared them out.

We opened a very large safe and there were stacks of paper money in it. We helped ourselves and, of course, took large notes – but re-membered in time to change them for smaller-value notes.

We stayed one night in the large house, and found large packing cases in the cellar full of clothes – all women's clothes, including fur coats which had been taken from the inmates of the death camps. (Up to that point we had not come across these camps, but were to do so in the next few days). There were also a lot of bottles of fruit and sides of bacon, legs of pork – and plenty of eggs. There were no men in the town, only women and children.

During the night we heard sounds of gunfire and a lot of screaming going on in the town, but we still had a good sleep on the first real bed for a very long time. The next morning we were told that a lot of raping and murders had taken place by the Russian slave workers who had been released. During the night we were bombed by aircraft and a lot of anti-personnel bombs were dropped. A boy picked one up and lost his hand. **"**

Heinz Deutsch (24) was a lieutenant (later 1st Lieutenant) with the 12th Paratrooper Storm Gun battalions. He recounts the events of 9/10 March 1945 in the vicinity of Wesel, when his unit was attempting to cross the Rhine.

" German troops had with-drawn, and we were on the left side of the Rhine about to cross by a railway bridge leading to Wesel. The German engineers, however, had blown this up earlier to prevent the Allies crossing there. So there we were with all our heavy weaponry. Some of our men had already crossed. I had been given the order to oversee the crossing of the bridge, so I had to wait until last. The bridge had been blown so that it was still possible for infantry to cross, but no vehicles. The engineers had to build a makeshift ferry to carry the guns.

The engineers put this together on the night of 8/9 March, with steel supports and wooden planks laid over these. It floated by means of empty air canisters. On 9 March, then, this ferry managed to carry across most of the guns.

When we reached Wesel, it had been completely destroyed. We were then told to withdraw to the north-east with our guns. But we had no reason to use them. The enemy troops were staying back. We didn't know exactly why. Perhaps they thought it was a trap.

Later there was an enemy landing from the air, partly with gliders. I shot down two of these gliders with the storm gun. The other two I could see had already landed, and it wasn't usual to fire at them when they were on the ground. We would point the storm guns at them and the infantry would take them prisoner.

Looking back at this time, morale among our men was surprisingly good. Our battalion were all volun-teers, and frankly, we wanted a bit of action. We thought the war could still be rescued. Of course, most of the time in action, you only have enough time to think of your own situation, not to be shot yourself. We were defending our Fatherland, and we thought we still had a good chance. I would say that politics never really entered into it for us. You never spoke about it, whether someone was in the party or had been in the Hitler Youth. We had a bit of doubt about the conduct of the war, but we were confident. There were no deserters.

I was awarded the *Ritterkreuz* (Knight's Cross) in April for knock-ing out 44 enemy tanks with my own gun in the space of eight weeks, and I was mentioned by name in the *Wehrmacht* Command Report.

About 10 or 15 years ago I went back to Wesel. I drove through this area, and I have a little story about something I saw. When we were withdrawing to build a position, there was a house standing behind us – it must have been one of the only ones still standing. Now I couldn't see this and so I ploughed into the back wall with my gun. When I looked to see what had happened, there were German soldiers in there roasting potatoes. When I went back, the house was still there and the wall newly built. We spoke to the people in the house, but I didn't tell them about the wall. **"**

◄ **Not all of the advance beyond the Rhine is a hard slog. American troops relax at the side of the road – for them the war seems as good as won.**

▼ **Americans cross the Rhine as it runs between its high, steep banks at Boppard. The construction of their pontoon bridge and actual crossing seems to be going ahead unopposed.**

Topham

CHAPTER 24

BATTLE DIARY

OCTOBER 1944

6	Russians renew Hungarian offensive
16	Horthy abdicates
19	Fall of Belgrade

JANUARY 1945

| 12 | Beginning of Russian drive to the Oder |
| 17 | Fall of Warsaw |

FEBRUARY

| 13 | Last Germans capitulate in Budapest |

MARCH

| 6 | Final German counter-attack in Hungary |

APRIL

16	Beginning of final drive on Berlin
18	Russians break through the Oder-Neisse line
22	First Soviet troops reach outskirts of Berlin
24	Berlin surrounded
26	Beginning of the battle of Berlin
28	Mussolini executed
30	Hitler and Eva Braun commit suicide

MAY

2	Fighting ends in Berlin
4	Ceasefire signed at Lüneburg Heath
7	Germany surrenders unconditionally
8	VE day

BATTLE OF BERLIN – BROTHERS IN ARMS

Berlin, the capital of Hitler's Third Reich, had suffered badly from 16 massive RAF raids between November 1943 and March 1944. Now it was the prestige objective for the Russian advance from the east. On April 16, 1945, General Zhukov's First Belorussian Front and Ivan Konev's First Ukrainian Front began the final offensive, having linked up to isolate the city and begin its final agony. On 25 April, men of the US First Army met with the Soviet Fifth Guards Army at Torgau on the River Elbe north-east of Leipzig. The Western and Eastern fronts had joined.

In a series of concentric attacks, the Russians used artillery and tanks at close range to fight their way through the suburbs into the central area. Among their opponents in the Reich's death throes were boys from the Hitler Youth and men from Occupied Europe who had volunteered for the Waffen-SS and now had no future.

The Reichstag building was captured on May 1, although Soviet troops had raised the *Hammer and Sickle* above the building in the half light of the previous evening. On May 2 General Karl Weidling, the recently appointed commander of the city, surrendered unconditionaly. The Russians took 136,000 prisoners. The Soviet High Command turned a blind eye to rape and authorised a degree of looting, with soldiers even permitted to send home a limited weight of goods. Hitler and Goebbels, meanwhile, had committed suicide in their bunker on April 30: the Reich they had created perished without them.

BROTHERS IN ARMS

The 'Ivans' are storming through the streets of Berlin – but the Germans are ready to fight to the last man, not just for honour, but for their comrades.

The two forces – Nazi Germans and Communist Russians – converge on the German capital, Berlin. A victory here would symbolise something more than just the winning of a battle – it would represent a triumph of one political ethic over another. Both sides recall the pressures of the battle and the personal tragedies.

Vladimir Shatilov was commander of the Russian 150th Rifle Division, which, on the evening of 28 April, fought through to the banks of the Spree – behind which lay the **Reichstag**, *Hitler's last resistance.*

❝ I went to the observation post of the 756th Regiment, commanded by Zinchenko. This regiment was to cross by the Moltke-the-Younger Bridge, seize the Foreign Ministry (we called this 'the white house') then, with Plekhodanov's regiment, was to be ready to attack the Ministry of the Interior – 'Himmler's House'.

Covered by artillery and mortar fire, our infantry rushed to the bridge. At first, small groups of soldiers under Sergeant Petr Pyatnitskii and Petr Shcherbina leaped through. Behind them came Lieutenant Ponkratov's company and finally the entire battalion of Captain Neustroev, with the Captain running in front and Political Adviser Berest and Chief of Staff Gusev running beside him.

The first to break into 'Himmler's House' were Davydov's and Neustroev's battalions. The fight inside the building lasted all night, and only at dawn on April 30 did our division's battalions completely clean out the buildings of the Interior Ministry. Then the fascists held only the *Reichstag* and the Kroll Opera House.

The Hitlerites brought new reinforcements into battle. We found facing us sea cadets from the Rostock naval college. They were ordered to stop, at any price, our troops' advance against the government buildings. It was Plekhodanov's troops who dealt with these cadets – the *Führer*'s last hope.

The Third Reich was living out its last days. There were very many prisoners, but I especially remember two Hitlerite generals, Major-General Schreiber and Lieutenant-General Wilhelm Brenckenfeldt. They were brought to me at the observation post, which at that time was close to the Spree. Seeing me, the two Germans fell on their knees, saying, 'We German generals bend our knees before the Soviet general . . .' The words sounded pathetic. It was revolting. ❞

Lieutenant-General Telegin was a member of the war council of the 1st Belorussian Front which, under Marshal Zhukov shared the Berlin operation with the 1st Ukrainian Front under Marshal Koniev.

❝ Captain Archangelsk's tank company was halted by gun and rocket fire near a massive obstacle at a crossroads near the *Reichstag*. The leading tank, trying to ram the obstacle, was set on fire and fell out of action in the centre of a square.

The tank commander and the turret gunner, badly wounded, just managed to pull themselves out on

▲ In spite of the SS efforts in sabotaging bridges in Berlin, the Russian Army had arrived on both sides of Berlin's Landwehr Canal by 29 April 1945.

◄ No longer able to contain his pent-up excitement, a Russian indulges in a victory dance in front of the Brandenburg Gate, early in May 1945.

► In a time of relative optimism before the Berlin battle, SS Panzer-grenadiers of the *Totenkopf* Division gather in a small town in Hungary, ready for the march towards the capital.

◄ By May, the struggle is over for the German forces. Russian tanks surround the Brandenburg Gate and the great capital of the Reich has been reduced to rubble.

Bildarchiv Preussischer Kulturbesitz

◀ In their frantic withdrawal before the advancing Red Army, the Germans pursue a scorched earth policy.

a full cup, and the boy, in a thin, grateful voice, said thank-you in German. The cook suddenly slid his wide palm affectionately over the curls. But, catching sight of us and not knowing how we would look on his behaviour, he blushed and immediately began to defend himself. 'I gave something to the child, Comrade General. I've seen all kinds of things in this war, but you know, my heart can't take hungry children.'

A boy of about seven, to whom a junior sergeant had poured some sweet tea out of his flask, gazed

to the paving stones through the lower hatch, and then sheltered behind the armour of the tank from enemy machine-gun fire. In the burning tank remained only the driver-mechanic, the Young Communist, Anatoli Ivanov – but after a few moments, the commander's hatch cover opened and Anatoli's head appeared, accompanied by his loud boyish voice, 'Forward, for motherland and victory!'

The burning tank, gathering speed, hurled itself at the obstruction – but another missile penetrated the tank's armour. The ammunition exploded and the tank was destroyed. Anatoli Ivanov likewise perished. The gap that Ivanov had succeeded in making was too small to allow tanks through.

Only a few minutes after the destruction of the tank, a fair-haired soldier jumped out from the window of a nearby house with a box of explosives on his back. He hurried to the place where Anatoli had met his end. Who was this hero? Most probably a soldier from the neighbouring assault group. The tank men covered this daring fellow with their cannon and machine guns. Wounded by an enemy bullet, he laboriously pulled himself along on his hands, crawling forward and dragging his box behind him. The tanks gave all the gun and machine-gun fire they could, and the hero crawled to the gap made by Anatoli Ivanov. He placed his explosives, lit the fuse, then collapsed. There was an explosion that threw the obstacle aside. The road to the *Reichstag* was clear – but the unknown hero had perished. **"**

 Lieutenant-General Nikolai Popel had served as a professional soldier for 40 years by the time of the battle for Berlin. By this time he was a member of the war council – the highest political/military group of the First Guards Tank Army. He remembers events towards the end of the battle for Berlin.

" Red flags had been put out on the roofs – signs that our men had passed this way. Without such indications in urban warfare, it would have been impossible to know which parts were one's own.

'And do you remember how we knew where the Germans were in 1941,' Mikhail Efimovich suddenly asked, 'especially towards evening?' 'Of course I remember. Wherever we saw flames, that's where the Germans were.'

We stopped our armoured personnel carrier near the entrance arch of a multistorey house, where a field-kitchen had been placed. It was the centre of a lively scene. Soldiers, NCOs and officers were getting food, waiting their turn, or already eating with healthy appetites. Among them, I spotted several German children. These little Berliners went up to our people and stretched out skinny little hands that tightly grasped cups and saucers. Beside the cook stood a curly-haired boy in ragged trousers. 'Eat!' he said. This was the first bit of Russian he had learned. The cook neatly poured him

Ullstein Bilderdienst

▲ **Open country fighting narrows down to street and house-to-house battle – and the storming Red Army winkles out the German defenders from their cover in the streets of Berlin.**

fixedly with hungry eyes at this delicacy, but overcame himself and, explaining that it was for his mother, carried the tea inside.

We watched anxiously some planes that were leaving a narrow white trail in the sky.

'Terrific speed!' said Kanukov, as he watched them with a calculating eye, 'It's all right if Hitler doesn't have many of them, but if there are a lot of them, things will get hot.'

This day, for the first time, we had encountered jet aircraft. Coming down like lightning on the column, a flight of them shot it up with machine guns. The sergeant who had poured tea for the German boy, was killed. **"**

 Untersturmführer
Heinz Landau, a Transylvanian Saxon fighting with the German Army against their mutual enemy – the Russians – had arrived on the outskirts of Berlin after fierce fighting.

" Nearing an open square, we could see a high-ranking *Feldgendarmerie* officer and half a dozen or so *gendarmes* with the unmistakable plaque around their necks. We immediately made towards them, welcoming their company, when to our horror, they opened fire on us with automatic weapons, instantly killing Willy and grazing Wolfgang and myself.

'Hey, you bastards, we're Germans! Are you short-sighted?' The next instant, firing broke out again, and we thought the Russians had caught up with us. It was one Schmeisser only – and I spotted the man firing it from another corner of the square into the *Feldgendarmes*.

We approached the sprawling bodies of the berserk gendarmes with caution. One was only just alive, cursing and moaning in Russian. We tore open their tunics – no shirt, no identification disc. Their facial structure and, above all, their smell, was unmistakably Russian.

The first bullets started to ricochet off the houses and the asphalt all around us, and there was not time to do anything about Willy.

That evening, to our surprise, we actually made contact with a large force of our regular army troops, just receiving their rations. To our delight, we were provided with some unexpected food, cigarettes and tobacco, a small bottle of schnapps each, and tablets to keep us awake.

We sat in complete darkness on the damp floor of the cellar of an otherwise completely destroyed building, eating, drinking and smoking and trying to snatch some sleep, while the Russian artillery started their night-shift. The shells and bombs rocked the ground like a

ceaseless earthquake, when an unseen body fell in amongst us, muttering a curse in Russian. All three of us had our bayonets or hunting knives out, groping in the dark. There was a short but violent tussle to my left, and, 'I've got him', from Wolfgang. A heavy body fell over me and a knife slashed a long tear in my sleeve and arm. I was frantically slashing and stabbing with my knife, and the body went limp. Out we scrambled as fast as we could – and not too soon. A couple of hand grenades

▲ **Russian Il-2** *Shturmovik* **ground attack aircraft fly unopposed over Berlin.**

▼ **Heinz Landau (right) in the last photo of his war, as Lt. of the Albert Speer** *Panzerjager Uberfall-kommando.*

Left: Süddeutscher Verlag; below: Novosti Press Agency

exploded in the cellar and we lay crouched in silence. Sure enough, half a dozen figures hove into dim sight and we emptied our Schmeissers with feeling.

As far as I could see, the sky was a gold-red, fires of assorted sizes were burning everywhere, the sound of several thousand Russian artillery and *Katyushas* was one endless clap and roll of terrifying thunder and lightning and, believe it or not, the well-known sound of German flak was adding its furious rapid bark to this infernal crescendo. Overhead, enemy aircraft were droning like endless swarms of mad bumble bees and bombs kept raining down on the tortured, but still defiant city.

We trooped out cautiously into the night. I peered carefully up and down the rubble-laden street. It was now getting quite light and nothing moved in the immediate vicinity. After waiting another ten minutes or so, we proceeded, leap-frogging in the usual manner, towards the west.

Ivan tanks were rumbling towards us in the distance – we immediately deployed.

Wolfgang and I, with a scratch unit of experienced *Panzerjäger*, ran towards the Russians under cover of

sights at 25 metres and took aim, noticing Wolfgang going through the motions with me, as if on an exercise ground.

Then 35 metres, 30 metres, 25 metres – and I squeezed the trigger. As I was flattening myself against the ground, I caught a glimpse of the spinning-top-like projectile racing towards the tank. In a split second, the tank veered to one side, flattening one of the trees, burst into flames and stopped. The hatch flew open and the crew, their uniforms already ablaze, jumped out as fast as they could. The lads behind us mowed them down.

The next in line turned off the road, crossing the ditch, then rattled into the field, hit a mine and lost one of its tracks. Wolfgang blew this one up with his *Panzerfaust*. I caught the third at a distance of 30 metres and, glory be, it must have been carrying ammunition or fuel, for it literally disintegrated, the huge wheels and tracks – even the long barrel of its gun – whirling through the air in slow motion.

To my horror, one of the tracks was hurtling towards me, and by thunder, it sure wasn't in slow motion any more. I was trying to dig

◄◄ A 'civilian', captured in street fighting in Hungary, turns out to be a Russian, hoping to avoid internment by adopting a civilian disguise.

◄ The tables have turned – and now it is the Russians who can amass a huge force with which to squash the German Army, East Prussia, late 1944.

the trees, carrying as many *Panzerfaust* as possible with us, our boots and belts bristling with hand grenades.

We took up our positions and waited. I noticed to my dismay, that I was shaking all over, and my poor loose teeth were making a noise like castanets. Also, once again, my stomach hurt, and I kept thinking, 'Oh God, don't let me be sick now'. I bit my jaws together, fought down the trembling and fused my hand grenades. The first T34 was now about 40 or 50 metres away. I set my

myself in deeper to the rather shallow ditch with my fingernails, when this monstrosity hit the ground with a thump and crunch – and I blacked out. I was only out for a second, as quite obviously Wolfgang had not even noticed the close shave I had had, but was busily preparing for the next target.

The Russians now stepped on the gas and thundered past us at speed, firing with everything they had. Someone managed to knock out the last but one. This stopped the last one with a bang, and Wolfgang and I

lips. 'Shoot me, *Kamerad*, for God's sake, shoot me.' His hand squeezed mine, then let go. '*Lebe wohl, Heinz.*' A quick burst through the head, and Wolfgang was at peace.

About three hours later, after almost ceaseless fighting, approximately 25 Germans, surrounded by an army of the brave, heroic Soviet Union, with tanks and artillery, fought their last battle.

There was an unexpectedly long lull in the fighting, giving me the opportunity to collect my wits – and this rather depressed me. The few lads and men around me were complete strangers, and we obviously weren't going to have the chance to

put a *Panzerfaust* in it. Further down the road, more tanks hove into sight and, watching them through my field glasses, I could see the massed Russian infantry behind them. Time to start moving back.

We held this square for the rest of that day and night, repulsing countless assaults and weathering furious artillery and aerial bombardments. We booby-trapped the buildings we were in and then retreated under the cover of a small, tough rear-guard.

By 27 April, the fighting was so confused that Wolfgang and I were not too surprised to come across a complete company of Russians, standing about in a huge open square, eating, drinking and talking. Many of them died on their feet as we opened fire with everything at our disposal. The whole thing was over in a matter of seconds. We were about 40 strong, and emerged completely unscathed from this encounter, which must have cost the Ivans more than 200 lives.

A day later, at 10 am, we knew the end, for us at any rate, was very near indeed. We realised we were encircled and that to expect outside help was ridiculous.

Wolfgang and I, with two others in tow, had just managed once again to shake off the enemy after a particularly nasty bit of house-to-house, room-to-room fighting, and were leap-frogging down a main road. I crouched in a doorway to give covering fire, when I saw a shell explode in the midst of my friends. About half a dozen of us ran back into the

Bildarchiv Preussischer Kulturbesitz

hail of Russian bullets, but all of them were either dead or terribly wounded – and we did not even have our usual first-aid kits.

I found what I dreaded most – Wolfgang minus his legs. I thought he was dead. I grabbed hold of my last friend's head and yelled in agony, 'Wolfgang, Wolfgang!' He opened his eyes and smiled – then realised what had happened. His lips moved, but his voice was so weak in all that din, I could not hear anything. I bent close with my ear to his

get acquainted. The end was just around the corner.

What worried me most was the fact that in this situation, one was dying like a dog – a stray dog – for who was there to report to whom, 'Sorry to inform you that your son has given his life on the field of honour'?

I knew only too well that, by the time it would be possible for the surviving Germans to come and sort out our mangled bodies, there would be no papers in our pockets, no boots on our feet, no rings on our fingers, no watches – nothing.

I took out my diary and fountain pen and wrote, 'Anyone finding this wallet, containing all my documents, photographs, money etc, please keep the money if it's any good. Send the rest to . . .' and the address of my parents. 'Please attach a few notes of your own, explaining that I hid these things in my last hours. The end for me came on 28 April 1945, here in Berlin, Köpenick.'

In one corner stood the huge terracotta oven. I wrapped my wallet in a piece of cloth and pushed it well behind the oven. Would anyone ever find it? Would the building even survive? Suddenly the safety of this building became very important.

We occupied the building across the road and waited for the curtain to go up on the last act. We did not have long to wait. Tanks and infantry started pouring towards us from every direction. It would have been senseless to try to meet them in the street with our *Panzerfaust*.

I took up a position on the ground floor in a corner room from which I could cover two major roads, and as the T34s started rolling past, I started firing *Panzerfausts*.

Two T34s were burning, their crews scattered all over the place. The roads were literally choked with dead and wounded infantry. One following tank veered off and buried itself in the wall of a building and got stuck. The others managed to reverse and open fire. I knocked out the one stuck in the wall, then grabbed an MG42 and joined the others in concentrating on the infantry. Several of our chaps were now dead, many wounded, and for these there was no choice but to carry on fighting or just lie still – or shoot themselves, which some of them did.

Some Ivans forced the entry, killing several of the men in their way, and the few of us still on our feet rushed to meet them – amongst others, a boy of 13 in his Hitler Youth uniform. We got them out of the building, but there were only five of us left. I left three at the entry, and took the boy down to the cellar, hoping to hide him somewhere. Ivan gave us no time, and I rushed to the narrow concrete window, firing my MG. Shrapnel whizzed past my head and went through the boy's face. Another rush by the infantry and my MG42 burst into ear-splitting cacophony in the confined space. There was a crash on my helmet – and my lights went out. **"**

▲ **High above the city, on top of the Brandenburg Gate, Russians raise their flags from the shattered statues – the image a defiant symbol of the Nazi defeat.**

◀ **Big, symbolic gestures are much easier than face-to-face combat, as this Russian soldier discovers as he takes a German prisoner after street fighting in Berlin.**

Jean Porter was 22 when she was sent from her home town of Antwerp in Belgium to work in a restaurant in Berlin in 1943. She stayed there until the end of the war and witnessed the final days when the Russians entered Berlin.

" I was sent to Germany in 1943. I got a letter, saying I had to go and work there. You had to report to a certain place; you were given money and coupons to buy some extra clothes. They asked you whether you wanted to work in a factory or privately, like in a restaurant or something, and I said I'd work in a restaurant, because I thought, you know, I don't want to go hungry. If you didn't go, they would find you and put you in prison. To tell the truth I was glad to go to Germany, because things were never that good at home. I had a stepmother, you see, and she didn't want me, so I went to live with an aunt, and she didn't really want me

soldiers on the corner of the streets with guns, lying dead. And when we got home, we just took what we could carry and went again to the shelter. And we could see on the bridge over the canal they'd piled up furniture ever so high, as a sort of barricade. I don't know how they could have built it so high. The next day we had to be evacuated, because the Russians were almost on the doorstep, so to speak. We walked all the way alongside the rails in the underground from one station to the other through the tunnels. We have to be very quiet, everybody was saying 'shsssh' . . . In the meantime they had tried to flood the underground to stop the Russians coming in. We were up to our knees in water, and if you fell over the rails that was your lot. You couldn't get up. You were so weak by then. In the underground there's like a ledge, and people were all trying to get up on there, but the people who couldn't get up were walking in the water. It was very hard to get up on the ledge, because it was every man for himself. We had to walk in the water, and there was one couple with a new-born baby, and it must have been dead, because I saw them

with me?' So I said, 'All right, I'll come.' Well, we went home, and, of course, there was nothing standing. There were bodies everywhere, half-burned bodies and horses as well. It was terrible. Anyway, we went to this girl's boss's house, and we stayed there the night. The Russians were knocking on the doors, and they said, 'Any Fräuleins here?' And the boss said, 'Oh no, no Fräuleins here, upstairs.' And so he sent them upstairs. The next day he told us we'd better go.

We walked all the way from Berlin to Potsdam, and that was 40 km. There were thousands of us, and when we got to Potsdam, there were loads of people there staying in a farm. The Russians there were burning down all the houses. I think they were mostly pretty uneducated people, they were just doing it for the hell of it. We had to sleep in the hayloft, and the lady there gave us food. I just followed this Dutch chap. He seemed to know where he was going, and we thought, well, if we get to Potsdam, we must be on our way home. There were loads of Dutch people there at the farm, and the next day the lady from the farm gave us a horse and cart and we set

either. So when the chance came to go to Germany, where I would at least have an occupation, I was secretly pleased.

So, they sent us on this train to Berlin. We didn't know where we were going at first. I worked in a café in the Anhalterstrasse near the Anhalter Bahnhof. Workers from the railway used to come in, lorry drivers, that sort of thing – there were a lot of people working you know, they weren't all in the war. They would all come in for a plate of stew, because you didn't need to use your coupons for it, as there was no meat in it. We stayed in a private house just round the corner. The boss rented this room. Me and this other girl from Belgium, Marie, stayed there. They were very good to us at the restaurant and in the house.

Life was very much the same from day to day. It was only at the end that the real action started for us. We knew there was something in the air. Nobody knew what was happening, but there were rumours going around that Russia was invading. The following day we went home to get some stuff. There were German

Jean Porter

▲ Jean Porter (center), with friend Marie and a Dutch comrade, sunbathing at a Berlin lido – an image of much happier times for them – and the city.

laying it down in the water. They had no food, and we had no food – we had no food for five days. We lived on a little bit of butter and sugar. The next day the Russians came into the underground and told us, 'All out, all out, the war is over.' So we all came out, and there was this girl there, and she said to me, 'I'm going to my boss, do you want to come

off. There were streams of people along the roads, moving out like us. Well, after a while, the horse would get tired, and so, what we did, we just let it go and took another one from the fields. The horses didn't mind, of course. At that time, nobody bothered, you see, everything was still a shambles. **"**

CHAPTER 25

BATTLE DIARY

FEBRUARY 1945
19   Landings on Iwo Jima – Operation Detachment
20   No 1 Airfield taken
23   Flag raised over Mount Suribachi
27   No 2 Airfield taken

MARCH
3   No 3 Aifield taken
4   First B-29 lands
6   P-51s and P-61s of USAAF 15th Fighter Group arrive
16   Iwo declared secure
26   Last Japanese survivors stage suicide attack
26–29   Kerama Retto seized

APRIL
1   Landings on Okinawa – Operation Iceberg
9–12   First assault on Shuri Line
12–13   Japanese counter-attack
16–18   Taking of Motobu Peninsula
16–24   Taking of Ie Shima
18–24   Outer Shuri defenses taken

MAY
4–5   Japanese counter-offensive. Major kamikaze attack on fleet
8   Americans open attacks on Inner Shuri defenses
31   Shuri town occupied

JUNE
4–11   Final battles at Oroku and Yaeju-Dake
18   General Buckner killed
22   US flag raised over Okinawa

IWO JIMA AND OKINAWA

Despite being only 8 miles square, and suffering from a massive air and sea bombardment, the volcanic island of Iwo Jima exacted a heavy toll from the US Marines of V Amphibious Corps. But, lying only two hours' flying time from Japan, the island's small airfields were strategically essential both as a base for short-range fighters defending B-29 bombers attacking the main Japanese islands, and as a bolt hole for damaged bombers which had to divert. The month taken for its capture early in 1945 cost 6,891 Americans killed and 18,700 wounded. The defending Japanese garrison suffered even more: of 22,000 men, only 212 chose to surrender. The island's dominant feature, the volcano of Mount Suribachi, was captured on February 23; Marines raising the *Stars and Stripes* on its summit were to provide one of the most memorable photographs of the war.

Okinawa, a Japanese island 67 miles long and 8 miles wide was attacked on April 1, 1945, by the US Tenth Army, a force of about 170,000 troops, following an air and sea bombardment which began on March 25. Although the island was heavily defended and the Americans expected to meet fierce resistance on the beaches, the landings were unopposed and by the end of the day they had 60,000 men ashore. But within a few days, they found that the Japanese had dug elaborate defenses in a few strategic positions. On May 3 and 4, the Japanese launched a suicidal counter-attack, which cost the Americans 12,513 dead and 36,600 wounded, before the island was declared secure on June 21. The Japanese losses were ten times as heavy, with 110,000 dead and only 7,400 surrendering as prisoners. Many Japanese civilians chose to jump to their deaths from the island's steep cliffs rather than face the indignity of surrender to the Americans.

LAST-DITCH BUSHIDO

Martyrs to their code of honour, the Japanese launch themselves as human bombs on the disbelieving Allies.

For the first time, the British Pacific Fleet joins in the action – and comes under *kamikaze* attack along with its American allies. As the US landing forces load more and more of their plentiful weaponry into the fray, the defending Japanese are running desperately short of any equipment with which to carry on . . . but still, some would do anything to avoid the word 'surrender'.

work with the British carriers. This was possibly the reason why, later on, they seemed to go for the bridges of British ships, with a view to killing our command personnel. But this was a silly thing to do – they could do far more harm to us by going for the hull of the ship. Damage to the actual lifts, while less spectacular, was a far more effective way of putting a carrier out of action.

Our first *kamikaze* started from

◀ As they struggle in the deep volcanic sands on Iwo Jima, the Marines advance slowly, bitterly contested by Japanese who are firmly dug into caves further inland.

US National Archives

▲ The British Pacific Fleet joins the fray at Okinawa – in the foreground is HMS *Whelp*, on which Prince Philip was serving, and in the background, the aircraft carrier, HMS *Indomitable*.

Peter C. Smith Collection

Admiral Sir Michael Denny was captain of the British carrier HMS Victorious, *which was part of the British Pacific Fleet. He recalls the fierce* kamikaze *attacks, which seemed to come at the most vulnerable moments.*

❝ Our anti-aircraft fire was pretty effective, and the *Victorious* was an immensely handy ship to handle, with a big rudder. I could spin her around quite rapidly and so I ruined both my *kamikaze* attacks.

They aimed originally for between the lifts – with American ships they could open up the flight deck and go right through into the hangar space below – but eventually they found that this didn't work on the British carriers' armoured decks.

Two *kamikazes* successfully striking an American carrier could put her out of action with regard to operating aircraft, but this did not

almost astern of us, and my turn put him on my beam. He tried to pull up and start again, but he was not quick enough. I crossed ahead of him pretty close, and his wheels touched the flight deck at right angles. The undercarriage sheared right off and his plane broke up, sliding 80 feet across the flight deck to crash over the side and on to the 4.5 inch guns.

From the first moment I started to swing the ship, he had been trying to adjust and steer up the flight deck – which would have given him the length of the ship in which to drop his stick and hit – but he missed.

It is interesting to recall that each pilot would react differently – there appeared to be no set formula for an attack, other than the aiming point and the run-in. One could never tell whether one was up against a first-class pilot or not, until the moment one swung the ship and watched the pilot's reactions. If one's timing was good, and the pilot was forced to rethink his attack, the majority of them would veer in at a lower angle, which at once reduced their effectiveness if they did hit. If one could lead an enemy pilot to make a large alteration in his course, or if he failed to make an alteration at all, one felt secure that he would not score a hit. The fatal thing to do was for a carrier to steer a straight course, for in that case he would always get you.

In the cases where more than one aircraft approached, in all cases they would make separate attacks. One could watch them pick their targets, through a good pair of glasses, and as soon as the leading aircraft went into his dive, his wing-men would open up on either side of him, hoping to hit you, no matter how you turned. "

Marine Robert Porter, after spending the early years of the war in the Mediterranean, was posted to the Pacific in 1945, to join the flagship of the Task Force 57, **King George V,** *in Operation Iceberg.*

" The Okinawa campaign was the first of the Pacific campaigns that the British Fleet was involved in. We were directly under the Americans and had to learn their signals and codes before the operation. Every ship in the Force – we were the 57th Task Force – had Americans on board teaching them signals and so on.

The job of the 57th Task Force was to bomb and annihilate the Sakishima group of islands. There were two particular airfields there called Ishigaki and Miyako. The enemy planes would take off from them to bomb us and the American Fleet.

By April we had already been sailing around the islands for about a month, waiting for the campaign to commence. Operation Iceberg, as it was known, commenced on April 1st 1945, when we attacked the islands and the Americans invaded Okinawa.

Our aeroplanes flew off the aircraft-carriers while we bombarded the islands from the battleships. We were about 8 miles from the shore, firing with the 14 inch guns. Those guns had a range of about 20 miles and did a lot of damage.

I was on the anti-aircraft guns – the 5.25s. We brought down quite a few planes as they took off from the islands. They would come over in groups of two or three – you were very aware of them most of the time.

▲ Gun crews on board USS *Missouri* look on, powerless, as a Japanese *kamikaze* plane attacks the ship. Without the steel decks of the British Pacific Fleet, the US carriers, too, were very susceptible to head-on attacks to their main decks.

The Japanese aircraft were suicide squads and very determined. They would never give way. The planes would come straight at you, flying straight through the flak. If they dropped the bombs and got a hit, they would go away, but if the bombs missed the ship they were after, they would go straight for it. They actually crashed on some of the carriers, causing serious damage.

You would often see the Japanese pilots in the water afterwards, if the plane had dived into the sea. Sometimes they were taken on board and sometimes they were left swimming in the water – it depended. Really, they wanted to sacrifice their lives for their Emperor, so probably

didn't want to be rescued.

We used to be at sea for three months at a time during the Pacific campaigns. It was the first time we were allowed beer in the British Navy. We were given one bottle a day, which was on top of the rum ration. It was a privilege allowed to us because we were at sea for so long. The Americans had dry ships and weren't allowed anything.

We used to get the beer at about 6 o'clock. It worked out very well because everyone was given a ticket for the beer and a lot of people didn't drink, so we got all their beer as well. When we were away from the danger zones, a gang of us used to go right to the top of the ship with

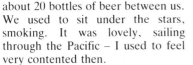

Vice-Admiral Richmond Kelly Turner, commander of US amphibious troops, was notified after a military conference in San Francisco in late September 1944 that the next objectives of the US Pacific campaign would be Iwo Jima and Okinawa – and that he would lead the assaults.

" We estimated that there were 13,000 Japanese troops on Iwo Jima (we were wrong, actually there were about 20,000). The scheme of manoeuvre called for landing two divisions abreast on the south-eastern beaches – the 4th Marine Division on the right and the 5th Marine Division on the left. The 5th Marine Division was to drive across the island, and then swing to the northeast. One Combat Team was to swing left and take Mount Suribachi. The right flank of the 4th Division was to wheel to the right and head for the East Boat Basin, while the rest of the division was to push to the centre of the island, overrun the main airfield, and then head for Motoyama Plateau. The 3rd Marine Division, in reserve, would land on the same beaches, either to assist the attack, or to occupy defensive positions.

Some 900 ships and craft were assigned to this operation and they began to move toward Iwo at the end of January. They were observed by Japanese submarines, so there was no surprise, either tactical or strategic. I had secured a generous amount of air bombardment, most of it high-level bombardment by B-24s and B-29s, flying out of the Marianas. But as we progressed, I found that the effect of the heavy bombardment did not appear to have caused appreciable destruction of specific installations or to have reduced the morale of the enemy. Once the Japanese had started moving their gun and mortar installations into concrete-lined caves, narrow ravines, tortuous gullies and cement-covered emplacements, the actual damage done was very little.

The pre-invasion naval bombardment started off on the wrong foot on D minus 3 because of rain squalls and poor visibility. Only about half the contemplated bombardment was actually delivered. On the second day the weather cleared and the heavy ships worked their way inshore during the morning. The Japanese were enticed to open up from a few well concealed batteries. At 11 o'clock in the morning the LCI gunboats moved in close to provide close support for the under-water demolition teams. Three unnoticed Japanese guns overlooking the beach from Mount Suribachi started firing just after the gunboats let go their rockets. The LCIs were hit hard, 11

▼ **The once orderly deck of USS *Enterprise* has become a mass of interwoven hoses and aircraft debris as the decks burn after a determined *kamikaze* attack has reached its goal.**

about 20 bottles of beer between us. We used to sit under the stars, smoking. It was lovely, sailing through the Pacific – I used to feel very contented then.

We were regarded as heroes when we got back to Australia. They were very excited about having the Pacific Fleet with them, and we were fêted everywhere. You could, perhaps, sense a little resentment because some people felt that the Americans had done all the work, and the British had come in at the last minute. However, when we went into Melbourne, so many people came on board to congratulate us that the ship actually sank to the bottom of the harbour and rested in the sand. **"**

of 12 were damaged, one was sunk, and they suffered 170 casualties. The battleship *Nevada* fired on the shore guns until they were silenced.

The landing plan called for putting 9,000 men ashore in the first 45 minutes. At 0805 naval gunfire was lifted and 120 aircraft shot rockets and machine gunned and bombed the beach area – some used napalm. At 0830 the first wave landed and hit the beach along the 3,000-yard front at nine o'clock. The troops moved forward for the first 350 yards under a rolling barrage of naval gunfire. Japanese fire was relatively light at first, but picked up so that at 0920 heavy fire was reported against the right flank beaches. Progress was rapid across the southern belt of the island but progress on the right flank was much slower.

Principal problems were the heavy swell, which swamped landing craft,

▶ Private First Class Galen A Brehm takes on the Japanese in a cave using a flame-thrower, while a rifleman waits to pick off any enemy who break out from the swath of enveloping flames.

▼ On Iwo Jima, Marine spotters have located an enemy machine-gun nest. One man calls instructions to be relayed to artillery and mortar units, requesting a concentration of fire on the nest.

came in one coordinated attack on February 21. The escort carrier *Bismarck Sea* was sunk, the escort carrier *Lunga Point* was damaged and so were the net tender *Keokuk Point* and LST-477. The fleet carrier *Saratoga* was hit by five suicide planes and damaged so badly she had to retire to an American Navy yard.

The Marines of the 28th Regiment of the 5th Marine Division raised the American flag on the summit of Mount Suribachi at 1035 on February 23.

The fighting was 'unto death' for the Japanese. On this day, Domei news agency in Tokyo said, 'This

man Turner shall not return home alive. He must not and he won't. This is one of the many things we can do to rest at ease the many souls of those who have paid the supreme sacrifice.'

After Mount Suribachi there was no question as to the outcome. On March 9 I turned over command to Rear Admiral Hill and departed for Guam to concentrate on preparations for the landings on Okinawa.

The landings were made on the Hagushi coral sand beaches, 11 miles north of the city of Naha. It was estimated that there were 65,000 Japanese troops on the island. This operation was under command of

and the volcanic sand on the beaches. The depth of the beach at water's edge varied from five to 90 feet, and the volcanic sand was treacherous. Troops struggled up the slopes ankle-deep in sand. Wheeled vehicles bogged down to their frames and a few tanks stalled in the surf and were swamped. As vehicles left the ramps, they sank down and their spinning treads banked the sand back under the ramps.

On D plus 1, the weather deteriorated, making the beach landings harder. Japanese suicide planes

▶ US Marines who have got past the worst of Iwo's volcanic sand banks start up a bombardment with field pieces – the opening of a bloody offensive in a hostile and bleak environment.

the US Tenth Army with 185,000 assault troops.

The scheme called for the Marines to capture Ishikawa Isthmus, and Yontan airfield north of Hagushi. The XXIV Corps would establish an east-west line across Okinawa and take Kadena airfield, then capture the southern part of the island. The small island of Ie Shima would be captured simultaneously, and then Northern Okinawa.

The Japanese did not seriously oppose the assault landings. Before dark on the second day, the XXIV Corps had reached the eastern shore of the island and the Marines were on their way to the Ishikawa

Isthmus, which they occupied on April 3. But from the outset, the fleet was bedevilled by Japanese *kamikaze* attacks. On the first day's shore bombardment, eight ships were damaged.

One of the most effective weapons that the Japanese developed, in my opinion, was the use of the suicide bombers. The suiciders hurt the Navy badly at Okinawa. Our chief method of defence was to spread out around the ships of the Amphibious Force, at a considerable distance, pickets composed of one to five ships, destroyers, destroyer escorts and small amphibious craft.

The cost, 368 ships damaged and 36 (including 15 amphibious ships and 12 destroyers) sunk during the Okinawa campaign. The carnage among naval personnel was equally heavy – 4,907 officers and men killed by the *kamikazes* and 600 more personnel killed than army soldiers fighting on the land, and 2,000 more killed than marines fighting on the island. **"**

Captain Kōichi Itō, Commanding Officer of the 1st Battalion, 32nd Infantry Regiment, witnessed the fight-to-the-death by many Japanese soldiers throughout the Pacific campaigns. Proudly he could say that his own battalion never surrendered at Okinawa.

" Early on 4th June, I took a roll-call. My battalion had been in the fighting since April, and our strength had dropped from a total of 700 to 120 men. That day, we arrived at the village of Zaawa from the Shuri Line. From 11th June onwards we fought off the enemy's overall offensive.

According to the US war history, the US forces sustained 1,500 casualties, killed or wounded, and lost 21 tanks in the fighting for Kuniyoshi, and the fierce Japanese counter-attacks made them rely on aircraft and tanks.

The Army's right and centre collapsed, and soon the extreme left collapsed also. Our battalion continued to resist stubbornly, but was cut off from battalion headquarters, so that the state of units under command was totally unknown.

One night at the beginning of July, I went on a tour of inspection with Kashiki, my adjutant, at the eastern end of Kuniyoshi Village on the south side of the plateau. We met two men who said they had escaped from Mabuni. It was through them we learned that the GOC, Lt-General Ushijima, had committed suicide on 23rd June. I felt a huge shudder pass right through my body.

Now the Army's organised resistance was at an end, we moved over to guerrilla warfare, to be fought by each unit in the place where it had survived. In the case of my battalion, the headquarters was at Kuniyoshi, and we made up units of 20 men each, from about 100 men who were still alive. In all, we could only muster ten rifles between us, but we did what we could to interfere with the enemy's mopping-up operations – but nine-tenths of the men were wounded or fell sick. I myself was suffering from a recurrence of amoebic dysentery, and for a long time I could not walk. If we put together all our arms and ammunition, we could seek a chance to die in one last attack on a nearby airfield, but although we put together a suicide unit, our physical condition was simply not up to it.

Then our food supplies began to run out. Our food supplies had come to us through the efforts of village girls who were attached to us. During the daytime they hid in trenches, but at night, they came down from the mountains and dug potatoes for us. I was amazed how much fitter and more cheerful these women were than the soldiers.

So to the night of August 14th. From time to time a cloud would pass over the moon, which was nearly at its full. As usual, enemy AA began to fire tracer then, as we watched, it seemed to spread over the whole island of Okinawa. I don't know how many thousands – tens of thousands – of star shells they fired. A red light criss-crossed with shafts of light from the searchlights, a stupendous barrage which went on until dawn. I heard that night my first and last noise of bombing by special attack planes. Everywhere the word for VICTORY was spelled out in V-shaped lights.

About August 22nd, I heard someone call out, 'Battalion Commander!' A Japanese Army corporal stood there, guiding a US Army officer. He said he had spent 17 years in Japan and spoke fluent Japanese – he told me Japan had surrendered.

No *kamikaze* planes had flown since August 14th – I knew that – and enemy leaflets had been dropped on us on the 18th, telling us that Japan had surrendered. I put these things together in my head – the premonition I had had became reality.

I waited for sunset that evening and went to see the regimental commander. We were to resist, whatever happened, I knew that – but I forced myself to recount the day's events to him. He seemed to be unconvinced, but in the end, ordered me to act as a peace envoy.

Two days later, I met the American, Morse, again, and asked for certain proof that Japan had surrendered. 'I'll bet you listened to the recording of the Emperor's Rescript ending the war,' he said, 'and the news from Japan. Captain Ito, please accept what has happened.'

'No, that's not proof enough,' I answered. 'Please have me meet our Chief-of-Staff at Army GHQ, who has already been taken into camp.' Lieutenant Morse kept his temper, but refused. 'Well, the parley's broken down. Let's take up our rifles again,' I said. The adjutant and the rest of the men were holding their breath. It was the work of a second. The enemy officer changed tack and granted my demand.

Straight away, I climbed into the jeep with Lieutenant Morse, and we turned towards Kadena, 30 km away to the north, where the US Army GHQ was. I had to get him to stop the jeep from time to time, for calls of nature, because of my dysentery – apart from that, the jeep sped on, through the shattered trees by the roadside. The mountains looked naked, as if they had been stripped bare, with a white, grainy texture like a coral reef.

Let me go back to the fate of the 10,000 officers and men who survived, and who were weaponless. They ended up in all sorts of ways –

All pictures: US National Archives

▲ A symbol of success to come – 'Old Glory' flies over the summit of Mount Suribachi on Iwo Jima, taken there by Marines of the 28th Regiment 5th Division.

◄ A fantastic criss-crossing of anti-aircraft tracer fire fills the skies over Yontan Airfield on Okinawa, 16 April 1945. F4U fighters stand ready for action in the foreground.

some were eventually killed in the fighting, some continued to resist, some escaped, and some surrendered. Some 3,000 men surrendered before the news of our defeat, and became POWs – thousands more ended up in US camps. So, even though organised combat by the army on Okinawa came to an end, it may be said there was no *gyokusai*, no fighting until annihilation. It was impossible to crush the Japanese soldier, however brave he was, even if he was weaponless.

Soon we reached US Army Intelligence HQ, and I listened hard to the recording of the Emperor's broadcast, which was very difficult to make out. I listened again and again. I asked for it to be repeated three times. 'Bear the unbearable . . . for the peace of the whole world . . .' the phrases stayed in my heart for ever.

Then north again, in the jeep. I met a colonel in a straw-thatched

village house. He showed me the *New York Times* and explained the situation, from the Soviet invasion of Manchuria to the end of the war. 'I have no proof, but I do believe Japan has surrendered. Please make your own decision, so that your men do not become casualties wantonly and pointlessly.' Tears welled in his eyes as he said this.

On the evening of August 25th, all 13 of our officers, with the regimental commander in the centre, assembled and sat in a circle. I reported, to the effect that I had verified that Japan had surrendered. The silence went on, and on . . .

Then the regimental commander, silent, his face full of anguish, said simply, 'We will obey. We will give up our weapons.'

I had one more duty to perform. I had to negotiate our conditions for disarming the 32nd Infantry:

1 The disarming would be on 29 August.

2 Between 27th and 29th, in an area of two square kilometres round our positions, our freedom of movement would be permitted.

3 All round the free-movement zone, the US Army would place sentries, and would prohibit the entry of US troops.

The US Army showed its respect for our unit and its fighting spirit by granting all these requests.

That is how the battle came to an end for us. Each unit, reduced to ten or twelve men, was placed under the command of the senior soldier pre-

sent, and we assembled, in ranks, in Kuniyoshi village. The soldiers' uniforms were faded and torn, and they could not conceal the pallor of fatigue. The US troops drove forward their vehicles to take up our casualties, and the severely wounded were taken to hospital. Next, a hundred local people from the area were removed to a camp for civilians. The girls who had helped our HQ wept in the trucks which were taking them away. They had helped so much, and now we could do nothing for them.

On the night of August 28th, we carried out the ceremony of burning the regimental flag, which had been the symbol of our tradition and honour ever since 1899. The officers gave a final salute to the flag as it went up in flames.

Next came the day of our disarming. The US Army, through me,

▲ Hard men of the US Marine Corps take time off from being tough and share a foxhole with an abandoned war orphan.

demanded that the regimental commander read the surrender rescript. The road through Kuniyoshi village ran from east to west, and by that roadside, we laid down 30 rifles. Next, the 300 officers and men formed up in ranks.

Colonel Hongo Kakuro stood facing Major Train, who was in command of a ten-truck unit, led by one jeep. Both commanding officers walked towards each other and shook hands. 'We give ourselves up to the US Army, by the command of His Majesty the Emperor,' said Colonel Hongo, choosing his words with great care. I had asked that we could say it this way, because to use the word 'surrender' was shameful.

And that is how Japan's 32nd Infantry Regiment never, right to the end, employed the word **"** *kofuku* – surrender.

CHAPTER 26

BATTLE DIARY

1931 to 1941

1931 British scientists Cockcroft and Walton split the atom

1932 James Chadwick discovers the neutron

1934 Frenchman Frederic Joliot-Curie discovers that bombarding unranium with neutrons produces artificial radioactive products such as plutonium. Enrico Fermi refines this work during the same year

1938 The first paper describing atomic fission is published

1939 Joliot-Curie confirms the chain reaction. Following Einstein's letter to him, US President Roosevelt sets up the Uranium Committee to oversee the development of an atomic weapon

1941 The basis for a practical atomic weapon is established

SEPTEMBER 1942

16 General Groves is placed in charge of the logistics of the bomb program Grove appoints J Robert Oppenheimer as scientific director

MARCH 1943

The Los Alamos research center becomes operational. Scientist Seth Neddermeyer suggests the implosion method of detonation

1944

Throughout the year, technical difficulties suggest that it might not be feasible to produce a practical atomic bomb at all

JULY 1945

16 The Trinity implosion device is exploded successfully at the Alamogordo bombing range in New Mexico

AUGUST

6 The 'Little Boy' uranium gun-type weapon is dropped on Hiroshima

9 The 'Fat Man' plutonium implosion weapon is dropped on Nagasaki

A BOMBS – UNDER THE CLOUD

Aware that the Germans had the physicists and knowledge to develop an atomic bomb, European physicists including Niels Bohr, Enrico Fermi and Leo Szilard proposed in 1939 that the United States should start work on an atomic weapon. A British committee was already working in the same field and in 1942 both countries combined their work under the cover name Manhattan Engineer District. Under the dynamic leadership of General Leslie Groves the project, with a budget of $500 million a year and a staff of 125,000, flourished in a large plant at Oak Ridge, Tennessee, and in another in Washington State. In December 1942, Enrico Fermi set the first sustaining atomic pile in operation and on July 16, 1945, awed physicists watched as the first atomic bomb exploded at Alamagordo, New Mexico.

The first atomic bomb, codenamed 'Little Boy' was dropped from the B-29 *Enola Gay* at 09.15 on August 6, 1945, over the Japanese city of Hiroshima. It detonated at a height of 800 ft (244 m) with the force equivalent to 29,000 tons of TNT, destroying about 5 square miles (13 square km) of the city and killing an estimated 70,000 people.

The second bomb, 'Fat Man', was dropped on Nagasaki, a substitute for its main target, Kokura, which was cloud covered. The hills surrounding the city sheltered many people from the blast, keeping the death toll down to a relatively low 24,000.

The shock of these attacks led the Japanese to accept surrender. If an invasion of the Japanese mainland had taken place the human cost for military and civilians alike would have been far greater.

UNDER THE CLOUD

Thousands of feet above, air crews of the US B-29s report a successful mission – below, the terror is only just beginning for the first atomic bomb victims

Popperfoto

◄ Colonel Paul Tibbets (right) and Captain William Parsons prepare to brief the servicemen involved in the A-bomb mission with the last-minute details.

◄◄ Twenty years later, Hiroshima has been rebuilt – but in this view from Mount Gold, the dominating feature is the graveyard dedicated to those who died in the 1945 bombing.

US National Archives

Unbeknown to the unsuspecting people of Hiroshima, they are about to become the victims of the first atomic bomb attack. High above their target, in the specially adapted Superfortress, *Enola Gay*, the pilot starts his bomb-run and the escort crews stand by to monitor the effects of 'Little Boy' as they happen.

Colonel Paul Tibbets was the man charged with piloting the **Enola Gay** *to drop the bomb on Hiroshima. After intensive work with the Manhattan Project, the time had come for him to perform the real mission.*

❝ I named the crews that were going to make these flights in each aeroplane and I said afterwards that there would be a further briefing at a certain time that evening to allow us to go in a little bit more detail into what these other crews – or more specifically what we wanted each one of them – to do; things we wanted them to look for and be prepared for.

Again, this intensified the atmosphere, so that when we got around to the point that we had all of the briefings over with and we had had a midnight supper (which was commonplace – whenever they were going out on an early morning run, they'd have a midnight supper), I found that it wasn't just the flight crews and the operations people that were there, but everybody was there – the whole organisation. Nobody was sleeping that night. They didn't know *why* they weren't, but they weren't sleeping.

So, when we finally got down to the aircraft and loaded on board (now they all knew that we had loaded the weapon, 'cos you can't hide the fact that an aeroplane has been loaded – they didn't see what was loaded, but everybody knew that that afternoon a bomb had been loaded in the aeroplane) and got to the time of take-off, this word has spread throughout the island.

I think the take-off possibly created a lot of interest on other people's parts – more so than on my own – because it had been decided earlier that there was a possibility that an accident could occur on take-off, so therefore we would not arm this weapon until we had left the runway and were out to sea. This, of course, meant that had there been an accident, there would have been an explosion from normal powder charges, but there would not have been a nuclear explosion. As I said, this worried people more than it worried me, because I had plenty of faith in my aeroplane. I knew my engines were good – I thought I was good. I wasn't anticipating any great problem that evening.

We started our take-off on time, which was somewhere about 2.45, I think, and the aeroplane went on down the runway. It was loaded quite heavily, but it responded exact-

◄ A year after the event, *Enola Gay* stands on display at La Guardia Airport in New York as part of the Army Day celebrations.

US National Archives

ly like I had anticipated it would. I had flown this aeroplane the same way before and there was no problem.

About 3.30 in the morning we had completed the loading of the nuclear portion of the bomb, and we had it armed. This had been done at an altitude of approximately 4,000 feet, to allow the people to be back in the aircraft unpressurised and working in conditions that wouldn't be too uncomfortable because of the chill of the higher altitude. Once the weapon had been armed, we had a radio contact or codes that we were using back to base to let them know the progress of things on the flight. We even had a prearranged code that we would refer to when we dropped the bomb, and this would indicate the results back to these people.

At the time the bomb was armed, we must have been somewhere close to five hours away from the target. Our next point was a rendezvous 600 miles away from Tinian. We had this rendezvous with Chuck Sweeney and George M . . . because they were going to fly aircraft that would escort me. These aircraft would contain scientific-type instruments that would be dropped from those aero-

planes at the same time my bomb dropped from my aeroplane.

We made the rendezvous quite successfully, then we had about an hour and a half or a little over that to go along in a lazy formation on a beautiful night out on the Pacific, with moon and clouds that looked like powderpuffs. It was quite peaceful, believe me, and nothing much went on – there was a bit of talk in the aeroplane, but that's always normal on a mission. But then you get a quiet period, and while we were going along there, I guess everybody had been dreaming or something, because it was quiet. But we had to start thinking about climbing up to the altitude, pressurising and getting ready to get on this bomb-run before we got to the coastline of Japan, and if my memory serves me correctly, it was something like 6.40 in the morning when we prepared a climb to altitude in order that we would be in our bombing altitude before reaching the coastline of Japan.

We arrived over the 'initial point' and started in on the bomb-run, which had about 11 minutes to go – rather long for a bomb-run, but on the other hand, we felt that we needed this extra time in straight and level flight to stabilise the airspeed of

the aeroplane, to get everything right down to the last detail.

After about three minutes on the bomb-run, I made the last-minute corrections. Now, when I did this, I

▼ **Under the propeller of his aircraft, *Enola Gay*, Colonel Paul Tibbets stands with the rest of the mission's crew after the return to Tinian after the mission.**

Associated Press

was also required to advise the crew that they must put on these dark glasses – we had been given dark glasses to shield our eyes from the glare that the blast was expected to produce.

The last three minutes of a bomb-run are quite important because of certain things that have to be performed in the cockpit of the aeroplane, and in this particular case, I wanted Sweeney and M . . . to know exactly what I was doing because they had things to do in their aircraft. As we came down to the last minute of the bomb-run, a tone was activated on the radio. It was a high-pitched tone that they were receiving in those other two aeroplanes to let them know we were only one minute away from the bomb-drop. At this particular time they had certain actions that they had to perform, which was to get their instruments ready to be released out of the bomb-bay. When the tone stopped in my aeroplane, this meant that the bomb had left the

bomb-bay of the aeroplane. It was a cut-off. They automatically opened their bomb-bay to release these instruments.

The problem after the release of the bomb is not to proceed forward, but to turn away, so I immediately went into this steep turn, as did Sweeney and M . . . behind me, and we tried then to place distance between ourselves and the point of impact. In this particular case, that bomb took 53 seconds from the time it left the aeroplane until it exploded. That's how long it took to fall from the bombing altitude. This gave us adequate time, of course, to make the turn. Now we had just made the turn and rolled out in level flight, when it seemed like somebody had grabbed a hold of my aeroplane and gave it a real hard shaking, because this was the shock-wave that had come up.

This was something I was glad to feel – it gave me a moment of relief, after all, having worked on that bomb for well over a year. You

know, that 53 seconds when I'm turning the aeroplane, I'm wondering, 'Is it, or is it not going to work?' and of course the shock-wave hitting us was an indication it had worked.

Now, after we had been hit by a second shock wave, not quite so strong as the first one, I decided we'd turn around and go back and take a look, because each of us in the three aircraft had hand-held cameras. We were looking through the front of the aircraft to take pictures as rapidly as we could of what was transpiring in front of us.

The day was clear when we dropped that bomb – it was a clear, sunshiny day. Visibility was unrestricted, so as we came back round again, facing the direction of Hiroshima, we saw this cloud coming up. The cloud by this time, in two minutes, was up at our altitude (we were at 33,000 feet at this time) and was continuing to go right on up in a boiling fashion. The surface was nothing but a black, boiling – the only thing I could say is a barrel of tar. That's probably the best description I can give. Where before there had been a city – distinctive houses, buildings and everything, that you could see from our altitude – now you couldn't see anything except black, boiling debris down below.

It was terrible to look at really – a

Popperfoto

Topham

◀ Once a cinema – now one of the only buildings which remain standing after the dropping of the bomb on Hiroshima. This distinctive dome is one of the only recognizable features left of the stricken city.

▲ A Japanese artist's impression of the after effects of the bomb – a very sanitized version of the gruesome images which typified the inferno.

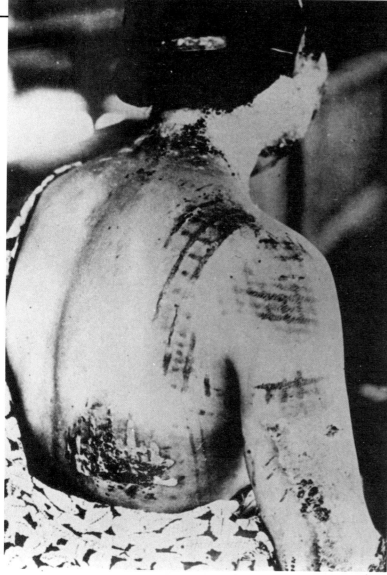

All photos US National Archives

for it.

I've often been asked how I felt, and I think I have what you might call a rather straightforward stock answer to the question. I had been assigned a military mission to perform. I was most anxious to do the best that I could possibly do in the accomplishment of that mission. I'd been trained for that. As far as my personal feelings are concerned, I never let my personal feelings enter into it. I learned this back in the days when I was flying out of England and bombing targets in Europe. I knew there were people down below, getting hurt by this, and I felt that if I let my emotions get carried away and I got to worrying about who's going to get hurt by something like this, that I wouldn't be effective at all – so I had to school myself not to think about it.

Now, from this point of view, I was not affected emotionally. I haven't been up to this day, because it was something that had to be done. I was convinced that it had to be done, and I was convinced it was the right thing to do at that particular time.

I've also been asked, would I do it again? My answer is, if you turn the clock backwards and get the same conditions existing today that you had in 1945, I'd probably do the same thing again with basically the same attitude.

You can't turn the clock backwards – you can't erase it. It has been done. Let's hope we've learned a lesson from it and that we don't have to do it in the future. **"**

▼ **A good distance from the epicenter of Nagasaki's explosion, trees have still been stripped by the heat of the blast.**

▲ **It is hard to imagine the intensity of the heat generated by the bomb – but this woman's kimono dye was burned on to her flesh.**

rather horrifying sight because you knew there were people underneath and you could speculate (but you didn't want to see) what the result was.

I didn't want to delay too long in this air – I don't think that I could have stayed in the Hiroshima area more than about six minutes. It took me about two minutes to make the first turn to come back and take a look at it, then about four more minutes of slow flight, just kind of looking around so we could take these pictures. Then I wanted to get away, because I felt that if I were Japanese and had seen anything like this happen, if it were humanly possible by any means of communication, and I had some fighters to get up into the air, I'd get them up after the aeroplane as fast as I could and make any sacrifice to get it.

Pretty soon it became a rather routine flight back home. As a matter of fact, it was routine enough that I let Bob Lewis and all the pilots fly that aeroplane and went back and got some sleep for about the first time in 30 hours – and I was ready

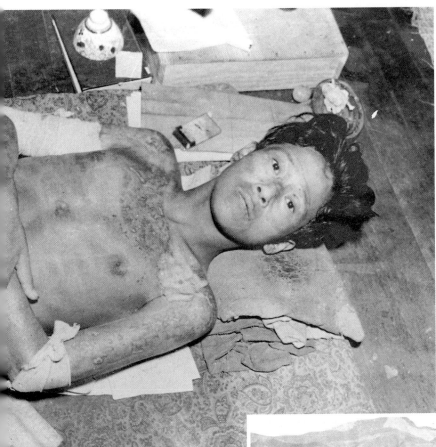

◄ **Burns from the intense heat of the blast were only to be expected – it was only in the following weeks that the effects of radiation became apparent – the new scourge of the atomic age.**

opposite direction, but a specified angle to put the greatest distance between the bomb and us on a slant-range that would be mathematically possible, because we had no idea what it would do to the aeroplane.

It takes 52 seconds for an object to drop approximately from 30,000 feet to 1,500 feet, and in that length of time, we were able to get 12 slant-range miles away from the explosion. Very shortly after the explosion, came a white light that just obliterated the very pale blue sky (which is so pale at that altitude). A white light just obliterated the whole sky. I'll never forget it. My back was to the explosion, of course. However, there was a man in the tail, a crew member, and shortly afterwards I heard him say something unintelligible. This was very unusual, because he was a very highly trained man – and he said it again. This was somewhat in opposition to training regulations because once a thing was reported, it wasn't to be reported again, so we could keep track of what things were being reported.

Major Charles Sweeney flew the B-29 which escorted Enola Gay *on the Hiroshima mission and was responsible for the scientific side of the operation. He was to drop instruments in canisters to record the results of the blast for scientific study.*

❝ We made our approach at 30,000 feet, as I recall. It was very close to 30,000 feet and the photographic aeroplane dropped back. I stayed in rather close formation with Colonel Tibbets.

The bomb-bay doors opened and we received a ten-second warning signal by tone, just before the release. Now I must describe the reason for our being there. We were carrying scientific instruments in canisters which were dropped by parachute and they were released by us at the moment that the bomb was released from Colonel Tibbets' aeroplane. Now, at a certain altitude, parachutes dropped those canisters gradually so that they could make recordings of blasts and radioactivity, and other things, and they were

telemetered so that three scientists in our aeroplane could make the readings necessary to determine what this thing had done in scientific terms.

Immediately the tone signal stopped, the bomb left Colonel Tibbets' aeroplane and we saw it start to plummet to earth. Our briefing was to turn as quickly as possible in the opposite direction – not quite the

Again he said something that to me was unintelligible and shortly thereafter the aeroplane was smacked on the bottom and my bombardier turned to me, then Captain Clement Behan and he said, 'Flak'. There was a little bit of panic in his eyes, and he thought we'd been hit by flak – but the aeroplane was still steady.

▲ **After the Nagasaki bomb, temple figures are a symbolic reminder of a national culture wiped out by the power of modern technology.**

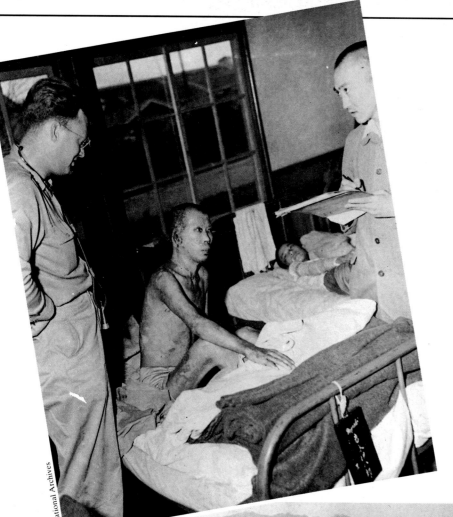

US National Archives

I could still feel the aeroplane flying well – and we were hit again and again, each time with a diminished force and in as much as Behan had been shot down four times in Europe, I had some confidence in his description of flak. It wasn't. The man in the tail was describing something that I guess human eyes hadn't seen before.

These were concentric rings of hot air coming up toward the aeroplane, or coming up radiating from the explosion. These were the things that hit the aeroplane and caused the smacking on the bottom. These diminished, of course, and went away. Afterwards we turned back and flew alongside back toward home base, 1,500 miles away. We saw off our right wing, the cloud coming up from Hiroshima. This was a cloud that, as it boiled up, had every colour in the rainbow and at about 25,000 feet the mushroom portion broke off and turned white – and of course we've all seen photographs of that.

We couldn't see the city – it was covered with smoke and, as I recall, even reconnaissance aeroplanes that flew over there almost constantly for the next two days, couldn't photo-

▲ Accompanied by his Japanese assistant, US Army Medical Corps Captain Thornton T Perry takes a clinical look at the damage done in the Nagasaki blast.

▶ The atomic cloud has gone – what remains of Hiroshima is a bleak wasteland. Even the ever-present Japanese bicycle – the hardiest of transports, able to survive even jungle use – cannot weather the effects of 'the bomb'.

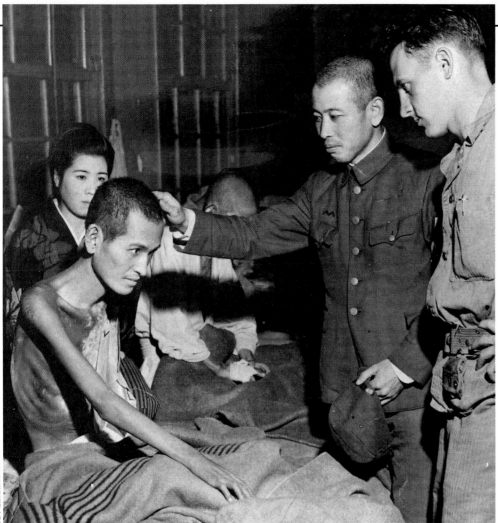

US National Archives

graph the city for – I've forgotten how long it was – 24 or 36 hours or whatever, because it was covered with smoke.

At that moment I felt that the mission had been executed properly and that this just might cause the Japanese government to say 'We're willing to end the war.' This was what it was all about. 🙰

🚩 *Seiichi Nagai was just ten years old when the bomb exploded over his home town of Nagasaki. He remembers his father, a professor at the town's Medical University, who had previously been studying the use of radium and X-rays and already had leukaemia – and the funeral of his mother killed in the bombing.*

🙰🙰 Our house was about 50 metres from the epicentre – but at that time I was at my granny's at Kiba in Miyamacho, about 7 km away. My mother was killed in the blast. I don't know when I first found out, really. I just knew she was no longer alive. When granny went to

meet her the day afterwards, she must have gone to our house in Urakami. Granny came back, but she didn't tell us straight away.

Father came back with the relief squad people on August 12. He had a triangular bandage tied around his leg and one on his head. I felt bad about that, but he was alive and he had come back – that was enough.

▲ **Flash-burn victims are studied in the US post-mortem.**

▼ **Impervious to the ramifications of their mission, the crew of *Enola Gay* toast success.**

At the time the loss of my mother was the same for the whole family, but the sheer joy that father was still alive was stronger than my grief.

From the book I wrote with my sister, I remember my mother's funeral. 'All four of us walked, bunched close up together, thinking simply that the four of us must keep together, whatever happened – that was what we promised Mummy. The gravestone had been blown down and the stone cross was bent. We unwrapped the white cloth, and stared a long time at Mummy. Those eight eyes stared at her, at that shape which had changed for ever. Our Mummy carried about in a bucket – however many times Kayano and I cried out for her, she would never come back again, would she? Our mother had been burned and reduced to fragments, the rays of sun shone into the bucket and were reflected by those white bones.

A hole was dug on top of where my sisters Ikuko and Sasano were buried, and Mummy's bones were placed in it. With a rustle and a clatter, our mother's bones were poured into that hole where her children were sleeping. We drew in our breaths, as if in greeting. The tears poured down my cheeks. Bending his face down towards his stick, Daddy was crying too. We each poured a little earth on top of Mummy's bones. A big pine tree inclined over the grave, and it was enveloped, as if by a perfume, with the fragrance of pine resin. On a new white cross were written the words: 'MARINA NAGAI MIDORI. DIED IN THE BOMBING, 9 AUGUST 1945. AGED 38 YEARS.' 🙰

US National Archives